W9-AYX-556

SEA BATTLES
IN CLOSE-UP

WORLD WAR 2

VOLUME TWO

U.S. Navy Memorial Foundation

Advisory

Council

Edition

CELEBRATING
50 YEARS OF
FREEDOM

A TRIBUTE
TO THE UNITED
STATES NAVY
1941-1945

Naval Institute Press

Published and distributed in the
United States of America by the
Naval Institute Press, 118 Maryland
Avenue, U.S. Naval Academy,
Annapolis, Maryland 21402-5035

Library of Congress Catalog Card
Number 87-63594

ISBN 1-55750-758-9

Manufactured in Great Britain

Front cover:
**Adm Vian's action in the
Second Battle of Sirte,
22 March 1942.** *From a painting
by Norman Wilkinson in the
collection of the National Maritime
Museum*

Right:
**HMS *Euryalus* ready to repel
an air attack with her 5.25in
guns at maximum elevation.**

Contents

Introduction

This book, like its predecessor *Sea Battles in Close-up: World War 2*, is a compendium of accounts of World War 2 naval battles originally published as individual volumes in the popular Ian Allan Ltd 'Sea Battles in Close-Up' series between 1973 and 1976. As before, the accounts are re-written by a new author and, where relevant, include new material which might not have been available to researchers in the 1970s. Also as before, a completely new sea battle is covered, in this case Leyte Gulf, the largest and most diverse engagement in naval history.

World War Two came at a time of decisive change in the nature of naval warfare. The gun-armed warship was no longer supreme but it was still important and sometimes decisive. In every battle described in this book except one, the Philippine Sea, traditional surface warships were the instruments or the objects of the action, often both. At Narvik British surface forces were able to assert their expected superiority over a quantitatively and qualitatively outmatched foe of similar type. At Crete surface forces denied the Axis the use of the sea and evacuated a defeated army. The story of the Malta Striking Force is a particular clear demonstration of the continued potential of the surface ship. Only when surface forces were based at Malta was the island able to play a decisive role in the interdiction of sea communications between Italy and North Africa. At Java Sea the surface ship-fired torpedo was the decisive Japanese weapon. Sirte is the classic defence of a convoy by surface forces from surface attack. The story of the efforts to neutralise the *Tirpitz* provide a classic example of the use of new technology to deal with a 'fleet in being' of the most traditional type. 'Neptune' depended on surface ships for escort and fire support. And Leyte Gulf marked the last major traditional gun and torpedo action in naval history.

Yet times had clearly changed. Only at Narvik, beyond the reach of the Luftwaffe's specially trained anti-shipping pilots, was the Royal Navy able to operate in its expected manner. Crete was a notable demonstration of the ability of 1940s air power to neutralise traditional command of the sea. The Malta Striking Forces were only able to operate because the Luftwaffe was somewhere else. Japanese command of the air was an important factor in the outcome of the Java Sea battle and Axis air power tragically snatched away the fruits of Adm Vivan's magnificent tactical success at Sirte. Air power also made possible the destruction of the *Tirpitz* 'at source'.

By 1944, the exercise of sea power had clearly become a struggle in three dimensions, on, above and below the oceans. Moreover sea power had acquired an ability for use against the shore unparalleled in naval history. In June the multidimensional nature of mid-Twentieth Century naval warfare was clearly shown on a global scale. In Europe the British organised the greatest amphibious landing in world history, Operation 'Neptune', the Normandy landings. And in the Pacific the US Navy fought the largest modern major fleet action ever, the battle of the Philippine Sea. Carriers had fought before, but never in such numbers. The striking weapons were submarines with torpedoes and aircraft in air-to-air combat. The decisive means of success were electronics and effective action information organisation. The true significance of Spruance's great victory has been hidden by a natural tendency to look for lists of ships sunk. It mattered little however that most Japanese carriers returned to base. Without aircraft they were useless — except as bait.

No nation had relied on technological superiority more than Japan. It was ironic therefore that she should be forced by Spruance's success in June to pit surface ships against carriers at Leyte Gulf in October. In one sense Leyte is a culmination. All aspects of naval warfare are there, amphibious landings, carrier strikes, submarine attacks, gun and torpedo battles, even (manned) missiles. Yet in another sense Leyte is a throwback, an aberration caused by an already defeated enemy being unwilling to accept defeat and an American commander who played directly into enemy hands. Hence the remarkable features of this most remarkable of battles, escort carriers being assailed by battleships and cruisers and veteran battleships slugging it out like aged boxers. Yet the parts of Leyte that mark the trend of the development of naval warfare confirm the lessons of Philippine Sea, the supremacy of the carrier and the growing power of the submarine, both to be the capital striking units of the second half of the century.

Thus the battles described, chosen primarily because of their coverage in the Ian Allan series of the 1970s, are, in fact, a series of demonstrations of the dynamics of a key turning point in naval history. Not only was technology changing, but the balance of naval power itself. The reader will find in the following the Royal Navy persistently demonstrating skill, courage, endurance and organisational ability of the highest quality. Yet Britain was clearly a power on the decline, unable any more to provide the wherewithal to fight three dimensional naval battles on a global scale. Even at Narvik the writing was on the wall as the Royal Navy only operated effectively where there was no air threat. By the time of Leyte Gulf the White Ensign had almost disappeared entirely. What is more remarkable in retrospect is the United King-

dom's role as the major partner in 'Neptune', perhaps the Royal Navy's swan song as a dominant actor in naval history.

In the spirit both of the original *Sea Battles in Close-Up* and the previous compendium, considerable emphasis is placed on technical detail both in the text and accompanying tables. This can throw interesting new light on actions, for example the types of torpedo available to the Japanese at Java Sea and the impact of this on who fired when and to what effect. Figures have been checked against the best available contemporary sources, the basic text being Conway's *All World's Fighting Ships*.

The main addition to the accounts has been the result of the revelations on signals intelligence that have appeared since the mid-1970s. This helps fill in missing pieces of the jigsaw in certain cases but it does not alter the main story. Code breaking is no substitute for the ships, aircraft and men who

have to act on the information provided. In certain cases, notably the contribution of *X-5* to the sinking of *Tirpitz* the author has put forward new views that might not find universal acceptance. There was insufficient space to provide full qualifications for every controversial point but it is hoped that readers who disagree with the author's analyses here and elsewhere will at least appreciate the stimulation of an alternative view.

Perhaps the points on which readers' eyebrows will most rise are the related criticisms of both Winston Churchill and his fixation with a Mediterranean strategy. Those who demur at the author's assessments are referred to Stephen Roskill's *Churchill and the Admirals* and Correlli Barnett's *Engage the Enemy More Closely* for more extended critiques. The author has, however, tried to avoid hindsight in making judgements about decisions and those who took them. Historians and their readers ought to always be aware that mark one crystal balls are not available to either planners or operational commanders.

The author has deliberately used modern naval terminology, as appropriate, to describe the forces engaged in the battles. Some may find this usage anachronistic but it helps make the experience described in these pages more accessible and, perhaps, more relevant to the modern naval practitioner. It also helps familiarise naval historians with useful modern terms such as 'surface action group'.

Working with the original volumes confirmed the author's memories as to their quality and interest. So he must therefore express his debt to their authors, too many of whom are no longer with us: Capt Peter Dickens (Narvik); Capt S. W. C. ('Bill') Pack (Crete and Sirte); Peter C. Smith and Edwin Walker (Malta Striking Forces); F. C. Van Oosten (Java Sea); Lt-Cdr Gervis Frere Cook (*Tirpitz*); Vice-Adm B. B. Schofield (*Neptune*); and W. D. Dickson (Philippine Sea). The author does not always agree with their accounts but his respect for all of them as historians is greater than ever. All mistakes are the responsibility of the present author not them.

Thanks are due to Simon Forty of Ian Allan Ltd for being very patient with an author struggling to balance too many obligations; Paul Kemp and staff in Department of Photographs at the Imperial War Museum, London; the helpful officials at the Naval Historical Center and National Archives in Washington DC, for assistance with picture research; Derek Law for producing the select bibliography; Dave Baker for pointing out flaws in the original draft; Irene Grove for sacrificing so much of her Christmas holiday to help with typing; and finally to Elizabeth Grove for putting up with the author spending much of his time at the word processor.

Eric Grove
Morden, Surrey

CHAPTER ONE

Narvik

In 1940, Hitler won the race for Norway; for some time both the British and the Germans had harboured designs on that huge but sparsely populated northern land. Interwar German naval strategists had formed the view that failing to take over Norway in World War 1 had been a great error as it would have been a way round the British blockade, a stranglehold that was fully restored on the outbreak of the new war. The protected sea route down the coastal 'leads' through Norwegian territorial waters was however even more important. Down it, especially in winter, went 40 per cent of Germany's supplies of iron ore. Winston Churchill, the enthusiastically aggressive British First Lord of the Admiralty, heckled his Cabinet colleagues for some offensive action to cut this supply line. The rest of the Government were understandably reluctant to act like Hitler and violate Norwegian neutrality but the desire to help the Finns against their Soviet invaders overcame qualms and plans were laid to invade both Norway and Sweden through the port of Narvik. Fortunately, this campaign, that would have seen Britain commit unprovoked aggression against Norway and Sweden and go to war against its future main military ally, was pre-empted by the end of the Russo-Finnish war in March 1940. Churchill, however, now resurrected an earlier plan just to mine the leads to force shipping out to sea where action could be taken against it. It was hoped this would lead to a violent German reaction that would see the Norwegians ask for British troops to be landed at the major Norwegian ports to give assistance in their defence.

Churchill had got fresh heart for this operation from the daring rescue carried out by the Home Fleet destroyer *Cossack* in a fiord near Bergen in February 1940; Capt Vian had liberated almost 300 merchant navy prisoners captured by the *Panzerschiffe Graf Spee* and clearly demonstrated

Below:

One of the first signs that all was not well off Norway were the reports sent by the doomed destroyer *Glowworm* that quite literally ran into the German invasion forces, severely damaging the cruiser *Hipper*. Sadly her sacrifice, that earned her captain, Lt-Cdr G. P. Roope, a posthumous VC, was not fully exploited. *Glowworm* was an interesting destroyer, having introduced experimentally the quintuple 'Pentad' torpedo mounting. *Real Photographs/Ian Allan Collection*

HMS *Hunter*, a classic interwar British destroyer, seen on 30 September 1936 running her trials off the Tyne. Note the destroyer director control tower on the top of the bridge structure ahead of the rangefinder. The director, introduced at the beginning of the 1930s, aided by a simple fire control computer, greatly aided accurate surface gunnery. The rangefinder was an MS 20 5ft baselength instrument. Less than four years later, together with her flotilla leader *Hardy*, *Hunter* would meet her end in Ofot Fiord.
Real Photographs/Ian Allan Collection

The impressive bulk of the modernised battleship *Warspite* which Vice-Adm Whitworth took into the confined waters of Ofot Fiord during the second Battle of Narvik. The picture was taken shortly after her reconstruction in 1937 — note the national markings on 'B' turret required for duty off Spain during the Civil War — but apart from her paintwork the ship was unchanged in April 1940. No electronic sensors of any kind were yet fitted, her advanced fire control system was still entirely optical.
Real Photographs/Ian Allan Collection

Germany's willingness to violate Norwegian neutrality when it suited her. Unfortunately, however, this affair also gave fresh impetus to the German Navy's commander Adm Raeder in his campaign to persuade Hitler to authorise a pre-emptive occupation of Norway. Given the command of the sea exerted by the British Fleet this operation would have to rely on speed, deception, surprise and daring — and the unproven capacity of the Luftwaffe to hold off superior British surface forces. The main problem was that Narvik lay in the north of the country beyond the Arctic circle and the key iron ore port. German forces landed there would be very exposed as would be the flotilla undertaking the landing. The Germans planned their pre-emptive strike, codenamed 'Weserubung' (Weser Exercise) for 9 April 1940. The British had planned to carry out the mining Operation 'Wilfrid' earlier but the desire to combine 'Wilfrid' with the mining of German internal waterways (Operation 'Royal Marine') and French cold feet about the latter operation caused a postponement to the 8th. Troops were standing by in cruisers and transports in the Clyde for the connected landings, Plan 'R4'.

The Germans achieved almost complete surprise. Indeed what indications of German movements that did leak out blunted rather than sharpened the British response. Fearing that a move by Germany's heavy ships into the Atlantic was imminent, the Admiralty ordered the disembarka-

HMS *Hunter*

Builder: Swan Hunter, Wallsend (launched 25 February 1936)

Displacement: 1,340 tons standard

Dimensions: 323ft x 33ft x 12.4 ft

Machinery: geared turbines, two shafts, 34,000shp, 35.5 knots

Armament: 4 x 4.7in guns (4 x 1); 8 x 0.5in AA (2 x 4); 8 x 21in torpedo tubes (2 x 4) ; 2 x depth charge mortars and one set over stern depth charge rails

Sensors: Type 124 sonar

Complement: 145

Notes: One of the eight 'H' class destroyers four of which, *Hunter*, *Hotspur*, *Hostile* and *Havock* were at the first Battle of Narvik making up with the leader *Hardy* the 2nd Destroyer Flotilla. HMS *Hero* took part in the second battle where she deployed the two speed destroyer sweep (TSDS) with which the class was fitted for minesweeping. *Hunter* was sunk at Narvik and only two of her sisters survived the war. The ships were typical of the standard British destroyers launched from 1929 onwards in nine classes lettered 'A' to 'I'. The 'H' class introduced new Mk XVIII mountings for the 4.7in guns with extra elevation.

HMS *Warspite*

Builder: Devonport Dockyard (launched 26 November 1913), reconstructed Portsmouth Dockyard (March 1934-March 1937)

Displacement: 31,315 tons standard

Dimensions: 639.5ft x 90.5ft x 29.1ft

Armour: 13in belt; 13in turret face; 11in sides; 10in maximum barbette; 5in middle deck over magazines, 3.5in over machinery; 3.1in main deck forward

Machinery: Four shaft geared turbines, 30,000shp, 23.5kt.

Armament: 8 x 15in (4 x 2); 8 x 6in (8 x 1); 8 x 4in AA (4 x 2); 32 x 2pdr AA (4 x 8); 16 x 0.5in AA (4 x 4)

Complement: 1, 124

Notes: A veteran of Jutland transformed in the 1930s into an effective modern battleship with guns increased in elevation, new fire control equipment, better horizontal protection, improved AA armament, completely new boilers and machinery, totally altered superstructure and provision for four torpedo-spotter-reconnaissance aircraft.

tion of the troops from the cruisers so they could revert to fleet duties. The escort for the transports — that contained troops intended for Narvik — was also sent to sea. Churchill did not consult any of his Government colleagues about this decision, which later came as a rude shock to the Cabinet. The Home Fleet sailed on 7 April but the minelayers and their covering forces were already at sea. Tasked with mining Vest Fiord were the destroyers *Esk*, *Impulsive*, *Icarus* and *Ivanhoe* all modified to carry mines rather than torpedo tubes and two of their 4.7in guns. In support were the fully armed destroyers of the Second Flotilla, led by its Capt (D) Bernard Warburton-Lee in HMS

Hardy. The rest of the flotilla were *Hotspur, Havock*, and *Hunter*. To the south was a covering force based around the modernised 15in gun battlecruiser *Renown* and commanded by Vice Adm Jock Whitworth, the Vice Admiral Commanding Battlecruisers whose relationship to Adm Sir Charles Forbes, the Fleet C-in-C, was exactly like that of Beatty to Jellicoe at the Battle of Jutland in 1916. He had left Scapa on 5 April. The seas were heavy and one of Whitworth's escorts, the destroyer *Glowworm*, had got separated looking for a man overboard. On 8 April she blundered into the German invasion fleet and Roope, her commanding officer, won a Victoria Cross for ramming the German cruiser *Hipper* after an unequal exchange of fire.

The 'unknown warship' report Roope was able to get off before his brave destroyer met her end added to British confusion about what was going on. At 1045 the Admiralty decided to withdraw the Vest Fiord mining force and concentrate it with Whitworth. This was another disastrous piece of back-seat driving by the Admiralty where Churchill's emotional and mercurial enthusiasm combined with First Sea Lord Sir Dudley Pound's centralising professional style to cause much unnecessary trials for the fleet at sea. Churchill and Pound had effectively uncovered Vest Fiord for the Narvik invasion force. For at that very moment a large German fleet was moving up the Norwegian coast. The damaged *Hipper* with four destroyers and 1,700 troops made for its planned target, Trondheim. The rest kept going northwards. There were the two 11in gun battleships *Scharnhorst* and *Gneisenau* providing cover and 10 destroyers carrying 2,000 mountain troops bound for Narvik at the head of Vest Fiord. These were the cream of Germany's destroyer forces, led by Kommodore Friederich Bonte in the *Wilhelm Heidkamp*. There were two full Flotillas: the Third with four more new Type 36 ships and the Second with four older Type 34As. The odd ship was the *Georg Thiele* an original Type 34 vessel from the 1st Flotilla. The seas were rough and the lack of seaworthiness of the overweight German designs was a great trial, both to their crews and even more to the embarked troops from southern Germany and Austria. The German destroyer crews were envious of the much better seakeeping of British destroyer designs.

Whitworth, obeying his orders from London, moved north ahead of the Germans and rendezvoused with the British Vest Fiord destroyers. He then moved to patrol to the west, expecting the mysterious German force to continue northwards. At 1850 on the 8th the Admiralty ordered Whitworth to 'concentrate on preventing any German force proceeding to Narvik'. Whitworth,

Right:
The German approach (1).

however did not obey and remained to seaward thinking that the Germans would not enter such dangerous waters in such atrocious weather. But the Germans had to take such risks if their plan was to succeed. At 2000, close to where the British had joined up a few hours before, Bonte bade farewell to the German battleships and moved into Vest Fiord for the final passage to his destination. The waters of Vest Fiord are broad but they are bound by treacherous pinnacles, rocks and islets that make even today's NATO exercises in the same area potentially very hazardous. There were some close shaves but the Germans' luck held; fortune favoured the brave. By 0300 on the 9th the destroyers were entering the more confined waters of Ofot Fiord. Having left ships and men to secure his rear Bonte arrived off a snowy and squally Narvik with three destroyers at 0415.

After some negotiation the 40-year old coast defence ship *Eidsvold* was dispatched with two torpedo hits from four fired by the *Wilhelm Heidkamp*. The Norwegians had decided to fight but had been unable to open fire, except for an initial shot across the *Heidkamp's* bows. Bonte had little alternative but he began to worry obsessively about sinking the old ship and killing all but eight of her crew. The *Bernd von Arnim*, a Type 34A destroyer, drifted through the murk to her chosen landing point, the Post Pier. As the destroyer edged ashore she was engaged by the other coast defence ship at Narvik the *Norge*. The Norwegians were unable to score hits with their old 8.2 and 5.9in weapons although the Germans also had problems making their torpedoes work. Finally the sixth and seventh German torpedoes to be fired exploded and the British built Norwegian veteran rolled over and sank; there were 97 survivors. It turned out the German G7a torpedoes were so deficient in depth keeping that they were of only dubious utility against shallow targets.

The local Norwegian army commander was a Quisling and had no intention of fighting and the town was quickly secured. Bonte, however was unhappy. The German whaler *Jan Wellem* was already at Narvik with fuel and stores but her slow pumps meant that the German destroyers would have to wait 24hr before being able to break out en masse. The British would be bound to be waiting. That morning the *Scharnhorst* and *Gneisenau* had made contact with Whitworth who had used the superiority of his modernised fire control to score three damaging hits on *Gneisenau* at 18,000yd. The Germans were surprised and their

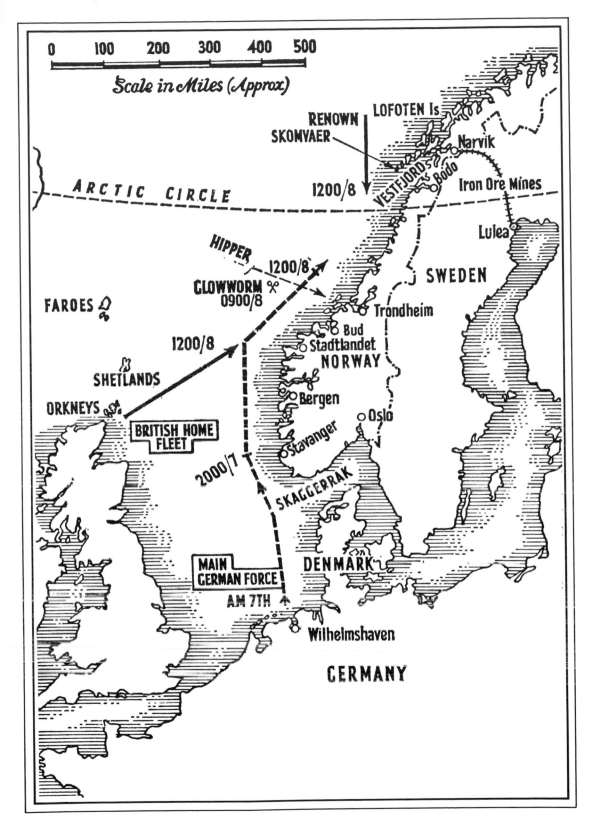

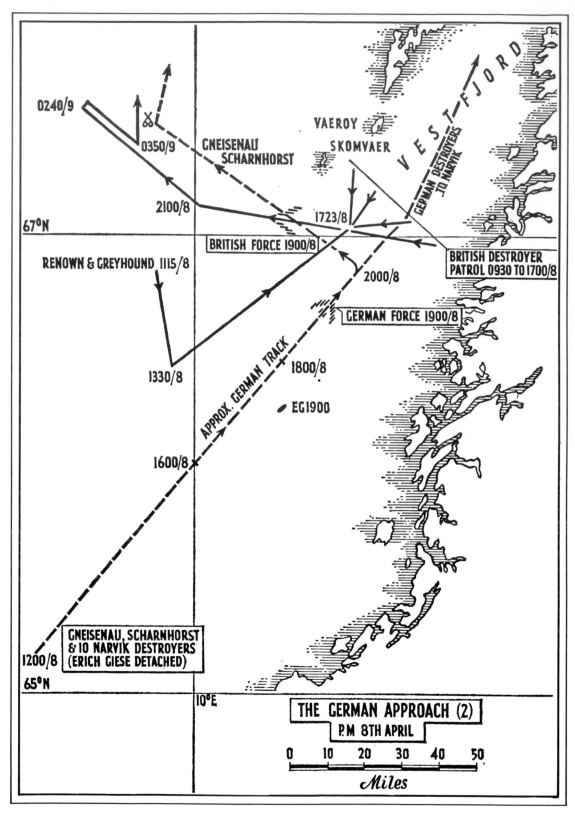

0240/9

0350/9

GNEISENAU
SCHARNHORST

VAEROY
SKOMVAER

VEST FJORD

GERMAN DESTROYERS
TO NARVIK

2100/8

67°N

BRITISH FORCE 1900/8

1723/8

RENOWN & GREYHOUND 1115/8

BRITISH DESTROYER
PATROL 0930 TO 1700/8

2000/8

GERMAN FORCE 1900/8

APPROX. GERMAN TRACK

1330/8

1800/8

EG 1900

1600/8

GNEISENAU, SCHARNHORST
& 10 NARVIK DESTROYERS
(ERICH GIESE DETACHED)

1200/8

65°N

10°E

THE GERMAN APPROACH (2)
P.M 8TH APRIL

0   10   20   30   40   50

Miles

11in shells made little impression on *Renown* when they did score two hits. During the battle the destroyers of the 2nd Flotilla made their minor contribution to the bombardment but in the conditions it is doubtful if the Germans noticed. Nevertheless Adm Lutjens, the battle group commander (who would later go down with the *Bismarck*) drew away to keep his fleet intact to cover the planned return of the Narvik destroyers. Whitworth had his own feelings about this and sent all nine destroyers and destroyer minelayers accompanying him back to the entrance to Vest Fiord to stop the Germans getting either in or out. At 0930 Warburton-Lee reported the establishment of his patrol line. Then Captain (D)2 was ordered by Forbes to send some destroyers up to Narvik to ensure that no German landing took place there. This had priority over another signal from Vice Admiral Battlecruisers ordering a rendezvous 50 miles SW of Skomvaer that evening. In addition HMS *Repulse*, *Renown's* much less heavily modernised sister ship, had been ordered forward from the main body of the Home Fleet. She was the core of quite a powerful group being accompanied by the 6in gun fleet cruiser *Penelope*, the destroyer *Hostile* (a 2nd Flotilla vessel that had been on detached service and had joined up overnight), a new 'K' class destroyer *Kimberley* and three big well-armed 'Tribals' *Bedouin*, *Punjabi* and *Eskimo*, built as answers to the powerful Japanese destroyers in the 1930s. All four of these latter destroyers were much more powerful than the small 'H' class vessels of Warburton-Lee's flotilla.

HMS *Hardy*

Builder: Cammell Laird, Birkenhead (launched 7 April 1936)

Displacement: 1,505 tons standard

Dimensions: 337.5ft x 34ft x 12.4ft

Machinery: geared turbines, two shafts, 38,000shp, 36.5kt

Armament: 5 x 4.7in (5 x 1); 8 x 0.5in AA (2 x 4); 8 x 21in torpedo tubes (2 x 4); 2 x depth charge mortars and one set over stern depth charge rails

Sensors: Type 124S sonar

Complement: 175

Notes: In the mid 1930s it was the custom to make the leader of a destroyer flotilla slightly larger than the rest of the 'boats' and add an extra gun between the funnels. She also carried a special echo sounding version of the latest destroyer sonar. The leaders of the 'G' and 'I' classes were generally similar.

Capt Spooner of *Repulse* had signalled his intention of joining Warburton-Lee at 0931 but now the Admiralty began to act as if his battle group was not there. It signalled to Warburton-Lee at midday that a 'small' landing from one ship had taken place at Narvik and that he was to use his discretion about taking up his destroyers to sink the ship and recapture the town. This interference, that bore all of Churchill's fingerprints, effectively put the 2nd Flotilla beyond the control of both Forbes and Whitworth. Warburton-Lee left *Greyhound* and the minelayers with Spooner and took his four destroyers up to the Tranoy Pilot Station in upper Vest Fiord to clarify the situation. With some difficulty it was elucidated that about six enemy destroyers were up at Narvik along with a U-boat and that the town was held in some force. The arrival of *Hostile* to join the Flotilla was thus especially welcome. She had been told by Spooner that she had better re-join her commander as he seemed bound for action up the fiord.

Warburton-Lee was a fine, aggressive and dedicated destroyer commander, one of the new breed trained in the interwar period not to repeat the poor showing of the British destroyers at Jutland. A letter dated 5 April 1940 was in the post to his wife in which he had said that 'The war is going to start properly soon and I'm going to start it'. His staff was of the same calibre as the Captain (D) and after the Tranoy visit they formed a council of war in *Hardy's* charthouse to discuss the situation. The officers felt bound to attack Narvik unless there were urgent and strong reasons against. Nevertheless the opposition seemed formidable — at least six German destroyers in inshore waters where their inferior sea keeping was less important than their more powerful and numerous guns. After half an hour with himself Warburton-Lee signalled London thus at 1751:

'Norwegians report Germans holding Narvik in force, also six destroyers and one U-boat are there and channel is probably mined. Intend attacking at dawn high water.'

At 1959, Whitworth, anxious about Warburton-Lee's weakness in the face of serious opposition ordered *Penelope*, *Kimberley* and the three 'Tribals' to support the 2nd Flotilla. Sadly, and to his everlasting regret, at 2038 the Vice Admiral cancelled this order fearing it conflicted with Admiralty intentions not yet vouchsafed to the men on the spot. Pound had apparently made it clear that Warburton-Lee's attack was none of his business. Complicating the operation with reinforcements might also cause delay and forfeit surprise — although there was still time for the cruiser and the big destroyers to be off Narvik at dawn, the obvious time for an attack. At 2059 the

Admiralty sent the 2nd Flotilla a signal giving some worse-than-useless tactical advice (which was ignored) and ordering an attack at dawn. This order was redundant as 'intend' implied action unless countermanded. The best part of a rather unnecessary signal was its conclusion wishing Captain (D)2 good luck; he would need it.

In order to be off Narvik at dawn on the 10th Warburton-Lee sailed in the opposite direction before turning for the rush up the fiord and this manoeuvre succeeded in confusing the enemy. U-boats had been taken off their normal *guerre de course* duties to protect the Norwegian gamble; three were on station in the Vest Fiord area — *U46* was at Ramnes and *U25* off Baroy guarding the narrow entrance to Ofot Fiord. *U51* was in the wider waters of Vest Fiord itself; she spotted the 2nd Flotilla sailing south-westwards and reported this comforting news to Bonte at Narvik. Thirty

minutes later Warburton-Lee turned his five destroyers round for their run in. Tranoy light was sighted half an hour after midnight and *U25* safely avoided. At 0145, after a spurt of 20kt, speed was reduced to 12.5kt as the fiord was now only 1½ miles wide. Asdic was used to aid navigation in the narrow waters.

The Admiralty sent another misleading signal at 0104 reporting that the Germans had arrived at Narvik in ore ships that were to be sunk. The destroyers were then to ascertain the strength of the Germans ashore. It seems clear that the First Lord, well dined as was his habit, was running through the options in his fertile mind. The great communicator could not resist communicating and he got Pound to draft yet another signal, sent at 0136. This reported that the two Norwegian coast defence ships might be in German hands. 'You alone' it went on, 'can judge in these circumstances if attack should be made. We shall support whatever decision you make.' Warburton-Lee had other things on his mind. At 0210 the Flotilla took emergency evasive action to avoid an apparent obstruction ahead but at 0240 it was back in order and Warburton-Lee wished his captains 'Good luck, let them have it.'

U46, blinded by the snow, was safely passed as was the destroyer *Diether von Roeder* on patrol outside the harbour. Warburton-Lee's plan was for

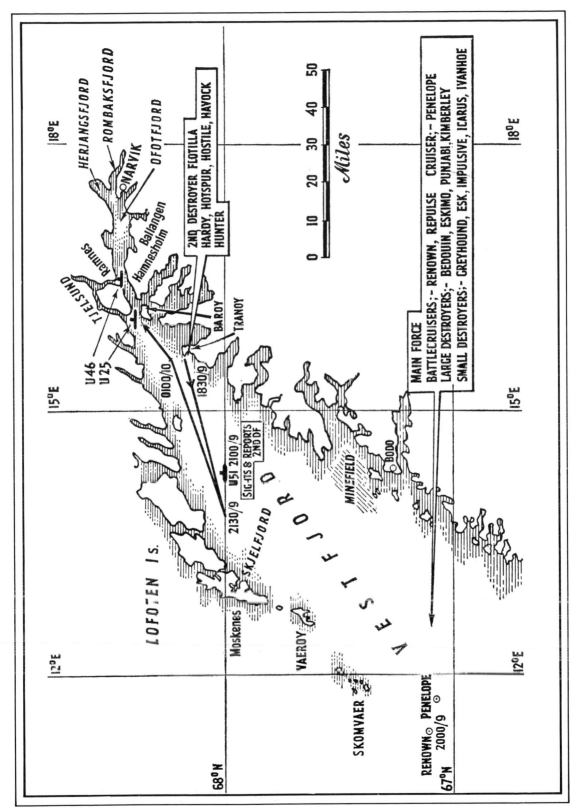

LOFOTEN IS.

HERJANGSFJORD

ROMBAKSFJORD

OFOTFJORD

NARVIK

Ballangen

Hamnesholm

Ramnes

TJELSUND

U 46
U 25

0100/10

BAROY

TRANOY

1830/9

2ND DESTROYER FLOTILLA
HARDY, HOTSPUR, HOSTILE, HAVOCK
HUNTER

Miles

0 10 20 30 40 50

MAIN FORCE
BATTLECRUISERS;— RENOWN, REPULSE   CRUISER;— PENELOPE
LARGE DESTROYERS;— BEDOUIN, ESKIMO, PUNJABI,KIMBERLEY
SMALL DESTROYERS;— GREYHOUND, ESK, IMPULSIVE, ICARUS, IVANHOE

2130/9

U51 2100/9

SIG-TS & REPORTS
2ND DF

Moskenes

SKJELFJORD

VAEROY

MINEFIELD

BODO

VESTFJORD

SKOMVAER

RENOWN PENELOPE
67°N   2000/9

68°N

12°E

15°E

18°E

15

Hardy, *Hunter* and *Havock* to attack the ships inside Narvik harbour while *Hotspur* and *Hostile* were to engage shipping and the suspected battery at Framnes. At 0343 Warburton-Lee signalled to his Flotilla that he was steering for the entrance to Narvik harbour; five minutes later the destroyers slowed to 6kt as they waited for sufficient light to go into action. The Flotilla turned to starboard together to skirt the southern entrance of the harbour and to give maximum room for manoeuvre for a torpedo attack, but this caused it to sail straight towards the land to the south of the harbour entrance. Some more rapid manoeuvring was called for as the Flotilla turned north still awaiting the dawn. In the murk the *von Roeder* entered the harbour without observing anything. Surprise was complete and Warburton-Lee decided to enter Narvik harbour on his own.

Inside, screened by merchantmen were all Bonte's big Type 36 destroyers, the recently anchored *von Roeder* to the north and the whaler *Jan Wellem* further south with the *Hermann Kunne* refuelling on the port side and the *Hans Ludemann* to starboard. Further south still were the *Anton Schmitt* and the *Wilhelm Heidkamp*, the latter with a sleeping Kommodore aboard. It was these last two *Hardy* spotted first, presenting a perfect torpedo target almost side by side. At about 0430 the British attack began. Lt G. R. Heppel, the Flotilla torpedo officer fired three Mk IXs. The first blew the bows off a nearby merchantman but the second hit the *Wilhelm Heidkamp* aft and exploded her after 5in magazine. In a brilliant flash the German destroyer's stern blew off and her after three guns flew through the air; Bonte and 80 other Germans died almost instantly. It could not have been a better opening for the British even though *Hardy* scored no further hits as she sped away. After herculean efforts by her torpedomen to train the tubes she fired three more torpedoes at the northern side of the harbour but all they hit were quays. *Hardy* carried eight torpedoes in all but one was fired prematurely by accident and the eighth was not fired at all because of a misunderstanding.

Hunter made the next attack, engaging merchantmen as well as the warships. She hit the *Anton Schmitt* with a 4.7in shell and then with a torpedo. Neither of the first two attackers had been hit but the return fire was getting stronger as the well-named Lt-Cdr R. E. Courage brought in HMS *Havock* at 0446. He fired three torpedoes towards the *Anton Schmitt*; one hit a merchantman and the force of the explosion diverted the second into another merchant ship. The third hit home on the already damaged *Schmitt*, sealing her fate. The explosion also damaged the *Hermann Kunne* which had slipped from *Jan Wellem* and was only 40yd away. As *Havock* swept out of the harbour

she was taken under fire by the *von Roeder* and the *Ludemann*. The latter got the worst of it however for the *Havock's* after 4.7s hit the *Ludemann* twice, knocking out her fore 5in gun and starting a fire aft that caused the after magazine to be flooded. Her steering was also wrecked.

Hotspur and *Hostile* had found no 'trade' around Framnes and now continued the attack into the harbour. *Hostile* stopped to take under fire the *von Roeder*. With her sighting telescopes frozen up and spotting very difficult she used the 'blind ladder' technique of gunnery — groups of three salvoes grouped 400yd apart. The probabilities were not favouring the Germans and the *von Roeder* was hit twice and seriously damaged. *Havock*, after laying a smoke screen to cover the exit of the first three 'H's from the harbour, fired torpedoes into the chaos that was now Narvik harbour, hitting two merchant ships. All five destroyers began to fire their 4.7s into the harbour eventually forming a rough anti-clockwise circle with each ship firing as she came abreast the entrance. The three surviving German destroyers replied both with guns and torpedoes. The virtually immobile *von Roeder* used its angling gear (not possessed by the British) to fire a spread of all eight of its torpedoes towards the harbour entrance. The G7as fanned out but

Wilhelm Heidkamp

Builder: Deschimag, Bremen (launched 20 August 1938)

Displacement: 2,411 tons standard

Dimensions: 410.1ft x 38.7ft x 13.1ft

Machinery: geared turbines, two shafts, 70,000shp, 38kt

Armament: 5 x 5in; 4 x 37mm AA (2 x 2); 7 x 20mm (7 x 1);8 x 21in torpedo tubes; depth charges; provision for 60 mines

Sensors: GHG hydrophones

Complement: 313

Notes: Numbered Z21 in the destroyer series the flagship of the Narvik force was the second newest destroyer in the German Navy having commissioned on 20 June 1939. Only her sister *Anton Schmitt* (Z22), also at Narvik, was newer (having commissioned 24 September 1939). All but one of the Type 36 destroyers were lost at Narvik, including all the slightly shorter (404.2ft) members of the class, *Diether von Roeder* (Z17), *Hans Ludemann* (Z18) and *Hermann Kunne* (Z19). The Type 36 destroyers were longer and beamier than their predecessors with modified hulls aft and cut down funnels. This was intended to improve both seaworthiness and handling. *Wilhelm Heidkamp's* wreck still lies at Narvik. The man after whom she was named, Wilhelm Heidkamp, had been serving in the battlecruiser *Seydlitz* at Jutland and was promoted for playing a key part in flooding the magazines and saving the ship, despite burns and gas poisoning.

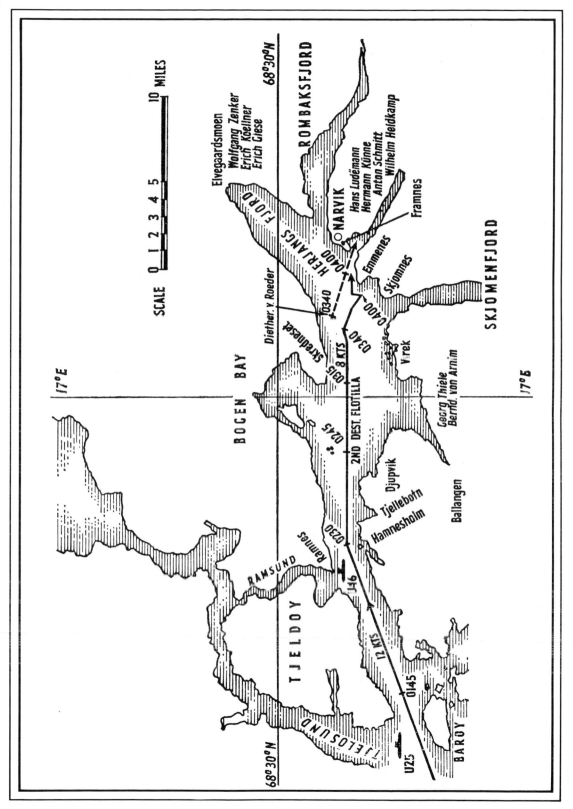

17

the British were saved by the poor depth keeping of the German weapons; they ran deep and not one exploded — two even ran harmlessly up the beach west of Ankenes! The *von Roeder* continued to be hit hard by the British gunfire and all she could do was to creep away to a safer berth by the Post pier. The British ships continued circling but, with return fire silenced and the harbour totally obscured, Warburton-Lee withdrew for a council of war with his staff.

Although Warburton-Lee seems to have been a little uneasy he felt that the attack ought to be kept up. The flotilla sailed back towards Narvik for *Hostile* to fire her so far unexpended torpedoes. Warburton-Lee ordered 20kt at 0544. *Hostile* came in closer than the rest and was hit by a 5in shell under the forecastle but with little damage. As the British drew away in line-ahead trouble was seen approaching down Herjangs Fiord to the north east. The German flotilla adjutant had belatedly sounded the alarm and now the cavalry was coming over the hill in the shape of the three Type 34A destroyers, *Wolfgang Zenker*, *Erich Koelner* and *Erich Giese*. The 4th Flotilla commander, the portly *Fregattenkapitän* Erich Bey (who would later go down with the *Scharnhorst*) had his ships in port quarterline which allowed all six forward 5in guns to bear. Hardy fired a full five-gun broadside simultaneously with the first German shots. The rest of the 2nd Flotilla joined in as runs on the harbour were completed but the range was long and no hits were scored by either side. The *Hans Ludemann* was equally unsuccessful with a spread of three torpedoes fired out of the harbour that were defeated once more by their defective depth keeping.

Warburton-Lee, mistook one of the big German destroyers for a cruiser and decided to withdraw. At 0551 he reported the situation to the Admiralty and sped westwards at 30kt, making smoke. Bey, appraised of the disaster in the harbour also decided to order break out but his orders were ignored by the *Georg Thiele* and *Bernd von Arnim* that had been lying at Ballangen to the west. The two destroyers had sailed on receipt of the alarm and, as they swept majestically up the Fiord they saw the enemy coming from the east. They swung to port to open their firing arcs and began shooting at 4,000yd. The British turned to port to do the same, *Havock* engaging the *von Arnim* while *Hardy* shot at the *Thiele*. Bey's pursuing German destroyers were plunged into confusion by the *Ludemann's* torpedoes as they continued their runs and took no part in the fight. The brave German pair did not need their help, however, for Warburton-Lee's luck had now finally run out. *Georg Thiele* straddled *Hardy* and hit with the fourth salvo and then started to score hits.

Four minutes after his enemy report Warburton-Lee made the Nelsonic signal 'Keep on engaging enemy' in the attempt to make sure that his Flotilla did not ignore the ships astern as well as the threat ahead.

It was the last signal he would ever make. Two 5in shells struck the area of *Hardy's* bridge destroying it and the forward 4.7s. Out of control, and carrying a Captain (D) mortally wounded in the head, the destroyer leader sped towards the southern shore of the fiord, her Flotilla in line astern. As they passed, *Georg Thiele* fired two torpedoes, *Bernd von Arnim* one, *Havock* five and *Hostile* four but none hit. Despite a shattered foot Paymaster Lt Stanning, Warburton-Lee's secretary, got down to the wheelhouse and turned to starboard eventually settling *Hardy* on a more or less westerly course. When an able seaman appeared to take over the helm Stanning went back up to the bridge. He considered ramming the Germans but the engines were finished. He therefore decided to put the wrecked *Hardy* ashore. The two victorious German destroyers turned to port to follow the British who were now both following HMS *Havock* and scoring hits on the Germans once more; *Georg Thiele* was struck in the boiler room. The German fire remained accurate, however, and seeing her consorts hit, *Havock* turned to starboard to draw the German fire, taking up station once more on *Hostile's* port quarter. This movement may well have deterred Bey from pressing forward to support the two engaged German destroyers.

The aggressive *Korvettenkapitän* Wolff of the *Thiele*, the German hero of this action, found himself pulling ahead of the British so he turned to starboard at about 0605. As the German destroyer turned she was hit three times. Number one gun was destroyed and the fire control room was knocked out; number two boiler room had to be shut down and fire fighting equipment was destroyed. The internal damage was the result of a single semi-armour piercing shell. The *Thiele*, however, continued to make good practice with her four remaining guns on local control, that was quite adequate at the short range. At 1,700yd she treated *Hunter*, now the leading British ship, to a deluge of 5in shells and 37mm tracer. She also seems to have fired three torpedoes one of which probably inflicted serious damage on *Hunter*, which suddenly stopped. *Hotspur* was half-a-mile astern. She fired two torpedoes which near-missed the *Thiele* but was hit by two 5in shells which cut the British destroyer's bridge communications.

Right:
Violation of Narvik Harbour, 0430 10 April.

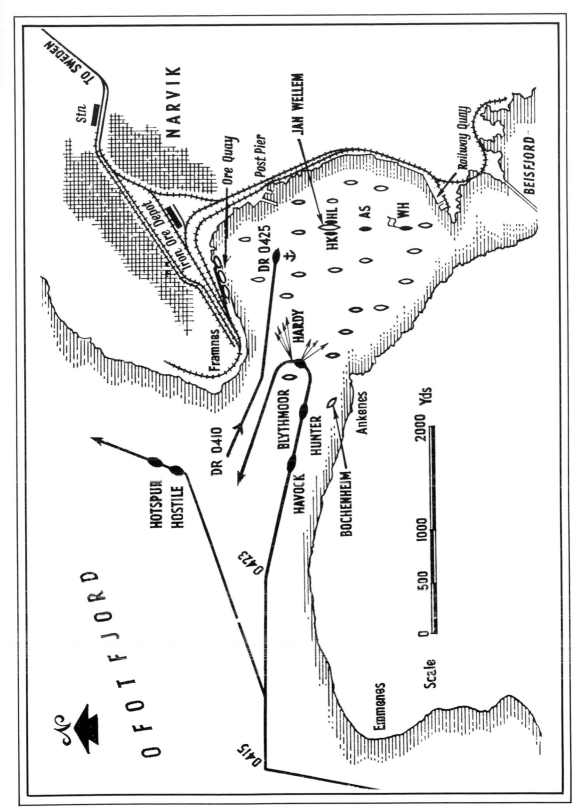

She swung to starboard and her officers could do nothing to avoid the disabled *Hunter*. At approximately 0615 the ships smashed into each other at 30kt; the sound of the collision echoed round the fiord. *Hostile* and *Havock* avoided the disaster and continued to the west.

The two ships in collision were now taken under a heavy fire from the *von Arnim*. *Hunter*, her siren screaming, heeled over to starboard and sank, one gun firing to the last. *Hotspur* extricated herself and found herself under fire from all five German destroyers; *Erich Giese* also fired a torpedo that went unnoticed. Using a human chain, Cdr Layman restored steering control in *Hotspur* and the ship's remaining gunners returned fire, damaging the *von Arnim* and keeping the timid Bey at bay. Using salt water in her boilers HMS *Hotspur* steamed westwards once more her jagged bow throwing up spray on either side. *Havock* and *Hostile* turned to protect her. Meanwhile, as her crew abandoned ship, *Hardy* fired her last gun and last torpedo at Bey's ships which returned fire; *Erich Giese* fired a torpedo which malfunctioned. Once it was clear the British were gone, Bey's three destroyers picked up *Hunter's* survivors. They did nothing to protect the ammunition ship *Rauenfels* coming up the fiord which was sunk in a huge explosion by HMS *Havock* as the British destroyers withdrew.

The remains of Warburton-Lee's Flotilla were met by the cruiser *Penelope* which was ordered up the fiord to support the destroyers' withdrawal and to patrol off the British minefield. As the survivors of the battle were congratulated a stopper

was placed in Vest Fiord to prevent movement in or out. British patrols penetrated as far as Baroy and the 'Tribal' class destroyers *Bedouin* and *Eskimo* were attacked by U25. The magnetic pistols of the G7as did not work in these high latitudes and the weapons exploded in the water and against the shore. The British thought they could have been mines and were worried about shore defences; they remained uncertain as to what actually still lay at Narvik. In reality Bey, who now assumed command, only had four undamaged ships, the *Kunne*, the *Zenker*, the *Giese* and the *Koellner*; the latter three were low on ammunition and empty of fuel. The *von Arnim* was unseaworthy with holes at bow and stern and a boiler out of action. The *Thiele* had lost both a gun and her fire control, her magazines were flooded and she had hull and machinery damage. The *Ludemann* had lost a gun and had a flooded magazine; the *von Roeder* was an immobile gun platform; the *Heidkamp* was sinking and the *Schmitt* was sunk. This was a good score for Warburton-Lee's Flotilla and disastrous news for the German

Below:
The Diether von Roeders Torpedoes.

Above right:
Battle in Ofot Fjord.

Below right:
Wolff turns west.

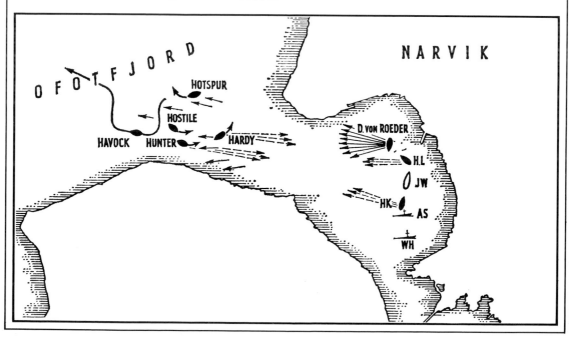

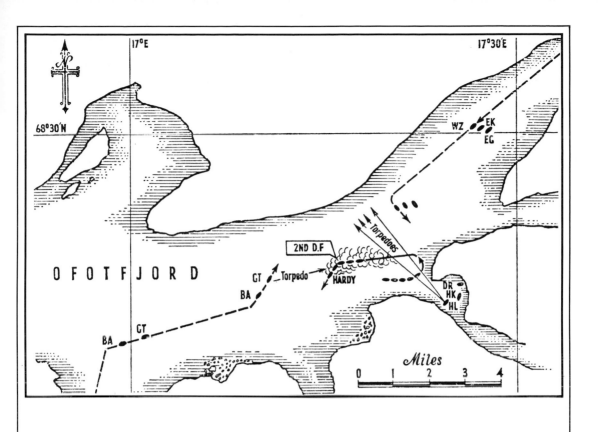

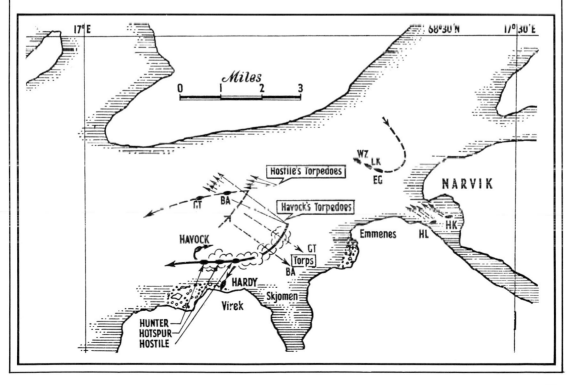

1457

Above:
Cossack **on her trials off the Tyne in 1938. The picture gives a fine view of the Rangefinder Director Mk II. Commanded by the famous Cdr Sherbrooke and with Lt Peter Gretton as her First Lieutenant** *Cossack* **was daringly handled in the second Battle of Narvik but was seriously damaged and went aground in Narvik harbour. She was eventually able to refloat herself in the early hours of 14 April but was only able to get out of Narvik stern first.** *Real Photographs/Ian Allan Collection*

Naval command. It would only be a matter of time before the British were back, and in over-whelming force this time. The German air power that was holding the Home Fleet at bay further south was not yet available so far north.

Bey tried a break-out with the refuelled *Zenker* and *Giese* on the night of the 10th but the sight of the British blockade caused him to turn back. The Admiralty again tried to take command and ordered *Penelope* and 'available destroyers' to attack Narvik but the cruiser captain suggested waiting until the 12th. Whitworth, understandably, complained of being constantly overridden by

HMS *Cossack*

Builder: Vickers-Armstrong, Tyne (launched 8 June 1937)

Displacement: 1,959 tons standard

Dimensions: 377ft x 36.5ft x 13ft

Machinery: geared turbines, two shafts, 44,000shp, 36kt

Armament: 8 x 4.7in (4 x 2) ; 4 x 2-pdr AA (1 x 4); 8 x 0.5in AA; 4 X 21in torpedo tubes (1 x 4); two depth charge throwers and one set over stern depth charge rails.

Sensors: Type 124 sonar

Complement: 190

Notes: The most famous member of a famous class built to counter the latest large Japanese destroyers. Some problem was faced by the Board of Admiralty in deciding what to call the type: 'Leader', 'Corvette' and even 'Support' were considered but in the event 'Tribal Class Destroyer' was chosen. The guns were in hydraulic Mk XIX mountings and had a realistic prolonged rate of fire of eight rounds/min per gun. The class pioneered director firing against aircraft although the 4.7in guns only had 40° elevation. The torpedo tubes were also new, power operated Mk IXs. Other members of the very powerful class at Narvik were *Bedouin*, *Punjabi* and *Eskimo*. As specialised 'destroyer destroyers' they were in their element. *Cossack* sank in October 1941 after being torpedoed by a German U-boat.

London. On the 12th the German supply ship *Alster* was captured and *Penelope* ran on to a rock off Bodo putting paid to her chances of leading an attack. In any case, her captain had been convinced by *Bedouin's* assessment of the supposed German defences that a run up the fiord was impossible.

The *Wilhelm Heidkamp* finally sank at 0600 on the 11th. Attempts were concentrated on the *Georg Thiele* to make her operational once more but this would take several days. Bey's problems increased still further that evening when the *Zenker* went aground and bent a propeller and the *Koellner* immobilised herself by grounding. The same day the Admiralty decided that the Narvik boil was to be lanced even if the Germans were disturbingly strongly established further south. The Home Fleet, moving northwards was ordered to mount 'an operation to clean up enemy naval forces and destroy shore batteries in Narvik...using synchronised dive-bombing attacks from *Furious* in combination with attack by surface forces. It is considered that the latter should consist of a battleship heavily escorted by destroyers.'

At 1615 on 11 April the Home Fleet was in position off Vest Fiord and the carrier *Furious* duly launched an air strike of nine Swordfish. The offensive capability of this multi-purpose biplane torpedo spotter reconnaissance aircraft with bombs was very limited and no significant damage was inflicted. The interwar Royal Navy had seen the surface ship as a more reliable striking weapon and had invested its limited resources accordingly. A surface attack was therefore required.

On the 12th Forbes' Staff Officer (Operations) Cdr Cecil Hughes-Hallet (later to acquire an unfortunate reputation as 'Hughes-Hitler') drew up an excellent set of orders for Operation 'DW'. The object was clear: 'Destruction of German warships, merchant ships and defences in Narvik area.' The means would be no less than the mod-

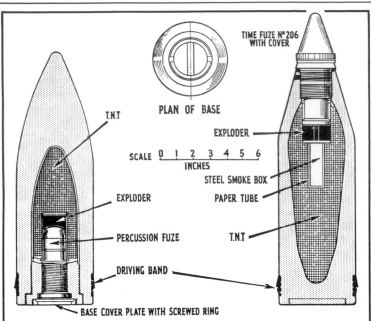

PLAN OF BASE

TIME FUZE Nº 206 WITH COVER

T.N.T

EXPLODER

SCALE 0 1 2 3 4 5 6
INCHES

STEEL SMOKE BOX

EXPLODER

PAPER TUBE

PERCUSSION FUZE

T.N.T

DRIVING BAND

BASE COVER PLATE WITH SCREWED RING

The two main types of British 4.7in destroyer shell.

Left: *Semi Armour Piercing (SAP) with small explosive charge and thick case which shattered into large fragments by the action of a percussion fuze in the base. It was British policy to use this type in the expectation of doing serious damage deep inside the target ship.*

Right: *High Explosive (HE) with thin walls, large charge and nose fuze, which could be either 'Time-Mechanical' against aircraft (as shown here) or instantaneous 'Direct Action'. This was the type favoured by the Germans because it would explode whatever it hit, even the thinnest plating.*

Left:
The two main types of British 4.7in destroyer shell.

Below:
Collision.

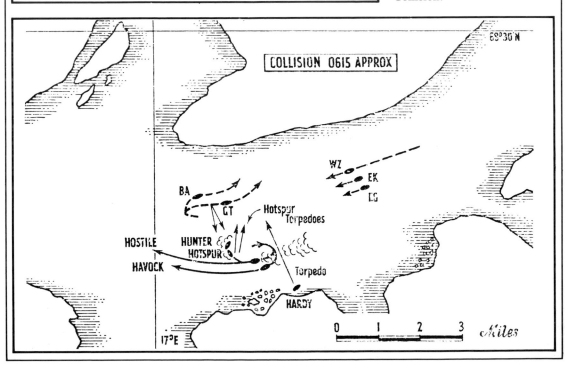

69°30 N

COLLISION 0615 APPROX

WZ
EK
LG

BA
GT
Hotspur
Torpedoes

HOSTILE
HUNTER
HOTSPUR
HAVOCK
Torpedo
HARDY

0 1 2 3 *Miles*

17°E

24

ernised Jutland veteran, the battleship *Warspite*, probably Forbes' most powerful all-round unit, accompanied by an overwhelming destroyer force consisting of *Bedouin*, *Punjabi*, *Eskimo*, *Cossack*, *Kimberley*, *Foxhound*, *Forester*, *Hero* and *Icarus*. The four last named were to be used as minesweepers. Whitworth had a special interest in commanding the operation and Forbes granted his request. He transferred by oared cutter from *Renown* that night, a hazardous feat in itself. The British force would attack on the following day, 13 April, a date that would be unlucky for one side or the other.

What was the state of the German forces? Much work had gone on to get the best out of Bey's battered force. Torpedoes had been transferred and repairs carried out. The state of each ship was as follows:

- *Hermann Kunne*: fully operational;
- *Hans Ludemann*: operational, four guns usable, after magazine pumped dry, four torpedoes;
- *Wolfgang Zenker*: operational, propeller damage but found to be able to go flat out without vibration, eight torpedoes;
- *Bernd von Arnim*: operational, repairs completed to shell holes but still feed water problem, capable of 33kt; undamaged gunnery system and six torpedoes;
- *Georg Thiele*: semi-operational due to lack of port main circulator and feed pump, capable of 27kt briefly, four 5in guns in local control only, six torpedoes;

- *Erich Koellner*: non-operational after grounding but usable as static battery;
- *Erich Giese*: non-operational, defect in machinery developed after break-out attempt and main machinery in pieces;
- *Diether von Roeder*: non-operational, only fore gun mountings manned, rigged for scuttling.

At 0838 on 13 April Bey received the news from Group West that German code breakers predicted an attack by capital ships and destroyers, possibly supported by carrier aircraft. He determined to fight it out. The *Koellner* was despatched to hobble down the fiord to take up position at Tarstad as an ambush with the *Kunne* protecting her and moving farther west as an advance picket. The poor machinery state of the other ships prevented further dispositions. Whitworth's powerful battle group began moving in before 1040 as the destroyer *Eskimo* kept *U48's* head down with depth charges. *Eskimo* then joined the starboard wing with *Bedouin* and *Punjabi*. To port were *Cossack*, *Kimberley* and *Forester* (which had ruined her minesweeping gear). In the centre steamed the great bulk of *Warspite* and ahead was the destroyer minelayer *Icarus* with bow paravanes, plus the more normal destroyers *Foxhound* and *Hero* with stern sweeps. The senior destroyer commander

Below:
After the battles Narvik harbour was littered with sunken merchantmen. *US Navy NH71406*

was Cdr J. A. McCoy who kept orders to a minimum, making it clear that he expected his captains to attack the enemy with as few restrictions as possible.

Warspite's Swordfish floatplane was catapulted off at 1152 overloaded with bombs on an armed reconnaissance. Lt-Cdr 'Bruno' Brown, the flight commander and as normal in prewar Fleet Air Arm practice, the observer, reported the *Kunne* off Tjellebotn steaming west but pressed on up the fiord. Next, at 1210, he saw the *Koellner* steaming westwards and a few minutes later the *Ludemann* in the harbour entrance. Then the shape of a U-boat was seen in Herjangs Fiord. She was the *U64* recently ordered into Vest Fiord and Brown did not stop his pilot attacking her. The submarine was hit by one 100lb anti-submarine bomb, near-missed by another and sank. The Swordfish then flew back over Narvik — passed at 1230 — to

Above:
The scene at Narvik after the first battle: in the foreground are the German destroyers *Hans Ludemann* (left) and *Hermann Kunne* (right) landing wounded and beginning to repair damage. The *Hans Ludemann*'s after guns are trained on the harbour entrance. Just visible in the bottom righthand corner of the photograph is the stern of the *Diether Von Roeder*. More destroyers are visible in the middle of the harbour among the chaos of sunk and damaged merchantmen.
Imperial War Museum (IWM) K4017

scout ahead of the group coming up the fiord. Another U-boat, *U46*, was in position to interfere with *Warspite's* majestic progress but she was unlucky and struck a pinnacle just as she was about to attack. The *Kunne* spotted ships approaching and turned east while exchanging long range fire with the British destroyers. The

Above:
The beginning of the second battle: the British destroyers sweep by Djupvik. *Redouin*, *Punjabi* and *Eskimo* are moving ahead of the minesweeping destroyers *Hero* and *Foxhound*. This and other aerial views were taken by *Warspite*'s Swordfish. *IWM A33*

Koellner had to find a spot closer to Narvik for her ambush and chose Djupvik, only to be spotted by Brown's Swordfish. Out of Narvik now came Bey with the *Zenker* and the *Ludemann*, followed by the *von Arnim*. As she turned in her tracks about 1245 the *Hermann Kunne* tried to lay a smoke screen to cover the German deployment but this was only partially successful and firing with the British destroyers began once more. At 1251 the *Ludemann* came within range of the British ships, as did the *Zenker* six minutes later; both were soon heavily engaged also. The Germans with single gun mounts had to zig-zag up the fiord to fire five-gun broadsides. The British with the twin mountings of the 'Tribals' and HMS *Kimberley* were able to keep a steady course and still fire four shots at a time. Then *Warspite* shook the mountains with her 15in guns but these were not good gunnery conditions and no one scored any hits.

As planned McCoy then took his starboard division destroyers ahead. He had the extra incentive to deal with the *Erich Koellner* which was spotted by *Bedouin* at 1305 and was under fire from all three 'Tribals' by 1310. The German ship was smashed by the concentrated fire of 24 4.7in guns and, if this were not enough, *Warspite* completed the demolition as she passed. The *von Arnim* joined the main fight in the fiord and *Cossack* had to avoid torpedoes fired by the *Zenker* and spotted by the Swordfish. *U25* fired two torpedoes at the advancing destroyers but with the predictable lack of effect. She then withdrew to attack the British on the way out. By 1330 the German destroyers were back at Narvik where they were joined by the *Georg Thiele*. *Zenker* had expended her last four torpedoes at the northern British destroyer group but it was McCoy's vanguard that began to attract most German attention. *Bedouin* was near-missed and damaged and *Punjabi* took avoiding action which left *Eskimo* leading the battle group. The *Bernd von Arnim* tried a torpedo attack but her defective weapons scored no hits despite one passing under *Cossack*. The German destroyer was bracketed with shells but suffered no damage.

The co-ordinated air strike appeared from *Furious* and the Swordfish bombed the weaving Germans. No hits were scored but the *Kunne* and *von Arnim* were near-missed; two Swordfish were shot down. The *von Arnim* and the *Zenker* were by now completely out of ammunition and at 1350 Bey ordered his ships to retire up Rombaks Fiord where they might be scuttled and their crews saved. Remarkably no one had yet scored a single hit except against the static *Koellner* because the ranges had been too long, the Germans had been

manoeuvring and the British were not firing with their proper broadside firing arcs open. Naval gunnery in 1940 was still a matter of chance and probabilities, despite the high degree of instrumentation and computerisation available. The superficially impressive gun armaments of contemporary warships were actually signs of that fact; lots of guns were needed to score a few hits. Ships were designed to fight on the broadside where the maximum number of shells could be fired most rapidly. It is not surprising therefore that with forward guns only the British destroyers were not having much success as their chances of hitting — slim enough in perfect conditions beyond 5,000yd — had been halved.

The battleship *Warspite* had special problems. She was designed for long range fleet action, not low trajectory work ahead. The gun blast of 'B' turret blew off the blast bags at the base of 'A' turret's guns and the lower turret filled with noise and fumes. The battleship's forecastle was also seriously damaged by gun blast. The gunsmoke

Below:
The fiery death of the *Hermann Kunne*. *IWM A36*

ahead obscured the main fire control director and fast manoeuvring destroyers were in any case not the easiest main armament targets for slow firing battleships. A final drawback was that at this stage of the war British battleships carried only armour piercing rounds. Nose fused high explosive would have been much more devastating against the kinds of targets that *Warspite* was actually engaging.

As the British approached the harbour at about 1400 they found the *Erich Giese* marooned in the harbour entrance, as far as she had got on her damaged engines. She engaged the *Eskimo* with torpedoes, but this was not her main danger — that was *Bedouin* and *Punjabi* coming into effective gun range to the south. These two British destroyers also fired torpedoes (which missed) and then became engaged in a gun fight with both the *Giese* and the *von Roeder*. *Punjabi* had her centralised fire control knocked out and had to switch her 4.7s to local control. The big British destroyer was hit four more times but she continued to close in to pom-pom range. *Warspite* joined in the bombardment of the *von Roeder* but with little success. *Bedouin* made undisturbed practice at the *Giese* and scored some hits but not enough to stop her

emerging bravely from the harbour when her engines were made serviceable again at 1405. She was hit first by *Bedouin* and then by *Warspite* but the 15in shells probably did not explode. The German destroyer was able to fire four torpedoes which were potentially very effective as they ran on the surface but the *Punjabi* had better luck with German torpedoes than with German gunfire and avoided the threat. *Bedouin* then closed to about half a mile of the *Erich Giese* and proceeded to hit her repeatedly but she stayed afloat until all her shells had been fired; only then was she abandoned with 83 dead left on board. It was one of the bravest actions in the short history of the German Navy.

The *Hermann Kunne* missed Bey's signal and when she also ran out of ammunition she was run ashore at Trollvik, in completely undamaged state. Her condition soon changed when her scuttling charges went off at about the same time a torpedo from *Eskimo* fired at 1413 was due to hit.

Below:
The *Erich Giese* burning and sinking after her brave fight against the odds. *IWM A22*

Above:
A view of Narvik harbour with *Cossack* (bottom left) still in action although hard aground.
IWM MISC 50674

Above right:
10 April the rescue.

Below right:
13 April 1230-1300.

Forester also attempted a torpedo shot at the *Kunne* before following *Eskimo* for the denouement in Rombaks Fiord.

At 1401 Whitworth ordered his destroyers to engage their German equivalents while he dealt with the 'shore batteries' — actually the *von Roeder* in the harbour. *Cossack*, commanded by Capt R. St V. Sherbrooke (later to find fame and lose an eye in the Battle of the Barents Sea) knew that there was indeed still a destroyer in the harbour and so moved towards Narvik, followed by *Kimberley*. They crossed *Warspite's* field of fire and she ceased fire. *Cossack's* first salvo was short and the *von Roeder* hit her fire control room and then six other parts of the famous British ship. As the *von Roeder* was only a floating battery, hits aft did not matter and her gun crews had the satisfaction of seeing the disabled *Cossack* drift ashore. The two static vessels traded shots until the *Roeder* was out of ammunition; *Kimberley* and *Foxhound* gave support also but the 25 brave German gunners survived. As *Foxhound*, which had cautiously closed her, rapidly backed away *Von Roeder's* crew blew her up.

The four remaining German destroyers sailed up Rombaks Fiord to die. The *Zenker* and the *von Arnim* went ashore first covered by the *Ludemann* and the *Thiele*. Neither ship had effective fire control and when the British hove into sight the Germans' shooting was poor. *Eskimo* shot much bet-

ter and put the *Ludemann's* after guns out of action. As the latter withdrew *Eskimo* and *Forester* smashed the *Georg Thiele* with repeated 4.7in hits. While swinging to port to complete the destruction of the German ship with a torpedo *Bedouin* spotted four enemy torpedoes approaching. They were the *Hans Ludemann's* parting shots and only masterly ship handling by Cdr Micklethwait avoided them. The *Thiele* fought on as *Hero* poked her forecastle round the fiord entrance and added her forward guns to the bombardment. The Germans had only two torpedoes left. One was fired by accident but the other ran true and on the surface. It hit *Eskimo* and blew off her bow complete with number one gun mounting. The British destroyer continued in action, however, and at 1452 fired a last torpedo at the stubborn German which missed. *Hero* now came further into the fiord to maintain pressure on the *Thiele* which fought to the last shell. *Korvettenkapitän* Wolff ran

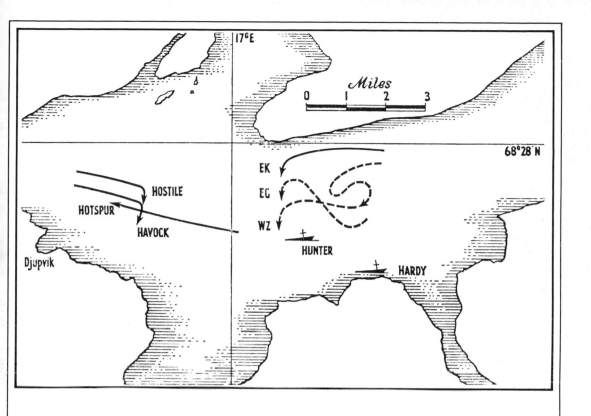

EK
EG
WZ
HUNTER
HARDY
HOSTILE
HOTSPUR
HAVOCK
Djupvik

Miles
0   1   2   3

17°E
68°28'N

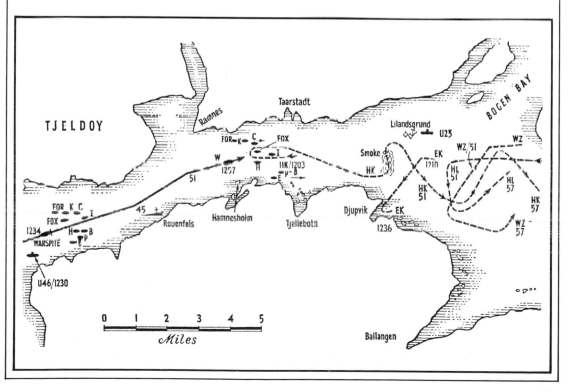

TJELDOY
Ramnes
Taarstadt
BOGEN BAY
Lilandsgrund
U25
FOR   K   C   FOX
Smoke
W
1257
HK/1203
P-B
HK
51
EK
1210
WZ/51
WZ
HL
51
HK
51
HL
57
HK
57
EK
Djupvik
1236
WZ
57
FOR   K   C
FOX
I
1234
WARSPITE
H   B
P
U46/1230
Rouenfels
Hamnesholm
Tjellebotn
Ballangen
51
45

Miles
0   1   2   3   4   5

31

Georg Thiele

Builder: Deutschewerke, Kiel (launched 18 August 1935)

Displacement: 2,232 tons standard

Dimensions: 392.5ft x 37ft x 13.1ft

Machinery: geared turbines, two shafts, 70,000shp, 38kt

Armament: 5 x 5in (5 x 1) ; 4 x 37mm AA (2 x 2); 6 x 20mm AA (6 x 1); 8 x 21in torpedo tubes (2 x 4); depth charges; provision for 60 mines

Sensors: GHG hydrophones

Complement: 315

Notes: The oldest German destroyer at Narvik, numbered Z2 in the 1930s destroyer ('Zerstorer') series. She was named after the commander of the 7th Half Flotilla of torpedo boats lost to British cruisers and destroyers on a minelaying mission in 1914. The Type 34 set the pattern for German destroyers being superficially rakish and well armed but with hidden weaknesses, notably poor sea keeping and mechanical unreliability caused by high pressure steam systems. Their bows had to be lengthened and a strengthening added to the hull. Four modified Type 34A ships were at Narvik, the *Wolfgang Zenker* (Z9, launched 27 March 1936), *Bernd von Arnim* (Z11, launched 8 July 1936), *Erich Giese* (Z12, launched 12 March 1936) and *Erich Koellner* (Z13, launched 18 March 1937). The Type 34As were slightly longer, 397ft, and Z9-13 displaced 2,270 tons standard. Other details were the same. The best feature of these ships was their heavy automatic AA armament which proved useful in surface combat also. The wreck of *Georg Thiele* was broken up in 1963.

his gallant ship aground having inflicted a serious delay upon the British. The German destroyer crews were able to get ashore to add their weight to that of the defending mountain troops. This more than doubled the German strength at Narvik.

The threat of further torpedo attack from the three ships at the head of the fiord delayed the British still further but eventually *Icarus*, *Hero* and *Kimberley* plucked up the courage to close in. They found the *Bernd von Arnim* in the centre, her bows in the air. The *Wolfgang Zenker* was still in process of being blown up and the destroyer turned over as the British watched. The *Hans Ludemann* looked intact and was fired upon. Attempts were made to tow her off as a prize but she was eventually sunk by a torpedo from HMS *Hero*.

So the naval Battle of Narvik ended with the annihilation of the German invasion flotilla, but the Germans had fought well and the destroyer crews

Right:
13 April 1330-1400.

Below:
The *Georg Thiele* after running ashore; she seems to have gone aground with some force. *IWM A24*

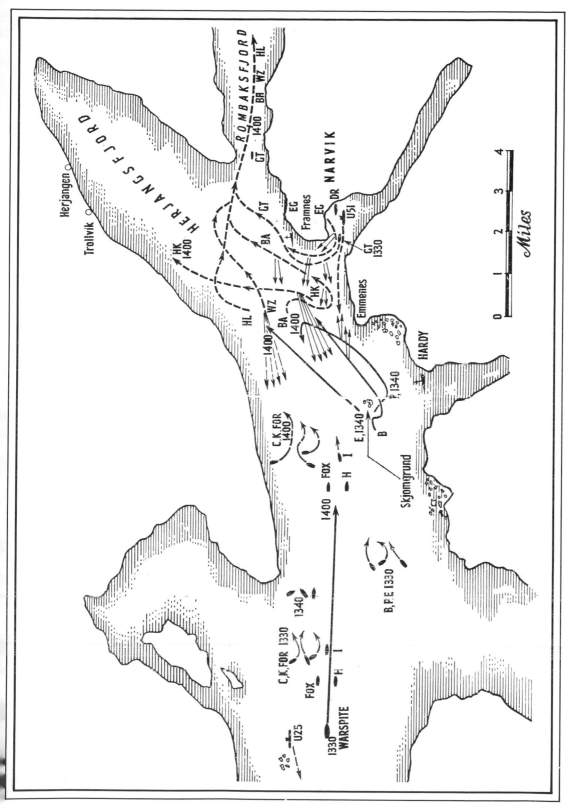

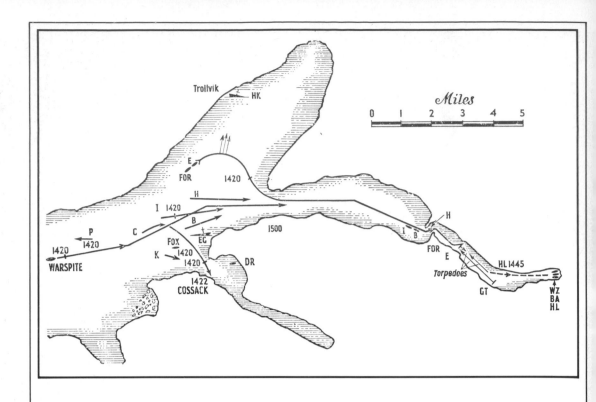

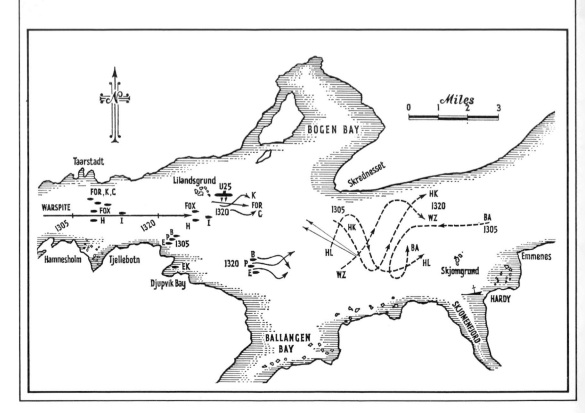

were to continue to show their mettle ashore in the defence of Narvik. As for the British, they had lost yet another opportunity. Although the Germans had more or less evacuated the town after the success of Whitworth's battle group there were no available British troops to occupy and hold this key port. When they did arrive they were not tactically loaded or equipped for the opposed landing that was by then required. By this time, German air power was also capable of reaching up even as far north as Narvik. The town only fell at the end of May by which time other disastrous events in France and Flanders necessitated immediate evacuation.

Given his responsibility for much of the confusion and failure it was ironic that Churchill should gain politically from the Norwegian débacle and replace Chamberlain as Prime Minister in early May 1940. His ability to play the defiant bulldog had been considerably helped by Warburton-Lee and Whitworth. The ability of their surface forces to exert command of the sea outside German bomber range meant that the German destroyer force had been halved. Given action damage to the rest only three German destroyers were running by the end of April; one operational flotilla of five destroyers had been reassembled by September. The German Navy was thus in no condition to contest command of the Channel with the British destroyer striking forces massed to oppose invasion. In this sense Narvik becomes one of the most significant battles of World War 2.

CHAPTER TWO

Crete

The Norwegian campaign had been won by air power. The Luftwaffe support for the invasion had come from *Fliegerkorps X* which contained those German aircrew best trained in maritime operations. Most of the strike aircraft were Heinkel He 111 high level bombers but *Fliegerkorps X's* 40-50 Junkers Ju 87 *Stuka* dive bombers had proved themselves especially useful as maritime weapons — once their pilots had got used to the special problems of attacking ships. The whole campaign had given an excellent demonstration of the need for fleets to command the air if they were to continue to command the sea or thrust power ashore from it. *Fliegerkorps X* also turned the tables on the British in the Mediterranean in early 1941 when it was deployed there to reverse the situation created by the successful British strike by the carrier *Illustrious* on the Italian fleet at Taranto. British carriers had not been designed or equipped to contest command of the air with a powerful land-based air force and only her armoured protection saved *Illustrious* from being sunk by the Stukas. She was soon replaced by her sister ship *Formidable* in March but the latter's limited number of low performance aircraft, useful though they were against the hapless Italian surface forces at Matapan at the end of March (see *Sea Battles in Close-up* Vol 1), did not promise much better results against the might of the Luftwaffe.

Below:
The Junkers Ju 87 *Stuka* dive-bombers were a formidable threat to warships once their pilots had mastered the arts of hitting moving targets; they could deliver their bombs with great accuracy.
IWM HU2924

The British had overstretched themselves following their crushing victories against the Italians in North Africa at the end of 1940 and the beginning of 1941. By the end of 1940 the British knew from intelligence reports, notably from cryptanalysis of Luftwaffe and Reichsbahn 'Enigma' traffic, that a major offensive in the Balkans was in the offing. In February 1941 Churchill overrode the doubts of his colleagues and his commanders on the spot — who wished to press on to Tripoli — and obtained a decision to send forces to Greece. All this did was to weaken the forces in Africa without giving sufficient protection to Greece. It also put a grave extra burden on Adm Andrew Cunningham, the C-in-C Mediterranean, who had to safeguard the maritime line of supply across the Mediterranean. The likely outcome was all too obvious. At the end of March the new German commander in North Africa Gen Rommel struck eastwards and a week later the Germans moved into Greece.

The tables were turned and within three weeks Cunningham was organising an evacuation of British forces from Greece: 21,000 of the 51,000 Imperial troops taken off were put into Crete, the Greek island which the British had occupied as an air and fuelling base since October 1940. Rommel's successes also increased German air cover over the Mediterranean. Despite this, Churchill rushed tank and other reinforcements to Egypt

through the Mediterranean in the 'Tiger' convoy in early May. The convoy got through but in the process *Formidable* was reduced to only four of her complement of Fulmar fighters. The arrival with the convoy of an extra battleship, *Queen Elizabeth*, and the cruisers *Naiad* and *Fiji* was only partial compensation for these aircraft losses, although *Naiad* was a 'Dido' class ship specially designed with 5.25in dual purpose guns to give anti-aircraft protection to the battlefleet. Cunningham already had two of these useful ships along with three old 'C' class cruisers converted into anti-aircraft ships with armaments of 4in AA guns and lighter weapons.

The Luftwaffe was enthusiatic about the idea of completing the Greek campaign with the conquest of Crete. The island's airfields were a threat to the Romanian oilfields and Crete might also be a useful German base for operations against Cyprus and the Suez Canal. An airborne invasion was therefore planned, Operation 'Mercury' to be carried out by the parachute and air landing troops of *Fliegerkorps XI*. Transport difficulties delayed the operation and in the event the Fifth Mountain Division that was already in Greece had to be sub-

Below:
Fast Junkers Ju 88s were also a significant menace, both as high level and dive-bombers. *IWM MH7517*

stituted for *Fliegerkorps XI's* air landing division. Moreover, part of the Mountain Division plus some heavy equipment would have to move by sea. To cover the landing was *Fliegerkorps VIII* with 280 Junkers Ju 88, Heinkel He 111 and Dornier Do 17 bombers, 90 Messerschmitt Bf 110 and 90 Bf 109 fighters and, most important for anti-ship work, 150 Junkers Ju 87 *Stuka* dive bombers massed on airfields in Greece. 'Enigma' decrypts from the famous 'Government Code and Cypher School' at Bletchley Park in England kept the British informed of the build-up and the German plans and Adm Cunningham made his preparations accordingly. Intelligence could not, however, provide an answer to *Fliegerkorps VIII* when the only fighters the RAF and Royal Navy could put on Crete were 24 Hawker Hurricanes, Gloster Gladiators and Fairey Fulmars, of which half were operational at any one time.

Cunningham's tasks were to prevent the seaborne assault and protect sea communications in the face of enemy air superiority. He formed four task groups: Force 'A' of the battleships *Queen Elizabeth* and *Barham* escorted by five destroyers to be deployed to the west to cover an intervention by the Italian Fleet; Force 'B' of the cruisers *Gloucester* and *Fiji* and two destroyers to be deployed between Cape Sapienza and Cape Matapan after landing an infantry battalion on Crete on 15 May; Force 'C' with the AA cruisers

Dido and *Coventry* and four destroyers to cover the northeastern coast of Crete; and Force 'D' with *Dido's* sisters *Naiad* and *Phoebe* with two destroyers to cover the northwest part of the island. *Phoebe* developed a defect and had to be replaced by the Australian cruiser *Perth* whose low angle

Below:
Crete as a barrier to the Aegean Sea.

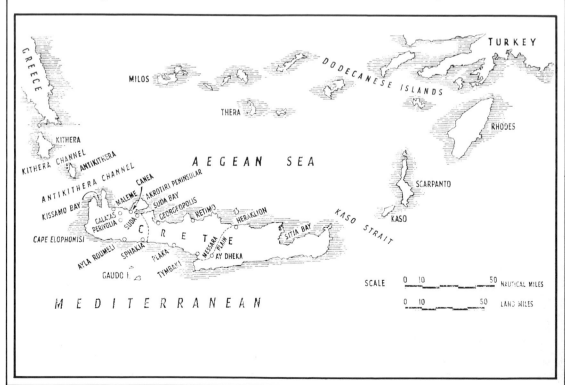

armament was less suitable for this exposed position. *Fliegerkorps VIII* made Suda Bay untenable and only motor torpedo boats were based in Crete itself. A relief battle group, Force 'A1' with *Warspite*, *Valiant*, the cruiser *Ajax* and eight destroyers would be held back at Alexandria along with the carrier *Formidable*, confined to port for want of fighters. Minefields were also laid by the fast minelayer *Abdiel* and submarine *Rorqual*. Cunningham decided to handle his dispersed forces from ashore.

It was Vice-Adm H. D. Pridham-Wippell, who had commanded the cruisers at Matapan, who took the combined Forces 'A' and 'D' to sea on the evening of 14 May. They covered a convoy to Crete as they moved to take up station. Force 'B' joined them on the 16th and the destroyers, reinforced to a total strength of 10, refuelled from the battleships. Meanwhile, Force 'C' moved independently towards the Kaso strait. The invasion date was known to be the 17th but on the 15th the Luftwaffe requested a 48hr postponement. This necessitated the relief of some of the British naval forces already deployed and Rear-Adm H. B. Rawlings took Force 'A1' to sea on the 18th. Rawlings relieved Pridham-Wippell south west of Crete on the 19th and was reinforced by two more destroyers. The other three forces returned to Alexandria to refuel, 'Enigma' having revealed a further delay in the German operation.

Below:
One of the victims on 'Black Thursday', 29 May, was Rear-Adm Rawlings' flagship HMS *Orion* hit twice by heavy bombs when crammed with 1,100 troops evacuated from Heraklion. She made it back to Alexandria with the survivors but was out of the war for almost a year.
Real Photographs/Ian Allan Collection

By the 20th — the invasion date — all surface action groups were back on station and composed as follows after some re-arrangement:

● Force 'A1' (Rawlings): *Warspite*, *Valiant* and destroyers *Napier*, *Hereward*, *Decoy*, *Hero* and *Hotspur*;
● Force 'B' (Capt H. A. Rowley): *Gloucester*, *Fiji* and destroyers *Greyhound* and *Griffin*;
● Force 'C' (Cdr H. A. King): *Naiad*, *Perth* and destroyers *Kandahar*, *Kingston*, *Nubian* and *Juno*;
● Force 'D' (Rear-Adm I. G. Glennie): *Dido*, *Orion*, *Ajax* and destroyers *Isis*, *Kimberley*, *Imperial* and *Janus*.

Force 'A1' was 100 miles west of Crete, Force 'B' was on passage to rendezvous with 'A1' 50 miles west of Crete on the 21st, Force 'C' was to the south of the Kaso Strait and Force 'D' was west of the Antikithera channel.

HMS *Orion*

Builder: Devonport Dockyard (launched 24 November 1932)

Displacement: 7,215 tons standard

Dimensions: 554.5ft x 56ft x 19.7ft

Armour: 3-3.5in belt; 1.25in over engines and boiler rooms, 2in over magazines; 1in on turrets

Machinery: Four shaft geared turbines, 72,000shp, 32.5kt

Armament: 8 x 6in (4 x 2); 8 x 4in AA (4 x 2); 12 x 0.5in AA (3 x 4); 8 x 21in torpedo tubes (4 x 2)

Complement: 570

Notes: One of the five 'Leander' class cruisers built in the early 1930s primarily for fleet work. The 6in mountings had 60° elevation and could be used against aircraft. The 4in armament had been doubled before the war. A director control tower and HACS Mk II were mounted on the bridge. After her bomb damage *Orion* was given a major refit in the USA that updated her light AA armament and added radar.

The German air assault on Crete began that day and Cunningham ordered his ships to close the island but to keep out of sight of land. Air reports of the suspected invasion fleet at sea caused Cunningham to order King and Glennie to patrol the northern approaches to Crete east and west of 25° East. When approaching Kaso Strait that evening King was attacked by the Italians, first with torpedo bombers and then with motor torpedo boats but no damage was inflicted on Force 'C'. That night Force 'E' of three destroyers was formed under Capt P. J. Mack to carry out a night bombardment of the Axis airfield on Scarpanto 50 miles east of Crete. *Jervis*, *Nizam* and *Ilex* duly shot the airfield up with numerous 4.7in shells but no aircraft were destroyed.

King found no invaders north of Crete that night and withdrew through the Kaso Strait just before sunrise to avoid the air threat. He also got the welcome support of two AA cruisers, *Calcutta*

HMS *Fiji*

Builder: John Brown, Clydebank (launched 31 May 1939)

Displacement: 8,524 tons standard

Dimensions: 555.5ft x 62ft x 19.8ft

Armour: 3.25-3.5in belt; 2in over magazines and engine rooms, 3.25in over boiler rooms; 1-2in on turrets

Machinery: Four shaft geared turbines, 80,000shp, 32kt

Armament: 12 x 6in (4 x 3); 8 x 4in AA (4 x 2); 8 x 2pdr AA (2 x 4); 16 x 0.5in AA (4 x 4); 6 x 21in torpedo tubes (2 x 3)

Sensors: Type 284 radar

Complement: 900

Notes: The first of the 'Colony' class of 8,000-ton cruisers, a size that the British preferred for reasons of economy and which they had tried to enforce on the rest of the world in the 1936 London Naval Treaty. The original preference had been to give these ships a fully dual purpose 5.25in main armament but production difficulties with the new mountings enforced a more conventional 6in fit that could use existing facilities. This was a pity as aircraft would be the cruisers' major opponents. *Fiji* was first of the class and had been fitted with radar in a 1940 refit that followed torpedo damage. Her AA armament had also been marginally increased. She had one director control tower and three HACS Mk IVs.

and *Carlisle*. Both German dive bombers and Italian high level bombers assailed the group that morning but the attackers at first got the worst of it against the powerful AA armaments of the cruisers and destroyers. At least one was shot down and two damaged but then, by unlucky chance, an Italian aircraft obtained direct hits on the destroyer *Juno*; one bomb penetrated the magazine which exploded and the ship sank in two minutes. The other British forces also suffered air attacks and their AA gunners, well hardened by experience, also scored successes. Only *Ajax* suffered significant damage, but this record was only obtained by the British ships at prodigious cost in AA ammunition.

That afternoon signals intelligence revealed the position of the invasion fleet and an RAF twin-engined Martin Maryland reconnaissance aircraft confirmed its presence about 80 miles north of Retimo. Force 'D' was tasked with its destruction with Forces 'A1' and 'B' guarding the Antikithera Strait to prevent Italian intervention. As Force 'D' entered the strait in 'a pleasing start to the night's operations' it shot down three out of four attacking Ju 88s. Force 'C' moved from the other direction to take up station on its beat and Force 'A1'

got more destroyer support in the shape of the four 'K' and one 'J' class vessels of Capt Lord Louis Mountbatten's Fifth Flotilla. Glennie, 18 miles north of Canea, spotted the enemy on radar at 2330 on the 21st. His three cruisers were now escorted by the destroyers *Janus*, *Kimberley*, *Hasty* and *Hereward*.

The invasion convoy was composed of about 25 small coasters and sailing caiques each loaded with about 100 German or Italian soldiers with artillery and ammunition to support the hard pressed parachutists ashore; the 2,331 Germans were mainly mountain infantry but the force also included a Flak battalion. The Germans were accompanied by an Italian marine detachment from the San Marco regiment. The convoy was led by the 670-ton Italian torpedo boat *Lupo* which was taken completely by surprise by the British attack. Totally outnumbered and outclassed *Lupo* laid a smoke screen and then tried to resist. She was closely engaged by all three cruisers and hit 18 times but bore a charmed life and was able to escape. Meanwhile, the British cruisers and destroyers were running down and shooting up the caiques and coasters all but three of which were sunk; none got to Crete. After smashing the convoy the British ships retired to the west, a shortage of ammunition causing the abandonment of plans to sweep northwards. The victorious Force 'D' was then recalled to Alexandria. Sadly, the forces ashore were unable to exploit this success and the attempted counter-attack on Malème airfield on the night of the 21st and morning of the 22nd failed. The Germans were

thus able to fly in reinforcements to replace the
men left bobbing in the Aegean. (Thanks to an
effective rescue operation, in which the brave *Lupo*
took a part, only 314 Axis personnel were killed in
the convoy action.) Force 'B' also made a foray
eastwards but found no enemy and was attacked
from the air. No hits were scored by the dive
bombers that appeared at sunrise on the 22nd but
holding them off depleted the cruisers' and
destroyers' holdings of AA ammunition still further.

By the 22nd *Fliegerkorps VIII* was beginning to
get the measure of maritime warfare. It deployed
its aircraft in six *Geschwaders*; *KG2* with three
Gruppen of Do 17s; *LG1* with three *Gruppen* of Ju
88s; *KG26* with one *Gruppe* of He 111s; *StG2*
with three *Gruppen* of Ju 87s; *ZG26* with two
Gruppen of Bf 110s; and *JG77* with three *Gruppen*
of Bf 109s. The Dorniers were at Tatoi north of
Athens, the Ju 88s were at Eleusis and at Molai on
the Elos peninsula; the He 111s at Eleusis; the
Stukas at Mycene and Molai, the Bf 110s at Argos
and the 109s at Molai. *Fliegerkorps VIII* was not a
specialised anti-shipping formation, as its performance so far had demonstrated, and high level
bombing was almost useless as a way of sinking
ships, although repeated near misses could have
serious effects. Even bombing that did not inflict

material damage however forced the ships
attacked to take up dispositions which were less
effective for surface action. It also forced the
expenditure of large amounts of AA ammunition
and inflicted psychological wear and tear.

Stuka Geschwader 2 (*StG2*) was intended to
engage precise targets and the crews of the '*Immelman Geschwader*', as it was nicknamed, had been
getting good on-the-job-training in the anti-ship
operations so far. By 22 May the eager *Stuka*
pilots were reaching the required standard actually
to draw blood against the Royal Navy. *LG1*'s Ju
88s were also capable of dive bombing and *JG77*'s
Bf 109s were fitted with bomb racks and were
capable of highly accurate low level attacks;
indeed, these little fighter-bombers were as great a
threat as the *Stukas*, perhaps even more so as they
could approach at low altitude, unobserved, preventing the avoiding action that was one of the
ships' main lines of defence.

King's Force 'C' was in an exposed position as
he was committed to a daylight sweep north of
Hraklion to prevent more seaborne invaders. His
destroyer screen was being strengthened by Capt
Mack with *Jervis*, *Nizam* and *Ilex*. Air attacks
began at 0700 and the British ships expended
more valuable ammunition in beating them off.
The threat could only get worse however, for, by
0830 King was only 60 miles south of the Milos
airfield and he was getting closer all the time. The
need to spread out Force 'C' to reconnoitre
conflicted with the requirements of effective air
defence. One or two surface targets were found.
Perth sank a caique as *Naiad* held off the bombers.

At 0909 destroyers were ordered to sink a small merchantman reported ahead by *Calcutta*. Then at 1010 King found what he was looking for, the largest Axis invasion convoy of 38 caiques and steamers escorted by the Italian torpedo boat *Sagittario*. The little Italian retired under a smoke screen, firing torpedoes as British shells fell all around her. The convoy was already on its way home having been recalled.

To its rescue came the Ju 88s of I/LG1. Their assault, plus the low speed imposed on his force by *Carlisle's* old engines, plus the Force's ammunition state, plus the tactical formation imposed

upon him by the air attacks led King to abandon his attack on the convoy and run to the west. Cunningham was very critical of this decision, arguing that the safest place for Force 'C' to have been was actually among the fleeing enemy transports sinking them. King, however, felt that such an attack would mean that his ships would have to spend so much time under attack from *Fliegerkorps VIII* that they would eventually suffer serious losses. Ammunition would run out and individual ships would be isolated from mutual support. Near misses would inflict decisive damage over time. In any case he was not fully aware of the size and importance of the convoy until he was committed to his run to the west.

As Force 'C' withdrew it was assailed by Ju 88s and Do 17s. No less than 181 bombs were dropped on HMS *Naiad*, 36 of which near-missed; the modern fleet cruiser began to suffer damage. Her plates sprang and all but two of her turrets were put out of action; *Naiad's* speed was reduced to 18kt. *Carlisle* received a direct hit on her bridge which killed her captain and started a fire but the damage did not prove serious. *Perth* had her main fire control put out of action by another near miss. Rawlings now moved east to give King support with his powerful battle group. Just as the forces met the *Immelman Geschwader* and *JG77*'s fighter-bombers mounted a fierce attack. Three Bf 109s took on the *Warspite* and attacked end on. One of the bombs exploded on the starboard side, wrecking the battleship's secondary batteries; damage to her boiler room intakes reduced *Warspite's* speed to 18kt. Then the destroyer *Greyhound*, which had detached from the mutual cover of the rest to sink a large caique was pounced upon by *Stukas*. Two heavy bombs caused catastrophic damage and the ship sank in 15min firing to the last.

Rear-Adm King was senior to Rawlings and took command of the combined force. He ordered *Kandahar* and *Kingston* to pick up *Greyhound's* survivors with *Gloucester* and *Fiji* in support. It had been found that even the low angle 6in guns of these ships had a significant deterrent effect on the German pilots. King was, however, unaware of the poor ammunition states of the two cruisers. When he found out at 1456 he ordered the rescuers to withdraw. By this time, despite the bombing and strafing, a number of survivors had been picked up. No ship had been hit but *Kingston* had been damaged by three near misses and the cruisers were on their last reserves of 4in AA ammunition. As they sped to rejoin the fleet they were therefore only able to put up weak and spasmodic AA barrages. This gave the *Stukas* and Bf

109s their chance. The dive bombers first attacked *Gloucester* and hit her with two bombs at 1527. One damaged a boiler room and put out the lights, the other demolished the after high angle director. After some shuddering near misses another bomb scored a direct hit on the port side; the port 2pdr pom-pom was wrecked and another bomb penetrated the mounting's platform and exploded on the deck below. Exploding 2pdr ammunition added to the general chaos caused by these two hits. The graceful cruiser lost way as her steam pipes were severed and at 1545 she was hit by three more large bombs. The wrecked ship now lay dead in the water ablaze and listing to port. Orders to abandon ship were given and she sank shortly after 1715.

HMS *Gloucester*

Builder: Devonport Dockyard (launched 19 October 1937)

Displacement: 9,400 tons standard

Dimensions: 591ft x 64.8ft x 20.6ft

Armour: 4.5in belt, 2in over boiler and engine rooms; 2-4in on turrets

Machinery: Four shaft geared turbines, 82,500shp, 32kt

Armament: 12 x 6in (4 x 3); 8 x 4in AA (4 x 2); 8 x 2pdr AA (2 x 4); 8 x 0.5in AA (2 x 4); 6 x 21in torpedo tubes.

Complement: 796

Notes: The last of the graceful 'Town' class cruisers completed in January 1939. She and her sisters *Liverpool* and *Manchester* were completed to a slightly broader beamed design with an extra main armament director control tower and improved protection. *Gloucester* had the thickest horizontal armour of the class but neither this nor her original AA armament hobbled by lack of ammunition could protect her from the *Stukas*. She seems never to have received any radar. The AA guns were controlled by three High Angle Control System (HACS) Mk IV directors.

Fiji, *Kandahar* and *Kingston* stood by as long as they could but the air threat forced them to withdraw after dropping life rafts. As an isolated force these three ships were vulnerable and they suffered numerous attacks, which went on for about two hours without much success. Then eventually at 1845 *JG77* inflicted the vital damage. One of its fighter bombers at the limit of its endurance, spotted *Fiji* and dropped its bomb close alongside to port. This blew in the cruiser's bottom plates and caused a list to port. The ship came to a standstill and lay there almost defenceless as she had finally run out of 4in ammunition. A *Stuka* now appeared to inflict the *coup de grâce* with three bombs, all of which hit. Captain William-Powlett gave the order to abandon ship and at 2015 *Fiji*, a new ship just over a year in commission, rolled over and sank. The destroyers dropped floats and withdrew to the south returning after dark to pick up 523 out of the cruiser's 780 man crew. During

the rescue the commanding officer of *Greyhound*, already rescued once that day lost his life trying to save a *Fiji* survivor in difficulty in the water.

The main force under Adm King had suffered some attacks that afternoon. At 1645 *Valiant* was unlucky enough to be hit by bombs from a high level attack but damage was slight. King now moved to place his force to intervene north of Crete by the eastern passage, which he thought might be a little safer. Although together he and Glennie had maintained a sea blockade of Crete the Ju 52s of *Fliegerkorps XI* had continued their airlift and built up German strength on the island. That night a battalion was landed from the large infantry landing ship (LSI(L)) HMS *Glengyle* to reinforce the defenders.

Because of a signalling error which said they were almost out of 2pdr pom-pom ammunition, Cunningham decided to recall his forces to Alexandria to replenish. Mountbatten's Flotilla was, however, first sent on an offensive night sweep in two groups north of Crete. *Kelly* and *Kashmir* sank two caiques and bombarded Maleme airfield, the German airhead. At dawn on 23 May as they withdrew to the west the pair were attacked by German aircraft. The first air attacks were high level and the nimble destroyers dodged the bombs. Then 13 miles south of Gaudo 24 *Stukas* of *I/StG2* appeared. *Kipling* which had been forced to detach because of engine trouble now regained contact and sped to give support. The destroyers were not easy targets and they manoeuvred to steepen the Ju 87s' dives still fur-

ther to try and put the pilots off their aim. Nevertheless, after avoiding six bombs, *Kashmir* was hit and mortally damaged. She sank in two minutes, one of her 20mm guns gaining a final revenge on a *Stuka* as she did so. Mountbatten's own *Kelly* sur-

---

HMS *Kelly*

Built: Hawthorn Leslie, Hebburn (launched 25 October 1938)

Displacement: 1,760 tons standard

Dimensions: 356.5ft x 35.75ft x 13.6ft

Machinery: Two shaft geared turbines, 40,000shp, 36kt

Armament: 6 x 4.7in; 4 x 2pdr AA (1 x 4); 8 x 0.5in AA (2 x 4); 10 x 21in torpedo tubes (2 x 5); two depth charge throwers and over stern depth charge rails

Sensors: Type 124 sonar

Complement: 218

Notes: Mountbatten's famous leader, although of the same size as the rest of the class. The leader's distinguishing feature was a longer after deckhouse. The 'Ks' like their predecessors the 'Js' had flawed AA fire control arrangements with a combined surface/AA director control tower that did not work well in the latter mode. After the trials of mid-1941 surviving members of the classes had their fire control arrangements modified. These late 1930s destroyers marked a reversion to an anti-surface warfare emphasis in British destroyer design with their heavy torpedo armaments.

Above:
Lord Mountbatten's famous flotilla leader *Kelly* **sunk by dive bombers on 23 May.** *IWM A4081*

Left:
The gallant destroyer *Kipling* **enters Alexandria harbour to the cheers of the fleet. She was carrying 128 survivors from HMS** *Kelly* **and 153 from** *Kashmir*. **Rescuing so many while under repeated air attack had been no easy task.** *IWM 4348*

vived a little longer but took a large bomb aft as she heeled under full helm at 30kt. She rolled further over to port and turned turtle even as she moved ahead. She stayed upside down for half-an-hour before sinking. The *Immelman Geshwader* pilots were a ruthless Nazi crew and they machine gunned the survivors in the water. *Kipling* was also hindered in her rescue work by high level bombing attacks that required violent manoeuvring but, despite being attacked by 40 aircraft with 83 bombs, she survived unscathed and returned to Alexandria with 153 survivors from *Kashmir* and 128 from *Kelly,* including the future First Sea Lord and Chief of the Defence Staff.

Stukas also attacked Capt Mack returning with Force 'E' from patrolling off Heraklion, but his destroyers were luckier and only suffered near misses which inflicted some damage on *Ilex* and *Havock.* As the fleet, with the King of Greece aboard, returned to its base on the 23rd, a disaster was averted by the C-in-C. The LSI(L) *Glenroy* had been sent to Crete with further reinforcements escorted by the AA cruiser *Coventry* and the sloops *Auckland* and *Flamingo.* Cunningham had called them off at 1117 as part of the general withdrawal but was then to be infuriated by a direct order from London for them to press on. Once more the Pound/Churchill backseat driving syndrome was making itself apparent. Cunningham was not a man to be trifled with and countermanded the instructions that would have offered the valuable *Glengyle,* her contents and her escorts as a sacrifice on the altar of German air power. Instead, *Fliegerkorps VIII* had to content itself with the annihilation of MTBs *67, 213, 214, 216* and *217* that had been active on search, patrol and transport missions along the coast of Crete; the attacks on the Suda Bay base also disposed of the patrol vessel *Severn.*

Cunningham was badgered by London about the continued need to prevent further seaborne landings, even at great risk to his fleet. He felt his first priority was the command of the Eastern Mediterranean for which Crete was not vital but his naval forces were. Such simple strategic wisdom seemed beyond Churchill and the Chiefs-of-Staff in London and the C-in-C's patience was stretched to the limit. Eventually he calmed down enough to draft a long dispatch to London on the 26th. It began with some fundamental strategic principles:

'It is not the fear of sustaining losses but the need to avoid losses which will cripple the fleet without any commensurate advantage which is the determining factor in operating in the Aegean. As far as I know the enemy has so far had little success in reinforcing Crete by sea'.

Britain's most aggressive Admiral needed no reminders as to the need to play a full part in the defence of Crete. As he had signalled to his ships on 24 May, when the shattering news came in about the loss of the *Hood* in the Atlantic:

'The Army is holding its own against constant reinforcement of airborne troops. We must *Not* let them down. At whatever cost to ourselves we must land reinforcements and keep the enemy from using the sea. There are indications that enemy resources are stretched to the limit. We can and must outlast them. *Stick it out*'.

On Sunday 25 May Force 'A' sailed once more under the command of Pridham-Wippell. It consisted of *Queen Elizabeth, Barham* and the destroyers *Jervis, Janus, Kandahar, Nubian, Hasty, Hereward, Voyager* and *Vendetta,* the latter two Australian vessels that had already been at sea searching for *Fiji* survivors. Force 'A' also contained a priceless asset in the carrier *Formidable* now operational again with 12 Fulmar fighters from 803 and 806 Squadrons, and 10 Albacore torpedo spotter reconnaissance bombers from 826 and 829 Squadrons. Another surface action group was already at sea following reports of landings in northwest Crete; this was composed of the cruisers *Ajax* and *Dido* and the destroyers *Imperial, Kimberley* and *Hotspur.* This found nothing in its night sweeps on the nights of the 24th/25th and 25th/26th. The fast minelayer *Abdiel* had been used to land troops in Crete after the *Glenroy* affair but now Cunningham sent *Glenroy* out again escorted by *Coventry* and two destroyers HMAS *Stuart* and HMS *Jaguar.* The was attacked by German bombers and Italian torpedo bombers which delayed its arrival and destroyed some of *Glenroy's* landing craft with near misses. Given poor beach conditions the operation had to be aborted once more. Another small convoy was also recalled the following day and only the ultra fast *Abdiel* was able to maintain communications, taking in reinforcements and evacuating wounded. Two destroyers accompanied the minelayer on her mission on 26th/27th and *Hero* was damaged by a near miss.

Force 'A' struck at the *Stuka* base at Scarpanto early on the 26th using *Formidable's* Albacores. It was not much of a counterattack with only six aircraft, two of which had to abort. Four Fulmars were sent off later in support. The bombers destroyed two aircraft and damaged others and the Fulmars strafed several other Stukas and Italian Fiat CR42 fighters that shared the field. The attackers achieved complete surprise but the limited resources available lessened their impact. Force 'A' was now joined by the cruiser group fresh from its search north of Crete: *Imperial, Kimberley* and *Hotspur* were short of fuel and were replaced by *Napier, Kelvin* and *Jackal.* The force opened the range from Scarpanto but came within range of *Fliegerkorps X* in North Africa. Only four Fulmars were serviceable when about 20 *Stukas* were seen coming from the south. The fighters were launched and directed to their targets as best they could be, given the primitive state of fighter control at the time; they shot down three Stukas and damaged another for the loss of one Fulmar. They were just too few to break up the attack, however, and *Formidable* was hit, seriously, on the starboard side forward. After some near misses a large bomb exploded on the starboard quarter. *Formidable's* damage control parties got the fires under control and the damaged compartments were sealed off, but it would be months before the crippled carrier would be operational again. The other damaged ship was the destroyer *Nubian* that had her stern blown off by a direct hit. Both ships were detached with destroyer escort to return to Alexandria. The crack pilots of *Fliegerkorps X* had done it again and neutralised the Mediterranean Fleet's carrier. Armour protection could not make up for too few aircraft.

The following day, the 27th, as Force 'A' covered the *Abdiel* group's withdrawal it suffered another *Stuka* attack which hit and near-missed *Barham.* The battleship suffered a serious fire and her bulges were flooded. At 1230 Pridham-Wippell was ordered back to Alexandria. On Crete the situation for the Imperial forces was getting desperate. Evacuation was in the air and Cunningham reassured his colleagues that his fleet would make another all-out effort to get the army off. At 0827 on the 27th, therefore, Wavell, the Theatre Commander was forced to reply to Churchill's

exhortations to resist that the grim reality was evacuation. The Chiefs-of-Staff approved with the priority for evacuation to go to personnel rather than equipment.

The enemy's command of the air meant that ships could only evacuate in darkness with a mere three hours spent at Crete. This allowed four hours steaming under cover of darkness there and back. At 0600 on the 28th Force 'B' set sail for Heraklion Harbour under Rawlings' command. It consisted of the cruisers *Orion, Ajax* and *Dido* and the destroyers *Decoy, Jackal, Imperial, Hotspur, Hereward* and *Kimberley.* The intention was the embarkation of the 4,000 men of the Heraklion garrison that night from the harbour. Force 'C' under Capt S. H. C. Arliss and consisting of the destroyers *Napier, Nizam, Kandahar* and *Kelvin* left two hours later for Sphakia with additional boats to lift the troops off the beach. Arliss arrived at his destination at 0030 and by 0300 had taken off 700 men. Food, rations and arms were landed for the 15,000 that had to be left behind that night. Ju 88s attacked the destroyers on their way to Alexandria but only minor damage was suffered and Force 'C' made Alexandria at 1700 on the 29th.

Rawlings was not so lucky as the Germans were concentrating on the situation at Heraklion. Force 'B' was attacked by high level bombers, dive

Below:
Stukas blew the stern off the destroyer HMS *Nubian* during their strike on the *Formidable* battle group on 26 May. This was despite the presence of the twin 4in AA mounting clearly visible on 'X' position. *IWM A16827*

bombers and torpedo bombers on the evening of the 28th. The destroyer *Imperial* was near-missed and suffered steering damage which did not seem serious at the time. Then *Ajax* had bombs fall close and her damage seemed serious enough for Rawlings to order her back to Alexandria. He could not afford lame ducks on this operation.

Rawlings arrived off Heraklion at 2330 on the 28th. The troops were smoothly taken off the quays by the destroyers and ferried out to the cruisers. Thanks primarily to the organisational skill of the local Naval commander, Capt M. H. S. Macdonald, the operation went like clockwork and all the troops were taken off down to the last rearguard. The concern was what would happen after daylight for the ships had not been able to get away until 0320 and it was a long way to Alexandria via the Kaso Strait. The ships left crowded with troops. *Orion* was carrying 1,100 in addition to her ship's company of 550; the destroyers each had 300 on board, twice their ships' companies of about 150 each. Then, at 0345, disaster struck: *Imperial's* damaged steering failed and she veered off out of control, her rudder jammed. There was no alternative but to leave her after transferring her troops and crew to *Hotspur* which was left behind to sink *Imperial* with a torpedo after the transfer was completed. It took two Mk IXs to finish off the doomed vessel and it was not until 0445 with dawn not far away that *Hotspur* started eastwards once more, with 900 men aboard.

At considerable risk Rawlings only proceeded at 15kt to allow *Hotspur* to catch up and the relieved destroyer rendezvoused with the rest of Force 'B'

at 0600 at the Kaso Straits. As the half-light brightened the Force set course for Alexandria 300 miles and 10 long hours away. Ju 88s were already in evidence and soon they were joined by Scarpanto's *Stukas* which pressed home repeated attacks. The British ships were skilfully handled once more, forcing the German pilots to steepen their dives. This forced early bomb release as the *Stukas* could not go beyond the vertical; early bomb release meant a less accurate trajectory. The dive-bombers shuttled back and forth to their nearby airfield and it was only a matter of time before one would score a hit. It came at 0625 on the destroyer *Hereward*. Again the cripple had to be abandoned and the damaged ship made for the coast of Crete, her AA guns spitting back frustrated defiance as more bombers closed in for the *coup de grâce*. *Hereward* finally blew up but Italian MTBs that had just brought Mussolini's main contribution to the invasion of the island picked up large numbers of survivors.

At 0605 *Decoy* was near-missed which reduced Rawlings' speed to 25kt and at 0730 this came down to 21kt as *Orion* was near-missed also. Then Rawlings received the extra blow; he was informed that because of an error in time zones he could not expect promised RAF fighter cover until 0840! The only additions to the ships' AA armaments were therefore the soldiers on deck with their machine guns and other small arms. Despite this hail of fire some of the braver *Stuka* pilots carried out low level strafing runs. One of these killed *Orion's* captain and slightly wounded Rawlings.

Below:
The Eastern Mediterranean.

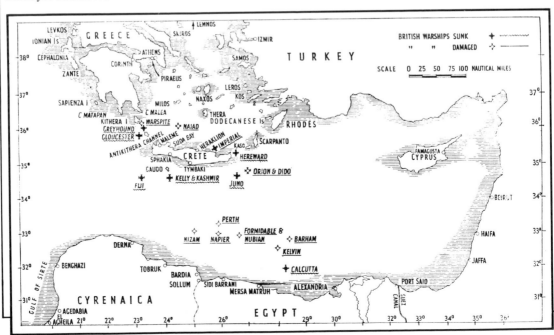

Then a bomb hit the cruiser's 'A' turret and caused a fire. *Dido* also had a turret put out of action by a bomb.

After a brief lull the *Stukas* returned refuelled and rearmed at 1045. Eleven dived in succession on *Orion*. One bomb passed through the bridge and exploded on the crowded mess deck below; 260 soldiers and sailors were killed and 280 wounded. Fires blazed and damage to compasses, steering and engine room telegraphs made navigation difficult. Despite the loss of vital officers, the brave cruiser maintained 21kt. Eventually two Fleet Air Arm Fulmars appeared but these were the only fighters to find Force 'B', testimony to the Admiralty's long-standing conviction that long distance navigation over the sea was beyond the ability of single seat fighter pilots. The Hurricanes may have got lost but at least they accounted for two Ju 88s. Three high level bombing attacks were endured but the 1045 attack was the last made by the dive bombers. *Orion* slowed as her fuel became more contaminated with sea water and her list increased but she and her battered Force 'B' arrived at Alexandria at 2000. Of the 4,000 soldiers lifted 800 had been killed, wounded or captured. It could have been much worse and Rawlings was right to be 'cheerful but exhausted' when he met the C-in-C on arrival.

Thousands of troops remained at Sphakia and Force 'D' had sailed on the evening of the 28th to bring them off. Under King, this force consisted of the cruisers *Phoebe*, *Perth*, *Calcutta*, and *Coventry* with the destroyers *Jervis*, *Janus* and *Hasty*. Also with the force was the LSI(L) *Glengyle* with her remaining landing craft and capacity for 3,000 troops. The events of the 29th however led to ships bigger than destroyers being taken off evacuation operations. After consultations with the Admiralty it was decided to confirm *Glengyle's* withdrawal because of the danger of too many eggs in that one large basket; the cruisers, however, were to carry on. By this time it was the evening of 29 May and too late; Force 'D' in toto was off the beaches with *Glengyle's* landing craft doing sterling work ferrying the men out to the warships as the two old AA cruisers stood off giving cover. Cunningham decided to retain the original plan but sent three more destroyers, *Stuart*, *Jaguar* and *Defender*, to act as extra escort and if necessary rescue assets. *Perth* had been near-missed by Ju 88s on the way across to Crete but her two specially embarked landing craft were undamaged and proved a useful supplement to *Glengyle's*. By 0320, 6,000 men had been taken off and King set sail, being joined by his extra destroyers at about 0650. This time the RAF were able to find the evacuation fleet and put up a spirited defence that held off both *Stukas* and Ju 88s

and shot down a couple of He 111s. *Perth* was hit by a bomb which put a boiler room out of action but there was nothing to compare with the carnage of 'Black Thursday'.

It was now estimated that about 8,000 assorted troops remained at Sphakia. Four destroyers had left Alexandria that morning to continue their evacuation. Arliss' Force 'C' of *Napier*, *Nizam*, *Kelvin* and *Kandahar* was halved in strength as *Kandahar* had suffered mechanical problems and *Kelvin* had to return to Alexandria after a near miss reduced her speed. His two remaining ships took off over 1,510 men using three landing craft that King had left behind and ships' boats. Again RAF cover was good on the return journey and the fighters shot down three Ju 88s and an Italian Cant 1007. The most serious attack was by a dozen Ju 88s between 0850 and 0915 and both destroyers were near-missed, reducing Force speed to 23kt. AA fire claimed one of the attackers, however, and three more were damaged. Force 'C' arrived at Alexandria without further incident.

There were still an estimated 6,500 men at Sphakia, and the real total was closer to 10,000. Cunningham was torn between his sense of duty to the Army and his task of preserving his fleet for its wider roles. The fate of Rawlings seemed to suggest that ships crammed with troops were not at peak fighting efficiency. With, however, personal requests from the Prime Minister of New Zealand landing on his desk there was little the C-in-C could do but agree to confirm a final rescue mission on the night of 1 June. Sufficient strength was to be sent to take off the estimated number, the minelayer *Abdiel*, the destroyers *Kimberley*, *Hotspur* and *Jackal* and the cruiser *Phoebe*, despite a considerable reluctance to risk any more of the valuable 'Didos'. Cunningham personally went on board the latter ship when she arrived with Force 'D' to tell *Phoebe's* crew the bad news that they were going back immediately. Not one man took the offer of being left behind. The cruiser became Vice-Adm King's flagship.

So Force 'D' sailed for the last time at 0600 on the 31st. News came in later that day that there were at least 9,000 men still at Sphakia but Cunningham refused to sanction another rescue mission. RAF aircraft provided effective cover on the outward voyage and three air attacks were beaten off. The RAF Hurricanes, like their German counterparts, were learning the skills of maritime warfare. To increase the Hurricanes' range they were flying with extra fuel tanks and with reduced ammunition loads.

The 4,000 men chosen for evacuation were the organised units that had done much of the fighting but many stragglers were successful in getting aboard and, in the end, the three battalions of the final rearguard were left behind. As in all evacuations not all showed great courage or self control, but that there was so much of this latter quality in evidence was a remarkable tribute to the human spirit in a less than perfect world. Most of those who were left behind were made prisoner but about 700 made their own way by boat to North Africa, almost 200 were taken off by submarine and as many as 500 found refuge in the hills.

King finally sailed at 0300 on 1 June. Cunningham sent out *Calcutta* and *Coventry* to give support but ironically enough it was the two AA ships that found themselves assailed from the air only 85 miles off Alexandria. Dive bombing Ju 88s missed *Coventry* but scored two direct hits on *Cal-*

HMS Calcutta

Built: Armstrong Whitworth, Walker (launched 9 July 1918) converted Chatham Dockyard 1938-9

Displacement: 4,200 tons standard

Armour: 1.5 -3in belt; 1in deck

Dimensions: 425.1ft x 43.5ft x 14.25ft

Machinery: two shaft geared turbines, 29kt

Armament: 8 x 4in AA (4 x 2); 4 x 2pdr AA (1 x 4); 8 x 0.5in AA (2 x 4)

Complement: 439

Notes: One of the second batch of old 'C' class light cruisers converted to AA ships in 1938-40. The conversion was kept simpler than in the first batch; advantage was taken of the new Mk XIX twin 4in mountings to put the guns on the existing 6in supports. The 2pdr pom-pom was placed in 'B' position. Two HACS Mk III systems provided director control.

---

cutta which proved two much for the old cruiser hull — she quickly sank. *Coventry* picked up 255 survivors then returned to base. Cunningham felt the loss of this ship especially deeply as he had once been her commanding officer. With the Germans' attention elsewhere and the RAF Hurricanes continuing their effective cover Force 'D' had an uneventful voyage and made Alexandria at 1700.

Cunningham has been criticised for not having tried just one more rescue but it is easy to sympathise with the harassed C-in-C who was seeing his fleet suffer steady attrition to Axis air power. Air cover was improving but it was still far from reliable. The Mediterranean Fleet was just too important to be totally neutralised to save what were, if all had gone according to plan, disorganised soldiers who would have been spread across the Imperial armies and whose survival would hardly have been noticed in operational or strategic terms. It was unfortunate that the units actually left behind included a valuable Royal Marine

battalion, one of the first Commando units and a crack Australian battalion. The Army and RAF commands in the area fully appreciated the effort that had gone into lifting over half the defenders off the island. The Mediterranean Fleet had also, despite a very unfavourable air environment, prevented a seaborne invasion. This had been achieved for the loss of two modern cruisers, an AA cruiser and six destroyers. As important was the serious damage to an aircraft carrier, two battleships, four cruisers and two destroyers. This meant that critical units would spend months in dockyard hands. Another cruiser and an AA ship plus five destroyers were facing weeks in repair yards and the Mediterranean Fleet was down to two battleships and three cruisers to face four Italian battleships and 11 cruisers. Cunningham's margin of superiority had disappeared and not even Bletchley Park could help Cunningham predict whether the Italians would exploit this very favourable situation.

Operationally, the lesson of Norway had been reinforced. Fleets could not operate for periods of days in waters dominated by an aggressively handled hostile air force if they did not have adequate air cover of their own. Even if they were not sunk they would be damaged sufficiently for the fleet as a whole to become a rapidly wasting asset. This is not to over estimate the effect of air power. Both *Fliegerkorps VIII* and the RAF demonstrated that without proper training and experience aircraft could be remarkably ineffective in attacking and defending ships. Nevertheless, as both sides found out, operational techniques can rapidly improve, both in attack and defence. Even with the new-found skill of the Desert Air Force's fighter pilots, the loss of *Formidable* greatly limited Cunningham's options. British command of the Eastern Mediterranean was looking very doubtful.

Now, however Hitler's grand strategy came to the rescue. The invasion of the USSR was due to start in June when sufficient equipment finally became available. Hitler's Balkan adventures had never been more than a flank-clearing exercise for the decisive bid for *Lebensraum* in the East. This would need every Luftwaffe squadron that could be spared. *Fliegerkorps VIII* moved east to resume its more traditional tasks supporting a land Blitzkrieg. *Fliegerkorps X* replaced it on the Eastern Mediterranean airfields and concentrated on this area rather than covering the still vital Axis supply routes in the Central Mediterranean. Pressure on Malta was reduced, indeed reduced sufficiently for the island to be used as a base for surface forces attacking Rommel's supply lines. Despite its recent travails, the Royal Navy thus had an opportunity to go on the offensive once more.

CHAPTER THREE

Malta Striking Forces

The Royal Navy has usually been in the business of sea control rather than sea denial; that is, it has been interested primarily in protecting the use of the sea rather than merely preventing someone else using it. It was a sign of Britain's faltering great power status that on several occasions in World War 2 she had no alternative but to attempt sea denial in situations of enemy predominance. One of the most notable of these cases was in the Central Mediterranean where the continued possession of Malta provided a base astride the Axis supply line between Italy and North Africa.

One way of dealing with Malta would have been an airborne invasion but Hitler would not countenance such a thing, especially after the pyrrhic casualties of the Crete victory. Capturing Malta would also have meant supplying it and Hitler preferred the British to pay the price of continuous resupply operations. Surgery being both risky and prone to dangerous long term effects it was left to the strategic anaesthetic of Axis air power to keep Malta's pain within bounds. This medication could be very successful. In March 1941 No 148 Squadron's Wellington bombers were forced to flee Malta leaving a single, battered squadron of Fleet Air Arm Swordfish torpedo bombers on the island. Although the British also established the 10th Flotilla of small 'U' class submarines at Malta — and these boats had their individual successes — they were unable to make much impression on the Axis troop and supply convoys. The Germans were able to send Rommel and his *Afrika Korps* to reinforce the Italians and supplies piled up at Tripoli in excess of the demands of the Axis armies. They could go no further because of the shortcomings of the transport system in North Africa itself.

In June 1941, however, the treatment stopped. With the invasion of the USSR about to take place the Luftwaffe in the Mediterranean had to be spread more thinly. After gaining air superiority over Malta, the main forces of *Fliegerkorps X*, which had already moved some squadrons to Libya, were transferred from Sicily to replace *Fliegerkorps VIII* in Greece and Crete. The remaining Italian threat to Malta was insufficient to prevent both the reinforcement of the offensive air forces in Malta and, more importantly, the basing of a powerful surface action group in the island. Such a group could annihilate a whole convoy at a single blow and allow Malta at last to make its presence really felt.

What might be achieved had been demonstrated in April 1941 when 'Ultra' decrypts from Bletchley Park revealed that elements of the 15th Panzer Division were about to embark for Tripoli. *Fliegerkorps X*'s activities were already becoming dissipated; both *Stukas* and Bf 110s had been transferred to Libya to support Rommel's offensive in March. Cunningham, that old destroyer man, thought it might now be safe enough to interdict the movement with surface ships based at Malta. Capt P. J. Mack, Captain of the 14th Flotilla arrived in the island on 11 April with four powerful destroyers, the 'Js' *Jervis* and *Janus* and the larger 'Tribals' *Nubian* and *Mohawk*. 'Ultra' did not give a complete window on to Axis communications — Italian naval communications were relatively secure at this stage — and Mack depended on the handful of reconnaissance Marylands of No 69 Squadron RAF based at Luqa airfield for detailed tactical intelligence. The first two convoys escaped but, at 1430 on 15 April Sqn Ldr E. A. Whitley and Flt Lt Arnold Potter in Maryland AR714 reported a troop and ammunition convoy that had sailed from Naples for Tripoli two days before. Covered by rain and low cloud, Mack duly sailed from Grand Harbour to make a perfect interception.

The first victim in the night attack off Sfax in the early hours of 16 April was the Italian destroyer *Baleno* that was quickly knocked out by accurate 4.7in salvoes from *Jervis* and *Janus* at 2,400yd, *Nubian* hit the ammunition ship and two of the four German troopships before becoming occupied with another Italian escort, the *Luca Tarigo*. The big 'Navigatori' class destroyer was also engaged by *Jervis* and *Mohawk* and suffered serious damage from both 4.7in shells and a torpedo. Another Mk IX accounted for the Italian ammunition ship that blew up in an appropriately massive explosion.

The Italian Navy's problems with operating and organising fleets should not mask a record of individual courage second to none and *Tarigo* added to that fine tradition. Her wounded captain con-

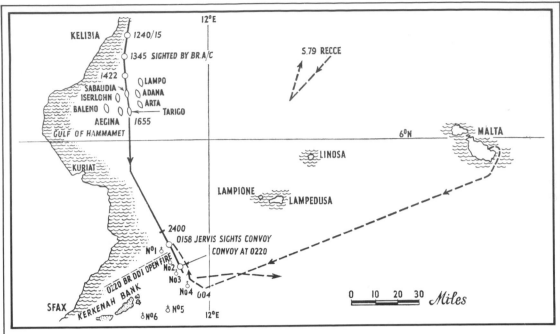

Above:
Convoy action of 15/16 April 1941.

Below:
Convoy action of 16 April.

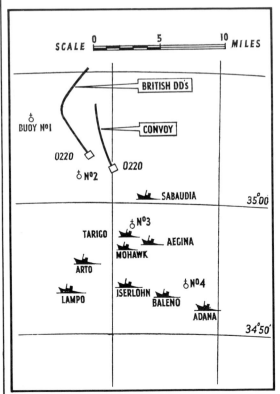

tinued to give orders until he bled to death and, despite being dead in the water, she fired two torpedoes both of which hit HMS *Mohawk*. One blew off the stern of the 'Tribal' and the other put a large hole in the destroyer's port side. She rolled over onto her beam ends with the after part submerged. *Janus* took her revenge by pouring fire into the wreck of the *Tarigo* until she was no longer a threat and *Nubian* disposed of the third escort, the destroyer *Lampo*, forcing her to run aground. She then damaged a third German troopship with gunfire and forced her aground also. *Mohawk*'s survivors were then picked up and the wreck was finally sunk with four 4.7in shells. The convoy had been wiped out with three ships

---

Luca Tarigo

Built: Ansaldo, Genoa (launched 9 December 1928)

Displacement: 2,125 tons standard

Dimensions: 358.5ft x 36.7ft x 11.1ft

Machinery: two shaft geared turbines, 50,000shp, 28kt

Armament: 6 x 4.7in (3 x 2): 7 x 20mm AA (7 x 1); 8 x 13.2 mm AA (4 x 2); 6 x 21in torpedo tubes; 2 depth charge throwers

Complement: 224

Notes: A two-funneled destroyer of the large 'Navigatori' class originally designated 'scouts' and built to counter large French 'contre torpilleurs'. The ships were much modified to improve sea keeping qualities that were never entirely satisfactory, even in Mediterranean waters. Both the *Tarigo* and her sister *Alvise Da Mosto* put up brave defences against the Malta Striking Forces.

sunk and two forced aground after suffering damage. One of the latter eventually also sank and the other was blown up by boarding parties from the submarine *Upholder*. A major Italian rescue operation saved 1,271 of the 3,000 men aboard the ships but 300 vehicles and 3,500 tons of stores were lost.

Mack tried to take out another convoy with a reconstituted striking force of four 'J' class destroyers in the early hours of 24 April. Due to a mix-up, however, the Flotilla sank an armed auxiliary and the convoy reversed course out of danger. Mack was then replaced by Mountbatten and his Fifth Flotilla of six 'Js' and 'Ks' with the cruiser *Gloucester* in support. *Fliegerkorps X* was taking a new interest in Malta by this time with both

Below:
The little 'U' class submarines of the 10th Flotilla at Malta provided useful support for the surface Striking Forces. They continued to operate when Malta was untenable for surface forces but they were unable to make the same impression as the surface action groups. *Ian Allan Collection*

bombing and aerial mining and when the Flotilla left Malta to attack a convoy HMS *Jersey* exploded a mine and blocked the harbour entrance forcing the abandonment of the attack. Other priorities, notably the 'Tiger' convoy of tanks to Egypt, meant that no more convoy strikes could be carried out, before Mountbatten left on 21 May for his nemesis off Crete.

The move of *Fliegerkorps X* to the Balkans and the Western Desert effectively raised the first 'air siege' of Malta and the island's air defences were also improved with the addition of no less than 228 Hurricanes flown in from the aircraft carriers *Ark Royal* and *Furious* in seven separate operations between 3 April and 30 June. More Swordfish arrived from *Ark Royal* for No 830 Squadron in July and the torpedo bombers were reinforced by specialist tropicalised long-range anti-shipping Blenheim IVs from No 2 Group RAF, operating in rotation.

No sooner had *Fliegerkorps X* disappeared than the British obtained another major advantage. The Italian medium grade cyphers used to send details of shipping movements had hitherto been

secure. The Government Code and Cypher School at Bletchley Park had only been able to help the Malta striking forces when information was obtained from German 'Enigma' codes. Now the Germans, who wrongly doubted the security of Italian codes prevailed upon their allies to adopt a new cypher, using a Swedish designed machine called the 'C38'. Bletchley Park was soon able to break into 'C38m' and from June was able to give Malta warning of Axis movements. To guard the 'ultra-secret' source reconnaissance aircraft were sent to 'find' the targets before attacks were carried out. Thus informed, the Swordfish and Blenheims began to operate with increasing effectiveness and together with the submarines accounted for significant percentages of Axis supplies. Nineteen per cent of Rommel's supplies went to the bottom in July and nine per cent in August. Rommel was worried, but need not have been. Sufficient supplies were still reaching North Africa to deal with Rommel's demands; his problems were caused by the difficulties in getting them to the front. The air reinforcement of Malta was stepped up. More anti-shipping Blenheims arrived, as did a second Fleet Air Arm torpedo bomber squadron (No 828 with Albacores), Wellington bombers and 93 more Hurricanes. Only surface forces, however, could put a real squeeze on the Afrika Korps.

Churchill sensed this and in August minuted Pound to consider 'the sending of a Flotilla, and, if possible a cruiser or two, to Malta, as soon as possible'. This resulted in the creation of Force 'K', the light cruisers *Aurora* and *Penelope* and the destroyers *Lance* and *Lively*. The two cruisers were small vessels of the 'Arethusa' class of 5,220 tons standard displacement. They had been built in the late 1930s primarily for work in the battlefleet as scouts and flotilla support vessels. They were armed with six 6in guns in three twin turrets and carried AA batteries of four twin 4in guns and two quadruple pom-poms. Both ships had radar for air search and the 284 surface fire control radar on their main armament directors; *Penelope* in addition had 285s on her high angle directors for control of her secondary armament. The two destroyers were brand new 'L' class vessels which carried eight 4in AA guns instead of their designed armament of six 4.7in guns. This had been forced by production difficulties but the substitute armament was not a bad one for service in the Central Mediterranean, especially as it meant they could carry their full complement of eight 21in torpedo tubes without detracting from their AA potential. Both were fitted with the latest fire control and search radar

The two cruisers came from the Home Fleet and the destroyers from Force 'H' at Gibraltar.

HMS *Aurora*

Built: Portsmouth Dockyard (launched 20 August 1936)

Displacement: 5,120 tons standard

Dimensions: 506ft x 51ft x 16.5ft

Armour: 2.75-3in belt, 2.75in over magazines, 1in over engine and boiler rooms; 1in on turrets

Machinery: four shaft geared turbines, 64,000shp 32.25kt

Armament: 6 x 6in (3 x 2); 8 x 4in AA (4 x 2); 8 x 2pdr AA (2 x 4); 6 x 20mm AA (6 x 1) ; 16 x 0.5in AA (4 x 4); 6 x 21in torpedo tubes

Sensors: Radar types 284 and 290

Complement: 500

Notes: She and her sister *Penelope* formed Force 'K'. They were half of the 'Arethusa' Class built as the smallest possible fleet cruisers at the beginning of naval re-armament. The extra AA armament and radar had been added in 1940-41. *Aurora* was transferred to the Chinese Navy in 1948, taken over by the Communists and sunk by Nationalist aircraft in 1949. She was raised and seems to have remained officially in service until the mid 1950s.

Force 'K' arrived in Malta at 0915 on Trafalgar Day 21 October, which proved to be an auspicious portent. The Force commander was the CO of *Aurora*, Capt William G. Agnew. 'Bill' Agnew was not cleared for 'Ultra' but obtained his orders from Vice-Adm Sir Wilbraham Ford, the Flag Officer at Malta who was authorised to receive the special intelligence. The air reconnaissance and target confirmation role was in the hands of a 'Special Duties Flight', three Wellington Mk VIIIs of No 211 Squadron, of RAF Coastal Command. Equipped with ASV radar these had been sent out in September to counter the increased use made by the Italians of darkness to run their convoys.

The system was not fool-proof and Force 'K's' first attempt to find a convoy on 25-26 October failed when the Wellington found nothing. In fact a northbound two-ship convoy escorted by an Italian destroyer had been at sea and arrived safely at Brindisi on 28 October. A similar failure of air reconnaissance occurred on the night of 1-2 November.

It was, therefore, with no certainty that action was in the offing that Force 'K' left Valetta Harbour on the night of Saturday 8 November. The expected convoy had been confirmed at 1400 that day by a Maryland daylight reconnaissance air-

craft; 40 miles off Cape Spartivento, steering due south at just over 10kt. The assigned ASV Wellington suffered wireless and radar failure but Force 'K' was able to find its quarry without its help — and the Malta command could rely on the earlier daylight sighting to safeguard security. The convoy consisted of seven ships: two German, — the *Duisberg* and *Dan Marco*; and five Italian — the *Maria*, *Sagitta* and *Rina Corrado* and the tankers *Minatitlan* and *Conte di Misurata*. The escort was quite a powerful destroyer group composed of six standard Italian fleet destroyers: *Maestrale*, *Libeccio*, *Grecale*, *Oriani*, *Euro* and *Fulmine*. This level of protection reflected the recognition that the threat to the convoys had become more serious. A covering force was, therefore, provided made up of the two heavy cruisers *Trieste* and *Trento*. The cruisers had their own escort of four destroyers, *Granatiere*, *Fuciliere*, *Bersagliere* and *Alpino*, all of the latest 'Soldati' class.

The officer commanding the convoy operation was Adm Bruno Brivonesi flying his flag in *Trieste*. Brivonesi planned to keep the covering force within sight of the convoy during the night by zigzagging astern or abeam of it at 16kt. The convoy was routed well to the east of Malta, outside of torpedo bomber range. Two Italian submarines, *Settembrini* and the *Delfino*, were given patrol areas between the convoy route and Malta in order to try to catch Force 'K' at sea. They were, however, unsuccessful as just after midnight on 9 November *Aurora* made a visual sighting of the convoy when the cruiser was in position 36° 55' north, 17° 58' east. Force 'K' was in line ahead in the order *Aurora*, *Lance*, *Penelope* and *Lively*, steaming 064 degrees at 28kt. Line ahead was the preferred tactical formation as it avoided recognition problems and allowed freedom of torpedo fire. In action escorts had priority over merchantmen because of the danger they posed to the attackers with their torpedoes.

The convoy was sailing south at 9kt in two columns about half a mile apart. The support force had ceased zig-zagging and was proceeding at 12kt on the convoy's starboard quarter about two miles astern. It was never identified as a threat by the British although it was sighted and assessed as a smaller portion of the convoy. *Aurora* sighted the convoy at a range of eight miles bearing 030 degrees. When the sighting was reported to the rest of the force, Capt A. D. Nicholl of *Penelope* was recorded as saying 'My God! There they are — bloody great haystacks!'. Agnew reduced speed to 20kt and led his force to port to put the convoy 'up moon' and to attack from the starboard quarter. At 0050 *Aurora* came abreast of the rear of the convoy and turned to starboard towards the 'tail end Charlie' escort *Grecale*. Her main armament

director crew monitored the correct range on the 284 radar so that the main armament could open up at any time. Agnew planned to keep the enemy fine on his port bow to present the least possible torpedo target. Force 'K's' captains had drilled their fire controllers and gunners to use their own initiative in engaging targets if circumstances required it. There had been many drills and exercises and everyone knew what to do.

Agnew was greatly assisted by the fact that the Italians thought Force 'K' was in fact their own support force. They were disabused at 0057 when the British opened fire, the bright moonlight providing excellent visual gunnery conditions even without radar assistance. *Aurora* immediately hit *Grecale* with her first three full broadsides. *Penelope* engaged *Maestrale*, the leading escort with equal success, obtaining hits with her first three radar directed broadsides. The destroyer turned away but *Penelope*'s gunners followed her with 16 more broadsides, although various problems prevented all six guns firing on a number of occasions. As 'Y' turret ceased to bear, the cruiser's secondary armament was allowed to join in and fired six salvoes, the first of which fell short. *Lance* engaged a merchant ship with her radar directed 4in guns and scored hits with her first salvo at 4,000yd. She then shifted her fire to the destroyer *Fulmine* which she also hit. A minute or two later *Lively* engaged the *Duisburg* and also proved remarkably accurate, all six of her salvoes scoring hits. She then shifted her fire to the destroyer *Euro*. After having demolished *Maestrale*, *Aurora* shifted her fire to a merchant ship, the *Rina Corrado*, sailing between the columns ahead of the unfortunate destroyer. Again her unerringly accurate gunnery officer, Michael Le Fanu (a future First Sea Lord), scored immediate hits with his four broadsides. The unfortunate merchantman burst into flames.

Shortly after 0100 Force 'K' turned once again to starboard to engage the convoy on the port beam. Still the Italians did not realise the true nature of their predicament. The merchant ships imagined that the shells were bombs and opened up with their anti-aircraft guns; the escorts on the far side of the convoy thought the attack was coming from their direction. In grim reality the destroyers on the starboard side of the convoy were in great trouble. *Fulmine* was hit repeatedly by *Penelope*'s 6in and 4in guns and at 0106 turned over and sank. *Euro* was also hit but was lucky in that the shells passed straight through without exploding. *Maestrale* was still operational and was making smoke to protect the convoy. She was, however, unable communicate by radio as her radio aerials had been shot away. This only increased Italian confusion and prevented the escorts getting their act together.

Force 'K' was able to sail along the starboard side of the convoy at between 2-4,000yd engaging in what was practically a practice shoot against the convoy. The merchant ships made no attempt to scatter as they ought to have done in the circumstances. They showed no initiative and the escort commander, Capt Bisciani, was unable to give the order. Adm Brivonesi was as confused as anyone and after an initial sighting report from *Bersagliere* deployed his ships to starboard and fired 207 rounds of 8in and 82 of 3.9in. Some shells did fall around *Penelope* and *Lively* but the British thought that they were being engaged by destroyers rather than cruisers. The Italians were greatly hampered by their lack of equipment for, and experience, in night action. They fired starshell but this was never effective enough to illuminate their targets sufficiently.

Blissfully unaware of the presence of enemy cruisers, Force 'K' set about the systematic destruction of the convoy. *Aurora* fired five broadsides with her main armament at the *Conte di Misurata* leaving her a blazing wreck. She then fired her port torpedo tubes and two of the three Mark IXs found targets. She then shifted her fire to the *Maestrale* and then to the tanker *Maniatitlan* which immediately caught fire. The ship was soon surrounded by blazing oil. Again Le Fanu shifted his guns to another merchant vessel but when two

more destroyers were sighted through their smoke screen they were engaged as priority targets.

Penelope fired six 6in broadsides and five 4in salvoes at another merchant ship. Within three minutes the unfortunate vessel was burning so the target was changed to another burning ship that seemed less seriously damaged. Ships' radar was notoriously unreliable at this time and now the cathode ray tube of *Penelope*'s 284 failed as a result of the repeated shock of firing. Moving to optical instruments the cruiser continued to enjoy excellent practice against yet another merchant ship which received six main armament broadsides. Then a tanker was fired at by *Penelope*'s forward turrets; five 'broadsides' from the four guns supported by the secondary armament again

Below:
Luckily an official photographer was working in Malta during the exploits of the Striking Forces and he has left an excellent record. This is *Aurora* entering Grand Harbour after the successful attack on the *Duisberg* convoy. On this negative the background has been blanked out for security reasons but this gives a clear view of the ship as she was at this famous time in her career. Preoccupied by blanking out the background, the censor has missed the 290 search radar at the masthead; this was a short-lived set, basically a 'small ship' radar of limited power and range. The main armament director above the bridge carries a 284 fire control radar. *IWM GM163*

Left:
Lively enters harbour at Malta after Force 'K's' success on the night of 8-9 November. Note the main armament of 4in AA guns; the 285 radar is clearly seen in profile on the director and the 286 'small ship' search radar at the masthead. *IWM GM165*

HMS *Lively*

Built: Cammell Laird, Birkenhead (launched 28 January 1941)

Displacement: 1,920 tons standard

Dimensions: 362.25ft x 37ft x 14.5ft

Machinery: two shaft geared turbines, 48,000shp, 36kt

Armament: 8 x 4in AA (4 x 2); 4 x 2pdr AA (1 x 4), 2 x 20mm AA (1 x 2); 8 x 0.5in AA (2 x 4); 8 x 21in torpedo tubes (2 x 4); 8 depth charge throwers and 2 depth charge racks

Sensors: Radars Types 285 and 286; Sonar Type 128

Complement: 224

Notes: An excellent modern fleet destroyer with a heavy three dimensional armament and the latest sensors. The 285 radar was mounted on the high angle/low angle director and the 286 at the masthead. *Lively* had a short but active career being bombed off Sollum in May 1942.

Above:
Cleaning out two of *Lively*'s well used 4in guns; note the names painted on the breech blocks. *IWM GM138*

caused a fire. At 0121 the 284 was operational once more and two four-gun 'broadsides' finished off the stricken *Miniatitlan*.

The cruiser then tried to shift fire to the starboard side to engage the Italian cruiser — thought by *Penelope* to be a 'destroyer' — whose shells were straddling the British ship. Because of fire control problems only the starboard 4in guns could be used but, as these were clearly ineffective at the long range, fire was checked after seven salvoes. *Lively* was unfortunate enough to have an Italian starshell burst overhead and she suffered near misses that caused holes in the funnel and a puncture in the steam pipe to the starboard siren. This was the only damage suffered by the British in the entire action. The destroyers were as preoccupied as the cruisers in making their contribution to converting the convoy into a shambles.

At 0125 Agnew led Force 'K' round ahead of the convoy to pass down its port side at a range of about 2,000yd. *Aurora* engaged a merchantman that seemed 'apparently whole' and which soon was not. He then shifted fire to the distant

Left:
Penelope returns shortly after 1300 on 9 November. Twelve hours previously she had been sinking an Axis convoy. Note that, unlike *Aurora*, she has 285 radars on her secondary directors as well as 284 on her main armament DCT. The masthead search radar is a 281, a proper high power, long range set for heavy ships. *IWM GM164*

'destroyers' but as they were disappearing moved back to merchantmen. At 0129 one was set on fire once more and at 0131 another ship that was already burning received a full broadside. This was an ammunition ship which blew up with great violence. *Penelope* finished off one of the escort destroyers and then also moved back to merchantmen. One of these was seen to blow apart; it was probably the same ammunition ship as that engaged by Le Fanu. As there were no merchant ships that were not on fire, *Aurora* altered course to starboard to engage the *Libeccio* and *Oriani* that were disappearing behind a smoke screen. *Penelope* also joined in this action after having set on fire the *San Marco*. Agnew now warned the whole force against wasting ammunition and Force 'K' ceased fire at around 0140. Five minutes later, Agnew altered course to sail round the rear of the convoy and, at 0205, as no fresh targets presented themselves, the victorious little surface action group set course for home at 25kt. It was vital to be back under cover of Malta's Hurricanes by dawn. At 0211 *Aurora* signalled to *Penelope* Agnew's 'heartiest congratulations'. Nichol replied, 'Congratulations to *Aurora* on her magnificent borealis'.

Above:

Heavy use blistered the paintwork on the guns; here are two of *Penelope*'s being scraped before repainting. *IWM GM145*

Right:

Capt W. G. ('Bill') Agnew of HMS *Aurora*, commander of Force 'K'. *IWM GM154*

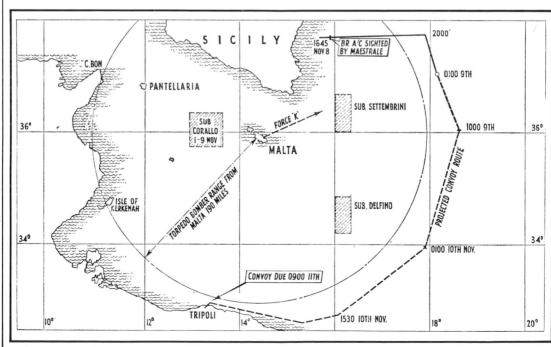

Congratulations were certainly in order. The entire convoy of seven merchant ships had been sunk, along with the destroyer *Fulmine*. Three more destroyers had been damaged: *Euro*, *Grecale* and *Libeccio* and the last named was finished off the next day by the submarine *Upholder*. Four Italian torpedo bombers attacked Force 'K' on the morning of the 9th but they dropped their torpedoes too far away and no hits were scored. Indeed, the Axis were unable to inflict any casualties at all on Force 'K' which entered Valetta at 1305. The order was received to 'splice the mainbrace' and Agnew was awarded an immediate CB. The Admiralty signalled to him their 'congratulations on your brilliant and successful action'.

Mussolini was highly disturbed by the annihilation of the convoy and both Brivonesi and Bisciani were relieved of their commands. It was indeed one of the most successful actions in the entire history of the Royal Navy. It became known as the 'Duisberg' Action' after the name of the larger of the German ships sunk. The loss of 34,473 tons of

Left:
The route of the Duisberg Convoy 8/9 November 1941.

Above left:
Capt A. D. Nicholl of *Penelope* standing on the left of Vice-Adm Sir Wilbraham Ford, Vice Admiral Malta. Ford and his staff played a key role in the operations of the Malta Striking Forces, being the channel by which 'Ultra' signals were translated into less highly classified orders. *IWM GM142*

Above:
The destroyer commanders of Force 'K': on the left Lt-Cdr. R. W. E. Northcott of *Lance* and on the right Lt-Cdr W. F. E. Hussey of *Lively*. *IWM GM162*

supplies at a single blow was of considerable significance; Force 'K' at a stroke had knocked out the equivalent of about half the usual monthly consumption of the Axis' North African armies. The Italians announced that Tripoli was 'practically blockaded' and suspended convoys.

The *Duisberg* action and the logistical crisis to which it contributed was excellent support for the British 'Crusader' offensive in the Western Desert that opened on 18 November. Force 'K' was used for diversionary operations to draw Axis air power away from advancing troops but then Bletchley Park reported that two Italian ships had left

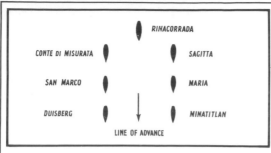

RINACORRADA

CONTE DI MISURATA   SAGITTA

SAN MARCO   MARIA

DUISBERG   MINATITLAN

LINE OF ADVANCE

Above:

Disposition of convoy.

Taranto on 14 November to pick up more supplies at Piraeus on the 17th which they were to
take on to North Africa. The Germans had forced
their reluctant allies to resume convoys.

Ford duly ordered Agnew to sail with his four
ships at 2330 on 23 November. Force 'K' was
spotted the following morning by the Italian submarine *Settembrini* and a rattled Supermarina, the
Italian Naval Headquarters, ordered all merchant
ships at sea to make for port. All received these
orders — except the *Bosforo* sailing under escort
from Benghazi to Brindisi and the two ships of the
convoy Force 'K' was hunting. This was made up
of the *Procida* and *Maritza* escorted by the small
torpedo boats *Lupo* and *Cassiopea*.

At 0950 a Cant reconnaissance floatplane began
to shadow Force 'K' and the British remained
under observation for the rest of the morning.
Lance and *Lively* used radio jamming to prevent

the shadowers vectoring in an attack. One of the
British reconnaissance Wellingtons succeeded in
locating the target convoy which was proceeding
southwest at 5kt. Force 'K' formed into line of
search on the opposite course and in the afternoon
HMS *Lively* was bombed by an Italian three-
engined Savoia-Marchetti SM-79. The destroyer
had little trouble in avoiding the bombs that were
released at high altitude. At 1522 *Penelope* and
Lively sighted smoke bearing 347 degrees, which
proved to be the two German steamers with their
Italian escorts.

Again the British ships benefited from mistaken
identity and the convoy's Ju 88 air cover initially
reported them as friendly. Eventually, the British
were correctly identified and the Ju 88s carried
out dive bombing attacks in the convoy's defence.
Penelope pressed in to attack the convoy, suffering
splinter damage from 3.9in shells fired by the
escorts. The gunnery conditions were not ideal for
the British cruiser but Lt J. S. Miller, *Penelope*'s
gunnery officer, opened fire at 1547 with his two
forward turrets. The two Italian torpedo boats
were laying a smoke screen to try to cover the
retreat of the two German merchantmen. *Lupo*
also bravely mounted two torpedo attacks which
forced Force 'K' to take evasive action. Sadly for
the plucky Italians, they were eventually driven
away and the two German merchant ships were
abandoned to be finished off by salvos from *Pene-*

Below:

Battle chart of the Duisberg action.

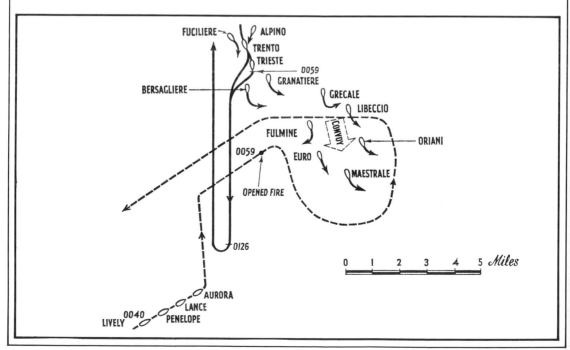

lope. Both blew up when their cargoes of petrol and ammunition exploded. At 1630 Force 'K' began its retirement at 28kt and it arrived at Malta at 0730 the following morning. The victory was, however, marred by disaster elsewhere. Prodded by Churchill, Cunningham had sent another striking force, Force 'B' under Rear-Adm B. Rawlings to intercept the convoys and had decided to cover the whole operation with his main fleet. Hitler had ordered U-boats to the Mediterranean to counter the Royal Navy's activities and this policy was vindicated when *U331* sighted Cunningham's battleships and mounted a daring attack. The battleship *Barham* was sunk, exploding as she heeled over in one of the best known images of naval war.

The loss of the two vital supply ships caused Rommel more serious concern, especially for his fuel situation. This was revealed by Bletchley Park's codebreakers and Churchill prevailed on the Admiralty to persuade Cunningham to send Force 'B' to Malta to complete Rommel's logistical discomfiture. The C-in-C Mediterranean had yet to notice any diminution in Axis air activity and was reluctant to send more ships to Malta given the island's own inadequate fuel supplies. Eventually, however, he gave in to the unrelenting pressure from London and at 0500 on 27 November Rawlings led Force 'B' out of Alexandria for Malta.

It was composed of the cruisers *Ajax* and *Neptune*, rather larger ships than the 'Arethusas', and two survivors from Mountbatten's flotilla, *Kimber-ley* and *Kingston*. For the first part of Force 'B's' passage it was escorted by Force 'C', the 'Dido' class AA cruisers *Naiad* and *Euryalus* and the destroyers *Griffin* and *Hotspur*. Because of poor fighter direction, shore based Fulmars were unable to keep away Axis reconnaissance aircraft but there was no major attack. Only one torpedo bomber appeared and its weapon was easily avoided. At 1820 Force 'C' detached and Force 'B' arrived at Malta at first light on the 29th. Rear-Adm Rawlings assumed command of the combined force and within hours an anti-convoy operation was being planned. Shipping bound for Tripoli and Benghazi had been reported and the four cruisers and three destroyers (*Lance* was in dock) sailed at 0500 on 30 November. The ships were the *Iseo* and *Capo Faro* bound from Brindisi for Benghazi escorted by the torpedo boat *Procione* and the *Sebastiano Venier* sailing from Taranto to Benghazi escorted by the large 1,900 ton 'Navigatore' class destroyer *Giovanni da Varazzano*.

In addition the armed merchantman *Adriatico*, which had taken refuge in Argostoli on its voyage to Benghazi, had left unescorted at 2300 on 29 November and the tanker *Iridio Mantovani* left Trapani at 1335 on 30 November for Tripoli. The tanker was escorted by another big destroyer, the *Alvise da Mosto*. It was a classic error of trade defence not to group all these ships into a single,

Below:
Routes to show the interception of the Procida and Maritza.

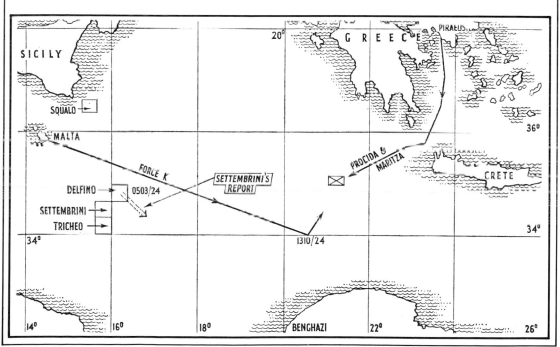

well escorted convoy. Instead the Italians took refuge in a powerful covering squadron composed of a battleship, four light cruisers and nine destroyers.

At 0918 Rawlings received news that heavy Italian forces were indeed at sea. Italian reconnaissance aircraft appeared at 1123 and at 1148 the submarine *Thunderbolt* (the salvaged *Thetis* that had sunk on her trials in a famous disaster) spotted a lone ship steaming south at 10kt. A few minutes later at 1155 the position of two more ships and their escort were reported to Rawlings by Ford, acting on 'Ultra' information. This was, in fact, a confusing signal as the only two-ship convoy had been attacked by Malta's Blenheims earlier that morning. The *Capo Faro* had been sunk and the *Iseo* and *Procione* took refuge in Argostoli.

It looked to Rawlings as if the three reported merchantmen were moving to a rendezvous. He was also aware of the position of the covering forces and decided therefore to move to pass ahead of the convoy after dark. Once the Wellington had finally confirmed the quarry's position the hunters could then mount an attack from whichever direction the moon's position dictated. Rawlings' forces suffered an ineffective torpedo bomber attack in the afternoon and as evening came on the cruisers and destroyers sped due east at 26kt to pass 32 miles ahead of the nearest Italian cruisers. Speed was reduced to 18kt to await aircraft reports but the reconnaissance Wellington spotted nothing to the northwest. Italian radio traffic to the north showed that there was still potential 'trade' although Rawlings was still without detailed positions. He was surprised when at 2248 the Wellington finally found a target 50 miles to the southeast , a single merchantman with escort on course 145 degrees at 8kt. Rawlings still expected his major target to be to the northwest but a bird in the hand could not be ignored. He decided to split his force: Force 'K' was sent to co-operate with the ASV Wellington (*Aurora* had

'Rooster' IFF that facilitated this) while Force 'B' waited for the 'main convoy'.

Rawlings had been let down by his intelligence services — there was no such convoy to intercept. Neither were there any covering forces as these had been withdrawn at 1745 that evening when a cruiser developed engine trouble. The air attack and sinking of the *Capo Faro* had made their presence less essential anyway. It seems strange that Rawlings was kept in the dark about the RAF's success. When Vice Admiral Malta sent his highly misleading signal at 1155 on the 30th it may well have been a case of too much trust being placed in the magic 'Ultra'; presumably the signals to which it referred had been sent before the Blenheims had attacked the little convoy. Perhaps one should not criticise the Naval HQ at Malta too much — there might well have been two convoys, given the Italian tendency to dispersion — but the failure to co-ordinate information with the RAF was regrettable. 'Ultra' also seems to have suddenly blacked out later that day. The Italian code routinely changed at the end of every month and it took time for Bletchley Park to break the cypher. Rawlings was left quite literally in the dark and after fruitless patrolling of the routes for Benghazi and Tripoli that night he turned Force 'B' in frustration for home at 0515 on 1 December.

Agnew, as usual, had better luck: at 0225 a sharp eyed Able Seaman, Richard Williams, made a visual sighting of a ship in the moonlight at a range of 12 miles. Force 'K' altered course to intercept and at 6,000yd *Aurora* opened fire from her forward turrets. The first broadside fell short but as the crew of the *Adriatico* ignored the 'abandon ship' signals from *Aurora* a second broadside was required, which hit the target. *Adriatico* was a warship and was armed with two 4.7in guns and two 13.2mm machine guns. She was carrying troops who had every intention of using their weapons. The Italians opened fire to which *Aurora* immediately replied hitting the armed merchantman heavily and setting her on fire. The Italians then abandoned the wreck but tried to avoid being rescued by the destroyer *Lively*. Only 21 survivors were picked up by the destroyer although more were rescued by the Italians. *Lively* also gave *Adriatico* the coup de grâce and the armed merchantman with her 366 tons of aviation fuel blew up.

As Force 'K' returned towards Malta shadowing aircraft were jammed and a rain squall also gave useful cover. At 1040 more 'trade' offered itself in the shape of the tanker *Mantovani* and her escorting destroyer. An aircraft had sighted these ships one hour before. Rawlings received the same report but decided that the ships would be dealt with by Malta's aircraft. An attack was indeed mounted by Malta's Blenheims which hit the tanker and left her dead in the water. Cdr del Anno of the destroyer *Da Mosto* took the valuable ship under tow. Unfortunately for the Italians Agnew decided at 1700 to attack the reported target; as usual he had received no news of the air attack. At 1714 Italian CR42 biplane fighters were seen circling over something 20 miles away. Agnew closed to investigate and at 1743 spotted the ships' masts.

Force 'K's' 4in guns drove off the fighters but the *Alvise da Mosto* bravely attacked the British force. *Aurora* used her usual tactic of keeping end-on to destroyers and using her forward armament only. The Italian destroyer began to lay a smoke screen and fire a torpedo. She then opened fire at a range of about 12,000yd. This was much too far for effective destroyer gunfire even with six 4.7in guns and the *Da Mosto*'s fire fell 6-800yd off *Lively*'s port quarter. Cdr del Anno tried a second torpedo attack but as *Da Mosto* turned into her smoke screen she was hit by the combined fire of the two British cruisers. The 6in shells easily penetrated the gallant ship's magazine and she exploded. A minute later *Aurora* shifted target to the tanker which was soon ablaze and the destroyer *Lively* picked up some grateful survivors. The destroyer finished off the *Mantovani* with a single Mk IX torpedo at 1953 and she blew up with her cargo of 5,332 tons of gas, oil and naph-

tha, 1,870 tons of petrol and 1,727 tons of benzine. Force 'K' returned to Malta the following day. Agnew paid fulsome tribute to the RAF reconnaissance Wellington with which he had co-operated. He wrote thus of Flt Lt Spooner, the aircraft's captain: 'He stayed in the air long past his endurance time in order to make certain that he homed me satisfactorily on to the target. In the past he has shown the most exceptional keenness in co-operating with Force 'K' and I am more than pleased to mention we brought off a kill together.'

In November as a whole the Axis supply route suffered 62% losses. Only 30,000 tons of supplies were delivered and Luftwaffe signals reported their operations to be in 'real danger' from fuel shortages; by mid-December there was only fuel for one sortie per aircraft per day. The Italians

Below:
***Sikh* leads the victorious British destroyers into Malta after sinking two Italian cruisers off Cape Bon.** *IWM GM202*

Right:
Legion follows. *IWM GM204*

Below right:
Maori leads in *Isaac Sweers*. *IWM GM210*

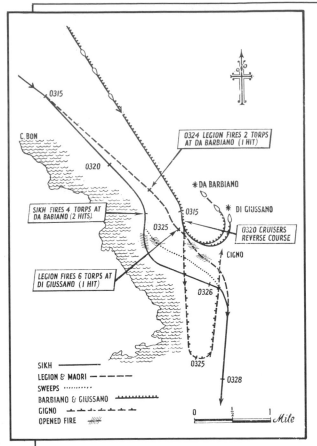

0315

C. BON

0320

0324 LEGION FIRES 2 TORPS
AT DA BARBIANO (1 HIT)

* DA BARBIANO

SIKH FIRES 4 TORPS AT
DA BABIANO (2 HITS)

* DI GIUSSANO

0315

0325

0320 CRUISERS
REVERSE COURSE

CIGNO

LEGION FIRES 6 TORPS AT
DI GIUSSANO (1 HIT)

0326

0325

SIKH ——————
LEGION & MAORI – – – – –
SWEEPS ·············
BARBIANO & GIUSSANO ▲▲▲▲▲▲
CIGNO ┼–┼–┼–┼
OPENED FIRE ╫╫╫

0328

0 ½ 1
Mile

Above:
The Cape Bon action. 13 December 1941.

were reduced to running fuel to North Africa in aircraft and warships. The loss of trucks in the land campaign meant that even what little was arriving could not be brought to the front in sufficient quantity and in early December Rommel was forced to retreat to shorten his supply lines.

As the Axis armies streamed back westwards Rawlings escorted the fast supply ship HMS *Breconshire* on a return journey after a supply mission to Malta. Rawlings then sailed again on an attempted interception mission but intelligence was still poor and nothing was found. The Admiralty had insisted that the Malta Striking Force continued to operate as normal in order to disguise the fact of the intelligence blackout. By 8 December, however, Bletchley Park had sufficiently broken the new month's settings to know that two light cruisers were to sail from Palermo to Tripoli the following day carrying 100 tons of petrol and 50 tons of other stores. These

two ships, *Alberico da Barbiano* and *Alberto di Giussano* were very fast vessels of the original 'Condottieri' type. Completed in 1931, they were armed with eight 6in guns but their protection was very light which allowed a maximum speed of 36.5kt, no bad quality in blockade runners. They left Palermo at 1720 on 9 December but British air activity that night caused them to turn back. The cruisers tried again at 1800 on 12 December, accompanied this time by the small torpedo boat *Cigno*.

Cunningham's fears about Malta's fuel situation had proved well founded and the enlarged surface Striking Force based on the island only had enough oil for one extended operation or two briefer sorties. The two Italian cruisers did not seem suitable targets and Cunningham who saw convoys as the main prize overruled Ford who wished to use Force 'K' against the blockade runners. Instead, four destroyers on their way east through the Mediterranean, were diverted to intercept. These ships were the two 'Tribals' *Sikh* and *Maori*, HMS *Legion*, the sister of *Lance* and *Lively*, and the 1,604 ton Dutch destroyer *Isaac Sweers*. The latter ship had been towed incomplete to Britain when the Germans invaded the Netherlands and had been fitted out with a British armament. Her main battery was six 4in guns and she carried eight 21in torpedo tubes. The passage group was commanded by Cdr G. H. Stokes and was being transferred from Force 'H' in Gibraltar to the Mediterranean Fleet at Alexandria to replace the Australian flotilla that had been called east to defend its homeland.

Stokes was ordered to sail in French territorial waters off the Tunisian coast in order to avoid minefields. His destroyers rounded Cape Bon at

---

Amberto di Giussano

Built: Ansaldo, Genoa (launched 27 April 1930)

Displacement: 5,110 tons standard

Dimensions: 555.5ft x 50.8ft x 17.75ft

Protection: 0.95in belt plus 0.71in splinter bulkhead; 0.8in deck; 0.9in turrets

Machinery: two shaft geared turbines, 95,000shp, 36.5kt

Armament: 8 x 6in (4 x 2); 6 x 3.9in AA (3 x 2); 8 x 37mm AA (4 x 2); 8 13.2mm AA (4 x 2); 4 x 21in torpedo tubes (2 x 2)

Complement: 520

Notes: The first of the first class of fast, lightly protected 'Condottieri' light cruiser classes built by Italy in the 1930s. The 'Giussanos' were built primarily to counter large French 'contre torpilleurs' but high speed was obtained at too high a price in lack of protection. On trials ships of this class made very high speeds, *Giussano* made 38.5kt for eight hours and her sister *Barbiano* made no less than 42.05kt for half an hour. Both habitability and seakeeping were poor. All four were sunk.

30kt, keeping as close as possible to the shore, and was surprised to find the Italian cruisers had turned back and were steaming back towards them. The Italians had become alarmed by the sound of aircraft overhead and were taking evasive action. This was a tricky situation as the British destroyers without angling gear had to swing to starboard to spread their torpedoes (the tubes were fixed in position before firing). Stokes waited until 0323 when there was enough sea room to

make the starboard turn. *Sikh* fired all four of her Mk IXs at a range of 1,500yd at the leading Italian ship, the *Barbiano*, two of which scored hits. She also took the other cruiser under fire with her guns.

The Italians were taken completely by surprise and the return fire of the *Giussano* passed over the Allied destroyers and hit the shore. Stokes had not co-ordinated his attack properly and Cdr Jessel in *Legion* was expecting *Sikh* to fire her torpedoes at *Giussano*. He also, therefore, engaged the *Barbiano* and hit her with one Mk IX. The lightly protected ship, aflame with burning petrol, quickly sank. With great presence of mind Jessel ceased firing torpedoes and swung again to point his remaining six torpedoes at the *Giussano*. This was the only occasion in the Royal Navy's history when a destroyer firing torpedoes shifted targets in this way. It was a worthwhile manoeuvre for one Mk IX struck the *Giussano* and the poorly protected vessel was also soon ablaze. Gunfire from all four destroyers added to the damage and the cruiser

Below:
A close up of the interesting Dutch destroyer *Isaac Sweers* showing the armament with which she had been fitted when completed in Britain. There is one 4in twin mount forward and two aft; a British high angle director has also been mounted on the bridge. Sadly the ship was torpedoed and sunk off Algiers in November 1942. She makes an interesting comparison with her sister *Gerard Callenburgh* completed by the Germans and illustrated in a later chapter. *IWM GM203*

soon sank. *Cigno* made her escape to the south.
Swordfish torpedo bombers from Malta now put
in an appearance but were unnecessary. The Italians picked up 645 survivors but over 1,000 Italian sailors lost their lives. When Stokes' force
entered Malta at dawn the following day the ships
of Forces 'B' and 'K' cheered them in. Cdr Stokes
was awarded the CB.

The Italians had determined on a major fleet
operation to force supplies through to North
Africa. It was codenamed 'M41' and the plan was
to run three convoys of eight ships in total to
Libya. It started disastrously when two ships were
sunk at 0230 on 13 December by the British submarine *Upright*. The following night two more
steamers collided and had to return home. The
remaining four, three Italian and one German,
sailed from Taranto during the night of
13 December with a close escort of five destroyers. It was covered by the two most powerful battleships in the Italian Navy, *Littorio* and *Vittorio
Veneto*, which sailed from Naples with an escort of
four destroyers and two torpedo boats. However,

the operation ended in complete fiasco when the
British submarine *Urge* hit the *Vittorio Veneto* with
a torpedo on the morning of 14 December. Supermarina had already cried enough when it thought
Cunningham was at sea with two battleships;
actually it was an operational decoy manoeuvre by
the minelayer *Abdiel* simulating *Queen Elizabeth*
and *Valiant* that were confined to harbour for lack
of escorts. All Axis ships had been ordered back to
harbour on the evening of the 13th. The only Axis
success was the sinking of the cruiser *Galatea* off
Alexandria by *U557*.

The Italians had another try on 16 December
with Operation 'M42'. The convoy was composed
of the same four ships which sailed from Taranto
at 1600 with a close escort of seven destroyers and
a torpedo boat. The Italian Navy made a maximum effort and produced both a close covering
force of the battleship *Caio Duilio*, three cruisers
and three destroyers and a distant covering force
composed of the battleships *Littorio*, *Andrea Doria*
and *Giulio Cesare* with two cruisers and 10
destroyers. Count Ciano, the Italian Foreign Minister, wrote in his diary: 'All the ships and all the
admirals are at sea — God help us'.

The British were already committed to a com-
plicated operation both to escort *Breconshire* in to
Malta and to take out the enemy convoy. Force
'K' — now back up to full strength as *Lively* had
completed her refit — together with Stokes' four

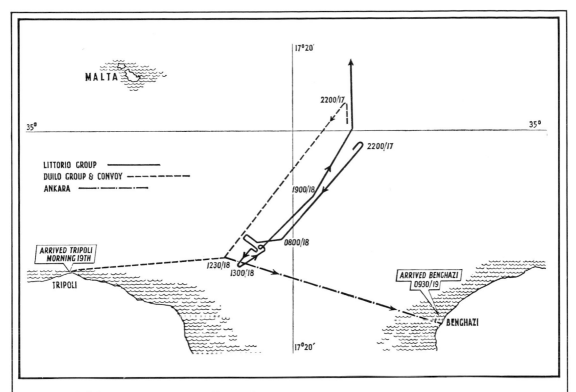

MALTA

17°20'

2200/17

35°   35°

LITTORIO GROUP ——————
DUILO GROUP & CONVOY ----------
ANKARA —·—·—·—·—

2200/17

1900/18

0800/18

ARRIVED TRIPOLI
MORNING 19TH

1230/18
1300/18

ARRIVED BENGHAZI
0930/19

TRIPOLI

BENGHAZI

17°20'

Above:

**The Italian Fleet and convoy movements during
M.42.**

destroyers left Malta at 1800 on 16 December to
rendezvous with the fast supply ship and her
escort; Stokes was to return with the Mediterranean Fleet ships to Alexandria. Agnew rendezvoused with *Breconshire* and her escorts —
Naiad, Euryalus, Carlisle and eight destroyers
under the command of Rear-Adm Philip Vian and
the combined force proceeded towards Malta
together through the daylight hours of 17 December. The group was shadowed by Axis aircraft and
attacked throughout the afternoon by Italian torpedo bombers and Ju 88s. No hits were scored
but the group had to manoeuvre to avoid the torpedoes.

In late afternoon it was reported that Italian
heavy warships were close by and their presence
was confirmed by the appearance of a battleship
reconnaissance floatplane among more bombers
and torpedo bombers. At 1742 the masts of the
Italian battlefleet were sighted and it looked as if a
major action was about to begin. The Italians
opened long range fire, which was disturbingly
accurate. *Breconshire* made a rapid getaway as
planned for these circumstances, escorted by the
destroyers *Decoy* and *Havock*. The rest of the
British ships moved to attack the Italians but
Vian, who was in overall command, recalled them
as the Italians did not seem to be closing and
action against the superior force was not essential.
Vian's destroyers had in fact scared off the heavy

ships. The Italian Fleet Commander , Adm
Iachino, with Matapan as a guide, had no intention of engaging British forces with their superior
night action skills in the gathering darkness.

Vian and Agnew split up after dark and the latter decided that his duties to the *Breconshire* took
priority over his orders to attack the convoy and
thus he continued to screen the supply ship. He
was reinforced by Force 'B', made up of the
cruiser *Neptune* and the destroyers *Kandahar* and
Jaguar (*Ajax* was confined to harbour with
mechanical problems). The strongly escorted *Breconshire* safely reached Malta at 1500 on the 18th.
Vian attempted an interception but did not succeed, and in receipt of an 'Ultra' signal that the
Italians were probably altering their compromised
plans, he returned to Alexandria.

When Vian was well to the east, decoded mes-
sages made the position of the convoy clear. It was
decided, therefore, to make a maximum effort
with the combined Striking Force which sailed at
1800 on the 18th commanded by Capt
R. C. O'Conor of HMS *Neptune*, the senior officer
present. It consisted of the cruisers *Neptune*,
Aurora and *Penelope* and the destroyers *Kandahar*,

Lance, *Havock* and *Lively*. Sadly, O'Conor led his force straight into a previously unknown minefield laid by the Italians with German contact mines 20 miles off Tripoli harbour. The mines were laid in some 100 fathoms of water, deeper than the British thought possible for moored mines. *Neptune* struck one on the port side at 0106 and as *Aurora* pulled out of line to starboard she too struck a mine. *Penelope* had taken the precaution of streaming paravanes and these saved the ship from serious damage when she too suffered a mine explosion. *Neptune* drifted on to two more mines at 0112 and 0125. *Kandahar* moved to stand by the stricken cruiser and Agnew ordered the other three destroyers to join *Aurora*. The mine had caused serious damage to the hull and *Aurora* listed to 11° before this was corrected by counter flooding. Her forward turrets were out of action because of damaged shell hoists. She made for Malta, working up to 18kt, and was escorted back to the island by *Havock* and *Lance*.

Penelope, escorted by *Lively* remained behind with the striken *Neptune*. At 0208 O'Conor signalled that he was preparing to be taken in tow and the destroyer *Lively* closed to take up position for this. The actual connection was delayed by a last minute decision to change the side of the ship for the tow and it had not yet been made when *Kandahar* struck yet another mine. Her stern was blown off and this caused *Penelope*, that was also closing to take up the tow, to turn away. *Neptune* now signalled 'keep away' and *Kandahar* signalled 'get out of it'. Capt Nicholl of *Penelope* still hoped to save the crews of the two mined ships but then *Neptune* drifted on to a fourth mine, which caused her to roll over and sink quickly. There was only one survivor. Nicholl had no alternative but to withdraw and leave *Kandahar*. Accompanied by *Lively* he arrived back at Malta at 1100 on 19 December. At 1625 the previous day the destroyer *Jaguar* had left Malta to try to offer assistance and at 0405 she sighted *Kandahar* which was submerged from her funnel aft. She succeeded in picking up 168 officers and men of the total ship's company of 235. The forepart of the ship refused to sink and *Jaguar* had to finish her off with a torpedo. An ASV Wellington provided invaluable help in homing the destroyer on to the wreck. The Axis convoy had to be left to Malta's aircraft and it was attacked by torpedo-carrying Albacores and Wellington minelayers. Damage was inflicted on one ship with a torpedo but the convoy arrived in its destination ports of Benghazi and Tripoli on 19 December. It landed 300 vehicles, ammunition, fuel and other stores and allowed Rommel to mount the counteroffensive in January 1942 that retook Cyrenaica.

Even without this disaster the days of the Malta surface Striking Force were numbered, for its very effectiveness had brought back the Luftwaffe. Already in October Hitler had decided that he ought to reinforce his overstretched *Fliegerkorps X* and the events of November made the matter urgent. On 2 December War Directive No 38 ordered *Fliegerkorps II* to Sicily and the setting up of a new *Luftflotte 2* command in Italy under Kesselring to control both *Fliegerkorps II* and *X* as well as German aircraft in North Africa. The Sicilian bases began once more to fill with German aircraft, Ju 88s at Catania, *Stukas* at Trapani and Bf 109Fs (that outclassed Malta's Hurricanes) at Gela, Comiso and San Pietro. The second air siege of Malta began in January 1942 and the island was immediately neutralised once more as an effective offensive base. After its brief moment of glory as a barrier to Axis logistics, Malta became a drain on British naval strength as the Royal Navy struggled to keep the island supplied. The cruisers and destroyers of the Striking Force had been the decisive instruments of Malta's success; now all its survivors could do was play their part in the desperate and debilitating struggle for their base's survival.

CHAPTER FOUR

Java Sea

Today, NATO's navies operate remarkably effectively as multinational forces. They have had, however, more than four decades to refine the techniques of working together. In December 1941 at much shorter notice a multinational squadron was thrown together to defend the East Indies from the Japanese. The experience was a far from happy one.

It seems surprising now but Dutch entry into the war against Germany in May 1940 did not lead to immediate discussions on mutual defence in the Far East. Talks on this did not begin until November 1940. The British were understandably reluctant to commit themselves too fully to the defence of Dutch territories in the East Indies, given the uncertainties of their own desperate strategic position and of whether the Americans would give any support. Talks between the British and the Australians with the Dutch and Americans as observers were held in Singapore between 25-29 November. The same month Roosevelt was safely re-elected as US President and the Americans were able at last to move towards plans and agreements with the British. At the crucial ABC-1 conference that commenced in Washington at the end of January 1941 the British Commonwealth and American participants came to the decision to deal with Germany first in any joint war. This was enshrined in a Staff agreement concluded on 27 March.

The Dutch were excluded from these deliberations but in February 1941 a further Anglo-Dutch-American (ADA) conference was held in Singapore. This reaffirmed the importance of the Singapore base as the first line of defence against Japan in the area. The British would have liked a firm declaration of alliance between itself and the United States and the Netherlands, but the United States still fought shy of any definite commitment. Nevertheless, Washington supported the idea of combined planning beginning with Pacific and Far Eastern defence: the US, British and Dutch planners duly met at Singapore at the end of April. Plans for safeguarding both sea lines of communication and Singapore itself were discussed and it was agreed between the British and the Dutch that the latter's ships would be placed under the command of the British C-in-C China in the case of Japanese attack. Nothing, however, was done about the crucial operational question of agreed procedures for tactical co-operation. In August 1941 the British assured the Dutch that they would support them against a Japanese attack and minor changes were made in the so-called ADB (American-Dutch-British) plans when the US and British Chiefs of Staff met in Argentia Bay, Newfoundland later that month — but the Americans still refused to confirm the plans! A further ADB conference was due in Manila in December 1941 but events intervened.

On 12 November Vice-Adm Sir Geoffrey Layton, the British Naval C-in-C China, issued his strategic plans for the employment of naval and air forces 'of the Associated Powers in the Eastern Theatre'. Known as 'Plenaps' these were intended to inform the countries concerned about strategy in order that detailed planning could take place. The Japanese attack on Pearl Harbor on 7/8 December 1941 prevented this process bearing fruit and forced the Allies into ad hoc co-operation. Already, on 30 November, two Dutch submarines had been placed under Layton's command. In the succeeding weeks the Japanese advanced rapidly; by 2 January Hong Kong and Manila had both fallen and the British battle squadron sent to Singapore had been sunk by Japanese aircraft (See *Sea Battles in Close-up*, Vol 1).

In many ways the Dutch East Indies were the main target of the Japanese expansion. Japan badly needed the East Indies oilfields from which it had been effectively cut off when the United States had frozen Japan's assets in protest at her occupation of Indo-China in July 1941. Japan had allocated its 16th Army, together with landing forces, to occupy the archipelago. The troops were to be transported by Vice-Adm Nobutake Kondo's Southern Force made up of battleships, cruisers, destroyers, minesweepers, submarine chasers, seaplane tenders and transports. In support was formidable strength in the air, not only the First Air Fleet, the carriers that had struck Pearl Harbor, but also two flotillas of the land based 11th Air Fleet and the 3rd Air Division of the Japanese Army Air Force.

To oppose this panoply of modern military power the Allies tried to pull together a command structure to co-ordinate their disparate forces. Gen Sir Archibald Wavell was appointed Supreme Commander of the so-called ABDA (American-British-Dutch-Australian) Command when the latter was agreed at the Arcadia Summit Conference in Washington at the beginning of 1942. Wavell arrived in Java on 10 January and held a conference which led to the command actually being set up five days later at Batavia (modern Djakarta). The Naval Commander (ABDAFLOAT) was an American, Adm T. C. Hart, with a British Rear Admiral, A. F. E. Palliser, as his Deputy. The Dutch were disappointed at being left out and Vice-Adm Helfrich, C-in-C of the Royal Netherlands Navy in the East Indies had no direct contact with the new headquarters. Surprisingly, he was never asked for any advice and had to rely on a Dutch liaison officer at the new HQ.

Who's who — Java Sea 1942	
Gen Sir Archibald Wavell	C-in-C ABDA Command
Maj-Gen Pownall	Chief of Staff, ABDA Command
Vice-Adm Sir Geoffrey Layton RN	British C-in-C, China Station; from 10 December 1941 C-in-C Eastern Fleet
Rear-Adm A. F. E. Palliser RN	Deputy Naval CDR, ABDAFLOAT
Cdre J. A. Collins RAustN	Commodore Commanding China Force (ie Cdr all British and Commonwealth Naval forces in area) from 22 February 1942.
Adm T. C. Hart USN	Naval Cdr, ABDAFLOAT
Vice-Adm W. A. Glassford USN	Cdr, US Naval Forces South Pacific
Vice-Adm Helfrich RNethN	C-in-C Royal Netherlands Navy, East Indies and Naval Cdr, ABDAFLOAT (in succession to Adm T. C. Hart USN)
Rear-Adm Karel Doorman RNethN	Cdr, Eastern Striking Force
Vice-Adm Nobutake Kondo IJN	Japanese C-in-C Southern Operations
Vice-Adm Ozawa IJN	Cdr, Japanese Western Force
Rear-Adm Nishimura IJN	Cdr, Japanese Escort Forces
Rear-Adm T. Takagi IJN	Cdr, Japanese Covering Forces

Another problem was the imposition of British concepts of centralised control of air power. The Dutch naval aircraft in the area were placed under command of the American, later British, air force Commander (ABDAAIR). The normal close co-operation between Dutch naval aircraft and warships promptly ceased. It did not help matters that ABDAFLOAT became separated from ABDAAIR when the latter was moved from the Grand Hotel at Lembang into Bandung itself at the beginning of February. Moreover, to compound confusion further the Dutch Naval Air Service personnel at Bandung were placed in a sepa-

rate building from the rest of the ABDAAIR staff. There was no single ABDA war room which made rapid decision making impossible and the various forces remained under national administration. In all, it was a complete nightmare.

The Japanese were much better organised. By 10 January two landing forces were at sea on their way to Tarakan and Menado. Dutch aircraft spotted the Japanese Tarakan force the day before the invasion on the 11th, the day the Japanese officially declared war on the Netherlands. Tarakan fell on the morning of the 12th after the oil installations had been set on fire. Naval forces in the area tried to make their escape but the minelayer *Prins van Oranje* was sunk by the Japanese destroyer *Yamakaze* and Patrol Boat *38*. The Menado force landed in northeastern Celebes on 10 January and Menado fell the following day becoming the headquarters of the Japanese Navy's 21st Air Flotilla. On 21 January the Japanese moved on from Tarakan to Balikpapan. One transport was sunk by American Army bombers and when the force anchored off its landing area the Dutch submarine *K17* sank another. During the night Vice-Adm W. A. Glassford's Task Force 5 (TF5) of four old American four-funnelled destroyers, the *John D. Ford*, *Pope*, *Parrott* and *Paul Jones* carried out a classic torpedo attack against the invasion fleet as it was silhouetted against the burning oilfields. This was the first surface action made by the United States Navy since the Spanish-American War and was understandably less than perfectly executed. Nevertheless, and despite the extra handicap of unreliable torpedoes (probably old Mk 8s), it did succeed in sinking three transports and damaging a patrol craft. The Japanese landings, however, still took place on schedule.

To the east the Menado force moved on to Kendari, whose airfield was in Japanese hands by 24 January. This put all of Eastern Java within range of land-based Japanese naval aircraft. From Kendari the Japanese moved on to Ambon, whose flying boat base had been bombed on 16 January. On 24 January Ambon was attacked by carrier-based aircraft from the *Soryu* and *Hiryu* and troops arrived from Davao via Menado on New Year's Eve. Ambon fell with little resistance the same day and by 5 February was being used as a Japanese air base. The only serious losses suffered by the Japanese were the sinking of the minesweeper *W9* and damage to her sister ships *W11* and *W12* from Dutch mines laid by the minelayer *Gouden Leeuw*. In the first days of 1942 the Japanese moved on Bandjermasin overland and down the coast in landing craft. The overland force had been landed at Tanahgrogot by the depleted transport squadron which had left to refuel at Palau. Bandjermasin fell on 10 February and Makassar had fallen to a force from Kendari on the 9th. The previous night the Makassar invasion fleet had been attacked by the American submarine *S37* which sank the destroyer *Natsushio*.

On 3 February 1942, against the better judgement of Hart and Palliser, a Naval Striking Force was formed to attack Japanese shipping in the Makassar Strait. Wavell and Maj-Gen Pownall, his Chief-of-Staff, had insisted on this. The Striking Force consisted of the American Washington Treaty heavy cruiser *Houston*, the old four-funnelled cruiser USS *Marblehead*, the American destroyers *Stewart*, *Barker*, *Bulmer* and *John D. Edwards* (all old four-stackers), the Dutch cruisers *De Ruyter* and *Tromp* and the destroyers *Van Ghent*, *Piet Hein* and *Banckert*. *De Ruyter* was a relatively modern 6,000-ton ship whose design had been stunted by financial considerations. She was armed with three twin and one single 6in gun mountings. *Tromp* was a 4,000-ton enlarged flotilla leader armed with three twin 6in gun mountings. She was a new ship designed to strengthen Dutch destroyers against their more powerful Japanese potential adversaries. The three Dutch destroyers were based on the classic interwar British design and were armed with four single 4.7in guns and six 21in torpedo tubes.

Below.
The cruiser USS *Houston*, taken in happier days at Southampton in 1930. By the time of the Java Sea she had acquired a small cap on her fore funnel.
Ian Allan Collection

The Striking Force commander, flying his flag in *De Ruyter*, was Rear-Adm Karel Doorman. Doorman was not a healthy man as he had contracted a tropical illness which exacerbated a tendency to be difficult with both others and himself. Nevertheless his stubbornness and determination made him popular with the Fleet and he was able to maintain morale at a remarkably high level. Doorman's first operation with the Striking Force

USS *Houston*

Built: Newport News (launched 7 September 1929)

Displacement: 9,050 tons standard

Dimensions: 600.25ft x 66.1ft x 19.4ft

Armour: 3-3.75in belt; 1-2in deck; 2-2.5in turrets

Machinery: four shaft geared turbines, 107,000shp, 32.5kt

Armament: 9 x 8in (3 x 3); 8 x 5in AA (8 x 1); 16 x 1.1in AA (4 x 4); 8 x 12.7mm AA (8 x 1)

Complement: 748

Notes: One of the USA's second type of Washington Treaty heavy cruiser, the 'Northampton' class, that established the pattern of three triple turrets that lasted for two decades. Originally six torpedo tubes were carried but these were removed to double the number of 5in AA guns. There was provision for four aircraft and two catapults were carried. Like her two sisters *Chicago* and *Augusta*, she was built as a flagship and had an extended forecastle to provide extra accommodation. She only had two-thirds of her main armament operational for the Java Sea battle, her after triple 8in turret having been put out of action by bombing. The heavy ammunition was manhandled forward from the after magazine to supply the forward mountings when they began to run short in the final days of the brave ship's life.

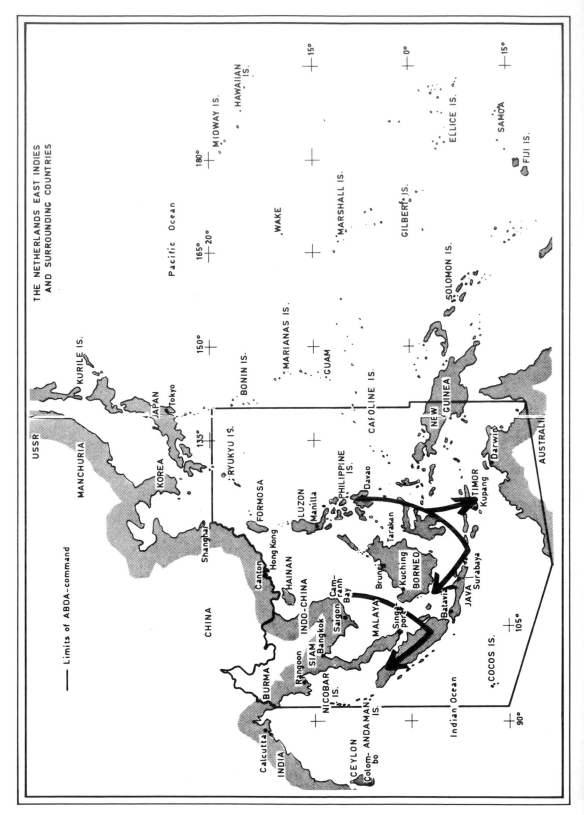

THE NETHERLANDS EAST INDIES
AND SURROUNDING COUNTRIES

Limits of ABDA-command

proved abortive when it sortied to intercept the Makassar invasion force. Attacks by 27 Japanese land-based Naval bombers caused significant damage to both American cruisers and lighter damage to *De Ruyter*. The old *Marblehead* had to return to the USA for repairs and the *Houston* lost the use of her after turret but remained on station. The force had to take refuge at Tjilatjap.

The Japanese had spread their invasion to the western part of the East Indies at the end of January. Airfields were taken to support an attack on Bankar and Palembang planned for February. Vice-Adm Ozawa was in overall command of an advance force that sailed from Camranh Bay on 9 February and the main force that sailed on the 11th. Japanese paratroops landed near Palembang on 14 February. It was decided to try to use the ABDA Striking Force against the two invasion forces. For this purpose it was strengthened with the British heavy cruiser and River Plate veteran *Exeter*, the Australian 6in cruiser *Hobart*, and the Dutch cruiser *Java* completed in the 1920s but of obsolete World War 1 conception. The Flotilla was strengthened by a fourth Dutch destroyer *Kortenaer* and two more old American destroyers, the *Pilsbury* and the *Parrott*. The force sortied on 13 February at 1600 to patrol through Gaspar Strait, along the north coast of Banka and then back to Tandjong Priok via the Banka Strait. In

Java

Built: Netherlands Dock and Shipbuilding, Amsterdam (launched 9 August 1921)
Displacement: 6,670 tons standard
Dimensions: 509.5ft x 52.5ft x 18ft
Protection: 2-3in belt ; 1.5-2in deck ; 4in gunshields
Machinery: Three shaft geared turbines, 72,000shp, 31kt
Armament: 10 x 5.9in (10 x 1) ; 8 x 40mm (8 x 1); 4 x 12.7mm AA (4 x 1)
Complement: 525
Notes: When *Java* and her sister ship *Sumatra* were authorised in 1915 they were large vessels intended to outclass foreign ships. They were not, however, completed until 1925-26 and were soon made outdated by Washington Treaty designs. They were fitted to carry seaplanes and a dozen mines but never carried torpedoes. Considerable German assistance was provided with materials and construction.

the early hours of 15 February it suffered its first loss when the *Van Ghent* went aground and had to be destroyed by its own crew. Later that day, the force was spotted by a reconnaissance aircraft from the Japanese cruiser *Chokai*. Land-based Japanese Naval bombers were soon called up once more and a mixture of lack of co-ordination at the

Below:
The Dutch cruiser *Java*, the largest Dutch ship to be lost in the Java Sea battle. Basically a World War 1 design, albeit somewhat enlarged, she was totally outclassed by the two Japanese cruisers that sank her. *Real Photographs/Ian Allan Collection*

ABDA command level and Japanese air attacks kept the 22 RAF Hurricanes at Palembang II airfield from intervening. Doorman, therefore, had little choice but to turn back, allowing the landing at Palembang to take place without difficulty.

While this operation was taking place, the Americans considered it politically expedient to remove Adm Hart from his clearly doomed command; reasons of health were quoted to justify his departure. The new ABDAFLOAT was Vice Adm Helfrich, a Dutchman with nowhere else to go. The new Naval Commander's job was made yet more difficult by the fall of Singapore on 15 February which effectively cut the ABDA area in two. On the 21st Wavell was ordered to defend Java to the last although he was to withdraw his headquarters from the island. On the 22nd, however, Wavell and the Dutch Governor General decided finally to put the wounded ABDA structure out of its misery and give command in the Dutch East Indies back to the Dutch. Vice-Adm Helfrich remained, of course, the overall Naval Commander with Doorman in command of the Striking Force. Glassford was left in command of US Naval Forces South Pacific and the remaining British Imperial Naval Forces were put under the command of the Australian Cdre J. A. Collins. The tri-service Dutch command was reorganised at Bandung but there was never a chance to rebuild proper air-sea liaison after the damage inflicted on it by ABDAAIR.

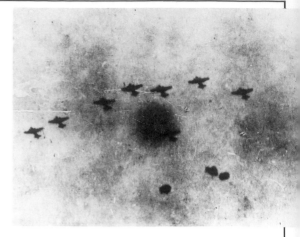

Above:
A formation of Japanese Mitsubishi G4M 'Betty' bombers carrying out one of the attacks of 15 February in the teeth of Allied AA fire. Japanese air superiority was a major advantage to them.
IWM HU50184

Right:
Sunda Strait.

Below:
The Dutch destroyer *Kortenaer* that was torpedoed and sunk in the 27 February action. All three of her sisters were lost in the same month.
Real Photographs/Ian Allan Collection

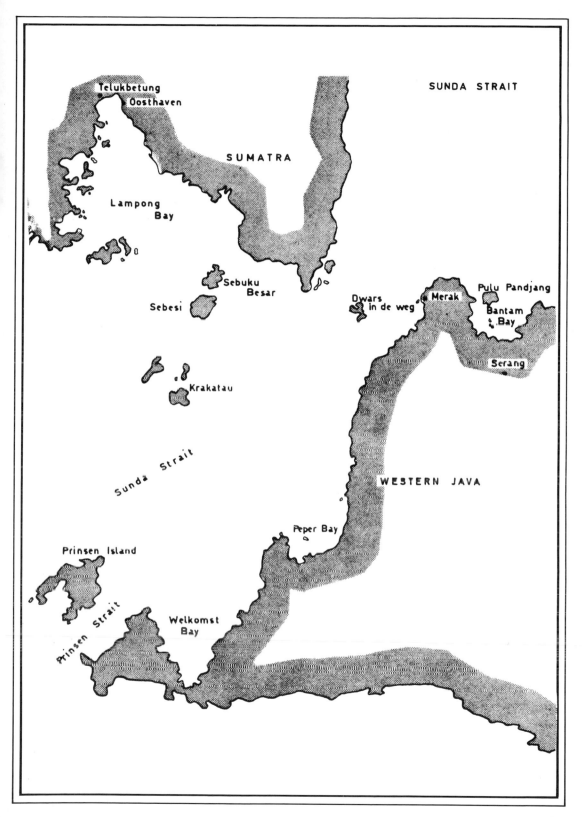

SUNDA STRAIT

Telukbetung
Oosthaven

SUMATRA

Lampong
Bay

Sebuku
Besar

Sebesi

Dwars
in de weg

Merak

Pulu Pandjang

Bantam
Bay

Serang

Krakatau

Sunda Strait

WESTERN JAVA

Peper Bay

Prinsen Island

Prinsen Strait

Welkomst
Bay

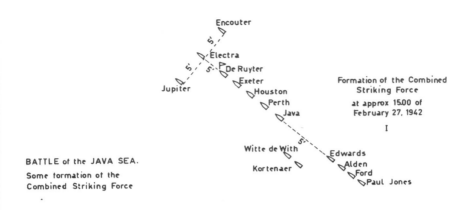

Encouter

Electra

De Ruyter

Exeter

Houston

Perth

Java

Jupiter

Witte de With

Kortenaer

Edwards

Alden

Ford

Paul Jones

Formation of the Combined
Striking Force
at approx 15.00 of
February 27, 1942

I

BATTLE of the JAVA SEA.

Some formation of the
Combined Striking Force

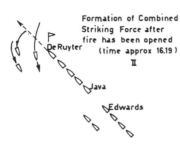

Formation of Combined
Striking Force after
fire has been opened
(time approx 16.19)

II

De Ruyter

Java

Edwards

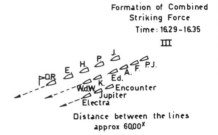

Formation of Combined
Striking Force
Time: 16.29–16.35

III

D.R. E. H. P. J.
K. Ed. A. F. P.J.
WdW Encounter
Jupiter
Electra

Distance between the lines
approx 60.00ˣ

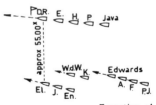

D.R. E. H. P. Java

approx 55.00ˣ

WdW K. Edwards
A. F. P.J.
El. J. En.

Formation of Combined
Striking Force
at 16.52

IV

5 cruisers

WdW. K. Ed. F.
A. P.J.
El. J. En.

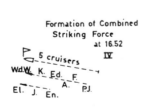

Formation of
Combined Striking Force
at 17.07

V

Formation and movements
of
Combined Striking Force
in the period of
17.08 – 17.40

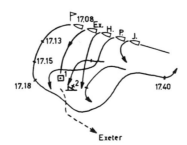

17.08
Ex. H. P. J.
17.13
17.15
17.18
17.40

Exeter

1. Exeter was hit by an 8"shell
   at about 17.07 and came to a
   stop(⊡)at 17.14

2. Kortenaer was hit by a torpedo
   at 17.13 and sank at 17.15

Left:
Battle of Java Sea.

On 17 February the Japanese embarked troops at Ambon to occupy Portuguese Timor (occupied by the Allies since 17 December). To cover the attack the Japanese carried out a major air attack on Darwin using both land-based aircraft and four carriers, *Akagi*, *Kaga*, *Soryu* and *Hiryu*. On 20 February Japanese Naval paratroopers co-operated with the landing forces and Timor effectively had been occupied by the 27th. Japanese Army troops, staging through Menado, had landed on Bali on 18 February and the airfield there was in Japanese hands by the following day. The ABDA Command, which was then still in existence, wanted to use Doorman's Striking Force against the Bali invasion fleet but first it had to be reorganised having been dispersed. Three Attack groups were formed, the 1st made up of the cruisers *De Ruyter* and *Java* and the destroyers *Piet Hein*, *Ford* and *Pope*. It sailed from Tjilatjap and carried out its attack at about at 2130 on 19 February. The cruisers went in ahead of the destroyers and had the benefit of complete surprise. The destroyers were less lucky and *Piet Hein* was sunk by gunfire and torpedoes from the Japanese destroyers *Hoshio* and *Asashio*. The two American destroyers launched torpedoes but could not see any results.

The 2nd Attack Group with four American destroyers leading the cruiser *Tromp* attacked at 0130 on the 20th. The USS *Pilsbury* torpedoed the Japanese destroyer *Michishio*. Both the *Tromp* and the destroyer *Stewart* were damaged by Japanese gunfire, the cruiser being hit 11 times. Finally, Dutch motor torpedo boats formed the 3rd Attack Group. Eight reached the target area from Surabaya but they were unable to launch their torpedoes. They retired back to their depot ship *Krakatau*. This action, which became known as the Battle of Badung Strait, was something of a disappointment for the Allies as no Japanese ships were sunk. Three destroyers and a transport were damaged. The Dutch cruiser *Tromp* had to be sent to Australia for repairs.

The Japanese were now ready to land on Bali. A Western Expeditionary Force was to land in Bantam Bay, with smaller beachheads at Eretam Wetan and Merak. Its Eastern counterpart was to land near Kragan. The Doorman Striking Force was split to deal with these landings, whose destination was known, thanks to Allied codebreaking. On 21 February Cdre Collins was placed in com-

Below:
A fine view of the newest British destroyer involved in the Java Sea defeat, HMS *Jupiter*. Note the replacement of the after bank of torpedo tubes by a 4in AA gun.
Real Photographs/Ian Allan Collection

mand of a Western Striking Force composed of the British and Australian ships *Exeter*, *Hobart*, *Dragon*, *Danae*, *Electra*, *Jupiter*, *Scout* and *Tenedos*. Hobart's sister ship *Perth* provided reinforcement three days later. The force was a mixed one of modern ships and World War 1-period veterans (the cruisers *Dragon* and *Danae* and destroyers *Scout* and *Tenedos*) but at least they all shared a common signals language and tactical doctrine. The Eastern Striking Force under Doorman was joint Dutch-US with the cruisers *De Ruyter*, *Java* and *Houston*, and destroyers *Witte de With*, *Banckert*, *Kortenaer*, *Paul Jones* and *Alden*. Six submarines, one British, two American and three Dutch covered the expected approach route of the Japanese forces. On 25 February a Dutch Consolidated PBY Catalina flying boat spotted the Eastern Invasion Fleet. Helfrich decided, therefore, to change his plans and concentrate a powerful force against this enemy threat. He moved *Exeter*, *Perth* and the modern British destroyers *Electra*, *Encounter* and *Jupiter* to Surabaya to join Doorman, who had been cruising off the north coast of Java and Madura to prevent unexpected landings.

On the arrival of the White Ensign reinforcements on 26 February, Doorman had a conference with his captains and their Staff officers. It was decided to sail to intercept the Japanese invaders that evening. There were some hopes of air cover by American Curtiss P-40 fighters being carried to Tjilatjap by the USS *Langley*, America's oldest carrier converted to a seaplane tender, Sadly, however, *Langley* was sunk by enemy aircraft 50 miles from her destination. At 1830 on

Right:
Battle of Java Sea 27 February 1942.

HMAS *Perth*

Built: Portsmouth Dockyard (launched 27 July 1934)

Displacement: 7,179 tons standard

Dimensions: 562.25ft x 56.7ft x 19ft

Armour: 4in belt; 2in over magazines; 1.25in over machinery; 1in turrets

Machinery: four shaft geared turbines, 72,000shp, 32.5kt

Armament: 8 x 6in (4 x 2); 8 x 4in (4 x 2); 8 x 21in torpedo tubes (2 x 4)

Complement: 570

Notes: Originally commissioned as HMS *Amphion* in the Royal Navy she was transferred to the RAN in July 1939. The design was a modified 'Leander' with machinery spaces and boiler rooms divided to make them less vulnerable to battle damage. During her last refit in Australia, *Perth* was fitted with radar but the precise type is unknown. During her service in the Mediterranean in 1941 she had briefly shipped a quadruple 2pdr pom-pom but this was removed at Port Said in July 1941.

Below:
HMAS *Perth*: after sterling service in the Mediterranean she met her end with the *Houston* in Bantam Bay. The Australian cruiser *Hobart* also involved in the Java Sea action was a sister ship. *Real Photographs/Ian Allan Collection*

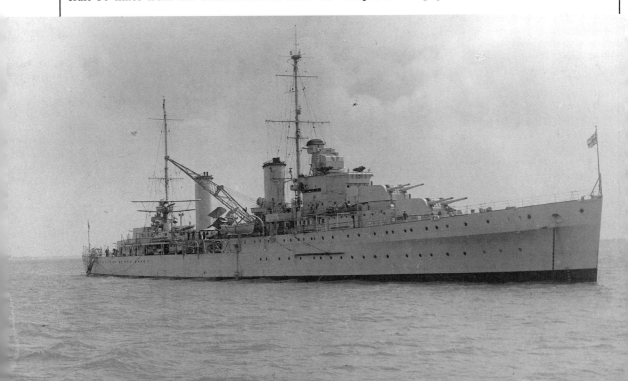

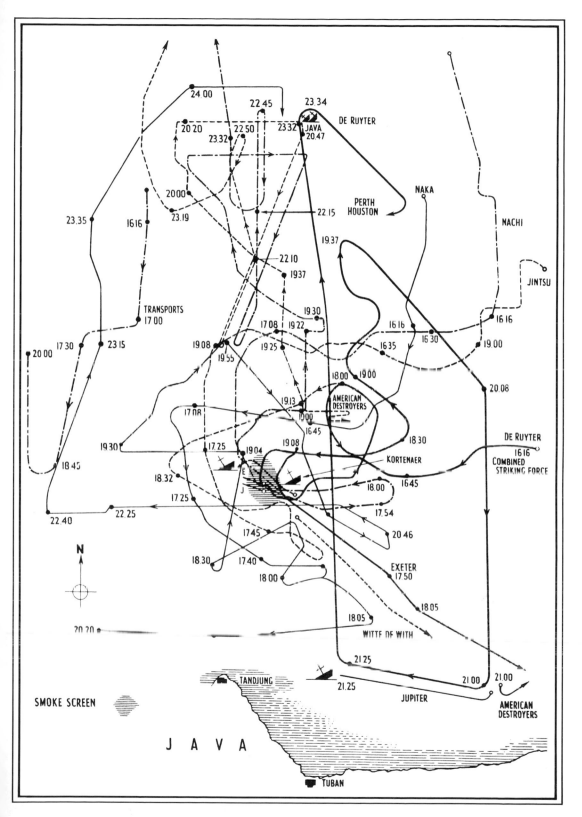

24.00

22.45

23.34

DE RUYTER

20.20   23.32   23.32   JAVA
        22.50   20.47

23.32

NAKA

2000
23.19

23.35   1616

PERTH
HOUSTON

22.15

NACHI

19.37

22.10

JINTSU

1937

1930

TRANSPORTS
17.00

1708   1922

17.30   23.15

19.08
        1955

19.25

1616   1630

1635

1616

19.00

20.00

1800   1900

20.08

1913

17.08

1000

AMERICAN
DESTROYERS

1645

19.30

18.30

DE RUYTER
1616
COMBINED
STRIKING FORCE

17.25   1904   1908

KORTENAER

18.45

18.32

1800   1645

N

17.25

22.25

17.54

22.40

20.46

17.45

EXETER
17.50

18.30   17.40

1805

18.00

20.20

1805

WITTE DE WITH

21.25

TANDJUNG

21.25

JUPITER

21.00   21.00

AMERICAN
DESTROYERS

SMOKE SCREEN

J A V A

TUBAN

85

the 26th Doorman's Striking Force left Surabaya to make a sweep along the north coast of Madura. After an abortive search, he turned back to Surabaya to refuel but at 1427 he received the news that a Dutch Catalina had spotted the invasion fleet near Bawean.

The ships of the Combined Striking force reversed course at about 1430 and made off for the northwest at 24kt. The force consisted of two heavy cruisers, *Exeter* and *Houston*, three light cruisers, *De Ruyter*, *Java* and *Perth*, five modern destroyers, *Electra*, *Encounter*, *Jupiter*, *Kortenaer* and *Witte de With* and four old destroyers, *Alden*, *John D. Edwards*, *John D. Ford* and *Paul Jones*. Their target was the 41 transports under Rear-Adm Nishimura who commanded a close escort of two destroyer flotillas, each of one light cruiser

and six destroyers. Nishimura flew his flag in *Naka*, the 5,195 ton leader of the 4th Flotilla. This consisted of seven large modern destroyers of the 1,961 ton 'Asashio' class and 1,685 ton 'Shiratsuyu' class. Of the former were *Asagumo*, *Minegumo* and *Natsugumo* armed with three twin 5in gun mountings and the rest were of the latter class with two twin and one single 5in guns. All carried eight 24in torpedo tubes for the formidable and unique oxygen fuelled Type 93 Long Lance long range torpedo. This could run without much of a track for 22,000yd at 49kt,

Below:
The old fashioned lines of the Japanese light cruiser *Jintsu* can be appreciated from this picture taken before the 1940 refit. Note the two twin torpedo tubes on the port side. Note also the seaplane catapult aft.
Real Photographs/Ian Allan Collection

Above right:
The 2,000-ton Japanese destroyer *Amatsukaze*, a fine new ship of the 'Kagero' class, fired a broadside of eight 'Long Lance' torpedoes on 27 February , at 1757. *IWM MH6230*

Below right:
The Japanese heavy cruiser *Haguro*. This picture was taken before her first major refit although the fore funnel has already been lengthened. During the refit the superstructure was lengthened and the single catapult (note the seaplane ahead of the after 7.9in guns) replaced by one on each side; the guns were replaced by more modern 8in weapons just before the war. *Ian Allan Collection*

35,000yd at just over 40kt and 44,000yd at 36kt. Western navies were not really aware of the capabilities of this extraordinary weapon. For comparison the British Mk IX mounted in its modern destroyers ran only 11,000yd at 41kt and 15,000yd at 35kt.

The other half of Nishimura's escort was the 2nd Destroyer Flotilla led by *Naka*'s sister ship *Jintsu*. It consisted of four destroyers of the latest 2,033-ton 'Kagero' class *Yukikaze, Amatsukaze, Tokitsukaze* and *Hatsukaze* and three older 'Shiratsuyus', *Yamakaze, Kawakaze* and *Humikaze*.

There was also a Close Support Group commanded by Rear-Adm T. Takagi. This was composed of the two 10,000-ton heavy cruisers *Nachi* and *Haguro* each armed with 10 8in guns and 16 24in torpedo tubes. Escorting the cruisers were two of the original 'Fubuki' class large destroyers *Ushio* and *Sazanami*. Both these and the other Japanese destroyers carried six 5in guns. Most destroyers carried eight tubes for Long Lances but the pair of 'Fubukis' had only six tubes and at this stage of the war were probably carrying Type 90 24in torpedoes with conventional heater engines

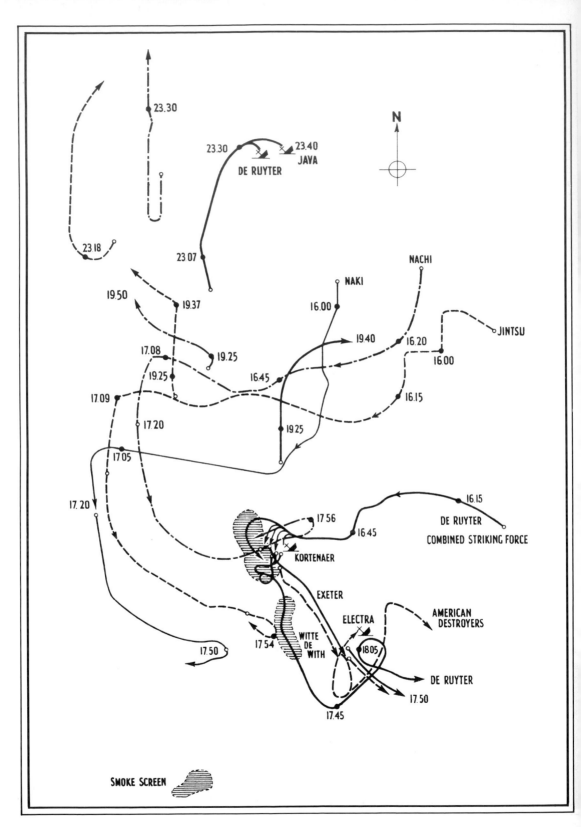

Battle of Java Sea 27 February 1942 (according to Japanese sources).

(range, 10,900yd at 43kt and 16,400yd at 35kt). Interestingly, *Ushio* and *Sazanami* did not fire any torpedoes in this action. The two light cruisers had been refitted with quadruple tubes in 1940 and were probably equipped with Long Lances; they certainly joined in the torpedo bombardment as did the heavy cruisers which had also been refitted to carry the oxygen fuelled weapons.

If the convoy was threatened by a powerful surface force Takagi planned to rearrange his forces, leaving one destroyer from each flotilla, *Natsugumo* and *Humikaze*, as close escort for the convoy and grouping the rest of his forces into a powerful Surface Action Group. His own destroyers were to operate as part of the 2nd Destroyer Flotilla. He would, therefore, take into action two heavy cruisers, two light cruisers and 14 of the world's most powerful destroyers.

Doorman was not only outnumbered but he was suffering under several major tactical disadvantages. Most importantly, his force was in no sense a unified group. There had been no combined exercises because of a lack of both time and

Below:
Doorman's flagship *De Ruyter* is near-missed by a bomb on 15 February. On the left is a Dutch destroyer and in the middle the cruiser *Tromp*.
IWM HU50182

a safe exercise area. No joint doctrine existed for either communications or fire control. Despite attempts to standardise on Anglo-French naval codes for tactical signalling and a standard air force code there were no joint signal books on board the Striking Force's ships. Nor was there a common flag signalling system. In order to overcome this the rather desperate expedient was resorted to of having British and American signalmen on board *De Ruyter*. There was a radio telephone system but this did not stand up to the vibrations of gunfire and *De Ruyter*'s searchlights

---

De Ruyter

Built: Wilton-Fijenoord (launched 11 May 1935)

Displacement: 6,000 tons standard

Dimensions: 560.1ft x 51.5ft x 16.7 ft

Protection: 2-3in belt; 1.25in deck: 2-4in turrets

Machinery: two shaft geared turbines, 66,000shp, 32kt

Armament: 7 x 5.9-inch (3 x 2, 1 x 1); 10 x 40mm AA (5 x 2); 8 x 12.7mm AA (4 x 2)

Complement: 435

Notes: Three cruisers were required in the East Indies but only two had been completed in the early 1920s. The third vessel was redesigned as a smaller ship with more economical layout of armament in three twin turrets — one forward, two aft. However, adding extra length to improve the speed and provide space for two seaplanes amidships enlarged the design once more and allowed an extra gun to be carried forward. The funnel carried prominent smoke deflection plates. She was originally to have been named *Celebes*.

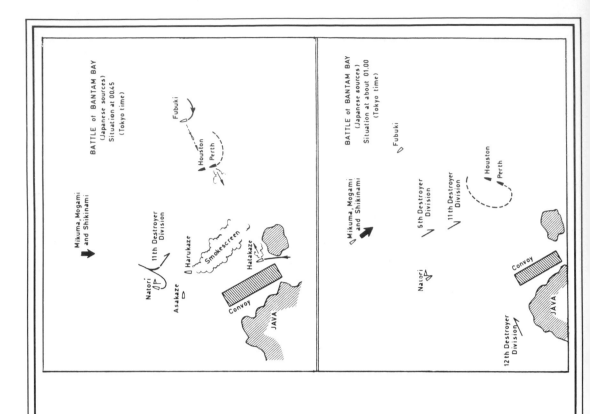

BATTLE of BANTAM BAY
(Japanese sources)
(from a letter of Naval Attaché Tokyo of 27-1-1949)

Japanese disposition at 24.00 February 28, 1942
(Tokyo time)

11th Destroyer Division

5th Destroyer Division

BABI IS.

Convoy

Bantam Bay

JAVA

SUMATRA

12th Destroyer Division

21th Torpedoboat Division

BATTLE of BANTAM BAY
(Japanese sources)
Situation at 00.45
(Tokyo time)

Mikuma, Mogami
and Shikinami

11th Destroyer Division

Natori

Asakaze

Harukaze

Smokescreen

Hatakaze

Convoy

JAVA

Fubuki

Houston

Perth

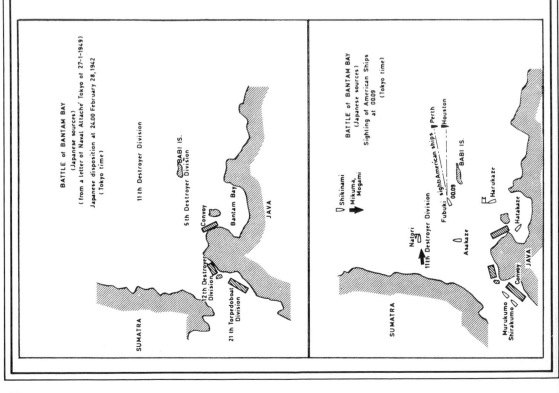

BATTLE of BANTAM BAY
(Japanese sources)
Sighting of American Ships
at 00.09
(Tokyo time)

SUMATRA

Shikinami

Mikuma, Mogami

Natori

11th Destroyer Division

Fubuki sights American ships

Asakaze

00.09

Perth

Houston

BABI IS.

Harukaze

Hatakaze

Convoy

Murukumo

Shirakumo

JAVA

BATTLE of BANTAM BAY
(Japanese sources)
Situation at about 01.00
(Tokyo time)

Mikuma, Mogami
and Shikinami

Natori

5th Destroyer Division

11th Destroyer Division

12th Destroyer Division

Convoy

JAVA

Fubuki

Houston

Perth

Above:
On 15 February Karel Doorman's striking force was attacked by bombers in the Gaspar Strait. *Exeter* was near-missed. *IWM HU50185*

were vulnerable to the blast of her guns. This meant the flagship could only communicate using hand signal lamps — in three parallel languages!

The other great problem was Doorman's lack of air cover. This was ironic as the Dutch admiral was himself a naval airman. His previous job had been commanding the very naval aircraft that the Allied Command system had recently taken away. At his last Staff conference on 26 February he had told the Naval Commander Surabaya that he hoped he would be able to rely on air reconnaissance and other help from the air. Sadly, however, by the end of February it was unlikely that this would be available. Most of the flying boats had been lost to Japanese fighters and what fighters there were left — about 30 — were under another command with different priorities. Reinforcement from Australia was impossible because of the Japanese conquest of Bali and Kupang. The Japanese were well supplied with reconnaissance aircraft both in their cruisers, both heavy and light, and in two seaplane carriers that established a base at Bawean. The Allied cruisers were without their air capabilities in part because of damage and resultant unserviceability, but more because of the intention to fight the Japanese at night. In such circumstances seaplanes and their fuel just added to ships' vulnerability.

At about 1530 Doorman's Striking Force was attacked by a Japanese bomber. Doorman asked

Left:
The Battle of Bantam Bay.

for fighter cover shortly afterwards but none was available as the Air Command, without telling its naval counterpart, had allocated all its limited number of machines to escort an attack by three US Army Douglas A-24 Dauntless two-seat dive-bombers on the invasion force. The cruising order of the Doorman force was *De Ruyter*, *Exeter*, *Houston*, *Perth* and *Java*; the three British destroyers were in line abreast ahead in the order port to starboard *Jupiter*, *Electra* and *Encounter*. *Witte de With* led *Kortenaer* on *Java*'s port quarter and the four US destroyers brought up the rear in the order *Edwards*, *Alden*, *Ford* and *Paul Jones*.

At 1612 *Electra* spotted a cruiser and destroyers bearing to the northwest sailing a course of 220 degrees. Four minutes later *Jintsu* opened fire on the British destroyer at 18,000yd with her 5.5in guns. *Electra* and *Jupiter* replied with their 4.7s, although the chances of hitting at that range were almost nil. As the two Japanese heavy cruisers appeared over the horizon and opened fire, the 2nd Destroyer Flotilla manoeuvred for a Long Lance attack. Doorman turned 20 degrees to port in order to prevent the Japanese from crossing his T. The Japanese, however, had superior speed because the destroyer *Kortenaer*'s boilers limited her to 27kt. Doorman was, therefore, forced further to port by the Japanese. The Allied cruisers were now in the front line with the destroyers in

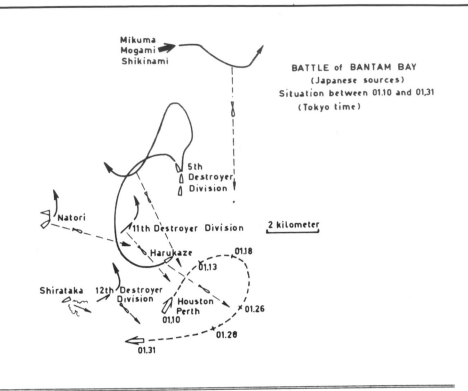

Mikuma
Mogami
Shikinami

BATTLE of BANTAM BAY
(Japanese sources)
Situation between 01.10 and 01.31
(Tokyo time)

5th
Destroyer
Division

Natori

11th Destroyer Division

2 kilometer

Harukaze

01.18

01.13

Shirataka   12th Destroyer
Division

Houston
Perth
01.10

× 01.26

01.28

01.31

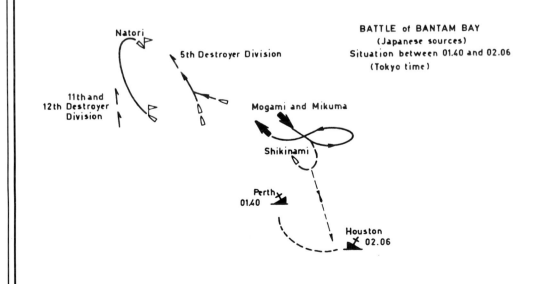

Natori

5th Destroyer Division

BATTLE of BANTAM BAY
(Japanese sources)
Situation between 01.40 and 02.06
(Tokyo time)

11th and
12th Destroyer
Division

Mogami and Mikuma

Shikinami

Perth ×
01.40

Houston
× 02.06

Left:
The Battle of Bantam Bay.

two lines on the disengaged side. The Allied cruisers were fully engaged with their six and 8in guns and the Japanese made effective reply. *De Ruyter* was hit twice but, luckily, the projectiles did not explode. The two Allied heavy cruisers were also both hit, but again not seriously at this stage. The Japanese do not seem to have suffered much damage either, although the Allies claimed some hits.

The Japanese relied on their torpedoes in such circumstances and *Naka* fired four Type 93s at 1633. She was followed by *Jintsu* two minutes later and by seven destroyers who between them launched 27 Long Lances by 1645. The cruiser *Haguro* completed the first attack with eight Long Lances in the water at 1652. *Nachi* could not fire because her compressed air system had been prematurely exhausted because of an accident with a valve. Doorman tried to close the enemy and at 1705 *Exeter* was hit by a torpedo which luckily failed to explode. Next, USS *Houston* was hit by yet another defective shell but she nevertheless decreased speed which caused some confusion in the Allied line. At 1708 confusion became complete as *Exeter* suffered a serious shell hit which penetrated her boiler room and put six of her eight boilers out of action. She sheered off to port, slowing down and the rest of the Striking Force

Asagumo

Built: Kawasaki, Kobe (launched 5 November 1937)

Displacement: 1,961 tons standard

Dimensions: 388ft x 33.9ft x 12.1ft

Machinery: 2 shaft geared turbines, 50,000shp, 35kt

Armament: 6 x 5in (3 x 2); 4 x 25mm AA (2 x 2); 8 x 24in torpedo tubes (2 x 4)

Complement: 200

Notes: One of the 'Asashio' class built under the 1934 programme and unaffected by the 1930 London Treaty. Fine ships, they suffered teething problems with their steam plants and steering gear, but this class set the pattern for the next two classes of Japanese fleet destroyer. A complete set of reloads was carried for the torpedo tubes. *Asagumo* fired seven Long Lances on 27 February, three at 1640 and four at 1807. She was sunk at the Battle of Leyte Gulf (see final chapter); by that time she had lost one of her after 5in turrets to increase her light AA outfit.

Below:
The destroyer *Asagumo*, an 'Asashio' class ship carried out two torpedo attacks on 27 February. She fired three 'Long Lances' at 1640 and four more at 1807. Just before the second attack she was damaged by gunfire, probably from *Exeter* and *Witte De With* and forced to a standstill.
IWM MH5945

followed her as they thought the Commander had ordered an alteration of course. As *De Ruyter* sailed blithely on ahead HMAS *Perth*, next in line to *Exeter*, laid a smoke screen around the damaged ship.

The four cruisers sailed into the four destroyers that were on their disengaged side. The Japanese reconnaissance aircraft that kept a constant watch on events must have been puzzled, if not amused, by the confusion below. Confusion was increased still further by the evasive manoeuvres of the Allied ships to avoid the 43 torpedoes fired at them and the explosions of the Long Lances as they came to the end of their runs without finding a target. One 24in torpedo, however, hit *Kortenaer* fair and square at 1713. The 6,000lb warhead blew the Dutch destroyer in half and she sank in two minutes. The Allies thought they were being attacked by submarines as the range was still so great. Actually the torpedo had probably been one fired by the cruiser *Haguro*.

Doorman ordered a destroyer counter-attack and *Electra* and *Encounter* disentangled themselves from the confusion and closed the enemy, followed by *Jupiter*. The two 'Es' engaged *Jintsu* and the 4th Flotilla which was hardly an equal contest. *Electra* was sunk but the three British ships managed to damage *Oshio* and *Sazanami*. Under cover of this attack Doorman sorted out his force and reformed the cruiser line in the order *De Ruyter*, *Perth*, *Houston* and *Java*; the four American 'fourstackers' followed astern. *Witte de With* was tasked with escorting the crippled *Exeter* back to Surabaya.

The Japanese mounted a second torpedo attack between 1748 when *Haguro* put eight more Long Lances in the water and 1807 when *Asagumo* fired her four. No less than 92 weapons were fired in all by the two light cruisers and all the other Long Lance-fitted Japanese ships except the *Minegumo* which had to take avoiding action to avoid torpedoes fired by her over-enthusiastic companions. Just before *Asagumo* fired she was engaged by the *Exeter* and *Witte de With* which succeeded in hitting her with a 4.7in shell. The destroyer came to a standstill and then moved to join the close escort forces after being stopped for 40min. Just as the Japanese ceased launching torpedoes Doorman ordered his American destroyers in to attack with their torpedoes. He soon thought better of this, however, and instead gave the old ships the more suitable duty of laying a smoke screen. This covered a withdrawal ordered by the tersely simple 'All ships — follow me'.

It seems that Doorman hoped to work his way round to the transports. The American destroyers soon tired of their passive duty and decided on their own initiative to make a torpedo attack after all. They launched 24 torpedoes between them but none of the old torpedoes scored hits. *Perth*, however, did succeed in hitting *Haguro* with a 6in shell that started a spectacular fire among the catapult aircraft. The fighting value of the Japanese cruiser was, however, unaffected. The Japanese now also withdrew as Takagi feared both a minefield and submarines ahead.

The first phase of the Battle of the Java Sea had been a victory on points for the Japanese. Doorman had lost his second most powerful cruiser and three destroyers and his USN destroyers had expended their entire torpedo complement; they were thus of dubious utility as surface action vessels as their old 4in guns were obsolete for engaging destroyers of the 'Special Type' and after. Only the *Asagumo* had been taken out of Takagi's group. Doorman wanted to find the convoy and signalled to Helfrich for information but the latter had no idea where it was. A Dutch Naval Catalina was about to take off but it would take until 2222 for it to find the invasion convoy. On the other hand Takagi's floatplanes, that dropped flares after dark, were able to allow him to keep his force well positioned between Doorman and the transports. The Dutch Admiral had to guess and he led his force round to the northeast and then to the northwest to try to get behind the escort. At 1927 he ran into the *Jintsu* and three of her flotilla. *Perth* and *Houston* opened fire and the Japanese cruiser fired torpedoes which forced Doorman's ships to turn away to starboard. Doorman then reformed his line on a southerly course turning to the west when he reached the 20m depth contour. The American destroyers were sent back to Surabaya for fuel and more torpedoes. At 2125 illluck struck once more when *Jupiter* struck a Dutch laid mine and quickly sank. At about this time Doorman turned north to search for *Kortenaer*'s survivors and Doorman detached his last destroyer *Encounter* that was short of fuel to pick up these men and then return to Surabaya.

So it was that Doorman was down to four cruisers only when he sighted the two Japanese heavy cruisers to port on a reciprocal course. The Japanese were matchless in night action (only the British came close) and the advantage was with the two heavy cruisers who turned about and engaged with both guns and 24in torpedoes. *Nachi* fired eight Long Lances at 2322 and *Haguro* four a minute later. Ten minutes after launch one of *Nachi*'s torpedoes hit *Java* and two minutes later one of *Haguro*'s smaller spread hit the flagship. *Java* took about 13min to sink and her final explosions killed almost all of her crew; *De Ruyter* lasted longer, perhaps for as long as 90min but her crew again suffered dreadful casualties caused by exploding 40mm AA ammunition and burning oil on the water surrounding the wreck. The men in both ships were physically exhausted. Only 92 of *De Ruyter*'s crew were saved and only 19 of *Java*'s. Doorman went down with his flagship. The other two cruisers, low on ammunition, retired to Tandjong Priok at 28kt. *Houston* only had 50 shots left per gun, *Perth* 20. As they approached their refuge they finally received air cover from three Hurricanes.

After refuelling, *Houston* and *Perth* headed for the open sea. They were bound for Tjilatjap but instead ran into the Western Invasion Force part of which was at anchor in Bantam Bay. It looked as if the Australian-American remnant of the Striking Force would be able to get some revenge and the two cruisers *Houston* in the lead, turned to starboard and opened fire as the destroyer *Harukaze* laid a protective smoke screen. The picket destroyer *Fubuki* fired nine torpedoes at the two cruisers from a parallel course to starboard with little regard for the safety of the Japanese ships beyond. The two cruisers seem to have turned to port to avoid the attack and the Type 90s ran by to sink a minesweeper and a merchant man in the anchorage beyond. Three Japanese merchantmen were damaged by the Allied cruisers' gunfire but the Japanese had powerful forces in the area. In the immediate vicinity were three Destroyer Divisions: the 5th with three old 1,400-ton unrebuilt 'Kamikaze' class ships (four 4.7in guns, six 21in torpedoes) *Asakaze*, *Harukaze* and *Hatakaze*; the 11th with three original 'Special Types', *Fubuki* (name ship of the class), *Shirayuki* and *Hatsuyuki*; and the 12th with two similar ships *Murakumo* and *Shirakumo*. *Fubuki* had already opened the action but the others now prepared to attack from the northwest together with their light cruiser *Natori* (seven 5.5in guns, eight 24in torpedo tubes). To the north and sailing to the sound of the guns were the 12,400-ton heavy cruisers *Mikuma* and *Mogami* (10 8in guns, 12 24in torpedo tubes) with another 'Fubuki' class destroyer *Shikinami*.

The 11th Division had opened the action with *Fubuki*'s attack and the remaining pair of destroyers turned to the southwest to engage the enemy who began to circle round to port. The old 'boats' of the 5th Division were not far behind on the port quarter of the 11th Division and *Natori* was in a supporting position on the starboard quarter. The 12th Division was coming up from the southwest out of the Sunda Strait where they had been protecting the other portion of the convoy. *Hatsuyuki* and *Shirayuki* turned to port and each fired full broadsides of nine Long Lances at 2340. The old 'Kamikazes' seem to have turned to port prematurely but made another turn to reverse their course. One of them, *Asakaze*, supported the attack of their newer cousins with a full broadside of six old 21in Type 6s at 2343 while *Natori* got off four 24in Type 8s (another old design) a minute later.

The two Allied cruisers turned to starboard to take avoiding action but this exposed them to a Long Lance attack from the heavy cruisers to the north; *Mogami* and *Mikuma* each fired six torpedoes at 2349. Eight minutes later *Mogami* fired the remaining six of her starboard battery at 2357. The target was disappearing however as the cruisers curved round to the southeast. There were too many Japanese ships to avoid, however, and the turn presented the cruisers broadsides just as more destroyers attacked. The 5th Flotilla closed in to use its old weapons and turning to port on a reciprocal course *Harukaze* fired five torpedoes at 2356 and *Hatakaze* six at 2357. At Midnight as the ships continued to circle, the two modern destroyers *Shirakumo* and *Murakumo* carried out a classic Long Lance attack with nine torpedoes each. This is the attack that seems to have done the damage as the torpedoes were fired at close range; they were set to run at maximum speed, 50kt, making fire control easier. *Perth* was hit on the port side at 0005 by two of the big torpedoes. She sank eight minutes later. *Houston* probably received at least two hits at about the same time and at 0029 the *Shikinami* fired a single Type 90 into the wreck. *Houston* sank some seven minutes later Three Japanese destroyers were damaged in the Battle of Bantam Bay as this part of the Java Sea action is sometimes called. *Harukaze* was hit laying her smoke screen and damaged in the bridge, engine room and rudder. *Shirayuki* was hit by *Perth* with a six inch shell on the bridge and *Shikinami*'s propeller was damaged by a near miss.

Almost simultaneously with the departure of *Perth* and *Houston* from Tandjong Priok *Exeter* escorted by HMS *Encounter* and the USS *Pope* left Surabaya for the Sunda Strait and Colombo. *Witte de With* should have gone also but was delayed by mechanical problems. The Allied ships ran into the Japanese forces covering the Kragan landing. The Japanese waited for reinforcements before engaging the Allied ships. Eventually they assembled four heavy cruisers, *Ashigara*, *Myoko*, *Nachi* and *Haguro*, the whole class, plus the 'Fubuki' class destroyer *Akebono*, the slightly later 'Akatsuki' class destroyers *Inazuma* and *Ikazuchi* and the Long Lance fitted 'Shiratsuyus' *Kawakaze* and *Yamakaze*. At 1115 *Exeter* was hit once more in the boiler room and her captain, faced with a total machinery failure decided to scuttle his cruiser. Before this could be done the *Inazuma* put a Type 90 torpedo into *Exeter*'s starboard side. She sank at about 1200. *Encounter* was overwhelmed by the gunfire of the more powerful Japanese ships and

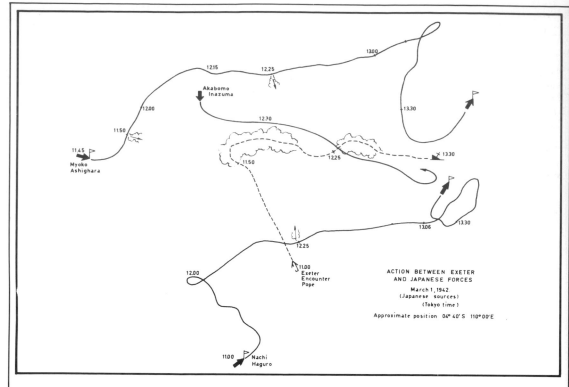

ACTION BETWEEN EXETER
AND JAPANESE FORCES
March 1, 1942
(Japanese sources)
(Tokyo time)

Approximate position 04° 40' S 110° 00' E

the *Pope* was sunk by half-a-dozen supporting Japanese bombers. *Witte de With* was eventually scuttled at Surabaya.

Other ships were luckier. HMAS *Hobart*, the old British cruisers *Danae* and *Dragon*, the old destroyers HMS *Tenedos* and HMS *Scout* and the Dutch destroyer *Evertsen* were ordered to Trincomalee. The Dutch ship, which was not fully worked up, became separated in a squall and was driven ashore at Sebuku Besar by two Japanese destroyers after being hit seven times and set on fire. The other ships, however escaped as did the American destroyers *John D. Edwards*, *Alden*, *John D. Ford* and *Paul Jones* which left Surabaya at 1700 on 28 February and reached Freemantle via the Bali Strait on 4 March. They successfully fought their way past three Japanese destroyers whose fire was so accurate that the Americans thought they were using radar — but not quite accurate enough.

All the Allied naval forces had succeeded in achieving was delaying the Japanese landings in Java by 24hr. These duly took place on 1 March and the following day Helfrich was ordered to leave. Command was transferred three days later and the Dutch surrendered the East Indies on 9 March. The doomed Doorman had probably done as much as he could. There had just not been time to work out the modalities of proper

Van Ghent

Built: De Schelde, Flushing (launched 23 October 1926)

Displacement: 1,310 tons standard

Dimensions: 322ft x 31.2ft x 9.75ft

Machinery: two shaft geared turbines, 31,000shp, 36kt

Armament: 4 x 4.7in; 2 x 3in AA (2 x 1); 4 x 12.7mm AA (4 x 1); 6 x 21in torpedo tubes; 24 mines

Complement: 129

Notes: First of a class of four destroyers based on the latest British Yarrow design. Sisters were *Evertsen*, *Piet Hein*, and *Kortenaer*. A second group with improved AA armament (1 x 3in, 2 x 2 40mm) was launched in 1928-30. Three of these were involved in the Java sea actions — *Banckert*, *Van Nes* and *Witte De With*.

Allied co-operation. That he had lost was not the fault of the poor, sick admiral, but rather that of the Allied Governments for not having got their act together sooner and for not having reinforced the theatre to the limit of risk elsewhere. Once again air power had been crucial in the surveillance role, if not as a strike weapon in itself. However, the main instrument of victory had been the surface ship, armed with a formidable underwater missile. Not until the Allies had carrier and land-based air power of their own in theatre and properly co-ordinated with their naval forces, would they have an answer to this threat.

HMS *Exeter*

Built: Devonport Dockyard (launched 18 July 1929)

Displacement: 8,390 tons standard

Dimensions: 575ft x 58ft x 21ft

Armour: 3-4.4in belt; 3in over magazines, 1.5in over machinery; 1in on turrets

Machinery: four shaft geared turbines, 80,000shp , 32kt

Armament: 6 x 8in (3 x 2); 8 x 4in AA (4 x 2); 16 x 2pdr AA (2 x 8); 6 x 21in torpedo tubes (2 x 3)

Sensors: Radar Type 279

Complement: 630

Notes. Second of two reduced size heavy cruisers built as a result of the Chancellor of the Exchequer, Winston Churchill's campaign against the Admiralty in the late 1920s to save money. Heavily damaged at the River Plate she had been given a 13-month retit at Devonport from which she emerged in March 1941 with new AA armament and radar.

Nachi

Built: Kure Dockyard (launched 15 June 1927)

Displacement: 13,000 tons standard

Dimensions: 661.75ft x 68ft x 20.75ft

Armour: 4in belt; 2.5-5in deck; 1.5in turrets

Machinery: Four shaft geared turbines, 130,000shp, 33.75kt

Armament: 10 x 8in (5 x 2); 8 x 5in (4 x 2); 8 x 25mm AA (4 x 2); 4 x 13.2mm AA (2 x 2); 16 x 24in torpedo tubes (4 x 4)

Complement: 773

Notes: Built to be the most powerful Washington Treaty cruisers the 'Nachi' class exceeded the treaty limits by almost 1,000 tons. Originally armed with 7.9in and single 4.7in guns they were given two major refits to bring them up to date; *Nachi* completed hers in July 1936 and March 1940. With their new gun batteries and Long Lance torpedoes they were formidable vessels in surface combat. *Nachi* was sunk by a carrier air strike in Manila Bay in November 1944.

CHAPTER FIVE

Sirte

The Gulf of Sirte lies on the coast of Libya to the west of Benghazi. It has become famous in recent years because of clashes between the United States and Libya but previously it gave its name to two naval battles fought to the north of it in the approaches to Malta. The first Battle of Sirte has already been described in Chapter 3. This was the successful defence of the fast supply ship HMS *Breconshire* by a combined force of cruisers under Rear-Adm Philip Vian and including Agnew's famous Force 'K'. The more important second battle, however, was an even more classic feat of convoy defence. Indeed, it must rank as one of the finest of its type.

The demise of the Malta Striking Force was not the only problem faced by Admiral Cunningham's Fleet in December 1941. Almost simultaneously the Italians mounted a daring human torpedo attack on the Mediterranean Fleet in Alexandria harbour. Both HMS *Queen Elizabeth* and HMS *Valiant* were effectively sunk and settled on the bottom of Alexandria harbour. It would take months for them to be put back into service. Happily, the two stricken capital ships had settled vertically and the British were able to maintain the deception that they were still operational. In effect, had the Axis command realised it, the combination of *Luftflotte 2* and the still intact Italian battlefleet was in a position to exert command of the Mediterranean. Convoys to maintain Malta could only be run through with considerable difficulty. Meanwhile the Italians were able to reinforce and resupply Rommel who mounted a major counter offensive in January which reached Gazala on 7 February and even captured Tobruk which had held out the previous year. Once again

Below:
HMS *Euryalus* ready to repel an air attack with her 5.25in guns at maximum elevation. On the horizon can be seen (left to right) *Breconshire*, *Penelope* and *Cleopatra*. *IWM A8172*

Rommel's advance gave the Germans useful airfields from which they could extend their air umbrella over the Mediterranean.

Malta was now more of a liability than an asset. In Correlli Barnett's brilliant phrase, it had become 'The Verdun of the Naval War' — an outpost that it took disproportionate losses to maintain and resupply rather than a useful base from which to blockade Rommel's army. Despite later claims by German officers, it was shortcomings in the Axis logistical system in Africa itself that caused the supply problems Rommel faced, not the limited effects of the air and submarine forces that struggled to operate from Malta under the weight of heavy air attacks that largely neutralised their effectiveness. Indeed the North African Campaign was to be turned on its head in 1942: rather than Malta supporting the land war in the Western Desert the Eighth Army was urged into offensive action to clear the North African airfields that were blockading Malta!

At the beginning of 1942 the only forces Cunningham had to screen the supply ships to Malta were Adm Vian's 15th Cruiser Squadron of 'Dido' class ships armed with 5.25in dual purpose guns *Naiad* and *Euryalus* were reinforced in December by *Dido* herself, her Crete damage having been repaired. Both *Naiad* and *Euryalus* had the full designed armament of five twin turrets but when *Dido* had been completed slow production of these advanced mountings had only allowed four turrets to be fitted. She had, however, received her fifth turret in 'Q' position ahead of the bridge during her recent major refit and repair. The 5.25in gun had been designed as the Navy's answer to the bomber threat and was an excellent modern dual purpose weapon with a maximum range of over 24,000yd and a maximum ceiling of 46,500ft. The 5.25 had an expected rate of fire of 10 rounds/min/gun. To add to the AA potential of his squadron Vian also had the AA ship HMS *Carlisle*, a World War 1 cruiser rearmed with four twin 4in anti aircraft guns. These fired at 12 rounds/min but their maximum range was less than 2,000yd and their ceiling 39,000ft. Multiple pom-poms provided the light anti aircraft armament for both types of ship. *Carlisle* could only make 29kt against the 33kt of the 'Dido' class and this meant that she was best used as close escort for convoys. In addition to the cruisers there were two flotillas of fleet destroyers and a flotilla of smaller escort destroyers. In addition to the above there were the remnants of Force 'K' at Gibraltar, the 6in gun *Penelope* and the destroyer *Legion*.

Cunningham lacked both battleships and aircraft carriers so his lighter surface forces were even more dependant on land-based air support.

Below:
Conflicting convoy movements in the Mediterranean.

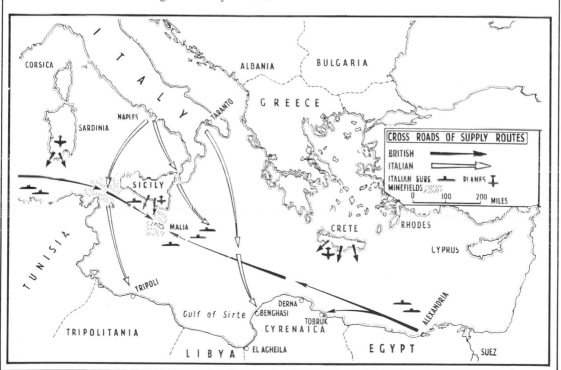

The previous year, Cunningham had waged a bureaucratic battle with Air Marshal Tedder, his RAF counterpart, to get a proper Mediterranean equivalent of Coastal Command established as a specially trained land-based maritime air force under Naval command. The best that could be obtained in the face of well entrenched Air Force prejudices about 'the unity of air power' was the designation of No 201 Group as a 'Naval Cooperation Group' for 'the conduct of operations at sea and co-operation with the Mediterranean Fleet as required by the C-in-C Mediterranean'. This took place in October but it took until January to get the Group operating properly, providing reconnaissance and fighter cover for the Fleet. The recapture of bases in Cyrenaica greatly assisted the airmen with their work. No 201 Group operating from recaptured Western Desert bases helped Vian escort the LSI(L) *Glengyle* to Malta and brought *Breconshire* back. A small convoy was run to Malta in mid-January, most of which got through and the fast naval supply ships were exchanged once more in February.

The Luftwaffe stepped up its pressure that month and a convoy operation failed because of heavy air attacks. In March *Fliegerkorps 2*'s pressure on Malta also increased despite the delivery of the first Supermarine Spitfire Vs by *Eagle* and *Argus* to replace the island's now outclassed Hurricanes. Under cover of the heavy attacks the Italians ran a convoy of their own unscathed in late February. In early March another Axis convoy

HMS *Cleopatra*

Built: Hawthorn Leslie, Hebburn (launched 27 March 1940)

Displacement: 5,600 tons standard

Dimensions: 512ft x 50.5ft x 16.75ft

Armour: belt 3in; 2in over magazines, 1in over machinery

Machinery: two sets geared turbines, 62,000shp, 32.2kt

Armament: 10 x 5.25in (10 x 2); 8 x 2pdr (2 x 4); 5 x 20mm (5 x 1); 8 x 0.5in AA (2 x 4); 6 x 21in torpedo tubes (2 x 3)

Sensors: Radars Types 281 and 285.

Complement: 487

Notes: *Cleopatra* and her sisters *Dido* and *Euryalus* were all carrying their designed five turret main armament at this battle. The 'Didos' had been designed as fleet escorts to protect heavier units from both light surface forces and aircraft. The enthusiasm felt for them by the Board of Admiralty was borne out by good results in action and the only real problem with the type was shortage of gun-mountings and a need to stiffen them forward to take the weight of the forward turrets. The Type 281 radar was at the masthead for air warning and a 285 was fitted to each HACS Mk IV director for AA fire control. *Euryalus* had a different radar fit from the others: Type 279 air search, 284 surface fire control and 282 for the 2pdr directors.

Below:
Vian's flagship at Sirte was the handsome 'Dido' class cruiser *Cleopatra*, seen here after the war with later AA armament. The quadruple 40mm Bofors AA mount replaced 'Q' 5.25in mount during a refit in the USA in 1943-44 following action damage escorting a later Malta convoy.
Real Photographs/Ian Allan Library

operation was reported and Vian was sent out from Alexandria to intercept with his three 'Didos' and nine destroyers. This would also cover the movement of another 'Dido', *Cleopatra*, and the destroyer *Kingston* which had reached Malta on their way to reinforce the Mediterranean Fleet. Unfortunately, the operation turned into a case of one for one replacement as *Naiad* was torpedoed by *U565* 50 miles off the Libyan coast. She sank in 20min, which allowed both Vian and his Flag Captain, Guy Grantham, to be saved. Vian took over the new cruiser as his flagship and took Grantham with him as his Flag Captain and Chief of Staff.

The two men made a good combination. Vian was a gunnery officer with a destroyer background having come to public attention as Captain (D) of the 4th Flotilla when his 'Tribal' class destroyer *Cossack* rescued the merchant seaman prisoners from *Altmark* in Josing Fiord in February 1940. He had been promoted Rear Admiral after only six years as a Captain in July 1941 and had been given command of the 15th Cruiser Squadron in October. He was regarded as a hard taskmaster, 'extremely efficient, merciless with the incompetent; and inclined to remain aloof' as one of his captains described him. He was exactly Cunningham's kind of officer and the C-in-C had an extremely high opinion of him.

Grantham was also a very able officer. He later rose to be C-in-C Mediterranean and Governor General of Malta. He had shown considerable

personal courage helping save his crew when *Naiad* was sunk. Vian went so far to describe him as 'that most brilliant and very capable officer; one could add that he is, and always has been, the very perfect knight, without fear and without reproach'. He had a truly excellent relationship with his other captains, H. W. U. McCall of *Dido* and Eric Bush of *Euryalus*. Both were dedicated and efficient officers. They all made an excellent team as McCall later wrote:

'The aspect that I cannot stress too strongly is that what was achieved was only made possible by teamwork: a complete and utter trust in our leader and the knowledge that this was reciprocated by him. Those of us who had served with him for some time could imagine how his mind worked, so that we could conform to his wishes with only the least amount of signalling, knowing exactly how much risk should be taken as each phase of the battle developed.'

In order to maintain the offensive spirit of his cruisers, Cunningham sent out McCall with *Dido* and *Euryalus* and half a dozen destroyers to bombard Rhodes. On completion of this mission the full squadron prepared to escort a Malta bound convoy due to leave on 20 March. Called MW10, it was composed of HMS *Breconshire* and three merchantmen — two British, *Clan Campbell* and

Below:
First Battle of Sirte 17 December 1941. See also Chapter 3

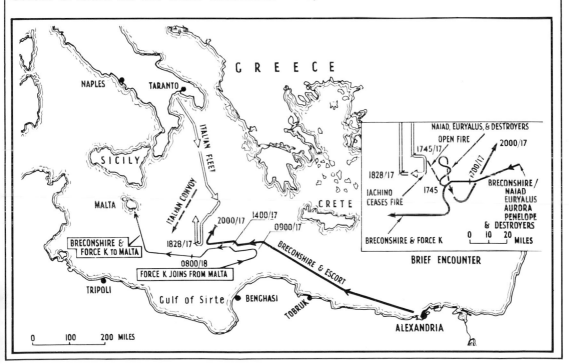

2926

Campus, and one Norwegian, Talabot. It was planned that these ships should arrive at Malta on the third day, 23 March. This maximised the time spent under cover of darkness, whose gloom was intensified by an early setting new moon. The main threat on the first two days would come from Axis aircraft operating from Greek and North African airfields. In order to diminish this threat RAF fighter cover would be provided and special forces, the Long Range Desert Group (LRDG), were to attack enemy airfields. By 22 March the convoy would be beyond the range of No 201 Group's fighters but the threat that day was expected to come primarily from the surface. MW10 would keep well to the south and would

Above:
Leading the other cruiser division under the command of Capt H. W. U. McCall was the name ship of the class, Dido, recently returned from an American refit following action damage off Crete. Note in this postwar shot how the ship has retained her multiple pom-poms. She received a full radar fit in 1943 while under refit in Liverpool. *Real Photographs/Ian Allan Library*

Below:
Lead ship of the mixed 22nd Destroyer Flotilla was Capt Micklethwait's HMS Sikh seen here prewar. By the time of Sirte, 'X' gun mounting had become a 4in AA twin rather than a twin 4.7. *Real Photographs/Ian Allan Collection*

L82

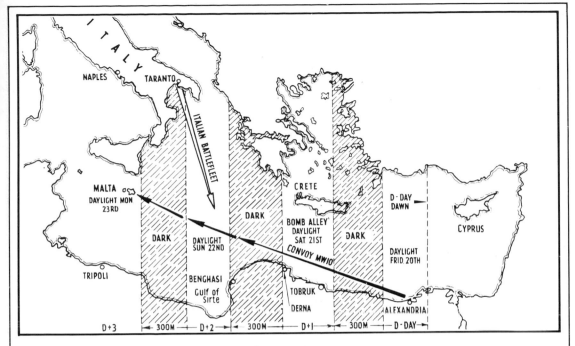

Above:

Plan to make best use of hours of darkness, Friday to Monday 20/23 March 1942.

be supported by British bombers. Force 'K' was to join Vian at first light on the 22nd to increase his anti-surface escort and five British submarines were sent to patrol off Taranto and in the Straits of Messina to give early warning of the Italian fleet's movements.

Given their short range, Vian sent the 5th Destroyer Flotilla of 'Hunt' class escort destroyers forward to Tobruk, which was then still in Allied hands, in order to refuel. This 5th Flotilla was composed of HMS *Southwold* (Cdr C. T. Jellicoe, Flotilla Commander), *Beaufort, Dulverton, Hurworth, Avon Vale, Eridge* and *Heythrop*. As they moved westwards the escort destroyers would also try to clear the area of submarines. All the 'Hunts' were of the slightly broader beam Type 2 and were armed with six 4in AA guns and depth charges. Once they joined the convoy their task would be close escort supplemented by HMS *Carlisle*.

Until the 'Hunts' joined, the destroyer escort of the convoy would be composed of Capt St J. A. Micklethwait's 22nd Destroyer Flotilla, a mixed bag of prewar vessels composed of the 'Tribals' *Sikh* and *Zulu*, the new 4in gun armed fleet destroyer *Lively* and the smaller prewar standard destroyers *Hero, Havock* and *Hasty*. This would then join the heavy covering force made up of Force 'B', Vian's own three cruisers escorted by Capt A. L. Poland's 14th Destroyer Flotilla made up of the four powerful sister ships *Jervis, Kipling, Kelvin* and *Kingston*. If surface action threatened on the 22nd, Vian hoped that the speed and initia-

tive displayed by a number of different small divisions of ships would so harass and threaten the superior enemy by repeated assaults and withdrawals that the enemy would be successfully held off from the convoy. Smoke screens were to be used liberally both to mask the convoy and to conceal the escorts as they made their attacks. If the enemy was sighted the escort was to form into three groups, a Striking Force to harass and attack the enemy warships, a Smoke-laying Division to lay smoke across the convoy and a Close Escort of anti aircraft destroyers.

The whole force was divided into seven divisions, five of which formed the Striking Force:-

- 1st *Jervis, Kipling* and *Kingston*
  (Capt Poland)
- 2nd *Dido, Penelope* and *Legion*
  (Capt McCall), in the event *Legion*
  operated with the 1st Division
- 3rd *Zulu* and *Hasty*
  (Cdr H. R. Graham of *Hasty*)
- 4th *Cleopatra* and *Euryalus*
  (Vian)
- 5th *Sikh, Lively, Hero* and *Havock*
  (Micklethwait)

The 6th Division were the smoke layers drawn from the Close Escort: *Carlisle* and *Avon Vale* commanded by Capt D. M. L. Neame of *Carlisle*.

Jellicoe commanded the 7th Division, the close escorts made up of the rest of the 'Hunts'.

Jellicoe's flotilla sailed from Alexandria on the night of 19 March but on the following day it was attacked by a submarine which sank HMS *Heythrop*. The remaining six escort destroyers fuelled at Tobruk but another fouled her propeller which reduced the flotilla to only five ships.

Littorio

Built: Ansaldo, Genoa (launched 22 August 1937)

Displacement: 40,724 tons standard

Dimensions: 780ft x 107.4ft x 31.4ft

Armour: 14.17in total belt, 6.65in total deck

Machinery: four shaft geared turbines, 128,200shp, 30kt

Armament: 9 x 15in (3 x 9); 12 x 6in (4 x 3); 4 x 4.7in (4 x 1); 12 x 3.9in AA (12 x 1); 20 x 37mm AA (8 x 2, 4 x 1); 28 x 20mm AA (14 x 2)

Sensors: Gufo EC3 radar

Complement: 1,950

Notes: One of three sister ships of the class, *Littorio* was out of action for some months after receiving damage in the Taranto air attack. The 4.7in guns were for firing starshell, a sign of the Italian navy's dependence on visual sensors at night. The battleship's radar was only made to work satisfactorily at the end of 1942 when a modified set was fitted. *Littorio*'s name with its Fascist overtones was changed to *Italia* after the fall of Mussolini. Powerful vessels, the impact of the 15in gun-Italian battleships was restricted by the dominating 'fleet in being' doctrine. *Italia* was slowly broken up between 1948 and 1955.

Above:
One of Micklethwait's mixed bag of 'boats' was HMS *Hero* seen here prewar. She still seems to have retained her full torpedo armament at Sirte; her sister *Havock* had lost her after set of tubes and shipped a 3in AA gun instead. Cdr R. L. Fisher did not fire *Hero*'s torpedoes in the action as the enemy was presenting a poor target and he wished to conserve his weapons for a possible night action. *Real Photographs/Ian Allan Collection*

Above right:
The battleship *Littorio* formed the core of the surface action group sent against MW10. She fired 181 rounds from her nine 15in guns. *IWM GM310*

Right:
First phase and tracks to 1640 22 March 1942.

MW10 sailed on time on the morning of Friday 20 March, and that evening, after dark, Vian's Force 'B' left base. It closed the convoy on the morning of the 21st, 70 miles north of Tobruk. The 5th Destroyer Flotilla was already present and its 6th unit, having cleared her propeller, joined that evening. No 201 Group gave very effective fighter cover and the only problem was *Clan Campbell*'s inability to make more than 9kt. This put the convoy behind schedule. The air threat was also kept down by the LRDG and RAF and Fleet Air Arm attacks on Axis airfields. This prevented reconnaissance and the Axis command

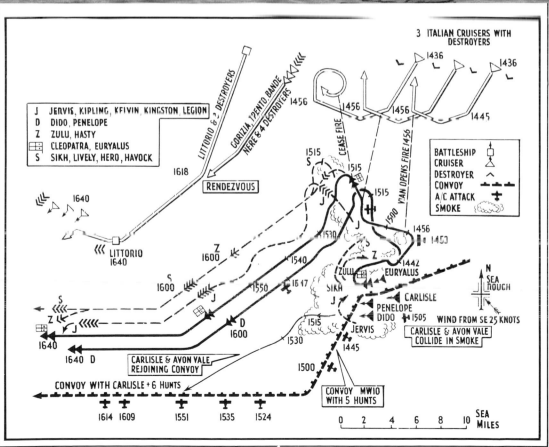

3 ITALIAN CRUISERS WITH DESTROYERS

J	JERVIS, KIPLING, KELVIN, KINGSTON, LEGION
D	DIDO, PENELOPE
Z	ZULU, HASTY
⊞	CLEOPATRA, EURYALUS
S	SIKH, LIVELY, HERO, HAVOCK

LITTORIO & 2 DESTROYERS

GORIZIA, TRENTO, BANDE NERE & 4 DESTROYERS

1456

1618

RENDEZVOUS

1436
1436
1456
1456
1445

CEASE FIRE

1515
S
1515
⊞ 1515

VIAN OPENS FIRE 1456

1590

BATTLESHIP
CRUISER
DESTROYER
CONVOY
A/C ATTACK
SMOKE

1640

LITTORIO 1640

Z 1600

1530

J

1456 1453

1540

1442

Z
ZULU
EURYALUS

N
SEA
ROUGH

S 1600

1540

1550

1617

SIKH

J

CARLISLE

S
Z
⊞
J

D 1600

1515

1530

PENELOPE
DIDO 1505

WIND FROM SE 25 KNOTS

CARLISLE & AVON VALE COLLIDE IN SMOKE

JERVIS

1640

1640 D

CARLISLE & AVON VALE REJOINING CONVOY

1445

1500

CONVOY WITH CARLISLE + 6 HUNTS

1614 1609   1551   1535   1524

CONVOY MW10 WITH 5 HUNTS

0   2   4   6   8   10
SEA MILES

105

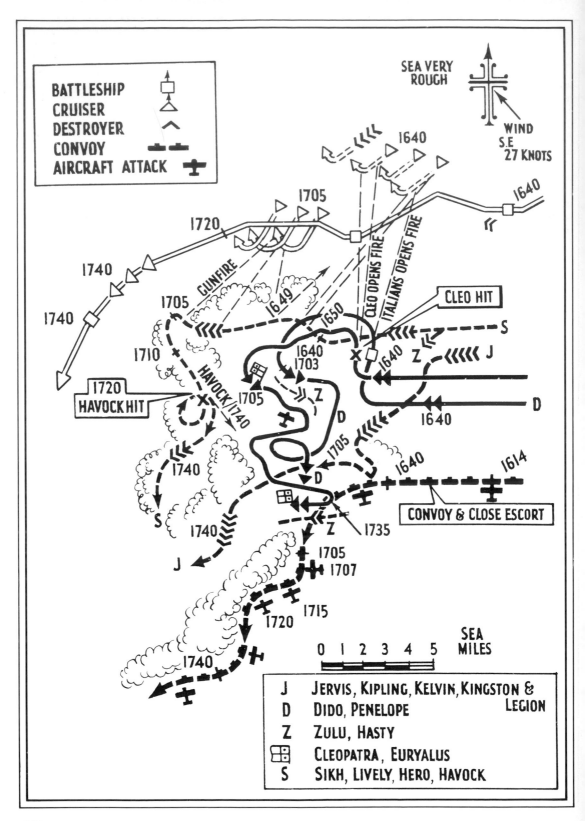

SEA VERY ROUGH

WIND S.E 27 KNOTS

BATTLESHIP
CRUISER
DESTROYER
CONVOY
AIRCRAFT ATTACK

1640

1640

1705

1720

1740

1740

1710

GUNFIRE

1649

1650

CLEO OPENS FIRE

ITALIANS OPENS FIRE

CLEO HIT

1705

S

1640

Z

J

1640

1640

HAVOCK/1740

1705

1640
1703

Z

D

D

1720
HAVOCK HIT

1740

1705

1705

1640

1614

D

CONVOY & CLOSE ESCORT

S

1740

Z

1735

J

1705
1707

1720   1715

1740

SEA MILES
0 1 2 3 4 5

J   JERVIS, KIPLING, KELVIN, KINGSTON & LEGION
D   DIDO, PENELOPE
Z   ZULU, HASTY
    CLEOPATRA, EURYALUS
S   SIKH, LIVELY, HERO, HAVOCK

was more preoccupied with a carrier operation in the Western Mediterranean to fly Spitfires into Malta. The convoy was not spotted until 1700 on the 21st by a German transport flying from North Africa to Crete. Shortly afterwards the Italian submarine *Onice* also made contact.

The news then came from 'Ultra' that the Italian fleet was sailing from Taranto and this was confirmed by the submarine *P36* early on the morning of the 22nd. Adm Angelo Iachino had sailed from Taranto with the 15in gun, 41,000-ton battleship *Littorio*, escorted by four destroyers. In addition, and not sighted by any British naval unit, a powerful cruiser force under Adm Parona had sortied from Messina at 0100 that morning. This was composed of the *Gorizia*, the 11,700-ton sister ship of the three heavy cruisers sunk at Matapan, the *Trento*, slightly smaller and older but armed with the same eight 8in guns and the 5,000-ton fast light cruiser *Giovanni delle Bande Nere*, a sister ship of the two cruisers torpedoed off Cape Bon. These ships were escorted by four destroyers. Vian was unaware of the existence of two enemy surface action groups as he only seems to have been warned in general terms that he was likely to encounter heavy enemy ships. The submarine report was the only hard news he had to go on as far as the composition of those forces. Bletchley Park was probably unaware of the second group as the Italians had modified their code at the beginning of March which made reading the traffic difficult and time consuming. Only at the end of the month did Bletchley Park get back to normal in the service it offered with the Italian naval cypher.

At 0800 on 22 March Force 'K' joined Force 'B'. At 0900 the last RAF fighter had to leave and half an hour later Axis air attacks began, both high level bombers and torpedo bombers. There were two screens, an outer anti-submarine screen of fleet destroyers and an inner screen of 'Hunts'. Both screens put up heavy AA barrages. This heavy defence caused the Italian SM79 torpedo bombers to drop their weapons at far too long a range. The convoy was in an open formation which allowed plenty of space for manoeuvre to avoid damage.

At 1230, with Iachino's group expected, Vian reformed his ships into the planned anti-surface disposition. The danger was confirmed by the appearance of an Italian floatplane an hour later which dropped a string of flares indicating the direction of the convoy's line of advance. While this was going on the British were being attacked by German Ju 88s. It was Eric Bush who sighted and reported smoke on the horizon bearing 350 degrees at 1410. Seven minutes later *Euryalus* reported that three ships were bearing in that direction. Shortly afterwards *Legion* did the same. Vian hoisted the executive signal for his divisions to concentrate in readiness to protect the convoy from the north. *Breconshire* and her three companions made off to the southwest with their smoke screen and close escort groups. At 1427 *Euryalus* reported four ships at 015 degrees and *Legion* one ship at 010 degrees distance 12 miles. Vian thought it was Iachino but in fact it was Parona's cruiser group. All the Italian Navy had been built for speed but this was only possible in calm weather and a developing southwesterly gale reduced the two groups to only 22kt. Iachino's group, that was not yet in sight, had also suffered the loss of one of its destroyers, *Grecale*, which had suffered a breakdown and had turned back for Taranto.

The only confused officer on the British side was Capt Nicholl of Force 'K' who had not received Vian's orders before leaving Malta. When he received the executive signal 'Carry out pre-arranged plan' he had no idea as to what plan to carry out. It was all worked out in a way that vindicated the seniority principle that sometimes seems strange to the other armed services. As Nicholl later wrote:

'The convoy and all the ships of the escort then began moving in various directions at high speed. I, unfortunately, had no knowledge of any pre-arranged plan; no previous orders of any kind had reached *Penelope*. However there is a well tried course of action I had learned in my time in destroyers: "When in doubt, follow father". So I tacked on to Vian's cruisers, and *Legion* joined the nearest destroyer division. Though I had no instructions, I had no difficulty in sensing what Vian wanted the cruisers to do.

'McCall in the *Dido*, however, knew that *Penelope* should have been astern of him. He had also noticed that the *Penelope*, though conforming to the movements of the other cruisers, was acting in a somewhat independent way. Vian led us towards the enemy at high speed and all the cruisers made smoke. The smoke, carried by a rising southeasterly wind, was lying perfectly. There was a long-range gun battle and a number of shell splashes fell close to the *Penelope*. But the enemy soon turned away and Vian at once led us back to the convoy.

'As soon as we were clear of the smoke, McCall signalled "What is seniority of captain?" "June 1939" I replied. "Take station astern" he signalled at once. Well, now I knew the *Penelope*'s position in the cruisers' battle formation. It was a great help.'

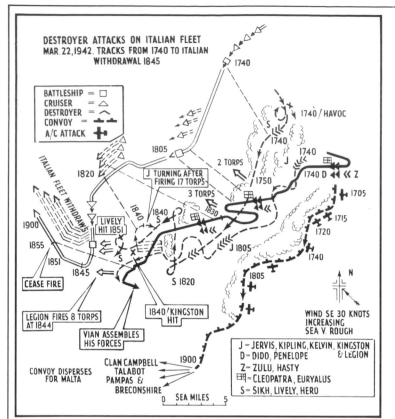

Right:
Another dramatic action shot as the cruisers lay smoke at the beginning of the battle. Note the bomb or shell splashes on *Cleopatra*'s starboard side. The flagship still appears to be engaging enemy aircraft with her after turrets. *IWM A8174*

Below right:
Euryalus firing at the Italian ships as both she and the flagship make smoke. *IWM A8168*

Left:
Destroyer attacks on Italian Fleet 22 March 1942. Tracks from 1740 to Italian withdrawal 1845.

At 1433 the Striking Force divisions turned east to lay smoke which was assisted by the wind. *Carlisle* and *Avon Vale* also carried out their smoke laying task and had a slight collision as both manoeuvred to avoid bombs. Both, however, were able to rejoin the AA screen of the convoy. The Italians soon lost sight of the convoy as they turned together to starboard to bring their guns to bear. Just before they made this turn, Vian identified his enemy and led with *Cleopatra* and *Euryalus* to close the range. At 20,000yd the two ships opened fire on the *Gorizia*. This caused Parona to turn away to the northwest. No hits were made by either side although the *Bande Nere*'s sharp shooting fire control officer did manage to get some 6in straddles on *Cleopatra* and *Euryalus*. By 1515 Parona had retired out of range to join Iachino. Given the primary Italian concern to keep their fleet in being, Parona was concerned to avoid surprise torpedo attack out of the smoke screen. He also rationalised his retreat by convincing himself that he was drawing the British on to the guns of the battleship.

Vian, thinking that the cruisers were the heavy ships reported by the *P36*, retired back towards the convoy thinking he had driven off the only threat. During the surface action the convoy had suffered a series of air attacks mainly from Ju 88s in both high level and dive bombing modes. These had been kept at bay by *Carlisle* and the escort destroyers but only at the cost of heavy expenditure of ammunition. The AA cruiser still had two thirds of her outfit of 4in shells but Jellicoe had to report that his 'Hunts' had fired off 60% of their ammunition supply. Vian, therefore, decided to reinforce the Close Escort with Poland's destroyer division. At 1535 Vian signalled to a relieved Cunningham, 'Enemy driven off'. However, Iachino was closing in, having altered course to 200 degrees at 1353 to make rendezvous with Parona. This occurred at 1618 in the rough sea and dense mist which, despite the 27kt winds, made visibility very poor. The combined Italian battle group came back into sight of the convoy at 1647, bearing northeast, distance 20,000yd.

They were first spotted by HMS *Zulu* and her sighting report was followed three minutes later by one from the sharp-eyed *Euryalus*. It was now clear that there were two groups of enemy ships: three cruisers and four destroyers in one and a battleship and three destroyers in the other. Vian led his striking forces to the north once more, except for Poland's division which stayed with the convoy. The material odds were with the Italians who were much more heavily armed for a surface engagement, but Iachino was hampered by his overriding instinct to maintain the fleet in being. One problem with the Italian Navy was that they had imagined before the war that they would have to face Anglo-French numerical superiority. When conditions changed they proved totally unable to exploit their own material and numerical superiority. Once doctrine is established it is hard to

change. In addition the Italians feared that Cunningham's battleships might be lying in wait behind the smoke.

Iachino thought he had three choices: a combined movement from either east or west or some kind of pincer operation. He decided on a combined attack from the west so he turned his force first west-northwest and then west-southwest paralleling the convoy and trying to get ahead of it. This also kept him clear of the dangerous smoke screen laid by the British. Both cruiser divisions, closing the Italians to the north, laid smoke screens and at 1643 *Cleopatra* and *Euryalus* both opened fire once more at maximum range,

Below:
Tracks of convoy, escort, and Italian ships 21-23 March 1942.

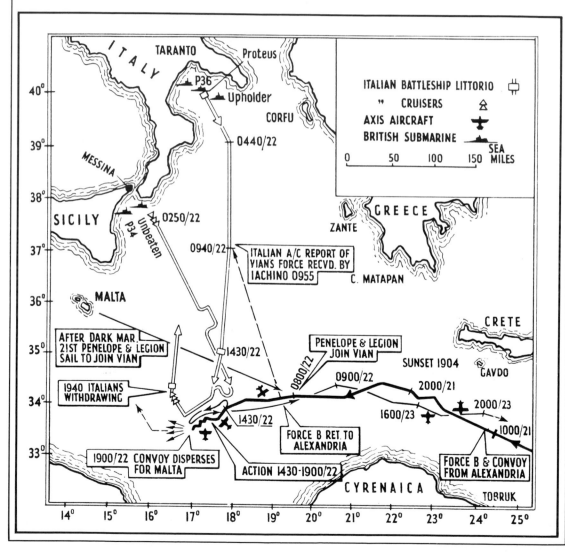

20,000yd. The Italians returned the fire, the sharp shooting *Bande Nere* scoring a hit on *Cleopatra* with her second salvo. This put the ship's radio and radar out of action.

Now, *Littorio* opened fire spectacularly with her 15in guns. She was shooting at *Euralyus*, which she spotted through a gap in the smoke screen. The big 15in shells straddled the little cruiser and inflicted splinter damage and Bush altered course to starboard to throw the battleship off the range. Of the two cruisers *Cleopatra* was the more vulnerable as she was, by definition, ahead of the smoke screen she was laying. She thought she was being fired at by the battleship also but it seems probable that the big shells exploding around her were 8in rounds from the heavy cruisers. She was lucky that her one hit came from the smallest calibre main armament available to the enemy. Neither member of McCall's group was hit.

At 1648 Vian led his division into the smoke screen, followed by McCall. At 1705 he altered course to the eastward to make sure no Italians were getting to windward of the smoke screen. This left Micklethwait's destroyers as the only force between the Italian battle group and the convoy. At 1720 a critical situation developed when it looked as if a gap in the smoke screen would allow the Italians to seize their chance. At 1720 *Havock* received a near miss from a 15in shell which damaged a boiler and reduced her speed to 16kt. Micklethwait sent her to join the convoy screen. He then turned northwards for a possible torpedo attack but as the range was so great decided instead to strengthen the smoke screen, moving to the south as he did so. The three destroyers opened fire with their main armaments on the Italians and the 4.7 and 4in shells landed disturbingly close to the *Littorio*, which straddled the *Sikh* in return at 1748. As the battle-

ship was clearly closing the convoy, Micklethwait tried to get her to turn away by firing two of *Sikh*'s Mk IX torpedoes. He also ordered the convoy to alter course to the south to avoid sailing into the Italians.

Vian had realised the danger and brought back the rest of Force 'B'. *Cleopatra* opened fire once more, this time on the *Littorio* at 1742. Vian's gunnery was masked by the smoke screen so he decided on a torpedo attack out of the smoke. A wireless mast had been erected and the signal was made at 1759. Three minutes later *Cleopatra* emerged from the smoke on her torpedo charge, sighted the battleship only 13,000yd away and opened fire with her 10 5.25s. *Euryalus* could use her 284 surface fire control radar while still in the smoke. The only other 284 in the force — *Penelope*'s — was unserviceable. At 1806 *Cleopatra* fired her starboard triple 21in torpedo tubes. The threat of the three Mk IXs caused the Italians to turn away. By 1806 Poland's destroyer division was also on its way to support Micklethwait.

Vian now decided to take another detour to the east, given the possibility that the Italians would move in that direction after their turn. At 1817, seeing that all was clear, he resumed his westerly course to give heavy support to his destroyers. Far from moving to the east, the Italians were persevering with their attempt to cut the convoy from a westerly direction. Micklethwait moved his destroyers on to a reciprocal course to extend the smoke screen in front of the convoy. As he duly laid his smoke screen, Poland made a torpedo attack having spotted the *Littorio* at 1834 bearing west-northwest at 12,000yd. He turned his flotilla together to the west in the order north to south *Jervis*, *Kipling*, *Kelvin*, *Kingston* and *Legion*. As the flotilla increased speed to 28kt four of the destroyers opened fire with their 4.7in guns. This

Above:
A dramatic picture of HMS *Kipling* taken during the Battle of Sirte from another destroyer of Capt Poland's division. *IWM A8165*

was a concentration shoot which placed all 16 guns under centralised control and which therefore enhanced the chances of scoring hits. *Legion* did not open fire with her two twin forward 4in mountings until the range was down to 8,000yd.

The Italians were steaming south in line ahead and the destroyers were closing the range at the rate of a mile every two minutes. The concentrated fire of the destroyers, coupled with the cruisers coming back into action, caused the Italian fire control officers to lose their aim and Italian fire was noted as being erratic. This was lucky for Poland as he had to run four miles beyond the smoke screen before he could make his firing turn. Here is the story in Poland's words:

'The moment seemed propitious for a torpedo attack on the enemy through the smoke made by Micklethwait's *Sikh* division. Accordingly I led round so as to pass astern of him and through his smoke while it was not too thick. When we emerged from the smoke we could see only one enemy ship which, instead of being four miles north-northwest of us (as signalled by Mickleth-

wait), was well over six miles away and bearing about west-northwest. The ship in sight also looked rather larger than the Italian 6in cruiser we had expected to see. However, the flotilla was ordered to take up formation for a torpedo attack and speed was increased to the maximum. Unfortunately some Italian torpedo bombers chose this moment to make an attack on us and we had to turn to comb the tracks of their torpedoes. This delayed us and had an adverse effect on our position relative to the enemy!

'It was very soon after passing through the smoke that a second enemy ship appeared out of the haze, also looking remarkably large, and a third, and a fourth. They also appeared to be an uncomfortably long way off and I remember enquiring more than once what the range of the nearest one was. The range seemed to close astonishingly slowly; the intervals between the ships seemed to be about three-quarters of a mile. They opened fire on us. My division opened fire with all the guns that would bear. Our cruisers were following us to support the attack, and firing as well.

'We went in in broad port quarter line, in the order *Jervis, Kipling, Kelvin, Kingston, Legion*. The range seemed to take an unconscionably long time to shorten, the fact being that we had not started, as we expected to do, from fine on the bow of the enemy, but from very broad on his bow; and so our rate of approach was much reduced. When the range of the nearest enemy from the *Jervis* was about three miles it was grand to see the second ship in the enemy line lose her nerve. She turned and steered straight away from us, making volumes of black smoke.

'Eventually the range was down from the six miles to two and three miles for which we had been waiting (one of the longest three miles I have ever steamed). We turned, and some 25 torpedoes started off towards the enemy line.'

The destroyers made their firing turn at 1841, Poland's regular flotilla turned to starboard but *Legion*, which had not seen the signal, turned to port. *Jervis* and *Kipling* fired five torpedoes each and *Kelvin* only two as she had fired two torpedoes in error by mistaking the run-in signal for a firing command. *Kipling* fired five, although her firing circuits were unserviceable and the tubes had to be hand operated. *Legion* fired a full spread of eight torpedoes. During her attack *Kingston* was hit by a 15in shell which passed through the ship and exploded on the other side. Her upper deck suffered extensive damage and there was a fire in the boiler room but, nevertheless, she was able to put Mk IXs in the water. None of the 28 torpedoes actually fired scored hits but they had the desired effect in forcing *Littorio* and the cruisers to turn away. A fire clearly visible on the battleship's quarterdeck and the British thought they had hit the battleship; actually it was the *Littorio*'s biplane Meridionali Ro43 seaplane that had been set on fire by the battleship's gun blast. *Kingston* came to a standstill as a result of her damage but her ship's company made her mobile once more and she was sent off to Malta for repairs.

Next it was Micklethwait's turn who saw an opportunity to attack the Italians on their starboard side as they moved to the northwest. At 1855 he turned to fire but smoke hid the target from *Sikh* and *Hero*. *Lively*, however, fired a full spread of eight Mk IXs. The range was about 8,000yd and all the torpedoes missed. At the moment of firing *Lively* was near-missed by a 15in shell which caused splinter damage and some

flooding. *Hero* did not fire as the Italian ships were turning and not offering a profitable target. The destroyers, had, however, drawn blood on their run-in. A 4.7in shell exploded above the *Littorio's* quarter deck to starboard causing some minor damage.

Often in naval warfare, threat is more important than destruction. The flotillas had succeeded admirably in their aim, for as evening was drawing on Iachino had no alternative but to continue moving north and back to base. After the fiasco at Matapan, the previous years had demonstrated the crushing superiority of the British in night operations, continuing the attack as the sun went down would have been courting disaster. Vian steered southward to close the convoy but as the latter was out of danger in the darkness and his fuel was running low he decided to return to Alexandria under cover of night for as far as possible.

Penelope and *Legion* made for Malta as did the damaged *Havock* and *Kingston*. The convoy was rapidly dispersing under orders from its Commodore, Capt C. A. G. Hutchison of HMS *Breconshire*. His idea was to allow both the fast ships and the *Clan Campbell* to arrive together at daylight to be concentrated with escorts to meet the expected air attacks. The merchant ships had indeed been fully engaged repelling air attacks all that day and both *Breconshire* and *Pampas* each claimed an enemy bomber had been shot down by their AA guns. Soldiers embarked in *Talabot* resorted to using Bren guns against the Ju 88s. Despite several near misses the merchant ships came through the columns of water unscathed.

The convoy also sailed through many 15in shell splashes, as the Italians seem to have fired through the smoke at long range. In these circumstances, hitting was a matter of luck and the Italians did not have any. British luck was mixed. The advisability of splitting the convoy was debatable, although the different speeds of the ships did make it tempting, given the proximity of Malta. *Talabot* and *Pampas* took a risky route over a known minefield but their luck held and they entered Grand Harbour between 0900 and 1000 on the morning of the 23rd. *Pampas* had been hit by two bombs, neither of which exploded.

Fliegerkorps II was making a maximum effort that day to salvage something from Iachino's failure and *Breconshire's* luck finally ran out. She was hit and disabled as she approached the island at 0920. Her escort was composed of three 'Hunts' and the AA cruiser *Carlisle*, which Cunningham had ordered to stay with the convoy. This was an unusual intervention as Cunningham did not normally believe in 'backseat driving'. The cruiser circled *Breconshire* while *Penelope* tried to take her in tow. This proved impractical and she was, therefore, anchored with the three escort destroyers forming an AA battery around her. The slow *Clan Campbell*, escorted by HMS *Eridge*, was still some 50 miles from Malta when the air attacks began. She covered 30 miles before being bombed and sunk. The destroyer picked up most of her crew. *Legion* was damaged by a near miss and was beached near Marsaxlokk, close to where *Breconshire* lay at anchor.

Unfortunately, the Germans stepped up the intensity of their air raids even further. More Spitfires had just been flown in by HMS *Eagle* but the British fighters were overwhelmed and the *Stukas* and Ju 88s were able to operate virtually undisturbed. *Breconshire* was towed to join *Legion* at Marsaxlokk on the 25th but the following day the destroyer was sunk on its way to Valetta. *Breconshire* was finally disposed of on the 27th. The previous day, disaster had overtaken the previously lucky *Talabot* and *Pampas* in Grand Harbour. Both were hit by bombs and sunk, the Norwegian ship having to be scuttled as her cargo of ammunition looked like exploding catastrophically. Although some of *Breconshire*'s oil was saved, only 7,500 tons of the 26,000 tons of supplies embarked at Alexandria got to Malta. It is hard not to agree with Capt Hutchison that it was a mistake to send a full scale convoy to Malta when Malta's aircraft were incapable of defending it on arrival. *Breconshire* might well have made a number of runs alone and delivered more material; the fast supply ship was fully capable of maintaining a schedule that would get it to Valetta at dawn.

The Italian fleet had its own problems returning to its bases. It avoided an attack by RAF Bristol Beaufort twin-engined torpedo bombers based in Egypt and Royal Navy Albacores from Malta. The storm had worsened and the conditions were far from those for which the Italian fleet had been built. The destroyers were in particular difficulties and both the *Scirocco* and *Lanciere* sank in the storm. The former ship had been sent out to reinforce the *Littorio* group on 22 March. The sharp shooting *Bande Nere* was also in particular trouble because of her light construction; speed is not

Below:
On board HMS *Breconshire* during the attacks on MW10. HMS *Carlisle* makes smoke ahead.
IWM AX110A

everything. She was badly damaged but staggered into Messina on 24 March. When she sailed again on 1 April after being patched up she was torpedoed and sunk by the submarine *Urge*. Adm Iachino, a good seaman, blamed the defects of his fleet on too slender hulls, inefficient watertight compartmentation and defective pumping. Even his relatively broad beamed flagship had shipped tons of water which had put out of action the electrically-powered firing machinery of one of the 15in turrets.

The less rakish, but far more seaworthy British ships had to reduce speed progressively as they steamed back to Alexandria head-on into the gale. Some ships suffered damage but although the crews became very uncomfortable as mess decks became feet deep in water the ships stood up well to their ordeal. Force 'B' became scattered and eight *Stukas* attacked the damaged destroyer *Lively* that was lagging astern. She survived, however, and made for Tobruk. RAF Bristol Beaufighters provided welcome fighter cover and the rest of Force 'B' arrived at Alexandria at dawn on 24 March.

As for the warships at Malta, *Carlisle, Beaufort, Dulverton, Hurworth* and *Eridge* sailed for Alexandria on 25 March. The damaged *Avon Vale* accompanied *Aurora*, which had been repaired in Malta Dockyard, to Gibraltar on the 29th. This left *Havock, Kingston* and *Penelope. Havock* tried to make for Gibraltar on 5 April but ran aground at high speed early the following morning when avoiding a minefield. *Kingston* was destroyed in dock on 11 April but *Penelope* which had also been hit by two bombs had managed to escape to Gibraltar, arriving the previous day. The many holes in her hull from bomb splinters gave her the nickname 'HMS *Pepperpot*'.

In many ways the Battle of Sirte is like the Glorious First of June of 1794. Tactically it was a brilliant success for the British but operationally and strategically it was a failure. Iachino had succeeded in forcing the convoy to manoeuvre so far south that Axis air power was able to act in synergy to ensure its destruction. Despite the peerless skill shown in their defence, MW10's supplies did little to assist in Malta's survival. The Second Battle of Sirte thus sums up the fundamental defect of Churchill's entire Mediterranean diversion, the squandering of valuable strength and skill to little

strategic purpose. What could not be gainsaid, however, was Vian's skill as an operational commander. Churchill, who was much better at putting words together than in assessing strategic priorities or giving operational naval commands, put it well in his message to Cunningham: 'That one of the most powerful modern battleships afloat, attended by two heavy and four light cruisers and a flotilla of destroyers should have been routed and put to flight...in broad daylight, by a force of five British light cruisers and destroyers, constitutes a naval episode of the highest distinction and entitles all ranks and ratings concerned, and above all their commander, to the compliments of the British nation.'

Trento

Built: OTO, Leghorn (launched 4 October 1927)

Displacement: 10,344 tons standard

Dimensions: 646.2 x 67.6 x 22.3ft

Armour: 2.8in belt; 2in deck; 3.9in turrets

Machinery: four shaft geared turbines, 150,000shp, 36kt

Armament: 8 x 8in; 12 x 3.9in (6 x 2); 8 x 37mm AA (4 x 2); 4 x 20mm AA (4 x 1); 8 x 13.2mm AA (4 x 2)

Complement: 781

Notes: An interesting contrast to *Gorizia* Adm Parona's other heavy cruiser was built for speed. She and her sister *Trieste* were Italy's only cruisers completed in the 1920s and were built under the Washington Treaty, whose displacement limit they slightly exceeded. They were originally built without funnel caps. *Trento* was sunk by the British submarine *Umbra* in June 1942.

Gorizia

Built: OTO, Leghorn (launched 28 December 1930)

Displacement: 11,712 tons

Dimensions: 557.3ft x 62.8ft x 21.9ft

Armour: 5.9in belt; 2.8in deck, 5.9in turrets

Machinery: 2 shaft geared turbines, 95,000shp, 32kt

Armament: 8 x 8in (4 x 2); 12 x 3.9in AA (6 x 2); 12 x 37mm AA (6 x 2); 8 x 13.2mm AA (4 x 2)

Complement: 841

Notes: The last survivor of Italy's best heavy cruisers with heavier protection than earlier and later ships. They were for a time classified as 'armoured cruisers'. Her three sisters were lost at Matapan. *Gorizia* fell into German hands and was sunk by an Italian human torpedo attack in June 1944.

CHAPTER SIX

Attack at Source — Tirpitz

'Attack at source' is a term in maritime strategy describing the use of striking forces to attack the enemy in his bases. Although, in one sense, it is just a modern expression of classical 'seek out and destroy the enemy' thinking, it rose to prominence with the advent of aircraft capable of assaulting the enemy in his bases at acceptable cost and without undue risk to one's own surface forces. The advent of the submarine also provided opportunities for greater security for the attacker than that possessed by surface torpedo craft in operations in enemy controlled waters. Although a post-war term, the concept of 'attack at source' was developed in both World Wars as the technology became practical.

A notable example of early thinking along these lines was Adm Beatty's idea in 1918 to use carrier-based torpedo bombers to attack the German High Sea Fleet. The latter showed little inclination voluntarily to place its neck on the chopping block of the North Sea for the Grand Fleet to cut its head off. Instead the High Sea Fleet operated as a 'Fleet in Being': that is, it was deliberately

Below:
The graceful but formidable lines of the *Tirpitz*. The picture seems to have been taken at Bogen Bay near Narvik, her base in the summer of 1942; note the anti-torpedo nets.
US Naval Historical Center NH71390

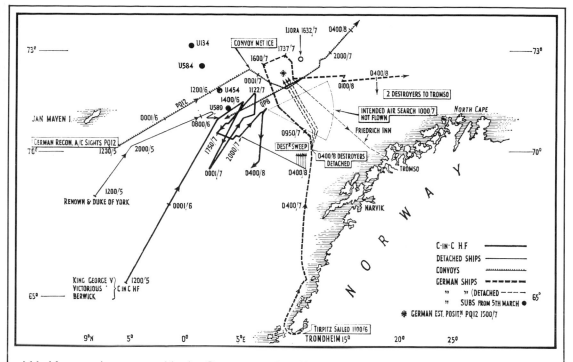

Inside the map:

IJORA 1632/7 · 0400/8 · CONVOY MET ICE · 1737/7 · 0400/8
1600/7 · 2000/7
73° — · U134 · — 73°
U584 · 0001/7
2000/7 · 0400/8
0100/8 · 2 DESTROYERS TO TROMSO
1200/6 · U454 · 1122/7 · INTENDED AIR SEARCH 1000/7 NOT FLOWN · NORTH CAPE
PQ12 · 1400/6 · U589 · FRIEDRICH INN
JAN MAYEN I. · 0001/6
0800/6 · 0950/7 · DEST SWEEP · TROMSO
GERMAN RECON. A/C SIGHTS PQ12 · 0400/8 DESTROYERS DETACHED
70° — · 1230/5 · 2000/5 · 0001/7 · 0400/8 · 0400/8 · — 70°
1200/5 · 0400/7 · NARVIK
RENOWN & DUKE OF YORK · 0001/6

C-IN-C H.F ————
DETACHED SHIPS ————
CONVOYS ············
GERMAN SHIPS – – – –
KING GEORGE V · 1200/5 · " " (DETACHED ----)
VICTORIOUS · C IN C H F · " " SUBS FROM 5TH MARCH ●
65° — · BERWICK · ✱ GERMAN EST. POSIT PQ12 1500/7
9°N · 5° · 0° · 5°E · TIRPITZ SAILED 1100/6 · 20° · 25°
TRONDHEIM 15°

Above:

Convoys PQ12: QP8. Operations Phase 1, 1200, 5 March 1942 to 0400, 8 March 1942.

withheld to continue to provide the German naval command with options that constrained the options of the Admiralty. The destruction of the High Sea Fleet would have meant more British resources could have been released for the direct defence of merchant shipping against the U-boat. Adm Scheer's capital ships provided invaluable support to the U-boats in preventing the re-allocation of fleet destroyers to convoy protection. The cream of the Royal Navy's officers and men had to be kept in Rosyth while Britain faced one of the greatest naval threats to her survival she has ever faced in the Western Approaches. No wonder Beatty wished that his Sopwiths really were Cuckoos when they arrived to lay their 18in torpedos in Scheer's nest!

In World War 2 the situation repeated itself. After various daring forays into seas commanded by the British and their allies had inflicted serious casualties — notably the loss of the *Bismarck* — the German Navy generally held back its remaining fleet assets as a 'Fleet in Being' to force the Allies to provide a British Home Fleet of significant strength to prevent a breakout into the Atlantic. Once convoys to northern Russian ports began in 1941 the Home Fleet also had to provide cover as the convoys passed disturbingly close to the *Kriegsmarine*'s forward operating bases in Norway. These convoys, of course also provided bait for the German battlefleet and opportunities to draw the German ships out to their destruction, but the constraints put on Allied battlefleet opera-

tions by both the U-boat threat and the Luftwaffe in Norway meant that such attempts could sometimes backfire with disastrous results.

The classic example of this was in July 1942 when the Home Fleet was held back to the west and the First Sea Lord, Adm Sir Dudley Pound, made one of the worst naval errors of the war and ordered PQ17 to scatter on the mistaken assumption that a powerful German battle group was about to attack. This sealed the fate of the convoy and out of the 36 merchant vessels which sailed only 11 reached their destination. U-boats and aircraft had done the actual sinking but, without the influence of the German battlefleet on the fatal decision to scatter their success would have been nowhere near as great. The German surface ships had never had to close the enemy to be effective and the attack on the battleship *Tirpitz* by the Soviet submarine *K21* was not even noticed.

One reason the German heavy surface units had not actually gone into action in July 1942 was that only a few months before the most powerful German unit, the *Tirpitz*, had almost been caught and sunk, in circumstances very like those that had led to the nemesis of her sister ship *Bismarck*. This near disaster for the Germans had occurred in March 1942 when convoy PQ12 had sailed from Iceland under the cover of the battlecruiser

Renown, the battleship *Duke of York*, the cruiser *Kenya* and six destroyers. Adm Sir John Tovey, C-in-C Home Fleet, and flying his flag in the battleship *King George V*, sailed from Scapa to join the covering force on 6 March. He was accompanied by the carrier *Victorious*, the heavy cruiser *Berwick* and six destroyers. In addition to PQ12, the Home Fleet was also covering the return journey of QP8 which left Murmansk on the 6th. The Germans had spotted PQ12 the previous day and ordered *Tirpitz* to intercept. There should have been powerful support in the shape of *Scharnhorst*, *Gneisenau* and *Prinz Eugen* which had carried out their successful escape up the Channel only three weeks previously. (See *Sea Battles in Close-Up*, Vol 1). Unfortunately for the Germans, however, both *Scharnhorst* and *Gneisenau* had suffered mine damage during the Channel Dash and *Prinz Eugen*, her location revealed by 'Ultra' decrypt, was torpedoed on its way to Norway off the approaches to Trondheim by the British submarine *Trident*.

Thus it was that the only support available to *Tirpitz* was a small destroyer force made up of the smaller Type 34A destroyers, *Hermann Schoemann* and *Friedrich Ihn* and the larger, 5.9in armed Type 36A *Z25*. The force, commanded by Adm Ciliax, fresh from his success in the Channel Dash, sailed from Trondheim at 1100 on 6 March. By midday on the 7th, *Tirpitz* was about 100 miles south of the convoys and 150 miles east of Tovey's portion of the covering force. Neither admiral was entirely happy. Ciliax did not know anything about the movements of the Home Fleet and wished to avoid action with its superior forces. Tovey was especially aware of the U-boat threat as he had been forced to send his destroyer escort away to refuel. Ciliax had also detached his destroyers but with the more offensive role of broadening his search pattern to find the convoy. This had limited success when the *Friedrich Ihn* found a Russian straggler from QP8, the *Ijora*, and sank her. Tovey picked up the distress signal and obtained a D/F bearing, which caused him to turn east-southeast but receiving 'Ultra' information that *Tirpitz* was on its way north he altered course in pursuit. He also took the risk of detaching his destroyers to search to the east. Unfortunately serious icing problems were preventing *Victorious's* aircraft from doing any flying.

Nothing was found as *Tirpitz* was some distance to the north searching for the convoy. She had to detach her destroyers to refuel but stayed on alone, moving first northwards and then to the west. The convoy was lucky to escape Ciliax's manoeuvres but the German admiral was not helped by a misleading signal he received from Group North on 8 March that the convoy had

turned back three days earlier! Ciliax, therefore, felt it was unwise to keep his valuable battleship at risk and at 2025 he turned to course 191 degrees to rendezvous with his escort off Vest Fiord before returning to base. Thanks to 'Ultra', Tovey had better information and he steamed to the northeast to intercept. The best intelligence, however, cannot inflict damage on the enemy and it was now up to the Home Fleet at sea to repeat the *Bismarck* treatment of a crippling air attack followed by battleship gun bombardment.

The prewar Royal Navy concept of the multi-purpose carrier aircraft meant that the only strike force available to Tovey had to be drawn from *Victorious's* 18 Fairey Albacore biplane torpedo/dive-bomber/spotter-reconnaissance aircraft. At 0640 Tovey ordered the carrier to fly off a third of these in the reconnaissance role, followed by 12 each carrying an 18in Mk XV torpedo. The strike was commanded by Lt-Cdr W. J. Lucas. Despite the continued poor weather, the aircraft took off safely and at 0802 one of the reconnaissance aircraft spotted *Tirpitz*, together with one of her destroyers, off Vest Fiord. The battleship tried to protect herself by launching two of her Arado Ar 196 floatplanes. These engaged the British reconnaissance and shadowing aircraft but this did not prevent Lucas and the striking force sighting *Tirpitz* at 0842. The Albacores had spotted the Germans on ASV radar at a range of 16 miles. Now, however, the British paid the price for their multi-role concept. Biplanes make excellent spotter reconnaissance platforms but poor striking systems. An Albacore had a maximum speed of 155kt; *Tirpitz* was steaming at 29kt into a headwind of 35kt. This meant it would take 30min before the Albacores could be in a favourable attacking position, 30min of severe icing conditions and with the possibility of German fighters appearing at any moment. In fact, the torpedo laden Albacores were only closing the enemy at 40kt and Lucas felt there was no alterna-

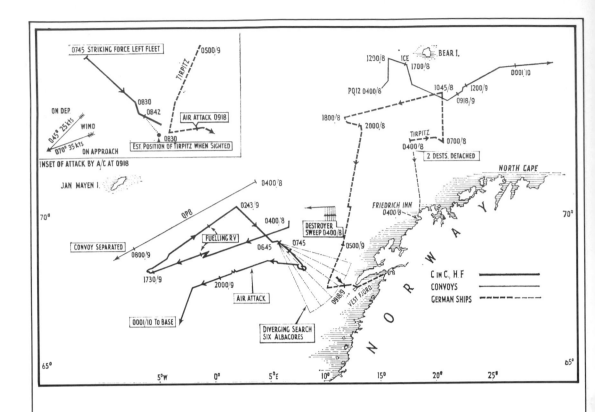

INSET OF ATTACK BY A/C AT 0918

0745 STRIKING FORCE LEFT FLEET

0500/9

TIRPITZ

0830
0842

ON DEP.
045° 25 kts
WIND
070° 35 kts
ON APPROACH

AIR ATTACK 0918

0830
EST. POSITION OF TIRPITZ WHEN SIGHTED

1290/8   ICE   BEAR I.
1700/8
PQ12 0400/8   1045/8   1200/9   0001/10
0918/9

1800/8   2000/8   TIRPITZ   0700/8
0400/8   2 DESTS. DETACHED

NORTH CAPE

FRIEDRICH INN
0400/8

JAN MAYEN I.

D400/8

QP8   0243/9
0400/8

70°   70°

CONVOY SEPARATED   FUELLING R.V.   0645   0745   0500/9
0800/9   DESTROYER SWEEP 0400/8

1730/9   0918/9   VEST FJORD

2000/9   AIR ATTACK

N O R W A Y

C in C., H.F.
CONVOYS
GERMAN SHIPS

0001/10 To BASE

DIVERGING SEARCH
SIX ALBACORES

65°   65°

5°W   0°   5°E   10°   15°   20°   25°

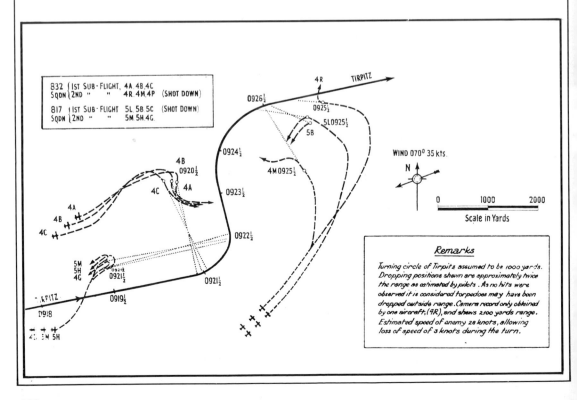

832 {1ST SUB-FLIGHT. 4A. 4B. 4C
SQDN {2ND "   "   4R. 4M. 4P (SHOT DOWN)

817 {1ST SUB-FLIGHT. 5L. 5B. 5C (SHOT DOWN)
SQDN {2ND "   "   5M. 5H. 4G

4R   TIRPITZ

0926½
0925½

5L 0925½

5B

0924½   4M 0925½

WIND 070° 35 kts.
N

4B
4A 0920½
4C   4A

0923½

4A
4B
4C

0922½

0   1000   2000
Scale in Yards

5M
5H
4G
0921½   0921½

0921½

TIRPITZ   0919½

0918

4G 5M 5H

Remarks

Turning circle of Tirpitz assumed to be 1000 yards.
Dropping positions shown are approximately twice
the range as estimated by pilots. As no hits were
observed it is considered torpedoes may have been
dropped outside range. Camera record only obtained
by one aircraft (4R), and shows 2100 yards range.
Estimated speed of enemy 28 knots, allowing
loss of speed of 3 knots during the turn.

tive but to order his sub-flights to attack independently.

The first dived on the German battleship's port beam at about 18,000yd and swung to starboard to drop its Mk XVs at a range of about a mile and a half. *Tirpitz*'s heavy anti-aircraft armament put up an impressive barrage as the battleship turned to port to comb the torpedoes. She had already begun to turn as the second sub-flight launched its torpedoes at a range of about a mile. The Mk XVs, set to run at a depth of 25ft and a speed of 40kt, all missed the target. The second pair of sub-flights attacked the battleship from the opposite side four minutes later; one Albacore was shot down and again *Tirpitz* avoided being hit. The main reason for the failure was not lack of bravery — some aircraft approached as close as 400yd to machine gun the battleship's upperworks — but lack of training. Lucas had only just joined *Victorious* and had never flown with its air group before.

He had not had practice in torpedo attack since 1937 and the rest of his men had not had much exercise in co-ordinated attack on enemy capital ships. Nevertheless, *Tirpitz*'s escape owed something to luck; one Mk XV passed within only 20yd of the battleship and her anti-torpedo manoeuvres had been so intense that her Chief Engineer warned the bridge that her steering gear was breaking under the strain.

Tovey was seriously disappointed by this failure. He had signalled *Victorious* before the strike on the 'wonderful chance' the carriers's aircraft had been offered to achieve 'most valuable results'. A mix of inadequate aircraft and insufficient training had thrown that chance away. Nevertheless, the operation did have an effect on the future of the *Tirpitz* as her narrow escape made the German Navy even more reluctant to risk its most powerful individual asset. This meant that the British were forced back to a series of 'attacks at source'. In fact, air attacks on *Tirpitz*

had begun a few days before on the night of 28/29 January 1942 when nine Handley Page Halifaxes and seven Short Stirlings of RAF Bomber Command attacked her at Trondheim. The icing conditions and complete cloud cover prevented them dropping any bombs, for the loss of one Stirling. Bomber Command tried again in greater strength early on 31 March, sending 34 Halifaxes to Trondheim. The fiord conditions made *Tirpitz* very hard to attack. She was covered with camouflage netting secured close alongside in a narrow fiord surrounded by high mountains. Dense smoke screens could be released as air attackers closed in. These defensive measures succeeded in protecting the battleship, especially as bad weather compounded the bombers' problems. Only one Halifax succeeded in finding the *Tirpitz* but none of the five bombs it dropped — one 4,000lb and four 500lb — caused any damage. Five Halifaxes failed to return.

Bomber Command tried yet again on 28 April. This was a sophisticated attack of high flying Avro Lancasters leading the way for a low level strike by Halifaxes. The latter were led by Wg Cdr Bennett, one of Bomber Command's best pilots who, later that year, would lead the new Pathfinder Force. Some 43 aircraft took off of which 32 made it to the target. These dropped 94 bombs (30 x 500lb, 20 x 4,000lb and 44 x '1,000lb Spherical Mines' — Naval Mk XIXs specially filled with Amatol high explosive and hydrostatistically fused to explode at 14-18ft). The idea was that these mines would be dropped close to the *Tirpitz* in the fiord but near misses could roll down the mountainside to explode alongside her — if they did not explode prematurely. Heavy AA fire and an effective smoke screen foiled the attack and no mines exploded close enough to damage the battleship but it clearly worried the Germans who took extra defensive measures. Five bombers were lost, including Bennett's, who avoided capture and escaped to neutral Sweden, returning to the UK five weeks later.

One of the shot down Halifaxes, a brand new Mk II of No 35 Squadron captained by Plt Off Donald McIntyre, which crash-landed on the surface of a frozen lake has since been salvaged and can now be seen in the Royal Air Force Museum at Hendon.

The attack was followed up the following night by 34 more Lancasters and Halifaxes but again the smoke screen proved effective and none of the 90 bombs or mines dropped 'blind' scored any damage. Two Halifaxes were lost.

Bombing having failed, the Royal Navy next tried a more novel approach. In December 1941, Italian two-man 'Maiali' human torpedoes had succeeded in disabling the two battleships of the Mediterranean Fleet. The Prime Minister demanded a copy and Sir Max Horton, Flag Officer Submarines, delegated the task to Lt-Cdr Tony Fell a former submariner who had been diverted into combined operations. A 'Maiali' captured in an abortive attack on Gibraltar was copied and became known as the British 'Chariot'. An unpowered prototype was ready by April 1942 and the first powered device was ready by June. The 'Chariot' was electrically powered and its batteries could drive it at just under 3kt for six hours. Its two-man crew, dressed in flexible diving suits with oxygen supplies designed by Cdr Geoffrey Sladen, sat astride the device, the forward member driving it. The rear member, facing backwards in the early model, acted as navigator, net cutter and warhead operator. The 'Chariot' carried a 600lb high explosive warhead, to be detached from the vehicle and then fixed to the target. A delayed action fuse gave the divers time to escape.

In order to solve the problem of taking the 'Chariots' within range of their target it was decided to use the 'Shetland Bus' fishing boat organisation based at Lunna Voe in the Shetlands. This ferried resistance workers and refugees to and from Norway and carried out other clandestine operations. Indeed, a 'Shetland Bus' officer, Lt David Howarth RNVR, had first suggested the idea of using human torpedoes against *Tirpitz*. It was decided, therefore to use the newly completed Norwegian fishing boat *Arthur*, which had been stolen by resistance worker Leif Larsen in order to return to Shetland after a minelaying operation in October 1941. Larsen jumped at the opportunity of assisting with the attack and a crew of three Norwegians and six British sailors was chosen for the attack. *Arthur* was to carry the 'Chariots' on board, along with a spurious cargo of untraceable peat, until she reached the Smolen Islands. At that point the 'Chariots' would be hoisted over the side and attached to *Arthur*'s keel. The 'Chariots' would then be taken sufficiently close to *Tirpitz* to mount the attack.

Carrying a complete set of forged papers, *Arthur* sailed first to join the depot ship *Alecto* and the battleship *Rodney* in a Shetland loch. *Rodney* was to act as target ship for practice attacks. The two 'Chariot' crews were Lt Brewster and Able Seaman (AB) Brown, and Sgt Craig of the Royal Engineers assisted by AB Evans. After successfully 'sinking' *Rodney*, the four men, plus the two sailors who would help them into their suits, were taken by Larsen to Lunna Voe in the *Arthur*. Details for both *Arthur*'s cover story and latest information on *Tirpitz*'s defences were smuggled out to Britain by the Norwegian resistance. The *Arthur* set sail for Norway on 26 October 1942.

Operation 'Title', as it was called, was dogged by ill luck from the start. On the 28th, as the little fishing boat approached Smolen, its engine broke down and it took three hours to get it started once more. The following day, the generator, carried to recharge the batteries of the 'chariots', broke down after only a quarter of an hour of use. It had been damaged by rough weather in the crossing and Brewster and his colleagues could only hope that their mounts had retained sufficient charge. German aircraft thwarted every attempt to uncover the 'Chariots' during the day then the weather deteriorated once more and hoisting out the 'Chariots' was delayed to the 30th.

The *Arthur* finally set off for the entrance to Trondheim Fiord at 1400 that day. Again the engine gave trouble but this was patched up overnight with the help of a local blacksmith. Despite the unexpected visibility of the 'Chariots' under the fishing boat, the expected examination by a German patrol boat went off safely. Then, however, disaster struck: a sudden and violent storm blew up which caused the 'Chariots' to break away and sink to the bottom of the fiord. As Lt Brewster wrote: 'I don't think anyone has ever been so disappointed as we were that night. We were within 10 miles of the pride of the German Navy; all our obstacles were behind us, and we might as well have been at the North Pole.' Larsen and Brewster decided to scuttle the *Arthur* and make for Sweden. All but AB Evans made it, the unfortunate seaman being wounded in a gun battle with police just short of the frontier. He had to be left and was later shot by the Germans as a spy. Improved 'Chariots' carried by submarines were later used with success in the Mediterranean.

Tirpitz, therefore, remained safely in her Trondheim Fiord anchorage through the winter of 1942-43. She carried out an extensive self-maintenance programme which even included a rudder change. In March 1943 the great battleship was operational once more and she joined the smaller 11in gun battleship *Scharnhorst* and six destroyers at Alten Fiord near the North Cape. They remained there as a potent threat, making one sortie on 9 September to destroy the supply dump and wireless station on Spitzbergen. This less than demanding operation was the only time that the mighty *Tirpitz* fired her eight 15in guns at a surface target in anger.

At the end of that month, the Royal Navy attacked her again but this time with a different kind of small submersible. This was the X-craft, a midget submarine 51ft long and 5ft in diameter of conventional diesel electric propulsion. The main armament were two 'side cargoes', one on each side, to be dropped under the target. Each cargo contained 3,570 tons of powerful Amatex high explosive and a time fuse with a delay of up to six hours. There were buoyancy tanks top and bottom of the charge to be flooded before dropping. The X-craft was the brainchild of a retired submarine commander, Cdr Cromwell-Varley, who had gained the support of his friend, Adm Sir Max Horton, Flag Officer Submarines and, more importantly, that of the Prime Minister to whom any kind of offensive gadget appealed. In the middle of 1941 an organisation was created for midget submarines; among the first officers appointed was Lt Donald Cameron RNR who would later take part in the Tirpitz attack.

The first prototype craft, X-3, was launched under cover of darkness at the Varley Marine Works on 15 March 1942 and in April volunteer officers were selected for 'special duties'. Training began in May and bases were set up at Port Bannatyne on the Isle of Bute and at the head of Loch Striven. In November 1942, X-3 sank in the loch but the crew managed to escape and the boat was successfully raised from the bottom. X-4 was, however, now complete, commanded by Lt Godfrey Place RN. Six operational boats had been ordered in May 1942 and these were modified in accordance with the results of trials with the pair of prototypes. X-5 was launched at Faslane on Hogmanay 1942 and X-6 arrived on 11 January 1943, closely followed by X-7, 8, 9 and 10. Unfortunately, however, the X-craft retained three serious defects: their miniaturised periscopes were unreliable being prone both to leakage and motor failure; their gyro compasses were incapable of standing up to the violent movements of which the midgets were capable; and the side cargoes' buoyancy tanks were prone to premature flooding causing serious trimming difficulties. It also seems to have been difficult to stop the midgets broaching to the surface when at their shallow operational depths.

The original intention was to use X-craft against *Tirpitz* in the spring of 1943 but the lengthening northern days made a summer attack hazardous and Barry, the new Flag Officer Submarines, felt that the operation was best postponed until the autumn to allow more training. This put the ball — quite literally — back into the court of the RAF. A special Coastal Command squadron, No 618, was formed to attack the *Tirpitz* with Mosquito IV aircraft each equipped with two 'Highball' bouncing bombs. These were Barnes Wallis-designed cousins of the 'Upkeep' weapons used to attack and breach the Ruhr dams in May 1943. Sadly the move to Kaa Fiord in the far north put *Tirpitz* way out of range and No 618 Squadron was never used as intended. It was now up to the X-craft.

These had to be brought close to their distant targets and this was one of the problems considered over the summer of 1943. Fishing boats like the *Arthur* had insufficient power and would probably arouse suspicion, especially after the failure of 'Title'. Attempting to use a depot ship, such as the *Bonaventure*, which had been allocated as mother ship to the midget submarines, would be even more dangerous and would alert the Germans to what was coming. It was eventually decided to tow the X-craft north with normal patrol submarines. The delay, as intended, also allowed the X-craft crews, now officially officers and men the 12th Submarine Flotilla (which also contained the 'Chariots'), to hone their skills in intensive training. *Bonaventure* was moved from Loch Striven to Loch Cairnbawn where exercises were carried out against units of the Home Fleet, fully protected by nets. After the accidental death of X-craft officer a specialist diver was added to the three man crew of each boat. The attack plans were aptly codenamed Operation 'Source' and intelligence was once again received from Norwegian resistance. Air reconnaissance was tricky as Alten Fiord was out of range of British airfields and only on 3 September, just over a week before the operation was due to begin, were detachments of RAF PR Spitfires able to arrive in the USSR for operations.

The moonlight condition dictated an attack between 20 September and 25 September. On the 11th, therefore, the submarine depot ship HMS *Titania* arrived in Loch Cairnbawn with a mixed flotilla of 'T' and 'S' class towing submarines: *Thrasher, Truculent, Syrtis, Seanymph, Stubborn* and *Sceptre*. Two more 'S' class boats were held in reserve at Scapa. Five days were spent on towing exercises. As luck would have it the initial Spitfire reconnaissance occurred during the Spitzbergen operation and it looked as if the birds had flown. However, by 10 September both *Tirpitz* and *Scharnhorst* were back at base.

The first boats to leave, at 1600 on 11 September were *Truculent* towing X-6 and *Syrtis* towing X-9. They were followed by *Thrasher* with X-5,

Right:

X5, *Platypus*, leaves on her daring mission towed by HMS *Thrasher*. Her fate remains a mystery, although it is quite likely she played an important role in disabling *Tirpitz*. Ian Allan Library

Below right:

The crews of X5, *Platypus*: back row (l-r), Lt Terry-Lloyd (passage CO), Midshipman Malcolm, Lt Henty-Creer (CO), S-Lt Nelson; front row (l-r), Stoker Garrity (passage), L/S Element (passage), ERA Mortiboys. Henty-Creer, Malcolm, Nelson and Mortiboys were all lost in the attack; Terry-Lloyd was awarded the MBE. IWM A19637

Below:

Track for Operation 'Source', 15 September to 4 December 1943.

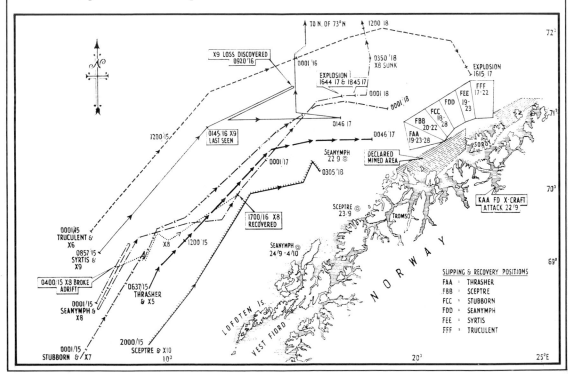

The crews of X6, *Piker II*: back row (l-r), Lt Wilson (passage CO), Lt Cameron (CO), Lt Lorimer; front row (l-r), S-Lt Kendall, ERA Goddard, L/S McGregor (passage), Stoker Oxley (passage). Cameron received the VC, Lorimer and Kendall the DSO, and Goddard the Conspicuous Gallantry Medal. *IWM A19635*

The crews of X7, *Pdinichthys*: back row (l-r), S-Lt Aitken, Lt Place (CO), Lt Whittam, Lt Philip (Passage CO); front row (l-r), L/S Magennis (Passage), Stoker Luck (Passage), ERA Whiteley. Place was awarded the VC and Aitken the DSO; Whittam and Whiteley were both lost. Philip was awarded the MBE; Magennis was later to receive the VC for his role in the midget submarine attack on the Japanese cruiser *Takao* at Singapore in 1945. *IWM A19636*

Seanymph with X-8, *Stubborn* with X-7 and *Sceptre* with X-10. The last boat left at 1300 on 12 September. After perusing the latest reconnaissance photographs, Adm Barry was able to signal precise targets to the midgets. The plan adopted was No 4: X-5 (Lt Henty-Creer RNVR, the operational commander of the mission), X-6 (Cameron) and X-7 (Place) were to attack *Tirpitz*. X-9 (Lt Martin RN) and X-10 (Lt Hudspeth RANVR) were to attack *Scharnhorst* and X-8 (Lt McFarlane RAN) was to attack the 'pocket battle-

ship' *Lützow* in Lange Fiord. The anchorages of the other two capital ships were further up Alten Fiord in Kaa Fiord, the stretch of water at its head. Details of the latest dispositions and defences were signalled to the attackers.

The first problem that faced Operation 'Source' was the weakness of the towing cables, some of which were made of rope and others of stronger nylon. First, X-8 broke its rope tow, then X-7. Both boats were able to regain contact with the larger submarines but X-9, which broke its rope tow in the early hours of 16 September was never seen again. The heavy swell, even beneath the waves, was causing the sterns of the towing submarines to rise and fall, so jerking and straining the tow rope. To counteract this effect X-9 was probably trimmed heavily by the bow, which would cause a fatal and uncontrolled plunge if the rope broke. On the following day, X-8 continued to have difficulties. Her side cargoes flooded, causing trimming difficulties. First one was jettisoned and then the other, a hazardous procedure as the explosive refused to be rendered safe. The resulting explosions so damaged X-8 that she had eventually to be scuttled.

Below:
Operation 'Source' location of shipping and defensive booms in Kaa Fjord.

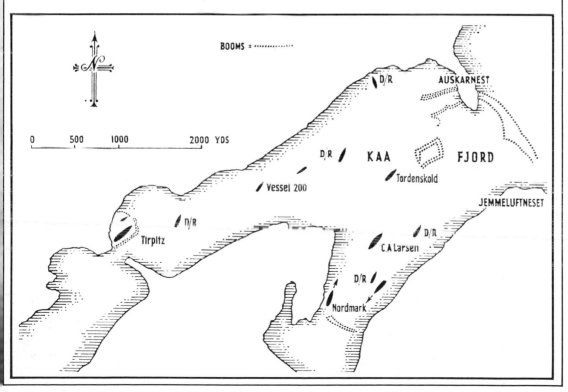

Above:
**HMS *Syrtis* towed X9 until the tow parted and then
assisted with the recovery of the X-Craft.**
Ian Allan Collection

The boats equipped with nylon tow ropes had
uneventful passages. The intention was to transfer
operational crews to the X-craft on 17 September
but this was delayed by bad weather. *Stubborn* and
X-7 attempted the transfer on the evening of
18 September and continued to have difficulty.
The tow parted twice during the transfer and it
took no less than five hours to complete. The
other three boats had less eventful transfers the
following day. By dawn on 20 September, all four
of the towing submarines with their X-craft were
in their designated slipping zones. The adventures
of *Stubborn* and X-7 had continued. They had
spotted a mine whose mooring line got caught in
the tow rope and came to rest on the midget submarine's bow. *Stubborn* could not inform Place of
this as the emergency towing wire had no communications. The X-craft's commander spotted
through the periscope that *Stubborn* had stopped
and came on the casing to push and kick the mine
clear. Somewhat to the surprise of the towing submarine he succeeded in doing this without an
explosion. Between 1830 and 2000, the four
remaining midgets, X-5, X-6, X-7 and X-10
slipped their tows and made their way towards
their targets. The four midgets had been chris-
tened unofficially by their crews, *Platypus*, *Piker II*,
Pdinichthys, and *Excalibur* and they will be referred
to as such for the rest of this account.

At 1630 *Pdinichthys* spotted an unidentified
large ship steaming northwards, this was probably
Excalibur's target, the *Scharnhorst*, steaming out
for routine gunnery practice — and out of danger.

This battleship's legendary luck would not desert
her for another three months. *Excalibur* was
already displaying the reliability problems that
dogged the untried X-craft. Her periscope was
giving trouble and the gyro compass had failed.
Hudspeth and his crew spent all day on the 21st
trying to make repairs and eventually *Excalibur*
tried to make its attack purely visually. Then the
periscope finally failed completely when its motor
burnt out, forcing the midget to the surface. At
0215 on the 22nd, the day of the planned attack,
Excalibur dived to the bottom for her crew to
repair the defects. They planned to attack their
non-existent target on the night of 22/23 September.

Cameron in *Piker II* planned to make his attack
at 0630 on the 22nd with a full six hour time
delay on the side charges in order to allow plenty
of time for the other two midgets to make their
attacks and retire. Unfortunately, the port side
charge refused to accept anything more than a
two-hour delay. Cameron had other problems
also; his starboard side charge was flooded causing
considerable trimming difficulties, especially as
the water became fresher, Also the periscope was
leaking and misting up and there was an air leak
in the forward ballast tank. Nevertheless, he
decided to press on, as his midget might be the
only one to get through. Cameron's troubles continued when, like *Excalibur*'s, *Piker II*'s periscope
motor also burned out and Engine Room Artificer
Goddard carried out a crude repair. At 0445,
barely able to see, Cameron approached the nets
at the entrance to Kaa Fiord.

Now his luck changed, for just at that moment
a coaster was passing through the boom. *Piker II*
surfaced and followed in the ship's wake using its
diesel. Cameron gambled that no one would

notice — and no one did. X-6 then dived and proceeded up the fiord blind while Cameron stripped the periscope once more to make it usable. When the submarine came back to periscope depth it had to dive again to avoid a destroyer's mooring cable. *Tirpitz* was, however, clearly visible behind her anti-torpedo nets by the northern side of the fiord. Keeping close to this shore, Cameron moved southwestwards towards the target using dead reckoning submerged. He was lucky to slip through a gap in the nets and then to be ignored when he accidentally ran aground on the western shore and broke surface — *Piker II* had been mistaken for a porpoise! There was no mistake, however, five minutes later at 0712 when the X-craft broke surface 75yd abeam of the German battleship. The Germans opened fire and Cameron dived but his periscope was flooded again and the compass out of action because of the grounding and the subsequent high angles of dive and rise. He groped his way in what he thought was the right direction, ran into an obstruction, broke clear and then surfaced right under *Tirpitz*'s port bow. *Tirpitz*'s crew opened fire once more with small arms and threw hand grenades. Cameron decided the game was up, dropped his side cargoes beside 'B' turret and ordered his crew to surrender. The last man out opened the Kingston valves and put the motor astern. This drove *Piker II* underwater, almost pulling an attached German picket boat with it.

Pdinichthys was at that moment laying her second side cargo further astern. Place had passed through the boom at 0350 without problems but then ran into the nets protecting an unused anchorage in the middle of the fiord. After an hour *Pdinichthys* broke free but the violent movements involved damaged the gyro and also a trim pump. Place attempted a deep passage beneath the torpedo nets protecting *Tirpitz* but the nets were lower than expected and the X-craft once again became entangled. She freed herself, came to the surface unnoticed, dived again and became entangled once more at a depth of 95ft. Again *Pdinichthys* became free but the gyro was now completely useless and Place had to surface to see where he was. To his pleasure and surprise Place found himself inside *Tirpitz*'s nets with the battleship only 30yd ahead. He dived to 40ft, hit the battleship abreast of 'B' turret and released his first cargo. He then dived to 60ft, turned, went astern under *Tirpitz* for about 180ft and released the other side cargo under the estimated position of 'C' turret; the time was about 0725. Place dived to 100ft to try to escape through the gap where he had entered. Without a compass, however, this was impossible and he again became entangled in the net. Nothing he could do could

find a gap and after repeated attempts, all of which resulted in the boat becoming entangled once more, *Pdinichthys* broke surface under heavy small arms fire. This got her over the net and she immediately dived to the bottom. Navigating blind, however, led Place straight back into the nets, in which he became entangled yet again.

What happened to *Platypus* will forever remain a mystery as Henty-Creer and his crew did not survive the mission. The official view is that the attack leader did not attack the target but recent work on the subject has produced a convincing case that Henty-Creer did in fact make an attack. It seems probable that he would have had the same kinds of problems with both the X-craft and the nets as those faced by Cameron and Place. Like the others, however, Henty-Creer may well have succeeded in laying his side cargoes under *Tirpitz* probably on the starboard side just forward of amidships. Given the mechanical and maneouvring difficulties *Platypus* was probably facing, Henty-Creer may have groped his way to the battleship and laid both charges together.

Cameron and his crew were taken on board *Tirpitz* and although they refused to say anything their attitude seemed to imply a successful mission. Kapt Meyer ordered the battleship to raise steam to take her to sea out of danger as soon as possible. At 0740, however, *Pdinichthys* was spotted trying to make her escape. Two nearby destroyers were ordered to drop depth charges and *Tirpitz* opened fire with her light AA guns. Meyer had no idea what weapons the midget submarines carried and he changed his plans to being torpedoed. In any case, the enemy midget had appeared on *Tirpitz*'s port bow and it was likely that any explosive charges laid would be on that side. It was, therefore, decided to haul the battleship's bow over to starboard using her anchors and cables. This had the effect of drawing *Tirpitz* away from the three charges laid by *Piker II* and *Pdinichthys* — but it may have brought the ship over Henty-Creer's side charges. At 0812 the charges exploded almost simultaneously as the shock of the first set off the rest. The first explosion was *Pdinichthys*' second charge abreast 'C' turret. Her first charge then went up and both of *Piker II*'s about 50-60yd off the port bow. Some Germans, however, clearly saw an explosion on the starboard side just below *Tirpitz*'s foremast. These were in all probability *Platypus*' charges.

The effect on the *Tirpitz* was catastrophic. The ship was lifted out of the water and then smashed back into it; after violent shudders the battleship eventually came to rest with a slight port list. Electronic and fire control systems were seriously damaged and all auxiliary machinery either thrown off its housings or damaged internally.

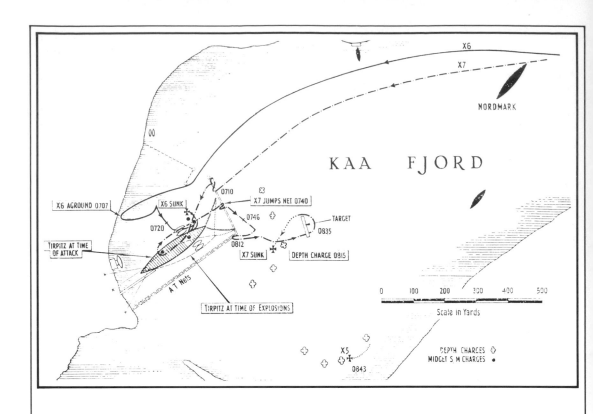

KAA FJORD

X6

X7

NORDMARK

X6 AGROUND 0707
X6 SUNK
0710
X7 JUMPS NET 0740
0746
TARGET
0835
0720
X7 SUNK
DEPTH CHARGE 0815
TIRPITZ AT TIME OF ATTACK
0812
TIRPITZ AT TIME OF EXPLOSIONS

A T Nets

0   100   200   300   400   500
Scale in Yards

X5
0843

DEPTH CHARGES
MIDGET S M CHARGES

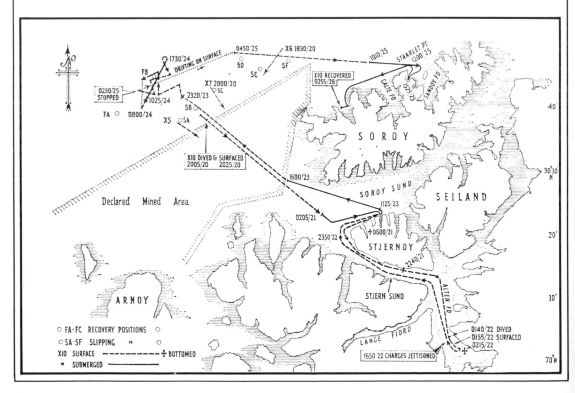

1730/24
DRIFTING ON SURFACE
0450/25
X6 1830/20
1010/25
STAARLET PT
1200/25
FB
SD
SE
SF
X10 RECOVERED
0255/28
GATE FD
1525/25
SANDOY FD
0230/25 STOPPED
X7 2000/20
SC
2320/23
1025/24
SB
SOROY
40'
FA
0800/24
X5
SA
X10 DIVED & SURFACED
2005/20   2025/20
1600/23
30'30 N
SOROY SUND
SEILAND
1125/23
Declared   Mined   Area
0205/21
+0600/21
2350/22
20'
STJERNOY
2240/21
STJERN SUND
ALTEN FD
10'
ARNOY
LANGE FIORD
0140/22 DIVED
0155/22 SURFACED
0215/22
FA-FC RECOVERY POSITIONS
SA-SF SLIPPING
X10 SURFACE   BOTTOMED
1650 22 CHARGES JETTISONED
70°N
SUBMERGED

Left:
Operation 'Source', the attack on the *Tirpitz* by the midget submarines on 22 September 1943 based on reports by the commanding officers of the midget subs X6 and X7 and a German plan.

Below left:
Approaches to Kaa Fjord showing the movements of X10, 20-28 September 1943.

Most of the bolts that held the battleship's machinery in place were broken. The aft fire control computer was a write off, as was the armament it directed. 'D' turret, despite its weight of 2,000 tons, was quite literally lifted from its rollers. When it crashed back on to them the bearings were so damaged that the turret could not be moved. 'B' and 'C' turrets were less seriously damaged but were also out of action.

One of the port 5.9in turrets was jammed and the 4.1in AA guns could only be operated in manual mode. The ship could not be moved as the bolts in the shaft bearings were broken and the shafting itself was cracked. The three main turbines and their mountings were all damaged and some of the steam pipes from the boilers were also broken. The steering was damaged, as was the port rudder itself and the main rudder shaft. The hull was not seriously damaged structurally, although the plating was torn and indented and the bottom suffered mild deformation. The battleship took in around 1,430 tonnes of water and several spaces were flooded. This flooding knocked out some of the turbo generators and other generators were put out of action by broken steam lines or severed cables. Power was only restored when two ships came alongside to provide it.

The explosion of the side cargoes also had the effect of shaking *Pdinichthys* free from the torpedo nets. Place put her on the bottom to inspect damage that was so serious that a return to Scotland was clearly impossible. He therefore decided to scuttle the boat after evacuating his crew and surfaced next to a battle practice target on to which he clambered, waving his white sweater in surrender. Unfortunately, *Pdinichthys'* ballast tanks were leaking and the boat sank almost immediately. Only one other member of the crew was able to escape and the other two exhausted their oxygen supply before they were able to get out under water. Henty-Creer appears to have waited in order to assess the results of the attack; alternatively he might have been trying to repair *Platypus'* defects. He then accidentally surfaced at 0843 about 650yd away from *Tirpitz* on the starboard bow. *Tirpitz* blazed away at the X-craft with both her heavy and AA batteries which scored some hits. Then the destroyer *Z-29* dropped depth charges but these do not seem to have destroyed

Platypus as the Germans continued to hear knocking noises on sonar. It is probable that Henty-Creer and his crew managed to effect some repairs and then made off into deeper water. The repairs proved inadequate and the submarine sank in water too deep for *Platypus* ever to be found. Considerable bravery had been shown by Henty-Creer and his crew and it is possible that his charges were those that inflicted some of the most serious damage. It seems doubly sad, therefore, that he did not receive a Victoria Cross like those justly awarded to Cameron and Place.

Excalibur was unable to cure her defects and Hudspeth decided to make for home when he heard the explosions under *Tirpitz*. After further adventures the fourth X-craft finally found *Stubborn* and at 2200 on 29 September, exactly 10 days after taking over *Excalibur*, Hudspeth handed back command to *Pdinichthys'* passage crew. Sadly, the tow ropes again proved fragile and in deteriorating weather *Excalibur* had to be scuttled by the passage crew. After carrying out uneventful patrols the other towing submarines were all back in Britain by 7 October. Adm Barry referred to the attack as 'one of the most courageous acts of all time'. *Tirpitz* had been effectively neutralised for six months at the cost of six midget submarines, a most cost effective trade off.

The Germans now set about repairing their injured battleship and the progress of the repairs was monitored by Bletchley Park. While the repairs were being carried out *Tirpitz* was attacked by 15 Soviet aircraft but only four found Kaa Fiord and only one scored a near miss which caused only minor damage. By 15 March 1944 the repairs were complete and *Tirpitz* carried out 14 days of trials in which she worked up to 27kt. She was due to sail on more trials on 3 April. The Home Fleet, however, had a surprise in store for her. It was decided to carry out a major carrier air strike on the German battleship, Operation 'Tungsten'. The fleet sailed in two groups, a fast Force 'I' commanded by the new C-in-C Home Fleet Adm Sir Bruce Fraser who had sunk the *Scharnhorst* in the Royal Navy's last major ship-v-ship gun battle the previous December. It was made up of the battleships *Duke of York* (flagship) and *Anson*, the carrier *Victorious* fresh out of refit and the cruiser *Belfast*. The destroyer screen was made up of a flotilla of five ships later relieved by one of six when the others had to go to the Faroes to refuel. Force 'II' was composed of four slow escort carriers reallocated to fleet work from their primary role, an indication of the Royal Navy's chronic shortage of fleet carriers. The CVEs were HMS *Searcher*, *Emperor*, *Pursuer* and *Fencer* and they were supplemented by the old fleet carrier *Furious*. Rear-Adm Bisset (RA escort carriers)

1555

commanded the force from the improved 'Dido' class cruiser *Royalist*. Surface protection was provided for Force 'II' by the cruisers *Sheffield* and *Jamaica* and there was a destroyer screen of five ships supplemented by the original five from the Force 'I' once they had refuelled. There were also two RFA tankers with Force 'II'. Fraser's original intention was to attack on the 4th but the 'Ultra' decrypts caused an advance by 24hr.

Force 'I' sailed to cover Russian convoy JW58 and then joined up with Force 'II' on 2 April. Fraser detached his flagship with a couple of destroyers and moved to the northwest leaving Vice-Adm Sir Henry Moore in *Anson* to carry out the strike. The force was re-arranged into groups, Force '7' with *Anson, Victorious, Furious, Jamaica* and six destroyers; and Force '8' with *Royalist, Sheffield,* the four escort carriers and six destroyers. The attack was timed for dawn on 3 April. Two TBR (Torpedo-Bomber-Reconnaisance) wings, each of 21 Fairey Barracudas were available, one from each fleet carrier. They would have to be used in the dive bombing mode as the net defences made torpedo dropping impractical. In order for the wings to strike as single formations, one squadron of each wing was transferred to the other fleet carrier. The Barracudas were carrying four kinds of bomb loads. Most were armed with three 500lb semi-armour piercing (SAP) bombs with delayed fuses. Others, however, carried a single 1,600lb armour piercing (AP) weapon and the rest either three 500lb instantaneously fused MC (Medium Capacity) high explosive bombs or 600lb anti-submarine bombs. The 1,600-pounders were intended for high level release — above 3,000 feet — in order to pierce *Tirpitz*'s armoured deck and the 500lb SAP bombs were intended to damage the area above it. The high

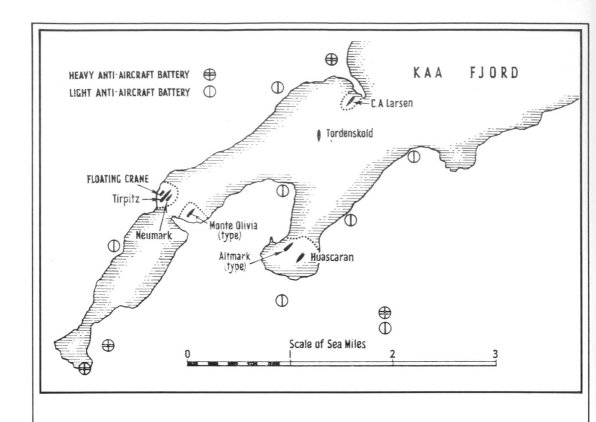

HEAVY ANTI-AIRCRAFT BATTERY ⊕
LIGHT ANTI-AIRCRAFT BATTERY ⏀

KAA FJORD

C.A Larsen

Tordenskold

FLOATING CRANE
Tirpitz
Neumark
Monte Olivia
(type)
Altmark
(type)
Huascaran

Scale of Sea Miles

0   1   2   3

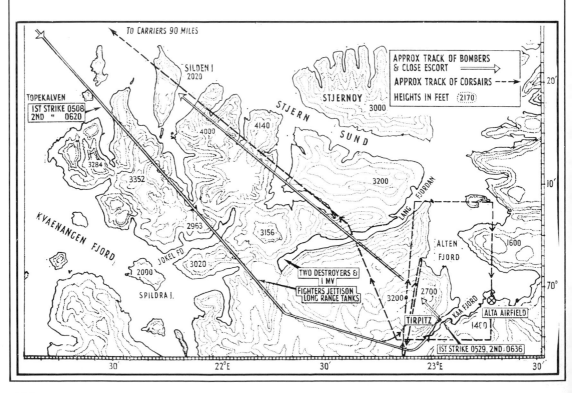

TO CARRIERS 90 MILES

SILDEN I
2020

STJERNOY
3000

STJERN
SUND

APPROX TRACK OF BOMBERS
& CLOSE ESCORT →
APPROX TRACK OF CORSAIRS - →
HEIGHTS IN FEET ⌷2170⌷

TOPEKALVEN
1ST STRIKE 0508
2ND " 0620

4000

4140

3284

3352

3200

LANG FJORDAN

2963

3156

KVAENANGEN FJORD

JOKEL FD

3020

2000

SPILDRA I.

TWO DESTROYERS &
1 MV
FIGHTERS JETTISON
LONG RANGE TANKS

3200

2700

ALTEN
FJORD

1600

3200

ALTA AIRFIELD

TIRPITZ

KAA FJORD

70°

1400

1ST STRIKE 0529, 2ND: 0636

30'   22°E   30'   23°E   30'

20'

10'

134

Fleet Air Arm attacks on the *Tirpitz*, 3 April 1944, in Kaa Fjord.

Below left:
An air track chart of the Fleet Air Arm attack on the *Tirpitz* in Kaa Fjord on 3 April 1944.

explosive bombs were for use against the ship's AA crews and the anti submarine weapons, set to 35ft, were to inflict underwater damage. It was found on the day that low wind over deck reduced depth bomb capacity to at most two. Fighter escort would be provided by Chance Vought Corsairs from *Victorious* and Grumman Wildcats and Hellcats from the escort carriers. More Wildcats as well as *Furious'* Supermarine Seafires would provide top cover for the fleet.

Victorious' Corsairs (from No 834 Squadron) began to take off at 0416 and eight minutes later the Barracudas, No 8 TBR Wing (Nos 827 and 830 Squadrons) took to the air. Simultaneously *Searcher* and *Pursuer* launched 20 Wildcats and *Emperor* 10 Hellcats (these aircraft came from Nos 800, 881 and 882 Squadrons). *Furious'* Seafires and Wildcats from *Fencer* kept guard above. The whole strike was formed up by 0437 and the aircraft headed for their target. Just as *Tirpitz* was weighing her second anchor, her crew noticed that the defensive smokescreen was being activated. At the same time 32 enemy aircraft were reported heading south at a distance of 43 miles. 'Tungsten' had achieved necessary surprise and although the Germans had their guns manned very little of the smoke screen covered the fiord. As the Corsairs flew top cover, the Wildcats and Hellcats came in low to strafe the battleship in order to suppress hostile fire. The Barracudas then began their dive bombing attacks at 0529. As errors of range exceeded errors of line the bombs were dropped along the battleship's fore and aft axis. The bombers dropped six 1,600lb AP bombs, 24 500lb SAPs, 12 500lb MCs and four A/S bombs. In order to achieve greater accuracy, the over enthusiastic Fleet Air Arm pilots dropped their weapons from too low an altitude for the armour piercing effect of the 1,600-pounders to work. Nevertheless, the first attack scored 11 direct hits and near misses and *Tirpitz*'s upper decks were reduced to a shambles.

As the first wave made their attack the carriers were launching the second wave. No 52 Barracuda Wing (Nos 829 and 831 Squadrons) was only able to launch 20 aircraft as one failed to start. Another crashed immediately after take off, killing its crew, so only 19 bombers made the attack. Escort was provided by 10 Corsairs from

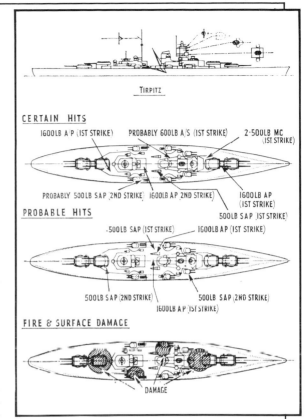

CERTAIN HITS

FIRE & SURFACE DAMAGE

Above:
Fleet Air Arm attack on the *Tirpitz* 3 April 1944. The Admiralty assessment of hits obtained (made on 3 May 1944).

No 826 Squadron, 10 Hellcats from No 804 Squadron and 19 Wildcats from Nos 896 and 898 Squadrons. Despite the warning, the smoke screen was still not effective and the British naval aircraft followed the same tactics, the fighters strafing the ship's upperworks for a minute before the bombers dived in to attack. No 52 Wing dropped two 1,600-pounders, 36 500lb SAPs, nine 500lb MCs and a single A/S bomb. It scored five direct hits and near misses against the alerted defences. There was no German fighter opposition to 'Tungsten'. One Barracuda in each strike was shot down by AA fire and one Hellcat was so badly damaged it had to be ditched.

The effect of the Fleet Air Arm's hits demonstrated a significant weakness in *Tirpitz*'s design. Although she and her sister ship *Bismarck* had very strong hulls their main armoured deck was one level too low, placing too many spaces and their often vital contents at risk to shell or bomb.

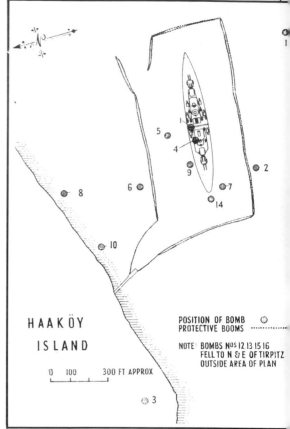

Above:
The sinking of the *Tirpitz* by Bomber Command, 12 November 1944.

This meant that although bombs did not penetrate beyond the armoured deck they could effectively put the battleship out of action. Damage was also increased by the Germans not having had a chance to close hatches or watertight doors. The anti-submarine bombs succeeded in causing some flooding but the serious damage was amidships. Two 5.9in turrets were knocked out and the boiler intake ducts were seriously damaged. Two heavy bombs caused particular destruction, one hit just aft of the port catapult and smashed its way below before exploding on the armoured deck, demolishing bulkheads, ventilation ducts and power cabling. Another, also dropped in the first attack, fell in the water but penetrated under the armour belt to explode in a fuel oil bunker. The explosion destroyed the side protection system in the areas of two compartments. Some 122 men aboard *Tirpitz* had been killed and 316, including the cap-

tain, wounded, many of the latter by the 0.5in bullets of the fighters.

Wearily, the Germans set to work to repair *Tirpitz* once more. The British tried another carrier air strike on 15 May, Operation 'Brawn', using 27 Barracudas from *Victorious* and *Furious*, escorted by 28 Corsairs, four Seafires and four Wildcats. This had to be aborted because of cloud cover and Operation 'Tiger Claw' planned for a fortnight later was also abandoned because of bad weather. Instead, the carriers attacked coastal shipping further south. On 17 June Operation 'Mascot' was mounted by the fleet carriers *Formidable*, *Indefatigable* and *Furious*. It was the day after Fraser had hauled down his flag to be replaced by Adm Moore as Home Fleet C-in-C. Moore's carriers launched no less than 44 Barracudas, escorted by 12 Fireflies, 18 Hellcats and 18 Corsairs. The attack went in when the midnight sun was at its

Above:
HMS *Fencer*'s ships company line up on deck for their triumphant return to Scapa after 'Tungsten'. HMS *Persuer* is taking up station astern.
Real Photographs/ Ian Allan Collection

lowest but there was more smoke and a post had been established on a mountain to direct *Tirpitz*'s fire, including that of her main armament, on any renewed air attack. *Tirpitz* put up a barrage of 39 15in shells and 359 5.9in, 1,973 4.1in, 3,967 37mm and 28,550 20mm rounds. The combination of smoke and gunfire held off the powerful British strike and only one near miss was obtained. A Barracuda and a Corsair failed to return and the British had to content themselves with sinking a trawler on their way home.

At the end of July, *Tirpitz* made what was to be her last movement as a fully combatant warship when she sailed for exercises with destroyers. On 22 August, the Fleet Air Arm began a final series of air attacks, coded 'Goodwood'. Four of these were mounted, using a Task Force of five carriers, the fleet carriers *Indefatigable*, *Formidable* and *Furious* and the escort carriers *Nabob* and *Trumpeter*. 'Goodwood I' went in on the afternoon of 22 August. It was a powerful strike of 32 Barracudas and nine Hellcat fighter bombers escorted by 24 Corsairs and eight Seafires. Low cloud, however obscured the target area and only the Hellcats were able to make attacks with 10 500lb SAPs. No hits were scored and the only successes of 'Goodwood I' were damage inflicted on two small supply ships and the destruction of seven floatplanes and flying boats moored in the fiord. *Tirpitz* fired no less than 62 rounds of 15in at the attackers. That evening six Hellcat fighter bombers from *Indefatigable* mounted another attack, 'Goodwood II', and although they thought they had hit the target they had not. Indeed, the Germans almost succeeded in turning the tables when a U-boat torpedoed HMS *Nabob*; the escort carrier was, however, able to return to harbour. Two Blohm & Voss flying boats were shot down as they attempted to shadow the British carrier battle group; one Barracuda, one Hellcat and one Seafire were lost in the operations.

'Goodwood III' was mounted on the afternoon of 24 August. The three fleet carriers were on their own and launched 33 Barracudas, each with a 1,600lb AP bomb, five Corsair fighter bombers, each with 1,000lb AP bombs, 10 Hellcat fighter bombers, each with a 500lb SAP bomb and 19 Corsairs and 10 Fireflies for fighter escort and AA suppression. At 1547 the Germans sounded the aircraft alarm and started the smoke screen. The aircraft attacked from all directions at heights between 6,500 and 10,000ft. Eighteen 1,600lb bombs were dropped, five 1,000-pounders and ten 500lb SAPs. A Hellcat landed one of the latter straight on top of 'B' turret, dishing in the top, destroying the quadruple 20mm gun mounted there and damaging the elevating gear of the starboard 15in gun. The other hit was by a Barracuda whose 1,600lb AP bomb was dropped at sufficient height, this time to penetrate the armoured deck. It completely defeated *Tirpitz*'s armour but having gone through almost 6in of protection failed to explode when it came to rest in No 4 electrical switchboard room. This weapon might even have caused fatal damage if it had worked properly. The 'Tirpitz' fired no less than 72 15in shells against this attack but proper AA ammunition for the lighter guns was beginning to run low. Two Hellcats and four Corsairs were lost.

'Goodwood III' had been the greatest success since 'Tungsten' but it was followed by another failure. Gales and fog delayed 'Goodwood IV' until 29 August. Some 60 aircraft were launched by *Formidable* and *Indefatigable* but the use of pathfinding Hellcats with target indicators could not make up for the Germans having reduced the notice on their smoke screens from 10min to seven. The aircraft had to bomb blind through the smoke and no damage was inflicted at a cost of a Corsair and a Firefly. All units engaged in the 1944 carrier strikes against the German battleship were allowed the battle honour 'Tirpitz'.

The Fleet Air Arm was again being let down by its aircraft. The Barracudas were too slow to overcome the Germans' warning system and their smoke screens. It was decided to try Bomber Command once more, using two weapons, the 12,000lb 'Tallboy' bomb designed by Barnes Wallis to penetrate the ground for earthquake effect and the 500lb 'Johnny Walker' (JW) bomb, an ingeniously shaped device designed to sink to the bottom and then rise up repeatedly moving laterally until it found the bottom of a ship. As Kaa Fiord was too far away from Scotland for Lancasters to make the round trip with the heavy loads No 617 Squadron, the 'Dam Busters', was sent with No 9 Squadron to mount Operation 'Paravane' from the Soviet Naval Air Force field at Yagodnik, near Archangel. The Lancasters had their mid-upper turrets removed and extra fuel tanks installed.

On 15 September under the command of Wg Cdr J. B. Tait, 27 Lancasters took off to attack *Tirpitz*. Twenty-one of the aircraft were carrying 'Tallboys' and the other six 12 JWs each. The plan was to approach from the south to get round the German radar early warning system and defeat the smoke screens, but these began to operate when the bombers were still five miles from the target. The Germans fired back with everything they had, including *Tirpitz*'s main armament with time fused shells but the main defence was the smoke. Five 'Tallboy'-equipped Lancasters and one JW aircraft decided to abort rather than bomb blind. The 'Tallboy' aircraft bombed down the axis of the ship, while the JW aircraft attacked across the target from southeast to northwest. Of the 17 Tallboys dropped, only one hit *Tirpitz*, forward 50ft from the stem. It passed through the ship to explode under it causing serious damage:

Below:
The old fleet carrier *Furious* took part in all but one of the carrier air strikes on *Tirpitz*. This picture was taken at about the time of 'Tungsten'.
Real Photographs/ Ian Allan Collection

the forward part of the battleship was flooded and her machinery shaken up once more. In fact, this bomb, which could have come from an aircraft of either No 9 or No 617 Squadron (both units claimed hits) finally knocked *Tirpitz* out as an operational unit. On 23 September 1944 Doenitz and the Naval Staff decided that it was no longer possible to repair her for active service.

Tirpitz was moved to a shallow anchorage close to Tromso for use as a floating battery. This brought her within range of Lancasters flying from Lossiemouth in Scotland, and the two squadrons involved in the first attack had their aircraft modified once more with extra fuel tanks to give them sufficient range for a low altitude round trip with 'Tallboys'. Modified bombs were also provided for this raid with larger fillings of more powerful Torpex explosive. Thirty-two Lancasters took part in Operation 'Obviate'. The Lancasters were worsted by a cloudbank that rolled in from the sea just before they mounted their attack. This prevented any hits but a near miss bent *Tirpitz*'s propeller shaft and caused some flooding. One Lancaster was hit by AA fire and forced down in neutral Sweden.

It took a third attack to inflict the *coup de grâce* on *Tirpitz*. On 12 November 32 Lancasters took off on Operation 'Catechism' and rendezvoused just over six and a half hours later 100 miles southeast of Tromso. The Lancasters climbed to 14,000ft to give their bombs sufficient velocity and with no fighter opposition and no smoke screen, it was almost like a practice attack. *Tirpitz* was hit on the port side, just abaft of the funnel and level with the mainmast. This bomb caused serious damage, blowing out the ship's plating and armour belt over a considerable area. Another

bomb hit between the two fore turrets on the port side but failed to explode. *Tirpitz* listed to port as more bombs exploded around her; as well as shaking her these bombs scoured out large enough craters for the great ship to capsize in the shallow anchorage. A third bomb seems to have hit *Tirpitz* on the port side forward of 'C' turret. This may have started a fire which spread to 'C' turret's magazine. Just after the last 'Tallboy' fell at 0950, a major explosion blew 'C' turret out of the ship. The loss of the turret affected the battleship's stability and *Tirpitz* suddenly rolled over to port and capsized. Some 950 officers and men were killed. There were 680 survivors, 87 men being rescued by cutting holes in the ship's bottom. The attack at source had finally succeeded; *Tirpitz* was no more.

Tirpitz

Built. Wilhelmshaven Dockyard (launched 1 April 1939)

Displacement: 42,343 tons standard

Dimensions: 813.7ft x 118.1ft x 28.5ft

Armour: 12.8in belt; 3.3-3.94in armoured deck; 7-14.25in on turrets

Machinery: four shaft geared turbines, 136,200shp, 29kt

Armament: 8 x 15in (4 x 2); 12 x 5.9in (6 x 2); 16 x 4.1in (8 x 2); 16 x 37mm AA (8 x 2); 78 x 20mm; 8 x 21in torpedo tubes (2 x 4)

Sensors: Seetakt Gema and Wurzburg radars

Complement: 2,608

Notes: A very powerful ship but with significant weaknesses, although the broad beam made for a stable gun platform. Above is the final armament; the torpedo tubes were added for raiding duties. The Gema radars were for surface search and, although director-mounted were of only limited assistance for fire control; the Würzburg was a partial solution to the problem of height finding.

CHAPTER SEVEN

Operation 'Neptune'

Although not normally regarded as a sea battle, the landings of the Allied armies on the beaches in Normandy, France, in June 1944 was one of the major naval operations of the war. The naval side of the operation was codenamed 'Neptune' and the naval commander was Adm Sir Bertram Ramsay, Allied Naval Commander Expeditionary Force (ANCXF). Ramsay was an exceptionally able officer whose career had not prospered in peacetime (he was mobilised from the Retired List and only officially restored to the Active List at the end of March 1944!) but who had proved himself as the organiser of the Dunkirk evacuation. Having evacuated the British Army in 1940, his task was to return it almost exactly four years later, together with its American and Canadian allies. Ramsay's Chief-of-Staff was Rear-Adm George E. Creasy, who would rise to be C-in-C Home Fleet after the war. Creasy had been

involved in invasion planning since 1943 and the joint British-American staff had had plenty of time to work efficiently and effectively.

Ramsay had become the Royal Navy's amphibious expert, having been Naval Commander for the North African landings in 1942 and Commander of the Eastern Task Force for the landings in Sicily the following year. His original target date for 'Neptune' was 1 May but there seemed little hope of acquiring sufficient ships and in March the operation was put back a month. It was also decided to postpone the proposed landings in the South of France in order to concentrate landing

Below:
As June 1944 came closer the ports on the south coast of England began to fill with the invasion armada; this is Dartmouth.
US National Archives 80-G-252243

craft on the Normandy operation. The demand for landing craft in 'Neptune' was huge: some 2,468 landing ships and landing craft, plus an additional 1,656 landing craft and other vessels to assist in moving material from larger ships to the beaches. When all vessels were taken into account, the total for the operation came to about 7,000 which required to be escorted and brought to the right place at the right time in the right sequence.

Above:
In their element at Normandy were the Royal Navy's monitors. This is HMS *Erebus* seen here between the wars. Her 15in guns were used against the batteries at Cape Barfleur and La Parnelle on the western flank of the landings.
Real Photographs/Ian Allan Collection
Below:
Operation Neptune, 6 June 1944. Convoy routes and Naval Covering Forces.

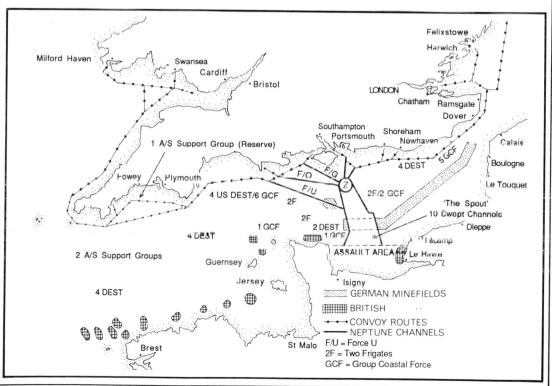

Ramsay issued his Naval Plan for 'Neptune' on 2 March 1944. The priorities were, firstly, to organise the safe and timely arrival of the troop convoys for the assault which would have to be supported by naval forces. The second task was to maintain the flow of reinforcements in the weeks after the landing. The opposition was not too serious compared to Allied strength but was none the less significant. The whole bay from the Seine Estuary on the left to Cape Barfleur on the right was covered by shore batteries. At Le Grand Clos north of Le Havre were three 15in guns originally intended for 'Bismarck' class battleships: their range of 22 miles allowed them to dominate the eastern part of the Baie de la Seine. There was a battery of three 155mm guns at Le Havre itself and at Villerville, Benerville, Houlgate, Le Mont and Merville there were batteries of 4-6 guns each. Three of these were equipped with 155mm guns in protected mountings and two had 150mm weapons in open sites. Between Isigny and Ouistreham there were three protected batteries of 155mm and one of 105mm guns plus two open batteries of 105mm guns and two of 100mm weapons. Along the eastern side of the Cotentin Peninsula were four batteries of 155mm guns in casemates as well as 24 captured Russian 152mm howitzers and 20 105mm field howitzers. The 155mm guns were former French weapons widely used by the Germans for coastal defence purposes. Numerous lighter guns and machine guns covered the beaches which were sown with obstacles, wire and mines.

As more mobile defences, the German Navy deployed the 5th Torpedo Boat Flotilla in the Cherbourg-Le Havre area. This was made up of the old 925-ton Type 23 boats, *Falke, Kondor* and *Mowe*, the slightly larger Type 24 *Jaguar* and the new 1,300-ton Type 39 *T28*. The Type 23 *Grief* had been sunk by a No 415 (RCAF) Squadron Albacore of RAF Coastal Command in the Baie de Seine on 24 May. These small destroyers, as the older boats had originally been classified, were armed with three or four 4.1in guns and six 21in torpedo tubes in two triple mountings. In the Channel area were also 23 S-boats (motor torpedo boats) in the 5th and 9th Flotillas at Cherbourg, the 2nd and 4th at Boulogne and the 8th at Ostend. In addition there were 116 minesweepers, 44 patrol vessels and 42 artillery barges.

Further south, at Bordeaux, losses to British surface forces had reduced German destroyer strength to a single flotilla, the 8th, with four destroyers and a torpedo boat. Three of the destroyers were powerful Type 36A class ships, *Z24, Z32* and *Z37*, armed with five 5.9in guns and eight 21in torpedo tubes; the fourth was *ZH1*, the former Dutch *Gerard Callenburgh* completed by the Germans and armed with five Dutch 4.7in guns, eight German 21in torpedo tubes and German AA armament. *Z37* was non-operational because of serious collision damage and her place had been taken by the last remnant of the 4th Torpedo Boat Flotilla, the Type 39, *T24*. Also between Brest and Bayonne were 146 minesweepers and 59 patrol vessels. Some 49 U-boats, nine of them equipped with snorkels, were assigned for anti-invasion duty, almost half of them at Brest and the rest at St Nazaire, La Pallice and Lorient. The German Navy still deployed significant heavy units and numerous other small craft but these were tied up in Norwegian waters and the Baltic. Considerable hope was, however, placed in newly developed midget submarines and manned torpedoes, as well as top secret pressure mines which it was thought would be unsweepable.

Although the Allies' superior management techniques allowed them to mobilise their strength much more efficiently than the Germans could, their commitments were extensive and global, and Ramsay had not got unlimited resources at his disposal. The combined forces of all the Allies would be required to meet the 'Neptune' requirement of 702 warships. These included battleships, monitors, cruisers and destroyers to neutralise the German coastal defences and to support the Army once it was ashore, plus frigates, destroyer escorts and corvettes to protect the convoys on passage, plus patrol and coastal forces to keep away the enemy fast attack craft and their more exotic mini submersibles. Thanks to the close proximity to the south coast of England, land-based air cover could be relied upon. Nine squadrons of fighters were allocated to cover the assault, six of RAF Spitfires and three of US Army Republic P47 Thunderbolts. In addition four squadrons of US Army Air Force (USAAF) Lockheed P38 Lightnings gave cover in the Channel.

Ramsay organised his vessels into two Task Forces, an Eastern commanded by Rear-Adm Sir Philip Vian flying his flag in the cruiser HMS *Scylla*, and a Western under Rear-Adm Alan G. Kirk USN, with his flag in the American cruiser *Augusta*. The Eastern Force covered the three British and Canadian beaches 'Sword', 'Gold' and 'Juno' while the other Force covered the two American beaches, 'Omaha' and 'Utah'. The nationalities of the landing forces was reflected in those of their naval support. The Task Force Commanders gave instructions to the bombardment forces even though the Commanders of the latter, eg Rear-Adm F. H. G. Dalrymple-Hamilton of the 2nd Cruiser Squadron possessed greater seniority.

The total of 702 warships did not include the massive number of mine countermeasures

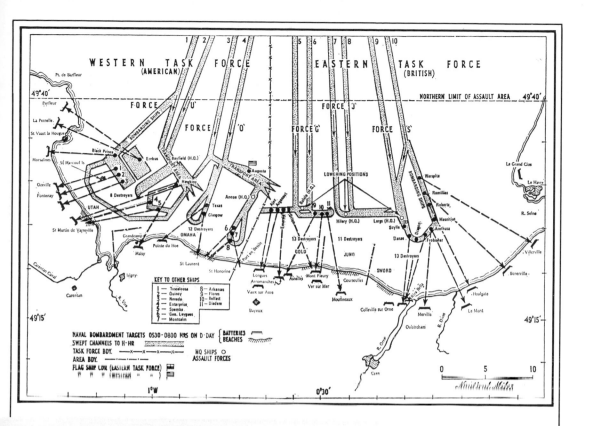

Above:

Operation Neptune: Assault Phase.

Left.

In order to spot for the guns over the beaches, American Navy pilots exchanged their slower seaplanes for British Spitfire fighters. These are Lts Robert F. Doyle and John P. Mudge of VCS7.

US National Archives 80-G-302124

(MCM) vessels required to sweep approach channels to the landing beaches. The plan was for two channels to be cut through the mine barrier for each assault course (each channel required a full fleet minesweeping flotilla), the clearance inshore of a coastal channel for bombardment vessels, the widening of the approach channels and the sweeping of any mines laid subsequently. Some 255 minesweepers and danlayers were required to cut and buoy the approach channels. The allocation of MCM vessels to each Task Force was: Eastern, 42 fleet minesweepers and 87 others; Western, 56 fleet minesweepers and 62 others. Only nine fleet minesweepers and 16 smaller craft in the latter totals were American, the rest were British Empire vessels (including Canadian ships).

The enemy's shore defences would be neutralised by a mixture of naval gunfire support and air attack. Specially trained fighter pilots would spot for the warships, whose priority targets were the heavy fixed batteries. Over 100 warships were allocated, including six battleships. Understandably, for such relatively undemanding duties these were some of the oldest of their type available to the Allies. The three British ships were HMS *Rodney*, powerful but slow and armed with nine 16in guns, the battered veteran of both Narvik and the Mediterranean; HMS *Warspite*, whose damage inflicted by a German guided bomb allowed only six of her 15in guns to be used; and the old unmodernised HMS *Ramillies*, which was reduced to only two operational turrets because of shortage of manpower. The Americans produced the Pearl Harbor survivor USS *Nevada*, launched in 1914 and armed with 10 14in guns; the even older *Texas*, similarly armed but with five turrets instead of four; and the veteran 'Dreadnought' *Arkansas*, armed with 12 12in guns. Also armed with heavy artillery were the two British monitors *Roberts* and *Erebus*, each armed with a twin 15in turret.

There were 23 cruisers available to supplement this heavy artillery. The British deployed two old 7.5in armed 'Hawkins' class ships and four old 6in cruisers of the 'D' and 'E' classes. One of the 'D' class cruisers was officially commissioned in the Polish Navy. There were, however, a number of newer cruisers, *Mauritius*, *Belfast*, *Glasgow*, *Ajax*, *Orion* and *Arethusa*. There were also five 'Didos' armed with eight to 10 5.25in guns and Vian's flagship *Scylla* which had never managed to acquire anything more powerful than eight 4.5in weapons. 13 of the above vessels were allocated to the Eastern Naval Task Force and five to the Western. The Americans contributed only three cruisers to the latter. All were armed with nine 8in guns, the prewar *Augusta* and *Tuscaloosa* and the the six month old *Quincy*. Also operating with the Western Task Force and assisting in the liberation

of their homeland, were two French cruisers, the 7,600-ton sister ships *Montcalm* and *Georges Leygues*, each armed with nine 6in guns.

If the cruiser portion of the bombardment was overwhelmingly British, the destroyers were more evenly matched. There were 28 British and two British-built but Norwegian-manned fleet destroyers, about 30 American destroyers (all from the almost identical 'Gleaves' and 'Benson' classes of just over 1,800 tons standard displacement and armed with four single 5in guns) and about a dozen British built 'Hunt' Class escort destroyers with 4-6 4in guns. About seven other 'Hunts' were with the escort forces. One 'Hunt' was Norwegian-manned, one French and two Polish. Finally the bombardment forces also included two Dutch gunboats, *Soemba* and *Flores*. These 1,500-ton vessels, built for local defence, were armed with three 5.9in guns. One was with each Task Force. Of the above bombardment vessels 73 were allocated to the Eastern sector and 33 to the Western. There were also a large number of specialist fire support landing craft. The escort forces included 31 frigates and destroyer escorts (21 British, six American and four French) and 21 corvettes including two French-manned and two Greek-manned vessels.

A major task for the Naval Command was the organisation of convoys, making the necessary ships and craft available, sailing them to the assembly anchorages and then to the correct beaches. Many ships were taken up from trade, especially large numbers of coasters for use as stores ships. Smaller vessels were more effective in putting ashore ammunition, petrol and other stores than larger vessels. The landing craft, landing ships, motor transport ships and personnel vessels as well as the hundreds of stores coasters assembled all round the British coast from the Thames to the Bristol Channel. The major loading ports for the assault troops were Newhaven, Shoreham, Portsmouth, Southampton, Torquay, Brixham, Dartmouth and Plymouth. The follow-up forces were to load in Plymouth and Falmouth for the Western Sector and Tilbury and Felixstowe for the Eastern. An efficient organisation was set up both to organise movements on the beaches and the movements of ships from the ports to the beachheads and back. In addition to all this, Rear-Adm E. W. Tennant, who had assisted Ramsay with the Dunkirk evacuation and had been one of the few officers to come out of the sinking of the *Repulse* and *Prince of Wales* with much credit (he had been Captain of *Repulse*), was put in charge of two specialised operations about which Ramsay was far from happy. One of these was the 'Mulberry' Harbour Scheme to set up artificial harbours off the beaches and the other was the

'Pluto' System to carry fuel across the Channel through pipelines laid across the sea. It was a tribute to Tennant that both these operations went off as well as they did.

On 10 April Operation 'Neptune' — Naval Orders began to go into typescript using a production line of WRNS typists. The orders themselves comprised 22 parts, 579 pages and the Administrative and Communications Orders brought the total page count to over 1,000. Correlli Barnett has called these documents and Ramsay's Naval Plan they reflected 'a never surpassed masterpiece of planning and staff work', eclipsing any of the performances of the German General Staff. On the 26th Ramsay moved from Norfolk House, London, to his Battle Headquarters at Southwick House near Portsmouth (now HMS *Dryad*). The exact timing of D-Day and H-Hour was not yet known. The landings had to take place between 12min before and 90min after sunrise at three to four hours before high water. There also had to be moonlight for the parachute landings. This limited the choice to between 5 and 7 June and the 18th to 20th. The preference was for the earlier period. H-Hour could not be synchronised because of tidal conditions at different beaches and the actual time of landing varied between 0630 in the west to 0725 in the east.

At the end of April and the beginning of May final rehearsals for the landings took place on various beaches along the south coast of England. As is now well known, the first of these went terribly wrong when a convoy on passage from Brixham and Plymouth to Slapton Sands, west of Dartmouth, was attacked by German S-boats. Two tank landing ships were sunk and a third damaged with the loss of 638 officers and men, 441 of them American soldiers. These were worse casualties than the American formations suffered in the landings themselves. Following this hard lesson, better cover was given to the later exercises at Slapton, Littlehampton, Bracklesham Bay and Hayling Island.

Below:
LST *289* limps into Dartmouth after being torpedoed by a German motor torpedo boat in the attack on the rehearsal landing at Slapton at the end of April 1944.
US National Archives 80-G-257908

Above:
There were casualties. LCI *85*, manned by the US Coast Guard limps alongside a transport to evacuate her crew after being fatally damaged by gunfire. *US National Archives 26-G-61044(4)*

On 25 May the Supreme Commander, Gen Eisenhower, informed Ramsay and his other subordinates that D-Day was to be 5 June. This decision effectively sealed off the landing forces from all unnecessary communications. On 28 May the British minelayers *Plover* and *Apollo*, four flotillas of motor launches and six flotillas of motor torpedo boats assisted by RAF Bomber Command finished laying 6,850 mines in protective fields, mainly between the Dutch ports and Brest. On the 31st, as loading of the assault force began, 10 sonic underwater buoys were laid to mark the edge of the German minefield where the minesweepers were to begin sweeping. The buoys were timed to come into operation on D-1. The weather, however, took a hand. By 2 June Eisenhower was informed that the meteorological situation was 'full of menace'. In the early hours of 4 June Eisenhower decided to postpone the invasion 24hr to 6 June. The signal was transmitted at 0515 to the invasion fleet, some of which was already at sea. The block ships which had sailed from Oban some days before and the bombarding ships from Belfast proceeded to their sheltered anchorages decided upon earlier for just such a contingency.

As the saying goes, however, 'there is always somebody who doesn't get the word' and in this case this was Group 'U2A', a convoy of no less than 138 vessels with four escorts and a rescue tug bound from Devon to 'Utah' Beach. Two destroyers were sent to find it but they ended up in a minefield and a Supermarine Walrus amphibian aircraft had to be sent out from Portsmouth to locate the convoy and persuade it to turn round. As the weather worsened farce turned to near tragedy when an American LCT, 2498, broke down and capsized; happily all were rescued. In fact, 'U2A' had had a very lucky escape: it had romped ahead of its allocated minesweeping flotilla and was sailing straight for the minefield in which the unfortunate destroyers found themselves. The minesweepers had abandoned their sweeping operation because of the bad weather and the two unfortunate destroyers had to wait for them to return when the weather improved. One of these mines scored the first German success in Operation 'Neptune', sinking the American minesweeper *Osprey* on 5 June.

In order to stop troops being landed in the wrong place in the British assault area, two Royal Navy midget submarines, X-20 commanded by Lt

Hudspeth RANVR (who had taken part in Operation 'Source') and X-23 were tasked with marking the beaches. They were towed across the Channel by two trawlers and made their way towards the French coast to be in position by 5 June. When news was received at 0100 that morning that the operation had been postponed the submarines moved out to sea to spend 5 June submerged at the bottom of the Channel. The submarines surfaced once more at 2315, received confirmation that the operation was indeed taking place and then moved back to their assigned positions. They were to wait there submerged until twenty minutes before H-hour when they were to surface and transmit on radio and sonar beacons. They were also to shine a flashing light out to sea and launch a dinghy with a pilotage officer, who was to anchor and use a powerful light to help give the landing craft some indication of their position relative to the beach. In order to avoid being run down, each X-craft displayed a large yellow flag and a white ensign.

As the midget submarines took their first fixes on the evening of 4 June the decisive meeting took place at Southwick House to decide whether the weather conditions would be good enough on the 6th to go ahead. It was decided to keep the 6 June date and this was reconfirmed on the morning of the 5th. The bad weather, in the end, proved an asset to the Allies as it lulled the Germans into a false sense of security. The Commander of German Naval Group West, Adm Krancke, for example, after having told Field Marshal von Rundstedt that his patrol craft could not leave harbour, left for Bordeaux on an inspection tour. When the first paratroops began landing at 0135 surprise was complete.

The assault and support forces began to get under way on 5 June, covered by a formidable umbrella of fighter aircraft. The weather was still rough, which caused some problems, but generally the movements went without a hitch. Some ships moved down Channel and the others moved up Channel to the area known as 'Area Z' or 'Piccadilly Circus', southeast of the Isle of Wight. From this area they proceeded southwards down 'The Spout' of swept channels. Vian left Spithead in HMS Scylla at 1630 and Kirk had sailed from Portland at midday to overtake the American assault groups as they reached 'Piccadilly Circus'. Even 'U2A' was able to get back under way after much hard work repairing storm damage. Some 128 of the 135 LCTs were ready for sea.

As the mass of shipping assembled, the minesweeping operations went into top gear. Leading the force were Harbour Defence Motor Launches fitted with minesweeping gear to protect the minesweepers themselves from hitting mines.

Five swept channels had been selected, leading south-southeastwards. Each split into two just before entering the minefields guarding the French coast, one for fast convoys, the other for slow. Each was swept by one of 10 flotillas of fleet minesweepers with 42 danlaying trawlers following behind laying lighted danbuoys. The main problem was with the minefield already mentioned, a small one laid by a German motor torpedo boat. The main German minefields proved much less extensive than expected. Indeed, the 1st Minesweeping Flotilla, cutting channel 9 in front of 'Sword' Beach, found no mines at all. During the sweeping operations, the positions of the minesweepers were checked by both radar and wire measuring gear and all flotillas laid their final buoys within 200yd of the planned position and within a few minutes of the planned time. The minesweepers then turned to sweep areas parallel to the beaches to provide safe anchorages and unloading points for landing ships and transports. They also had to sweep bombardment channels for the warships. As the Germans were strangely unresponsive and their shore batteries remained silent, their major problem was to keep out of each other's way. They then went on to begin sweeping the spaces between channels 3 and 4 and 5 and 6. It was a considerable oversight on the part of the Germans not to have reinforced their mine barrier or laid more influence mines in shallow water.

One reason for the lack of reaction was that the RAF had systematically put out of action the Kriegsmarine's surface warning radar system during the preceding week. What stations still existed were systematically jammed. The stations north of the Seine were left sufficiently operational to detect the decoy 'convoys' formed of barrage balloons towed by motor launches. The actual invasion fleet was not detected until 0230 off Utah and when coastal forces were ordered to sea by the Germans the effort was spread both north and south of the Seine. As late as 0500 the Germans were still confused and had little idea of what was going on.

At Utah Naval Force 'U' was commanded by Rear-Adm D. P. Moon USN flying his flag in the 16,000-ton attack transport Bayfield. He had 116 amphibious ships and craft in company in 'U2A(1)' when he anchored at 0229, 11.5 miles offshore. In support were the battleship USS Nevada, the monitor HMS Terror, two American heavy cruisers, the Quincy and Tuscaloosa, the 7.5in gun British cruiser Hawkins, the 6in cruiser Enterprise, the 5.25in armed improved 'Dido' Black Prince, the gunboat Soemba and eight USN destroyers. 'U2A(2)' was due at 0330 after all its adventures. Eighteen British and 16 American

minesweepers were completing their work, although their efforts were partially vitiated by the German use of delayed action mines that needed multiple stimulation before going off. The Germans had also laid influence mines on the Cardonnet bank offshore. Two PC-type patrol craft and four Landing Craft Control (LCC) acted as navigational aids for the long run in from the transport area to the shore. It took two hours to move from the transports to the shore and an LCC and an LCT were lost to mines on the Cardonnet Bank.

At 0505 a German shore battery opened fire on the destroyers *Fitch* and *Corry*. A quarter of an hour later the batteries were heavily bombed but they continued in action. When one heavy battery started to attack the minesweepers HMS *Black Prince* replied. The whole bombarding squadron commanded by American Adm Deyo in *Nevada* gave the order for the full bombardment to begin 14min early at 0536. For three quarters of an hour the ships pounded the Germans ashore. At 0610 aircraft began to lay smoke to shield the landing craft but there were gaps and in one of them the destroyer USS *Corry* became a target for the shore batteries. Her manoeuvring took her over a delayed action mine which exploded, breaking the destroyer's back and sinking her.

As the troops landed British fire support LCGs (Landing Craft Gun) opened fire on the beach defences with their 4.7in guns at 700yd and 17 British Landing Craft Tank (Rocket) let fly with their banks of about a 1,000 5in rockets. This had the fortunate effect of putting up such a dust storm that the landing craft allowed themselves to be carried by the tide away from the designated landing ground to a more lightly protected area of beach. The naval gunfire support proved invaluable in neutralising the shore batteries and smashing any opposition to the landing before it could create problems. By 1800 some 21,328 troops, 1,742 vehicles and 1,695 tons of stores had been landed.

The other American beach, 'Omaha', was a different story. Faulty intelligence underrated the opposition and the terrain favoured the defenders. Force 'O' was commanded by Rear-Adm John Hall USN and his bombardment force, coded 'C' was under Rear-Adm C. F. Bryant flying his flag in the USS *Texas*. Force 'C' was a mixed Allied group composed of the American battleship *Arkansas*, the British cruiser *Glasgow*, the French cruisers *Georges Leygues* and *Montcalm* and seven American destroyers. Group 'O1' following contained Hall's specialised command ship *Ancon*, 15 transports, 33 large infantry landing craft and two Landing Craft Headquarters (LCHs); it was escorted by two American and three British destroyers. Finally there was Group 'O2', the slow convoy of 267 craft of various kinds.

The bombarding ships anchored at 0220 and at 0250 'O1' anchored in the transport area 11 miles offshore. This created immediate problems as the waters were less sheltered than off 'Utah' and were less suitable for lowering and manning the small assault craft. As at 'Utah', German shore batteries opened fire first and *Arkansas* fired in reply at 0530, 20min before the bombardment was due to begin. The planned bombing of the defences went astray and the bombarding ships did not have enough time to neutralise the defences which took a heavy toll of the American soldiers as they waded ashore. Some of the LCCs drifted out of position which added to the confusion. The troops in the Western section of 'Omaha' were particularly hard pressed as many of their amphibious tanks had sunk on the run-in. The situation was saved by the destroyers closing the beach to blast away opposition with well placed 5in shells; these ships were also supported by armed landing craft. Hall kept the troops flowing ashore and by the middle of the day the landings were becoming established. Much effort was wasted against a battery of telegraph poles that was thought to be a powerful shore battery at Pointe de Hoc. This consumed the efforts of the battleship *Texas*, a British 'Hunt' class escort destroyer and an American destroyer as well as three companies of US Rangers, all of which might have been better employed elsewhere. By 1715 the US Army's 1st Division was able to establish its HQ ashore but it had already lost some 4,000 men killed and wounded.

Things were better at 'Gold' Beach. Force 'G', of 243 amphibious vessels, was commanded by Cdre C. E. Douglas-Pennant in the 9,100-ton HQ Ship (LSH(L)) *Bulolo*, a former armed merchant cruiser bristling with antennae for communications equipment. His associated bombardment squadron, Force 'K' consisted of the 6in cruisers *Orion*, *Ajax* and *Emerald*, the 5.25in cruiser *Argonaut*, the gunboat *Flores* and 14 destroyers. In the Support Force were three Landing Craft Gun (Large), seven Landing Craft Tank (Rocket), four Landing Craft Support (Light) armed with 2pdr armoured car or 6pdr tank turrets forward, 20mm guns and a smoke mortar, seven LCFs (Landing Craft Flak) with 20mm guns and 2pdr pom-poms and 16 armoured LCTs (LCT(A)s) carrying Centaur close support tanks armed with 95mm howitzers. The bombardment began at 0545 and all but one battery was silenced. The four casemated 6.1in guns at Longues proved hard to destroy but after they had forced *Bululo* to shift berth they were finally knocked out by *Ajax*. Another strong point at Le Hamel missed being engaged by the LCT(A)s and it also proved impervious to destroyer fire; it was finally knocked out at 1600 by LCG(L)s and LCFs. Vian was able to share in the action at 'Gold' when HMS *Scylla* fired 40 rounds of 4.5in at Arromanches that was taken at 2100 that evening.

The terrain at 'Juno' was potentially a problem but the defences were not strong being manned by a formation with a high proportion of Russians and Poles. Cdre G. N Oliver was in command of the 187 amphibious ships of Force 'J' in the 11,250 ton LSH(L) *Hilary* and the bombarding Force 'E' under Rear-Adm Dalrymple Hamilton comprised the cruisers *Belfast* and *Diadem*, eight British and two Canadian destroyers and one Free French 'Hunt'. The Support Force was made up of seven LCG(L)s, eight LCT(R)s, six LCS(L)s, six LCFs, eight LCT(A)s, and eight unarmoured but Centaur-equipped LCT(HE)s. Navigational errors and heavy weather postponed H-Hour to 0745-55 but the heavy bombardment by the Bombardment and Support Force vessels, coupled with numerous air strikes helped the Canadian troops establish themselves ashore without undue difficulty. Useful support was also given by nine Landing Craft Assault (Hedgerow) armed with 24 6pdr mortars. In the late morning the Reserve Brigade Group began to come ashore and in the evening Gen Montgomery's Army Group HQ and the 51st Highland Division arrived in Group L1, 13 LSTs , the dock landing ship (LSD) *Northway* and four coasters.

'Sword' Beach, like 'Juno' was not well protected, although the Allied command was worried about its proximity to the heavy batteries in the Le Havre area. Ramsay and his staff need not have worried quite so much as air bombardment put out of action the heaviest battery of 15in weapons and other heavy batteries thought to be in the immediate area were either not manned or had been removed. Nevertheless Rear-Adm A. G. Talbot commanding the 285 vessels of Force 'S' from the 5,850-ton LSH(L) *Largs* was allocated a strong bombardment group, Force 'D'. Commanded by Rear-Adm Patterson flying his flag in the cruiser *Mauritius* it consisted of the partially operational 15in gun battleships *Warspite* and *Ramillies*, the similarly armed monitor *Roberts*, the 7.5in cruiser *Frobisher*, the small 6in cruisers *Arethusa* and *Danae* and the latter's Polish sister ship *Dragon*. There were 13 destroyers and the Support Force of Force 'S' was made up of three LCG(L)s, five LCT(R)s, three LCS(L)s, four LCFs and eight LCT(A)s.

The battleships, monitor and *Arethusa* anchored without incident in their bombarding positions and the rest of the cruisers from Force 'D' reinforced by Vian's flagship *Scylla* took up position in their swept loop. As the amphibious ships were entering the area for them to lower their assault craft the Germans' 5th Torpedo Boat Flotilla put in a daring attack. *Kondor* had mechanical defects and stayed at Le Havre but the other four boats launched 15 torpedoes. Two passed between the pair of battleships and one near-missed *Largs* which had to take avoiding action. Less lucky was the Norwegian destroyer *Svenner* of the British 'S' class which was hit amidships, broke in two and sank. *Warspite* used radar to engage the German ships with her 6in secondary battery and *Ramillies*, *Mauritius* and *Arethusa* all opened fire also but the Germans escaped unscathed.

The other opposition came from shore batteries and *Warspite* had to shift berth to avoid the fire of one especially troublesome 155mm battery at Bennerville. Repeated bombardment was necessary to keep the batteries subdued. *Mauritius* and *Arethusa* also provided gunfire support for the paratroopers dropped to secure the vital bridges leading from the beach head. The main problem at 'Sword' was congestion rather than enemy action but nevertheless seven landing craft were lost to obstacles, mines and mortar bombs during the morning of 6 June. Total losses of landing craft on all beaches on D-Day were as many as 304, about half to mined obstacles, but nevertheless over 70,000 troops had been landed in the British-Canadian sector alone.

Allied commando forces were landed on the flanks of the main landings. Some of these operations ran into trouble, like No 47 Commando's attempt to take Port-en-Bessin. This only suc-

Above right:
The modified 'Dido' class cruiser *Diadem* supported the landings at 'Juno' beach and was later damaged in collision in the great gale. Her initial targets were the four 105mm guns at Beny-sur-Mer.
Real Photographs/ Ian Allan Collection

Right:
An LST moves into the 'Mulberry' harbour at St Laurent off 'Omaha' beach. The life of this Mulberry was cut short by the great gale.
Ian Allan Collection

ceeded on 7 June, covered by the 6in guns of HMS *Emerald*, a battery of 25pdrs near Arromanches and RAF rocket firing Hawker Typhoons. No 41 Commando also was unable to take its first objective at Lion-sur-Mer until the 7th despite two hours of bombardment by supporting destroyers the previous afternoon. All the Allied forces continued to receive welcome NGS in the days after D-Day which materially contributed to their advances. The Germans were prevented from making effective counter-attacks as much by the fire of the warships as by air attacks, the big shells of the battleships proving especially effective. Both ground and airborne spotters were used. On 8 June the USS *Nevada* had a particularly effective shoot when she destroyed 110 German vehicles with 70 14in shells fired at 23,500yd. The German shore batteries some of which remained in action until actually overrun, were ineffective in reply in the early days after the landings. Smoke, electronic countermeasures and bombardment prevented a single hit being scored.

To defend the landings area the Task Force Commanders divided the assault area into various sub-areas (see map). Kirk placed a division of destroyers in sub-area 'Prairie' and radar pickets in the northern parts of 'Kansas' and 'Ohio'. The 'Mason Line' was patrolled by motor torpedo boats. Later coastal forces, both MTBs and larger steam gunboats (SGBs) were place in the northwestern part of sub-area 'Mountain' to catch enemy forces rounding Cape Barfleur. In the Eastern area Vian anchored fleet minesweepers half-a-mile apart in a line six miles offshore. From the eastern end of this line another known as 'Trout' ran at right angles towards the eastern edge of 'Sword'. The latter was kept by LCGs and LCFs anchored 200yd apart. Three divisions of MTBs were stationed in the northwest corner of Vian's defence perimeter and destroyers patrolled north and south in the western part of sub-area 'Tunny'. A Captain of Patrols commanded the eastern defences from a frigate or destroyer in the inner defence area; Vian used *Scylla*'s newly-developed operations room where the radar picture was compiled into a surface plot to control his sector with the cruiser anchored 5,000yd inside the northeastern corner of the outer defence line. This action information organisation was of more importance than the light calibre of the cruiser's main armament.

The German plan of campaign was to use the S-Boat flotillas at Cherbourg to mount torpedo attacks and lay mines in the American assault area while the flotillas at Boulogne were to do the same in the British and Canadian sector. The flotilla at Ostend was to operate in the Eastern Channel and

another flotilla, the 6th, was redeployed from the Baltic. The S-boats laid influence mines with magnetic and acoustic pistols but the most important weapons were those with the new pressure fuses for which Hitler had finally granted release. Aircraft were also used as minelayers after 9 June once the Luftwaffe's stock of pressure mines had been delivered from Magdeburg. Delayed action and anti-sweeping devices made mine countermeasures difficult and the new pressure mines were either unsweepable or only sweepable in suitable weather, depending on the type. If they had been laid prior to the landings they might have disrupted the entire invasion . As it was, 11 vessels were mined in the 10 days after D-Day in the Eastern Sector; these included two hospital carriers and a minesweeper but only one ship was actually sunk, the Trinity House vessel *Alert*. In the American sector the problem was greatest in the west off 'Omaha' and the destroyer *Glennon* and destroyer escort *Rich* were sunk. Two MCM vessels were sunk and 25 other craft damaged. Eventually a pressure mine was accidentally dropped ashore and dismantled; it was discovered that slowing down to four knots in danger areas defeated the new fuse.

On the first night after the landings the Germans mounted air attacks. A trawler shot one aircraft down over Vian's sector and shortly after dawn a German bomber hit HMS *Bulolo* with an incendiary bomb. This inflicted a few casualties but caused no serious damage. In the American sector the USS *Ancon* was near missed but, more seriously, the Germans scored a direct hit on the destroyer *Meredith* with an Henschel Hs 293 radio-controlled glider bomb. The ship later sank. One enemy aircraft was shot down in these attacks. There was also a battle between S-boats and British coastal forces off Le Havre in which the Germans suffered some damage. On the night of 6-7 June the 5th and 9th S-boat flotillas were engaged by the Allied patrols off Cape Barfleur. Some of the German MTBs penetrated 'The Spout' and attacked a convoy of LCTs and large infantry landing craft (LCI(L)s). The convoy was ably defended by the motor launch ML *903* assisted by the fire of the landing craft but two of the latter were sunk and another damaged. The Germans lost two of the attackers to mines on their way home. The following night the S-boats were back attacking Convoy EBC3 of 17 vessels. There was an escort destroyer present this time, the old 'V/W' HMS *Watchman* and she drove the Germans off. Less lucky was ECM1 of 16 LSTs and 15 Motor Transport (MT) ships attacked on the western flank to the east of Cape Barfleur: LSTs *314* and *376* were sunk.

The torpedo boats at Le Havre mounted attacks on the night of the 6/7th, 8/9th, 9/10th and 12/13th but without result. On D-Day the 8th Destroyer Flotilla was ordered north to join them. The departure of the three destroyers from Bordeaux was soon known to the British who launched a strike of 14 Canadian rocket-firing Bristol Beaufighter aircraft to deal with them. Another squadron of 17 Beaufighters flew in support to suppress AA fire with their guns and a further eight flew in escort. The fighters spotted the enemy 30 miles west of the Isle de Normoutier at 2030. One group of four rocket-firing Canadian aircraft near missed *ZH1*, the leading ship, trying for hits below the waterline but no damage was inflicted. Then nine rocket firing aircraft took on Z32 and the last Beaufighter to attack took on *Z24*. Although the Canadians inflicted superficial damage and killed 25 officers and men the attack was a failure and the destroyers reached Brest to join *T24*. It seems strange that the Allied aircraft were not more heavily armed, with bombs or even torpedoes, but range was probably a problem.

Both Type 36As had their AA armament augmented before venturing forth again. The four ships of the 8th Flotilla sailed from Brest escorted by minesweepers on the evening of 8 June to attack the landings off Normandy. It was the German Navy's most important throw and the Admiralty took no chances. Forewarned by 'Ultra' it ordered C-in-C Plymouth to send the powerful 10th Destroyer Flotilla from Devonport to intercept. The Allied force consisted of the 19th Division with four 'Tribals' — HMS *Tartar* and

Ashanti, and HMCS *Huron* and *Haida* — and the 20th Division, with two Polish ships the 2,000-ton, 39kt *Blyskawika* built at Cowes in the late 1930s and rearmed like an AA cruiser with eight 4in guns, and the British-built 'N' Class ship *Piorun*; the rest of the Division were British-manned, the 'Tribal' HMS *Eskimo* and the slightly smaller *Javelin*.

The Allied ships spotted the German flotilla on radar at just after 0115 and turned to starboard to make a torpedo attack. This exposed them to the moonlight and the Germans in turn spotted the enemy just as *Tartar* illuminated with starshell. The Germans turned to port to comb the expected torpedoes and to mount their own torpedo attack. The three leading German ships each fired four G7as forward on the starboard beam. The British were overhearing the German tactical radio net and the 19th Division turned to port in good time to avoid the German weapons. The 'Tribals' used one forward mount for starshell and the other for effect and in line abreast hit the Ger-

man destroyers hard as they turned to port across the Division's bows creating perfect targets. *Z32* was hit twice and *ZH1* six times, two serious 4.7in hits in the boiler and turbine rooms bringing the ship to a standstill. Then it was the turn of *Z24*, whose wheelhouse and charthouse was destroyed and whose forward 5.9in turret was isolated. She sheered off leading *T24* out of further danger but received more hits as she did so.

Z32 ran northwestwards into the other Allied destroyer division which hit her about 20 times with 4in and 4.7in shells. The German ship fired four torpedoes and then made off to the west. This attack caused confusion to the Polish and British ships; *Blyskawica* turned away, and lost contact with *Piorun*; the RN pair thought this was a turn to launch torpedoes and fired a total of seven Mk IXs. They then formed up on *Blyskawica*. *Z32* now ran into *Tartar* and *Ashanti* once more and another fire-fight developed. Hits were scored by both sides and the big German shells slowed *Tartar* down and set her on fire. As *Z32* retired to reload her tubes *ZH1* moved to the centre of the action. She engaged the damaged *Tartar* but then had her bows blown off by a Mk IX torpedo from *Ashanti*. Having attempted to continue to engage her attackers with both guns and torpedoes *ZH1* was scuttled by her own crew with depth charges.

Z24 and *T24* made off to the south pursued by the pair of Canadian destroyers. The latter were, however, called back to look after *Tartar*. The two German ships turned back but were then released by Kapt von Bechtelsheim in *Z32* to return to Brest when the extent of *Z24*'s damage was signalled through. The leader, however, was sighted by the Canadian destroyers which gave chase to the eastward, the rest of the 10th Flotilla in pursuit. The German sailed right over an Allied minefield which caused the Canadians to break away but then turned back, not wanting to be caught in daylight too far up Channel. The two Canadian destroyers intercepted and a running fight developed on parallel westerly courses. The German destroyer was outnumbered and blasted by repeated 4.7in hits. After being reduced to one gun, running out of ammunition and being unable to launch more torpedoes after a last pair of G7as at 0445 because of damaged davits, the battered *Z32* was run ashore on the Isle de Batz. RAF Coastal Command Beaufighters shattered the stranded and evacuated wreck with bombs and rockets later in the day.

On the night of the 9th, Boulogne S-boats successfully attacked two ammunition carrying coasters after an unsuccessful attack on a convoy. The following night S-boats did especially well, blowing off the bows of the American built frigate HMS *Halsted* with a torpedo and sinking four Allied tugs two of which were hauling parts of 'Mulberrys'. On the night of the 11/12th another part of a 'Mulberry' was sunk although the 'Hunt' class destroyer HMS *Talybont* sank two S-boats. The last time the German fast attack craft were able to mount attacks was on the 12th/13th when three were sunk by aircraft on the return journey after abortive missions.

On the evening of 14 June, at Ramsay's request, the whole panoply of RAF Bomber Command was unleashed on Le Havre: 335 Lancasters and 13 Mosquitoes escorted by Spitfires of No 11 Gp ADGB dropped over 1,000 tons of bombs including 22 12,000lb 'Tallboys' courtesy of No 617 Squadron. The German Navy based there was massacred. *Falke*, *Jaguar* and *Mowe* were sunk along with 10 S-boats — the main target of the attack — 17 minesweepers and patrol craft, three landing craft, a gun carrier and five tugs. *T28*, four S-boats, four minesweepers and eight other craft were damaged. One reason for this 'catastrophe' as Adm Krancke called it, was that the AA guns had been silent to allow the Luftwaffe to operate. On the following evening Bomber Command neutralised Boulogne also and the S-boats were reduced to isolated minelaying sorties. The Luftwaffe could only claim a limited revenge; it bombed and sank the 'Captain' class frigate *Lawford* on the night of the 8/9th and a merchantman on the 9/10th.

Much had been expected of the German U-boats but the '*Landwirt*' pack (as the 36 boats on anti-invasion duty were known) had little success against massive defences informed by 'Ultra' decrypts. Despite orders from Doenitz, the U-Boat Commander, Rear-Adm Godt, only sent Schnorkel-equipped boats into the landing area; it would have been suicide for the other submarines. The non-Schnorkel boats at Brest were sent on the surface to patrol between the Lizard and Hartland Point. Operation 'Cork', concentrated patrolling by aircraft and surface ships in what Ramsay called a 'solid wall' led to 22 attacks in the South Western Approaches in the first 48hr. *U970* and a boat returning from the Atlantic were sunk and seven others had to return to base with damage. Between 8-10 June, despite revised orders to proceed submerged, four more non-Schnorkel U-boats were sunk and the remainder of those without Schnorkels were ordered home from the Western Channel on 11 June. The eight Schnorkel boats in '*Landwirt*' were reinforced by four more from Germany which were sent into the Channel straight from their passages south. On 15 June the Schnorkel U-boat *U621* attacked a convoy of LSTs but was let down by her torpedoes which exploded prematurely; she had to be

Above:
The old target battleship HMS *Centurion* was sunk at one of the 'Gooseberry' breakwaters to provide shelter for the beaches.
US National Archives 26-G-2963

satisfied with a small landing craft that was hardly worth the T5 homing torpedo used. U-boats also had two successes against the Channel anti-submarine patrol lines. They were able to sink two British frigates, the 'River' class ship *Mourne* and the 'Captain' class *Blackwood*. Nevertheless no British major amphibious or merchant ship was sunk by a U-boat in the 21 days after 6 June; this was a considerable success for the ASW forces given the poor radar and sonar conditions. Two ships were, however lost to shore batteries when transitting the Dover straits.

The main naval problems post invasion were organising the mass of shipping required to support the build-up of the Allied armies. Over 200 supply ships and major amphibious vessels arrived off the beaches every day. From the 7th onwards the blockships, coded 'Gooseberrys', began to arrive to be sunk to protect the anchorages; these included old warships, the French battleship *Courbet*, British target ship *Centurion*, Dutch cruiser *Sumatra* and British cruiser *Durban*, flagship of the sad convoy of doomed vessels. Problems arose as the delivery of men and material fell behind schedule at 'Omaha', but despite unloading difficulties and the loss of the American transport *Susan B. Anthony* to a mine on 7 June, deliveries were back on schedule by 13 June. In the circumstances, mistakes and foul-ups were remarkably few. By the 15th the 'Mulberrys' themselves were taking shape — 'A' off 'Omaha' and 'B' off 'Gold', but early on 19 June a great gale blew up that suspended convoys and destroyed Mulberry 'A'. Eight-hundred craft of all kinds were driven ashore and limited deliveries only began again as the gale blew itself out on the 22nd.

The gale was the greatest problem 'Neptune' faced, being more significant than any challenge launched by the Germans. As mines with delayed action fuses became activated and new mines were laid the focus shifted from the American sector — where 10 warships and 324 other craft were lost or damaged in the first two weeks — to the British. Between 23-24 June only the destroyer USS *Davies* was mined in the West while 12 warships and seven other vessels were mined in Vian's area. The destroyer *Swift*, a trawler and two small minesweepers were sunk along with three MT ships and an LCH. Even *Scylla*, Vian's flagship, was damaged and the Admiral's Staff had to transfer to HMS *Hilary*. After this the mine threat

Legend:
- LCA FORMATIONS
- HEADQUARTERS SHIP
- LS INFANTRY
- LC INFANTRY
- LC TANKS
- LC HQ's & MLs
- MAJOR SUPPORT CRAFT

GROUP		GROUP COMPOSITION	LEAVE L P	TOUCH DOWN
1	ML — LCH — LOWERING POSITION	2 LC (NAVn) 1 LC (HQ) 1 ML 8 LCT DD Tanks 3 LCS (L) 3 LCG (L) 8 (LCP)	H -125	H -7.5
2	10 LCA — LOWERING POSITION — 10 LCA	1 LCH 10 LCT (AVRE) 20 LCA Ass Coys 2 LCF 9 LCA (HR) 8 LCT (A) 1 LCT (CB)	H -90	H HOUR
3		5 LCT (R)	H -76	
4	GRP4A 33rd FD RT GRP4 76th FD RT GP4B 7th FD RT	18 LCT (SP) 3 MLs	H -65	GP4= H +75 GP4A= H + 105 GP4B= H +195
5	22 LCA 18 LCA	2 LCF 40 LCA Res Ass Coys LCOCUBE	H -60	H +20
6	8 LCA 6 LCA 8 LCA	2 LCI (L) 14 LCA (C'dos) 8 LCA (Towed) RE	H -50	H +30
7		9 LCT (Priority Vehicles) 3 LCT (Wading Tanks)	H -40	H +45
8	18 LCA	3 LCI (L) 18 LCA (Reserve Bn)	H -20	H +60
9		12 LCI (S) Commandos	H +35	H +75
9A		10 LCI (S) Commandos	H +65	H +105
10		9 LCT (2nd Priority Vehicles) 2 LCT Stores	H +35	H +120

faded but mobile gun batteries put pressure on 'Sword' beach. Several vessels were hit and it was decided to close the beach, first to personnel and then to all traffic.

The Germans tried another U-boat offensive but 'Ultra' gave good warning and all available Support Groups were sent from the Atlantic to seal off the Channel. *U971* was sunk by aircraft on 24 June and the following day the frigate *Bickerton* sank *U269*. Her sister *Goodson* had her stern blown off by a T5 later on the 25th but the frigates *Affleck* and *Balfour* dispatched *U1191* that night. The continuing bad weather that followed helped the German submarines which crippled the corvette HMS *Pink* on the 25th and sank the troopship *Maid of Orleans* on the 28th, 35 miles south of Selsey Bill when convoy FXP18 was attacked. The following day, close by, four Liberty ships were torpedoed but none was sunk in convoy ECM18 and finally *Empire Portia* in northbound convoy FMT 22 was torpedoed but again not fatally. That evening off Start Point *U988* was damaged by a Consolidated B-24 Liberator and finished off by the four frigates of the 3rd Escort Group the following morning. The U-boats continued to struggle against the ASW defences in the Channel but 30 were sunk in July and August and the offensive was an expensive failure.

The destruction of Mulberry 'A' made the capture of a port more attractive and the last phase of 'Neptune' became operations against Cherbourg and its defences. These were formidable with three batteries of 11in and 20 of 5.9in guns, most in protected installations, as well as numerous lighter guns. When it became clear that resistance at Cherbourg would not collapse, as originally hoped, Task Force 129 was formed under Rear-Adm Deyo. It consisted of two units: Group 1, with the cruisers USS *Tuscaloosa* (flag), USS *Quincy*, HMS *Glasgow*, HMS *Enterprise* and the battleship USS *Nevada* escorted by six US destroyers; and Group 2 with the battleships USS *Texas* (flagship of Rear-Adm Bryant) and *Arkansas* and five American destroyers. Each Group had an attached Minesweeping Flotilla: the 9th supported Group 1 with its eight fleet minesweepers, four danlayers and five motor launches while the 159th supported Group 2 with eight American minesweepers, a danlayer and four motor launches.

TF 129 assembled at Portland and sailed at 0430 on 25 June. The American Army commander ashore cancelled the long range fire plan as he feared casualties to his own troops and the two Groups closed the coast to provide close support. The German batteries met them with the heaviest fire of the whole 'Neptune' operation. Deyo ordered off the minesweepers which were sitting ducks and which had found no mines. The two British cruisers then duelled with the battery at Querqueville which hit *Glasgow* in the hangar and the after superstructure. USN Kingfishers and RAF Spitfires provided spotting. It took 318

rounds of 6in to silence the battery, and then only temporarily. The American ships in Group 1 tried to support the troops ashore but they too had to shift fire to the shore batteries because of the latter's accurate shooting.

Bryant got involved with the naval 11in guns of the 'Hamburg' battery south of Cap Levi. These four weapons should have been silenced by the *Nevada* firing from their blind side in the long range preliminary bombardment. It was left to the *Texas* to take the battery under fire and the old American 'Super-Dreadnought' scored a direct hit on one gun with a 14in shell. Despite a destroyer smoke screen the German naval gunners got their revenge at 1316 when they hit the battleship on the bridge structure killing the helmsman. The warships stuck it out until 1500 at the request of the troops ashore and when TF 129 withdrew all but one of its major ships had been hit or damaged by fragments; the captain of *Enterprise* had been wounded. Three of the destroyers had also been hit and all the rest near missed. Fourteen men in the force had been killed but Gen Collins of VII Corps was appreciative of the support given by the ships and the diversion they achieved. The last resistance in Cherbourg ceased on the 27th but it took great efforts by salvage and mine disposal teams to get the port back in action once more. It was fully operational in September 1944.

With the capture of Cherbourg, Ramsay began to disperse his forces involved as both the Admiralty and the US Navy had pressing commitments elsewhere. The landing beaches still had to be defended however, especially as the Germans started using the *Kleinkampfmittel Verband*, the Small Battle Force or 'K' Force, formed by Vice-Adm Hellmuth Heye earlier in the year. A device called 'Neger' ('Nigger') had already been employed by the 'K' Force in the Mediterranean in April. It consisted of a electric torpedo fitted with a pilot's compartment carrying a similar torpedo with a warhead slung beneath it. The *Neger* operated awash and was designed to close enemy ships and release its armed torpedo towards the enemy. In May, despite Allied air attacks, the 'K' Force began to redeploy to the Atlantic coast and by the end of June a base for manned torpedoes had been established at Villers Sur Mer, 11 nautical miles east of the invasion area. The base also received improved equipment, the lengthened 'Marder' ('Marten'), that was capable of submerged operation. The sources are confused as to whether the human torpedoes used in the attacks on the Normandy beach head were *Negers* or *Marders*; both seem to have been used and the following will use the generic term 'manned torpedo'. In addition to these devices, 30 'Linse' explosive motor boats were sent to Le Havre.

These were intended to be pointed at their targets by their pilots who would then abandon them leaving them to complete their runs under the control of radio equipped command boats.

The first to attack were the *Linsen* on the night of 25-26 June but it all ended in fiasco. The range of the boats was insufficient to reach the landing area unassisted and they had to be towed by motor minesweepers. Nine explosive boats and eight radio control boats were committed but the weather was bad. One explosive boat blew up sinking its tow, *R-46*, and other *Linsen* foundered in the choppy sea. Half a dozen boats reached the Orne and tried to attack but were driven ashore.

The manned torpedoes had their turn on the night of 5-6 July. The anchored minesweepers of the offshore defence line were at most risk and two, *Cato* and *Magic*, were torpedoed and sunk. The 'Captain' class frigate HMS *Trollope* was also damaged. At least four manned torpedoes were sunk by Allied forces and only 13 returned. Twenty-one tried again on the night of 8-9 July and one piloted by Midshipman Potthast, a veteran of the *Neger* attacks off Anzio, torpedoed and blew the stern off the old Polish cruiser *Dragon*; the former British ship was expended as a Gooseberry. Potthast was spotted by the minesweeper *Orestes* and his craft shot up with 20mm fire; the intrepid operator was wounded and taken prisoner. The same night the minesweeper *Plyades* was sunk and two more were damaged; a manned torpedo also exploded when under fire from MTB *463*, taking the boat with it. None of the manned torpedoes returned, four being finished off by Fleet Air Arm Seafires on the morning of the 9th.

The 'Trout Line' was strengthened to cope with these attacks. A Support Squadron Eastern Flank was formed under Cdr K. A. Sellar. He deployed about 80 vessels, shallow draft armed landing craft in fixed positions, LCFs, LCGs, LCSs and even LCT(R)s, with Motor Launches patrolling behind them. MTBs and MGBs formed an outer picket and heavier warships also patrolled the area, not without hazard. On the night of 19-20 July the prewar destroyer HMS *Isis* was on patrol watching out for the 'K' Force when she was sunk by a large underwater explosion. Manned torpedoes were out that night and might have been responsi-

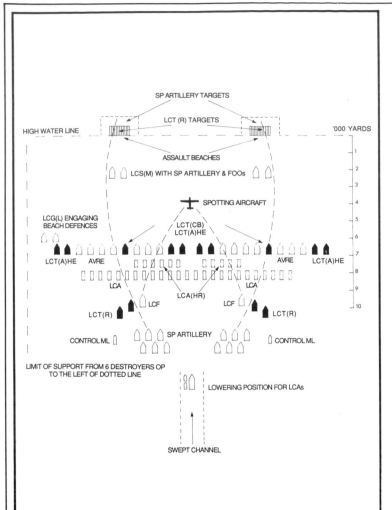

SP ARTILLERY TARGETS

LCT (R) TARGETS

HIGH WATER LINE

'000 YARDS

ASSAULT BEACHES

LCS(M) WITH SP ARTILLERY & FOOs

SPOTTING AIRCRAFT

LCG(L) ENGAGING
BEACH DEFENCES

LCT(CB)
LCT(A)HE

LCT(A)HE   AVRE

AVRE   LCT(A)HE

LCA

LCA(HR)   LCA

LCF   LCF

LCT(R)   LCT(R)

CONTROL ML   SP ARTILLERY   CONTROL ML

LIMIT OF SUPPORT FROM 6 DESTROYERS OP
TO THE LEFT OF DOTTED LINE

LOWERING POSITION FOR LCAs

SWEPT CHANNEL

Left:
Typical deployment for the close range support of the left-hand brigade of a divisional assault.

Below right:
Map showing defence lines and patrol areas established by Eastern and Western Task Forces.

ble but the more likely cause of the ship's loss was a mine.

Kapt Bohme, the director of 'K' Force operations, planned a major attack to break the 'Trout Line'. This took place on the night of 2-3 August. Kapitanleutnant Bastian of Small Battle Unit 211 placed in command of the attack was now operating 28 explosive *Linsen* and 16 control boats from Houlgate only 15nm from the invasion area. Bohme supported Bastian with no less than 58 manned torpedoes, all *Marders* on this occasion. The withdrawal of the 'K' Forces was to be further supported by S-boats which should have been carrying the new T3d '*Dackel*' ('Dachshund') very long-range pattern running torpedo. Allied bombing of Le Havre prevented the German MTBs obtaining their new equipment but aircraft supporting the 'K' Forces' attack were equipped with the latest pattern running airborne torpedoes.

Bohme's aim was to draw the Allies northwards with the first wave of *Marders*. There are reports that the Germans also dropped decoys, plexiglass buoys, to simulate the appearance of the real manned torpedoes and cause extra confusion. The first *Marder* operators launched their armed torpedoes at about 0200. The wreck of the *Dragon* proved a tempting target and was torpedoed again but more serious was a hit on the 'Hunt' class escort destroyer *Quorn* that was sunk. As the northern end of the 'Trout Line' became a confusion of starshell, depth charges and tracer the *Linsen* mounted their charge. The armed trawler *Gateshead* and ML *185* exploded four with gunfire almost immediately, the first of 18 kills by the defenders. There was only one confirmed success for the boats, LCG(L)-*764*. The armed landing craft succeeded in sinking a control boat but was then rammed by two explosive *Linsen*. In the confusion of the combined attacks the armed trawler Gairsay was also sunk and two merchantmen badly damaged, one terminally.

As the surviving Linsen withdrew the second wave of Marders moved in. In the dawn twilight their crews had little chance. Although the Marder could submerge it had to operate on the surface for its pilot to see anything. MTBs sank five with gunfire and other vessels disposed of another 10. With the dawn six more were destroyed by RAF Spitfires as the MTBs held off the supporting S-boats. Attempts were made to recover both a Marder and Linse (dubbed 'Weasel' by the British) but none succeeded and the escort destroyer Blencathra was slightly damaged by the Marder it was trying to pick up exploded.

The combined attack had not really repaid the investment. Linsen were used again on the night of 8-9 August, but were held off by the defences. Some 28 were committed, 16 explosive and 12 control boats, and only eight of the control boats survived. Up to five Linsen were destroyed by 4in and 20mm fire from LCF-1 and four by MTB-714 in close range combat. Dackel torpedoes also began to be fired into the anchorage off the beach-head using S-boats and rafts and the Luftwaffe continued to drop pattern runners. No ships were sunk but two repair ships deployed to salvage the many damaged landing craft, the former cruiser Vindictive and former seaplane carrier Albatross were damaged as was a freighter and a minesweeper.

The 'K' Force made its last throw on the nights of 15-16 and 16-17 August. On the first night 14 Marders were despatched of which half were lost in the poor conditions for no result. On the second night a massed attack by 42 manned torpedoes was largely wasted as their pilots were diverted into attacking the blockship Courbet which the Allies deceived the Germans into thinking was a fully operational Free French battleship. She absorbed two torpedoes that might have found more valuable targets. The only successes for the Germans were an LCF and a barrage balloon vessel sunk in return for 26 of their manned torpedoes. LCS(L)-251 succeeded in recovering a Marder that it had disabled with 6pdr. and 20mm fire. This was the last attack on the Normandy beach head by these devices that had proved to be more dangerous to their operators than to the enemy.

By the end of the month 22 larger one-man midget submarines of the 'Biber' ('Beaver') type were brought to Fécamp near Le Havre and 14 sortied on the night of 29-30 August. Weather was poor and, although the midgets claimed two torpedo hits, no results were achieved. The Bibers had many of the problems of the other weapons used by the hapless 'K' Force — they were hard to control and had to attack on the surface against a foe sensitised to small, moving objects. In the end, they had to be destroyed only the day after their first attack when the Allied forces closed in on their base. The 'K' Force had never been a serious

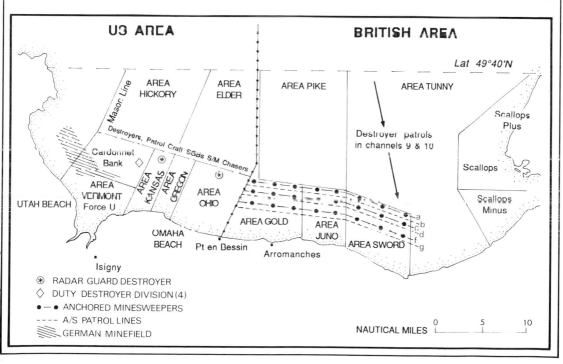

threat but it had been a significant nuisance to the Allies and it necessitated much effort in counter-measures.

As the Allied armies moved up the French coast Ramsay's remaining warships continued to give support, *Warspite* assisting in operations against Brest and Le Havre. The capture and opening of ports allowed the Normandy beaches to be finally closed and the last one ceased receiving cargo on 7 September 1944. Sadly, Ramsay, who trans-ferred his HQ to France on 8 September was killed in an air crash on 2 January 1945. He thus did not live to see the final victory which his abili-ties had done so much to bring about. Ramsay was a modern kind of officer, able to motivate a staff and as skilled in the politics of Alliance and inter-service relations as in leadership in action. It requires intelligence, judgement, determination and moral strength of a high order to take deci-sions and to keep up the momentum of often tedious staff work far from the stimulation — and

distraction — of the sound of the guns. Modern maritime warfare is about organisation and the synergy of diverse forces operating in three dimen-sions. No one was better able to direct a complex modern operation better than Ramsay and Opera-tion 'Neptune' was one of the finest victories in naval history.

Linse

The Germans got the idea for explosive motor boats from their Italian allies. The German design was derived from the Italian MTM and was first used by SS commandos in the Mediterranean in April 1944. Naval Small Battle Unit Flotillas were then equipped as Kleinboote Verbande. The 1.3 ton *Linse* was 18.9ft long and 1.75ft in beam. Made of wood it was powered by two 95hp V8 Ford engines through two screws. The boats were supposed to be capable of silent running at speeds of up to eight knots; maximum speed was in the region of 35kt. After problems in early operations caused by the need to be towed to the target area the action radius in later examples was extended to 60 miles. The operator sat amidships with the explosive charge of about 400kg (880lb) behind. There were also control boats equipped with a second man with a radio transmitter similar to that used to operate remotely controlled demolition tanks ashore. The men in the armed boats put them on a collision course with the target and then abandoned ship. The control boat then made sure the armed *Linse* kept on course by observing shielded lights at bow and stern. The boat's course and speed could be altered and the charge detonated if necessary by remote control if the boat was not going to strike the target. If it did so there was a contact exploder, a metal framework around the bow, that ignited a small charge. This blew off the bow and allowed the boat to sink before a time delay exploded the main charge. Unarmed *Linsen* were also used as delivery vehicles for frogman assault teams.

Biber

This proper one man submarine was designed at the beginning of 1944 by Kapt Hans Bartels, a long standing enthusiast for such craft. The prototype was built in six weeks by Flenderwerke, Lubeck and this was accepted for service use by Doenitz at the end of March. Bibers were first deployed by 'K' Flotilla *261* and a total of 324 were built. Characteristics were:

Length: 29.5ft

Beam: 5.25ft

Draught: 4.5ft

Displacement: 6.5 tons

Machinery: 32hp petrol engine and 13 hp electric torpedo motor

Maximum speed: 6.5kt surfaced, 5.3kt submerged

Range: 130 miles at 6kt surfaced, 8.6 miles at 5kt submerged

Safe diving depth: 100ft

Armament: two underslung 21in torpedoes or two mines.

Notes: Although equipped with a periscope the *Biber*, like the manned torpedoes, normally operated awash. It was unstable under water and could not keep a constant depth. The operators had breathing gear with 20hr supply but death to carbon monoxide poisoning from the engine's exhaust was common. *Bibers* never scored any successes with torpedoes but proved to be quite effective minelayers in the Scheldt.

Neger and Marder

The German manned torpedoes were developed at the torpedo testing establishment at Eckenforde by Richard Mohr. Mohr is one of the German words for negro and this led to the first model being given its name. The aim was to develop a system specially for dealing with Allied invasion forces. Details were as follows:

Length: Neger 25 ft, Marder 27.2 ft

Beam: 1.6 ft

Draught: 3.5 ft

Displacement: *Neger* 2.74 tons, Marder 2.95 tons

Machinery: 12hp electric torpedo motor

Maximum speed: 10 knots

Range: 48 miles at 4 knots

Diving depth: (Marder only) 100 ft

Armament: one 21in torpedo.

Notes: Attempts to give the original *Neger* a flooding tank and compressed air blower proved unsuccessful and the design had to be lengthened to allow this to be added, so creating the *Marder*. The torpedoes operated awash with the operator's head in a plexiglass dome just 18in above the surface. Only the simplest of controls and sights were provided and the device was only realistically usable against stopped targets. The earliest Negers had fixed domes but later examples had a dome release mechanism. This caused its own problems as the manned torpedo was easily swamped. The operator was equipped with breathing apparatus but cases of asphyxiation were common. The manned torpedo was highly unstable after torpedo release but an alternative hazard was malfunction of the torpedo release gear which would convert the manned torpedo into a true suicide weapon as the more powerful armed torpedo took control. About 200 *Negers* and 300 *Marders* were built and up to 400 were lost to various causes. Not for nothing would Doenitz not allow regular U-boat crews to serve in manned torpedo units. The operators were a mixed bag of volunteers from the Navy and Army.

CHAPTER EIGHT
The Philippine Sea

On the same day that the Normandy landings took place, 6 June 1944, equally momentous events were about to take place on the other side of the world in the Marshall Islands. The main American battlefleet, 'Task Force '58' (TF58), set sail from its anchorage at Majuro to cover Operation 'Forager" the landings in the Marianas. What was about to take place was unique in naval history, the only time when large battlefleets of aircraft carriers engaged each other in decisive action.

When the American Central Pacific Drive, commanded by Adm Chester W. Nimitz in Hawaii, opened with the attack on the Gilbert Islands in November 1943 the next step had still not been settled. The US Navy wanted to follow its prewar 'Orange' Plan, concentrate on the Central Pacific and draw the Japanese Navy into a decisive battle around the Marianas. The US Army Air Forces supported this plan as they needed bomber bases in the Marianas to strike against Japan. Gen D. MacArthur, however, the vice-regal Southwestern Pacific commander wished to continue his own offensive and it took until March 1944, when the Central Pacific forces moved on to the Marshalls, before it was finally decided to assault the Marianas in mid-June.

These American deliberations made it difficult for the Japanese to formulate their defensive strategy. As the US Navy expected, they planned to unleash their battlefleet in full strength to strike the next American thrust. At the beginning of March a '1st Mobile Fleet' was created. This was an important move as it effectively placed the surface forces, including the battleships, under the command of Japan's carrier fleet commander, Vice-Adm Jisaburo Ozawa. The Japanese thought of unleashing Ozawa on the American base at Majuro but the death of Adm Koga, Combined Fleet Commander and Ozawa's superior, threw a spanner in the works. Koga's replacement Adm Soemu Toyoda, hoisted his flag on 2 May 1944. The following day he issued Combined Fleet Order 76 that set out plan 'A-Go', a combined offensive by the 1st Mobile Fleet and the land-based 1st Air Fleet, to be executed when the Americans moved further west. The Japanese had all too little fuel because of the American subma-rine offensive against their tankers and relied for oil on the Borneo Balikpapan and Tarakan fields whose refinery capacity was restricted. The only way the 1st Mobile Fleet could operate in defence of the Marianas was therefore by putting volatile Tarakan crude directly into the tankers and then into the bunkers of the fleet at its advanced anchorage less than 200 miles away at Tawi-Tawi in the southern Philippines. Tawi-Tawi was otherwise a poor fleet base. It had no airfield for pilot training and it was surrounded by waters normally infested by enemy submarines. Despite all this the 1st Mobile Fleet concentrated there on 16 May 1944.

Both sides used submarines for reconnaissance and inflicting attrition on the enemy. The USS *Lapon* found a powerful force of carriers off the west coast of Borneo on 13 May and *Bonefish* was duly ordered to carry out a surveillance operation on Tawi-Tawi in case the force was bound there. By 16 May *Bonefish* was at the anchorage and reported the whole Japanese fleet impressively arrayed. Adm Lockwood, COMSUBPAC at Pearl Harbor, brought more of his boats in. *Puffer* fired six torpedoes at the light carrier *Chitose* but, although one scored a hit, none exploded. American submarines, even at this relatively late stage of the war were still being troubled by ineffective torpedoes. Nevertheless, this narrow escape and other submarine sightings had the important effect of forcing the 1st Mobile Fleet to stay in the protected anchorage, preventing the carriers from engaging in any flying. *Puffer* had better luck the day before the main American fleet sailed from Majuro when she despatched the aircraft stores ships *Ashizuri* and *Takasaki* in the Sulu Sea. Over the next two days the USS *Harder* sank no less than three Japanese destroyers around the anchorage itself.

By contrast, Japanese submarine operations were a complete disaster. A patrol line of new 600-ton coastal submarines of the 'KS' class, was set up 120 miles southeast of the Admiralty Islands. Thanks to American 'sigint' (signals intelligence), the position of the line was revealed to American hunter-killer groups. One American destroyer escort, the USS *England*, sank no less than six submarines in 13 days, an especially

remarkable achievement for a new ship with only about 10 weeks at sea. In addition to the *England*'s kills, 11 other Japanese submarines were sunk by American surface ships and aircraft in the area of 'A-Go' operations between 17 May and 19 June 1944. With their submarine reconnaissance thus neutralised the Japanese had even less idea where the American blow would fall. The focus of the submarine losses seemed still to indicate a southern drive and Toyoda placed his

forces on six hour alert on 20 May with the signal 'Start A-Go'. The following day Adm Ozawa called his commanders to meet on board his flagship, the fine new fleet carrier *Taiho*. He emphasised that the coming encounter was to be a decisive battle. All units were to press home attacks regardless of damage; all ships were to be considered expendable.

On 27 May MacArthur's forces invaded the island of Biak off the coast of New Guinea. This

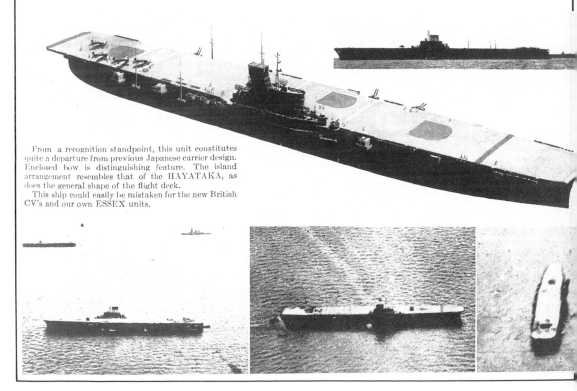

From a recognition standpoint, this unit constitutes quite a departure from previous Japanese carrier design. Enclosed bow is distinguishing feature. The island arrangement resembles that of the HAYATAKA, as does the general shape of the flight deck.

This ship could easily be mistaken for the new British CV's and our own ESSEX units.

Taiho

Built: Kawasaki, Kobe (launched 7 April 1943)

Displacement: 29,300 tons standard

Dimensions: 855ft x 90.9ft x 31.5ft

Armour: 2.2-5.9in belt; 3.1in flightdeck; 4.9in lower deck

Machinery: four shaft geared turbines, 160,000shp, 33.3kt

Armament: Air group — 27 A6M5a 'Zero' fighters, 27 D4Y1 'Judy' dive-bombers, 3 D4Y1c 'Judy' reconnaissance aircraft, 18 'Jill' torpedo-bombers; Defensive — 12 x 3.9in AA (6 x 2); 51 x 25mm AA

Sensors: Radars types 21 and 13

Complement: 1,751

Notes: An excellent and well protected carrier thrown away by execrable damage control. The armoured protection did not prevent a powerful air group being carried. It is possible that the Japanese were influenced by the survivability demonstrated by HMS *Illustrious* in the Mediterranean in January 1941. The British carrier, however, had much less offensive capability.

caused much uncertainty for the Japanese, who moved forces southwards to reinforce the defenders and to be ready if the US fleet moved in this direction. On 10 June Ozawa despatched his largest surface assets, the 18in super battleships *Yamato* and *Musashi* to the south: they were spotted and unsuccessfully attacked by the submarine *Harder*.

On 11 June, a day early in order to confuse the enemy, TF58 began softening up the Marianas with a sweep by over 200 Grumman F6F Hellcats and eight Avengers against the islands' airfields upon which were almost 500 aircraft. Eleven Hellcats were lost but 36 Japanese aircraft were destroyed in the air and on the ground. As well as the usual Mitsubishi A6M 'Zeros', twin-engined Nakajima J1N1 Gekko ('Irving') Navy fighters and Army single-engined Nakajima Ki44 Shoki ('Tojo') fighter-bombers were reported shot down in combat. That night, Mitsubishi G4M 'Betty' torpedo bombers from Truk attacked the northernmost of the American carrier task groups but no hits were scored and one 'Betty' was shot down. Attacks on Saipan, Guam, Tinian and Rota were repeated on the morning of the 12th, 468 sorties in all, directed against both airfields and shore installations. By 13 June there could be no

doubt in Japanese minds that the Marianas were the major target and at 0900 the 1st Mobile Fleet sailed. This was actually a planned sortie to find better bases in the Philippines but it became a combat move as Ozawa made up his mind about American intentions. At 1727 he signalled 'Prepare for A-Go Decisive Operation'. The main forces sent south were ordered to rendezvous with the rest of the fleet in the Philippine Sea. The rest of the 1st Mobile Fleet, its departure noted by the US submarine *Redfin*, made first for the Guimaras anchorage between Panay and Negros which it reached on the 14th to refuel.

At 0844 on 15 June, US Marines landed on Saipan's beaches. Eleven minutes later Adm Toyoda sent the 1st Mobile Fleet the following order: 'On the morning of the 15th a strong enemy force began landing operations in the Saipan-Tinian area. The Combined Fleet will attack the enemy in the Marianas area and annihilate the invasion force. Activate "A-Go" Operation for decisive battle.' Five minutes later he sent Adm Togo's Tsushima signal of 1905 : 'The rise and fall of Imperial Japan depends on this one battle. Every man shall do his utmost'

The core of the 1st Mobile Fleet was made up of three carrier divisions. The Japanese had still not really filled the gap in their forces made by the loss of the four carriers sunk at Midway. Only the 1st Carrier Squadron, commanded by Adm Ozawa himself, was made up of real fleet carriers. Its flagship was the 30,000-ton carrier *Taiho*, completed only three months before. She was a fine ship, combining an armoured flightdeck with a large air group of 75 aircraft. There were also the two veterans of virtually every carrier battle except Midway, *Shokaku* and *Zuikaku*. These 26,000-ton ships had armoured hulls but unprotected hangars and decks and each carried the same air group as *Taiho*'s. The carriers were screened by two 13,000-ton heavy cruisers, the sisters *Myoko* and *Haguro*, each armed with 10 8in guns and the 10th Destroyer Flotilla. This was led by the 6,700-ton, 6in cruiser *Yahagi* and consisted of a mixed group of seven modern destroyers. Four were fine new 2,700-ton vessels of the 'Akitsuki' class built specially for carrier escort and each armed with four twin 3.9in rapid firing dual purpose guns. The other three were of the slightly older 'Kagero' and 'Asashio' classes. These ships had each lost one of their three 5in twin mountings in 1943-44 to allow the addition of extra light AA guns. This fast (33kt) battle group was designated Force 'A'.

The next Carrier Squadron, the 2nd, was slower and based around ships that had been converted into carriers rather than built from the keel up as such. *Junyo* and *Hiyo* had both been laid

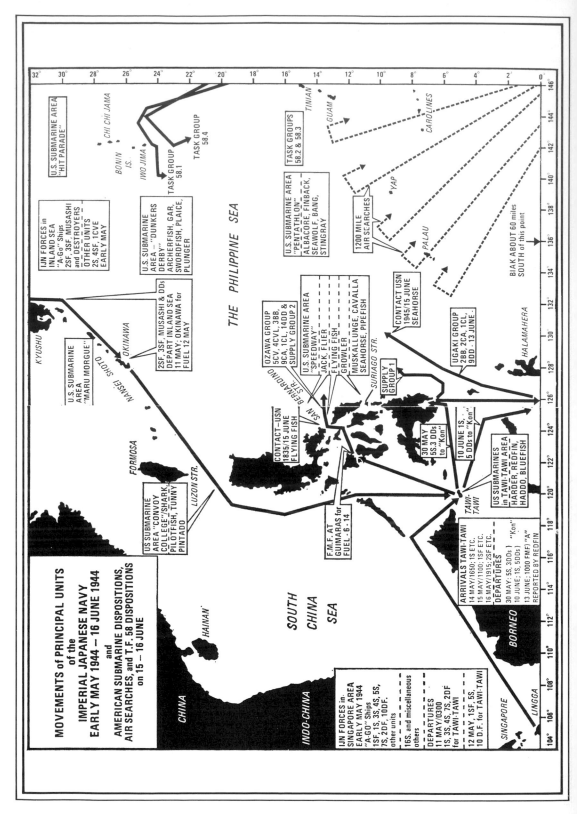

MOVEMENTS of PRINCIPAL UNITS
of the
IMPERIAL JAPANESE NAVY
EARLY MAY 1944 – 16 JUNE 1944
and
AMERICAN SUBMARINE DISPOSITIONS,
AIR SEARCHES, and T.F. 58 DISPOSITIONS
on 15 – 16 JUNE

THE PHILIPPINE SEA

SOUTH CHINA SEA

CHINA

INDO-CHINA

HAINAN

FORMOSA

KYUSHU

OKINAWA

NANSEI SHOTŌ

LUZON STR.

BORNEO

SINGAPORE

LINGGA

HALAMAHERA

TAWI-TAWI

BIAK ABOUT 60 miles
SOUTH of this point

CAROLINES

GUAM

TINIAN

YAP

PALAU

BONIN IS.

CHI CHI JAMA

IWO JIMA

SAN BERNARDINO STR.

SURIGAO STR.

U.S. SUBMARINE AREA "HIT PARADE"

TASK GROUP 58.4

TASK GROUP 58.1

TASK GROUPS 58.2 & 58.3

1200 MILE AIR SEARCHES

IJN FORCES in INLAND SEA "A-Go" Ships
2SF, 3SF, MUSASHI and DESTROYERS
OTHER UNITS
2S, 4SF, 1CVE
EARLY MAY

U.S. SUBMARINE AREA — "DUNKERS DERBY"
ARCHERFISH, GAR, SWORDFISH, PLAICE, PLUNGER

U.S. SUBMARINE AREA "PENTATHLON"
ALBACORE, FINBACK, SEAWOLF, BANG, STINGRAY

U.S. SUBMARINE AREA "MARU MORGUE"

2SF, 3SF, MUSASHI & DDs DEPART INLAND SEA
11 MAY; OKINAWA for FUEL 12 MAY

OZAWA GROUP
5CV, 4CVL, 3BB, 9CA, 1CL, 14DD &
SUPPLY GROUP 2

U.S. SUBMARINE AREA "SPEEDWAY"
JACK, FLIER
FLYING FISH
GROWLER
MUSKALLUNGE, CAVALLA
SEAHORSE, PIPEFISH

CONTACT USN 1945/15 JUNE SEAHORSE

UGAKI GROUP
2BB, 2CA, 1CL, 9DD - 13 JUNE.

CONTACT—USN 1835/15 JUNE FLYING FISH

SUPPLY GROUP 1

30 MAY 5S.3 DDs to "Kon"

10 JUNE 1S, 5 DDs to "Kon"

US SUBMARINES in TAWI-TAWI AREA
HARDER, REDFIN, HADDO, BLUEFISH

US SUBMARINE AREA "CONVOY COLLEGE" SHARK, PILOTFISH, TUNNY, PINTADO

F.M.F. AT GUIMARAS for FUEL - 6 - 14

ARRIVALS TAWI-TAWI
14 MAY/1650; 1S ETC.
15 MAY/1100; 1SF ETC.
16 MAY/1915; 2SF ETC.
DEPARTURES
30 MAY: 5S, 3DDs } "Kon"
10 JUNE: 1S, 5DDs }
13 JUNE: 1000 FMF/ "A"
REPORTED BY REDFIN

IJN FORCES in SINGAPORE AREA
EARLY MAY 1944
"A-GO" Ships
1SF, 1S, 3S, 4S, 5S, 7S, 2DF, 10DF.
other units
16S. and miscellaneous others
DEPARTURES
11 MAY/0300
1S, 3S, 4S, 7S, 2DF for TAWI-TAWI
12 MAY, 1SF, 5S, 10 D.F. for TAWI-TAWI

166

down in 1939 as liners; they displaced over 24,000 tons standard and could carry 51 aircraft each, but they were very vulnerable to both aerial and underwater attack having poor watertight sub-division and almost no armour protection. Their air groups were each made up of 18 'Zero' fighters, nine 'Zero' fighter-bombers and six Nakajima B6N 'Jill' torpedo bombers; *Junyo* carried nine Yokosuka D4Y 'Judy' and nine Aichi D3A 'Val' dive bombers and *Hiyo* 18 'Vals'. The third carrier in the Squadron was the 13,000-ton *Ryuho*, a light carrier converted not very success-fully in 1941 from the submarine depot ship *Taigei*. *Ryuho* was mainly used for training; her presence in the frontline was a sign that the Japanese were scraping the bottom of the carrier barrel. Her air group comprised only 33 aircraft, 18 'Zero' fighters, nine 'Zero fighter bombers and six 'Jill' torpedo bombers. She limited the speed of the whole group to no more than 23kt.

This Squadron was commanded by Rear-Adm Joshima flying his flag in *Junyo*. His low speed allowed the deployment of a 25kt battleship as part of his screen: the 39,000-ton *Nagato*, com-pleted in 1920 but rebuilt in the mid-1930s. She was armed with eight 16in and 16 5.5in guns but more useful were the eight 5in dual purpose guns and a recently enhanced armament of 68 25mm light AA weapons. Also assigned was the 12,200-ton heavy cruiser *Mogami*, rebuilt after being heavily damaged at the Battle of Midway as a sea-plane carrying cruiser and carrying only six 8in guns, all forward. The destroyer screen was made up of eight ships from two separate flotillas. The 4th Destroyer Division of the 10th Flotilla com-prised two 'Asashios' and a 'Kagero'; the 27th Destroyer Division of the 2nd Flotilla was a mix of two older 'Shiratsyus', a 'Kagero' and the two new 2,100-ton fleet destroyers of the 'Yugumo' class. The whole battle group was designated Force 'B'.

The weakest Japanese aircraft carrier squadron was the 3rd, commanded by the aggressive Rear-Adm Obayashi in the light carrier *Chitose*. She, and her sister *Chiyoda* had been built in the 1930s as seaplane/midget submarine carriers; they were converted into 11,200-ton light aircraft carriers after the Midway disaster. They carried 30 aircraft each, six 'Zero' fighters and 15 'Zero' fighter bombers, with three 'Jill' and six Nakajima B5N 'Kate' torpedo bombers. The third member of the squadron was the similar *Zuiho*, originally com-pleted as a submarine support ship *Takasaki* and converted just before Pearl Harbor. She carried the same air group as *Chitose* and *Chiyoda*. These ships could all make 28kt. They were assembled in a mixed carrier battle/surface action group, Force 'C', under the command of Vice-Adm

Takeo Kurita. He flew his flag in the heavy cruiser *Atago*; his command had only come together when the surface forces returned from their wild goose chase to the south.

The surface ships or 'Heavy Screen Group' were the main striking power of Force 'C'. The Group consisted of the four main squadrons of the Japanese surface fleet. The 1st Squadron was the pair of mighty 62,000-ton battleships *Yamato* and *Musashi* armed with nine 18.1in guns and a massive AA armament of over 100 guns of various calibres. The 3rd was composed of the two surviv-ing fast battleship rebuilds of World War 1 'Kongo' class battlecruisers, *Kongo* and *Haruna*. These displaced about 32,000 tons and were armed with four twin 14in turrets.

The 4th Squadron was made up of the four formidable and aggressive looking 'Takao' class cruisers, *Atago*, *Takao*, *Chokai* and *Maya*, built at the beginning of the 1930s and variously mod-ernised between 1938 and 1942. The first two had been extensively rebuilt and now displaced 13,400 tons standard. *Chokai* and *Maya* had been less heavily modernised but the latter had been badly damaged the previous year and on repair had lost a twin 8in mount to be given extra AA guns. Finally there was the 7th Squadron with the pair of 12,400-ton (standard) 'Mogami' class cruisers still armed with five twin 8in gun mountings, *Kumano* and *Suzuya*; and *Tone* and *Chikuma*, the pair of 11,200-ton cruisers built for scouting duties with carrier forces and armed with eight 8in guns forward, leaving space aft for five seaplanes.

The destroyer screen was made up of most of the 2nd Destroyer Flotilla led by the cruiser *Noshiro*, a sister of *Yahagi*, and consisting of four 'Yugumos', a 'Kagero' and the 2,600-ton experi-mental 40kt destroyer *Shimakaze* armed with four 5in guns, 16 x 25mm AA guns and 15 x 24in tor-pedo tubes.

In support of these three main battle groups were two Supply Forces. One was made up of the newly built fleet tanker/seaplane carrier *Hayasui* and three converted merchant tankers accompa-nied by three destroyers and a new 1,300-ton destroyer escort. The 2nd Supply Force had two former merchant tankers, and was escorted by two warships.

Ozawa hoped that significant attrition would be inflicted on TF58 by Japanese land based aircraft. Then his carriers would strike, exploiting the superior range of their aircraft. Force 'C' would go ahead to act as a lure, shield, and a scouting force. Splitting the carriers into separate groups made them vulnerable to defeat in detail but after the experience of the Battle of Midway, when a concentrated force were sunk almost at one blow, it was considered the lesser of the two evils. It also

Above:
**Vice-Adm Marc Mitscher, commander of Task
Force 58 (TF58), taken during the battle.**
US National Archives 80-G-236857

fitted out as a flagship. The main fighting component of the 5th Fleet was TF58, commanded by the experienced airman and carrier commander Vice-Adm Marc A. Mitscher flying his flag in the carrier *Lexington*. TF58 was composed of four Carrier Task Groups and a Heavy Surface Strike Group. The main platforms of the carrier task groups were the 27,000-ton 'Essex' class fleet carriers and the 10,600-ton 'Independence' class light fleet carriers. The 'Essex' class were excellent ships with a complement of up to 98 aircraft, making them the most powerful warships in the world. Their hangars were open and unprotected, allowing aircraft to be warmed up for the rapid launch of large strikes. (The British adopted this system for their last carriers, the abortive 'Gibraltar' class, abandoning the much vaunted but flawed armoured hangar/limited capacity design.) The hulls of the 'Essexes' were, however, armoured with belts of 4in maximum thickness, hangar deck protection of 2.5in and internal armoured decks over the belt of 1.5in. Maximum speed was 32.7kt. The 'Essex' class had been laid down under the 1940 'Two Ocean Navy' programme and the first, *Essex*, had been launched in July 1942. Six were available to Spruance by June 1944.

The 'Independence' light carriers were an emergency programme designed to provide additional carrier hulls as rapidly as possible. They were built on standard 'Cleveland' class light cruiser hulls and all nine were commissioned in 1943. Spruance had all but one of the class available off the Marianas. They could each carry up to 35 aircraft, mainly fighters, and allowed the fleet carriers greater concentration on the strike role.

Task Group 58.1 was composed of the 'Essexes' *Yorktown* (flagship of Rear-Adm Ralph E. Davison) and *Hornet,* and the light carriers *Belleau Wood* and *Bataan*. *Yorktown* carried 42 Hellcat fighters, 40 Helldiver dive-bombers, four Dauntless dive-bombers, 17 Avenger torpedo bombers and four Hellcat night-fighters; *Essex* had 37 Hellcats, 33 Helldivers, 18 Avengers and four Hellcat night-fighters; *Belleau Wood* had 26 Hellcats and *Bataan* 24, while both light carriers carried nine Avengers. In support of the carriers were Task Unit 58.1.2 made up of the first three heavy cruisers of the new and large 'Baltimore' class, *Baltimore, Boston* and *Canberra*. The Group Screen, TU58.1.3 was made up of the smaller AA cruiser *Oakland* armed with 12 5in dual purpose guns and two Destroyer Squadrons (DesRons). DesRon 46 had nine ships, all new and powerful 2,325-ton (standard) 'Fletcher' class ships, probably the best destroyers of their time. DesRon 6, composed only of DesDiv 11, had four older prewar destroyers of the 'Gridley' class and one

gave scope for 'encircling' the enemy. Tactically, the Japanese Fleet was in 'Number One Battle Disposition (Modified)'. The two main Japanese carrier battle groups had the flagship carrier at the centre with another carrier on each quarter. Heavy surface ships were deployed ahead of the main carrier with the destroyer screens in a circle around the whole force. Force 'C' was in the lead deployed in a line (see diagram). Under attack, however the Japanese formations tended to go to pieces. Weaknesses in numbers and weight of AA guns led Japanese commanding officers to try to outmanoeuvre their attackers individually.

The Japanese fleet was weak not only in armament but in sheer numbers. It was facing the most powerful naval force the world had yet seen, the American Central Pacific Fleet. This was the 5th Fleet when commanded by Adm Raymond A. Spruance and his staff, and the 3rd when commanded by Adm Halsey. Spruance, the 'Quiet Warrior' was in command for Forager and flew his flag in the heavy cruiser *Indianapolis*, specially

Above:
The screens of the Carrier Task Groups were reinforced before the battle by AA cruisers of the 'Atlanta' class; this is the *Oakland* of Task Unit (TU) 58.1.3. *Real Photographs/Ian Allan Library*

'Bagley' class. These were primarily surface warfare vessels with high speed (38.5kt) and heavy torpedo armaments of 16 21in tubes each. All mounted four 5in dual purpose guns but the 'Gridleys' could mount no AA guns bigger than 20mm.

TG58.2, commanded by Rear-Adm Alfred E. Montgomery in the *Bunker Hill*, consisted of two 'Essexes', the flagship with 38 Hellcats, 33 Helldivers, 18 Avengers and four Hellcat night-fighters; and *Wasp* with 35 Hellcats, 32 Helldivers, 18 Avengers and four Hellcat night-fighters. The two CVLs were *Monterey* (21 Hellcats and eight Avengers) and *Cabot* (24 Hellcats and nine Avengers). In support were the 6in cruisers of TU58.2.2, new ships of the 'Cleveland' class, *Santa Fe*, *Mobile* and *Biloxi*. The screen, TU58.2.3, was composed of an 'Atlanta' class AA cruiser, *San Juan* — one of the older units armed with 16 5in guns — DesRon 52 of nine 'Fletchers', and the small DesRon 1 composed of three prewar 'Farraguts'.

TG58.3, the nerve centre of TF58, contained the last remaining American carrier veteran of the original Pacific War battles, the 20,000-ton fleet carrier *Enterprise*, commissioned in 1938. She had a maximum speed of 32.5kt and had a 4in armoured belt, with a 1.5in armoured main deck. She carried 31 Hellcats, 21 Dauntlesses, 14 Avengers and three Corsair night-fighters. She carried the flag of Rear-Adm John W. Reeves, Group Commander, and was accompanied by *Lexington*, the flagship of the whole Task Force, with her 37 Hellcats, 34 Dauntlesses, 18 Avengers and four Hellcat night-fighters. TG58.3 had two CVLs, *San Jacinto* and *Princeton*, each with 24 Hellcats and, respectively, eight and nine Avengers. The cruiser support unit, TU58.3.2, consisted of the 'Cleveland' class light cruisers *Cleveland*, *Montpelier* and *Birmingham* with Spruance's flagship *Indianapolis* attached. The destroyer task unit, 58.3.3, supported by the AA cruiser *Reno* (12 5in guns) was the entirely 'Fletcher' equipped DesRon 50 with 13 'Fletchers'.

TG58.4 commanded by Rear-Adm William K. Harrill had the *Essex* herself with 38 Hellcats, 36 Helldivers, 20 Avengers and four Hellcat night-fighters. The two CVLs were *Langley* and

Cowpens, each with 23 Hellcats and nine Avengers. The 'Cleveland' class light cruisers *Vincennes*, *Houston* and *Miami* provided TU58.4.2 and the screen, TU58.4.3, was made up of the AA cruiser *San Diego* (16 5in guns) and two Destroyer Squadrons. DesRon 12 had two Divisions: 4 with four 'Fletchers' and 23 with three slightly older 'Bristol' class destroyers and a prewar 'Mahan' class destroyer. DesRon 23 was composed of six 'Fletchers',

Harrill's main task was to support TG58.7 which had the impressive appearance of a traditional battlefleet. This was Vice-Adm Willis A. Lee's Heavy Surface Strike Group, a 'battle line' of seven modern battleships each armed with nine 16in guns. These ships were intended to sup-

port the carriers with both heavy gunfire, if required, and with AA protection. The ships were of three classes: *Washington* (flagship) and *North Carolina* were the first two US battleships of post-World War 1 conception, both commissioned in 1941. Displacing 37,500 tons standard they had 12in belt and 16in turret armour and could make 28kt. Secondary armament comprised 20 5in dual purpose guns, and over 100 light AA guns, 40mm and 20mm. Next came the 38,000-ton 'South Dakotas' completed in 1942, *South Dakota*, *Indiana* and *Alabama*, built shorter with heavier 13in belt and 18in turret protection. *South Dakota* had 16 5in and 68 40mm guns, the other two 20 5in dual purpose guns and 56 40mm. All carried 40 20mm guns. Speed was 27.5kt. Finally, there were the first two of the fast 48,000-ton 'Iowas', specially built to support the carriers. *Iowa* and *New Jersey* were 200ft longer than the 'South Dakotas' and their engines of over 200,000shp (40% more powerful than in the earlier ships) could speed them through the waves at 32.5kt. Armour was 13in thick on the belt and 19.7in on

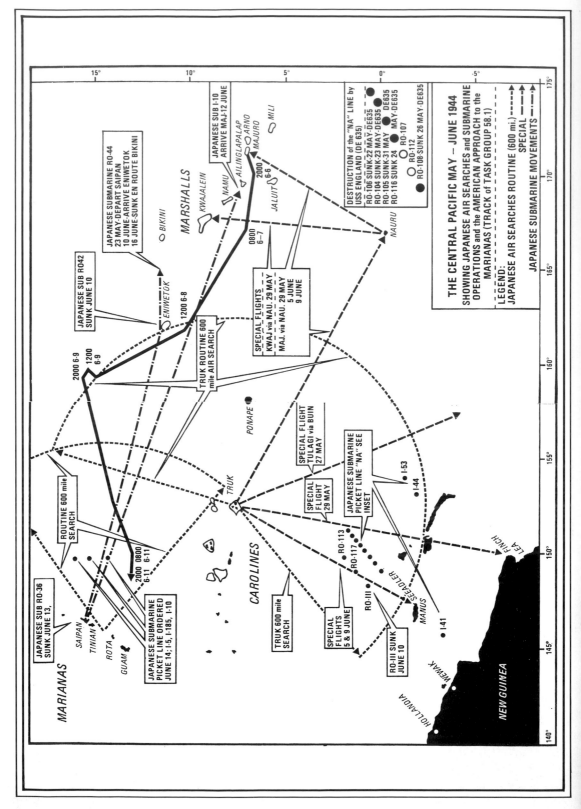

THE CENTRAL PACIFIC MAY – JUNE 1944

SHOWING JAPANESE AIR SEARCHES and SUBMARINE
OPERATIONS and the AMERICAN APPROACH to the
MARIANAS (TRACK of TASK GROUP 58.1)

LEGEND:
JAPANESE AIR SEARCHES ROUTINE (600 mi.) ------
SPECIAL ------
JAPANESE SUBMARINE MOVEMENTS ------

DESTRUCTION of the "NA" LINE by
USS ENGLAND (DE 635)
RO-106 SUNK-22 MAY-DE635
RO-104 SUNK-23 MAY-DE635
RO-105 SUNK-31 MAY   DE635
RO-116 SUNK 24 MAY-DE635
RO-112
RO-107
RO-108-SUNK 26 MAY-DE635

JAPANESE SUB I-10
ARRIVE MAJ-12 JUNE

JAPANESE SUBMARINE RO-44
23 MAY-DEPART SAIPAN
10 JUNE-ARRIVE ENIWETOK
16 JUNE-ARRIVE EN ROUTE BIKINI

JAPANESE SUB RO42
SUNK JUNE 10

SPECIAL FLIGHTS
KWAJ via NAU. 29 MAY
MAJ. via NAU. 29 MAY
5 JUNE
9 JUNE

TRUK ROUTINE 600
mile AIR SEARCH

SPECIAL FLIGHT via BUIN
TULAGI
27 MAY

SPECIAL
FLIGHT
29 MAY

JAPANESE SUBMARINE
PICKET LINE "NA" SEE
INSET

I-53
I-44

RO-113
RO-117

RO-III

TRUK 600 mile
SEARCH

SPECIAL
FLIGHTS
5 & 9 JUNE

RO-III SUNK
JUNE 10

I-41

ROUTINE 600 mile
SEARCH

JAPANESE SUBMARINE
PICKET LINE ORDERED
JUNE 14; I-5, I-185, I-10

JAPANESE SUB RO-36
SUNK JUNE 13,

MARIANAS

SAIPAN
TINIAN
ROTA
GUAM

CAROLINES

PONAPE

TRUK

BIKINI

ENIWETOK

MARSHALLS

KWAJALEIN

NAMU

AILINGLAPALAP

ARNO

MAJURO

MILI

JALUIT

NAURU

NEW GUINEA

HOLLANDIA

WEWAK

MANUS

SEEADLER

LEA FINCH

2000 6-9
1200 6-9
1200 6-8
2000 6-6
0800 6-7

2000 0800
6-11 6-11

MARIANAS

the turret: secondary armament comprised 20 5in dual purpose guns and 120 or more light AA guns, half 40mm and half 20mm. Both had been completed in 1943.

The battleships, TU58.7.1, were supported by TU58.7.2 with four 33kt heavy cruisers each armed with nine 8in guns. The *Wichita*, completed in 1939, was a unique ship of just over 13,000 tons full load displacement. The other three were the *New Orleans*, *San Francisco* and *Minneapolis*, of the prewar 'New Orleans' class whose two surviving sisters were off the Normandy beaches. The screen was made up of two Destroyer Squadrons, DesRon 45 had one division of older destroyers, three 'Bagleys' , one 'Mahan' and a large prewar 'Porter' and DesDiv 89 with five 'Fletchers'. DesRon 53 had only one division of four 'Fletchers'

In addition to TF58, the 5th Fleet contained a separate amphibious force supported by older battleships and escort carriers. Under Lockwood's command at Pearl Harbor were the US submarines operating as a distant reconnaissance and

striking line. There were four packs of these boats operating in support of the 5th Fleet , made up from a number of related classes of 'fleet submarine' of 2,000-2,400 tons submerged displacement, launched from 1936 . The pre-1939 submarines had four 21in torpedo tubes fore and aft but later boats had a six-tube forward salvo, significantly increasing their striking power.

The Americans had over 900 aircraft, double the 450 available to the Japanese but that was not

Below:
TG 58.4 was supported by new 'Cleveland' class 6in cruisers, including the *Miami* seen here. These ships carried equal numbers of 6in and 5in dual purpose guns. *Real Photographs/Ian Allan Library*

Bottom:
During the air attack on the American fleet one of Rear-Adm Turner Joy's 'New Orleans' class cruisers in TU58.7.2, supporting Lee's battle line, puts up a heavy AA barrage and lays smoke. *US Naval Institute 80-G-238218*

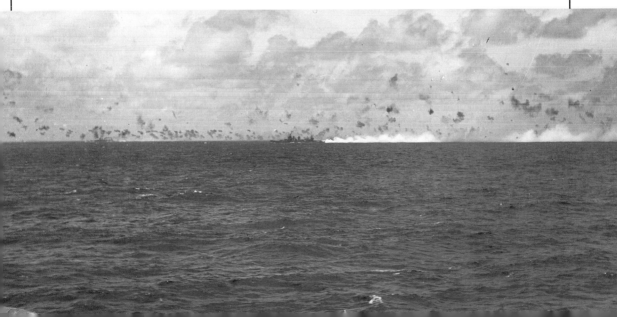

their only advantage. The standard US Navy fighter, the F6F-3 Hellcat, was slightly faster than the 'Zero' in the latter's latest A6M5 version; it was also more strongly built with an engine of almost twice the power. Its six 0.5in heavy machine guns could inflict terrible damage on the more flimsy Japanese aircraft. The 'Zero' was quite well armed itself with two 20mm cannon and three machine guns but lacked both armour and self-sealing fuel tanks. Only the latest A6M5bs in *Chitose*, *Chiyoda* and *Zuiho* had the armoured glass and automatic fire extinguishers fitted as standard in Allied aircraft. The Japanese advantages were in manoeuvrability and rate of climb but the Japanese pilots could not exploit them. Japanese training had suffered badly through fuel shortages and the need to replace the heavy casualties of the war so far. In the previous winter of 1943-44, combat familiarisation had been abandoned for the best pilots coming from basic training and, although this decision was reversed in the spring, the damage had been done. Many potentially good pilots had been killed prematurely on operations and most of the pilots in the 1st Mobile Fleet were fresh from training school with very little actual combat experience. Many were seeing action for the first time. The average Japanese naval pilot had only 275hr of flying time compared to 525hr for an American.

Japanese Air Group 601 of the 1st Carrier Squadron was a mix of skilled survivors of previous battles, seaplane pilots and freshly trained personnel. It had been able to carry out training at Singapore but the inability to carry out flight operations around the Tawi-Tawi base caused a serious degradation of flying skills. Air Group 652 of the 2nd Carrier Squadron had suffered serious attrition in the fighting around Rabaul. The replacements for these losses had been hastily brought together in Japan and could not receive proper training because of shortage of petrol. The experienced pilots in the fighter-bomber squadrons were from bomber backgrounds and were untrained in air-to-air combat. Even the Japanese considered the 652nd a poor group. Again, deployment to Tawi-Tawi prevented any further training. Air Group 653 of the 3rd Carrier Squadron was almost as bad. The majority of its pilots were of the September 1943 or January 1944 graduates, mainly the less able class members who had not been rushed into combat. Average duration for pilot training for each group were six months for the 601st, two months for the 652nd and three months for 653rd. This should be compared with the prewar course length of 3½ years.

This lack of pilot skills was a particularly serious problem as the Japanese aircraft depended on the kind of superiority that had been displayed by the first generation of Japanese pilots in the months after Pearl Harbor. Both the new Yokusuka D4Y Suisei (Comet) dive-bomber (Allied codename 'Judy') and the Nakajima B6N Tenzan (Heavenly Mountain) torpedo bomber ('Jill') were high performance machines, being light, fast and manoeuvrable. Their range was good but they were also difficult to fly. The Japanese were also still using a higher proportion of older aircraft. The 'Val' dive-bombers and 'Kate' torpedo-bombers were unchanged from the aircraft that had bombed Pearl Harbor.

The American pilots were, on the other hand, both well trained and combat hardened. If anything, combat hardening had gone too far as many of their aircraft were in need of overhaul; fuel consumption was therefore higher than normal, a factor which made their range disadvantage even worse. The Avenger torpedo bomber was, however, relatively fast and well armed and armoured. The Helldiver dive bomber was even faster than the Avenger and could absorb much punishment but it was not as manoeuvrable as its slower predecessor the SBD-5 Dauntless which, much to the delight of its pilots, was still in service in TG58.3 and in small numbers in the *Yorktown*.

There were as many Hellcats in Spruance's carriers as Ozawa had total aircraft and the American aircraft had another advantage, modern fighter control. By June 1944 the US Navy had a well established system of Combat Information Centers (CICs) where radar operators plotted enemy raids. They then passed range and bearing information to plotters who put the target on a plexiglass screen. Raids were allocated numbers and the position of friendly fighters displayed. The status of all the fighters being controlled by the ship was placed on another board. There was a fighter direction officer (FDO) at Task Force and Task Group levels and one in each carrier. The Task Force FDO allocated raids to Task Group FDOs, and the latter the raids to individual ships. As the fighter director officers (FDOs) observed and evaluated raids, they would vector their standing combat air patrols (CAP) on to the interception point, giving estimates of the size of raid, altitude, course and speed.

When the CAP made visual contact its commander advised the FDO as to the raid's actual course, speed and composition and then attacked. A CAP committed to intercept a raid would be replaced by another group of fighters to provide an immediate reserve. All this allowed enemy raids to be engaged out to 60 miles. Attackers had to face 15min of air combat, which meant that not many would reach their targets. The advanced system worked remarkably well. The electronics

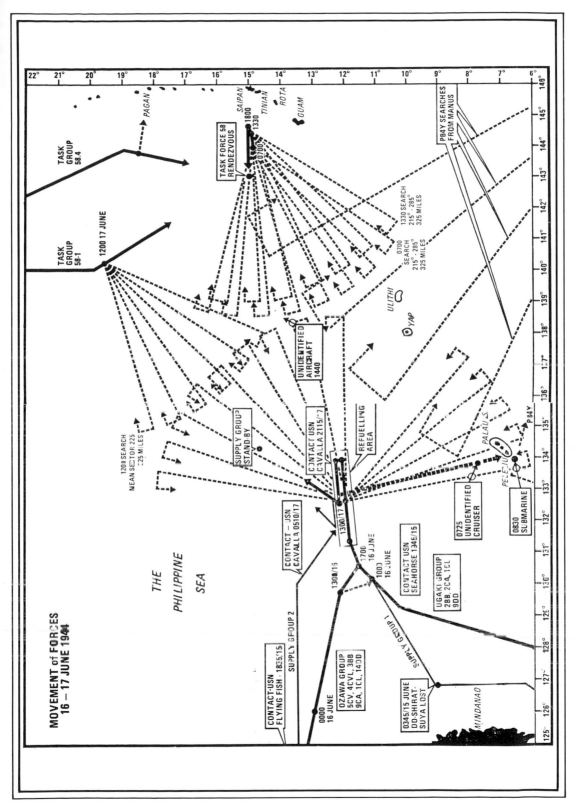

MOVEMENT of FORCES
16 – 17 JUNE 1944

THE PHILIPPINE SEA

TASK GROUP 58.4

TASK GROUP 58.1

1200 17 JUNE

PAGAN

SAIPAN

TINIAN

ROTA

GUAM

1800

1330

0700

TASK FORCE 58 RENDEZVOUS

PB4Y SEARCHES FROM MANUS

1330 SEARCH 215° - 285° 325 MILES

0700 SEARCH 215° - 285° 325 MILES

ULITHI

YAP

UNIDENTIFIED AIRCRAFT 1440

1200 SEARCH MEAN SECTOR 225 325 MILES

SUPPLY GROUP STAND-BY

CONTACT USN CAVALLA 2115/17

REFUELLING AREA

PALAUS

P 34 V

PELELIU

0725 UNIDENTIFIED CRUISER

0830 SUBMARINE

CONTACT – USN CAVALLA 0510/17

1300/17

1300/15

1700 16 JUNE

1000 16 JUNE

CONTACT USN SEAHORSE 1345/15

UGAKI GROUP 2BB, 2CA, 1CL 9DD

SUPPLY GROUP 2

SUPPLY GROUP 1

CONTACT-USN FLYING FISH 1835/15

0000 16 JUNE

OZAWA GROUP 5CV, 4CVL, 3BB 9CA, 1CL, 14DD

0345/15 JUNE DD-SHIRAT-SUYA LOST

MINDANAO

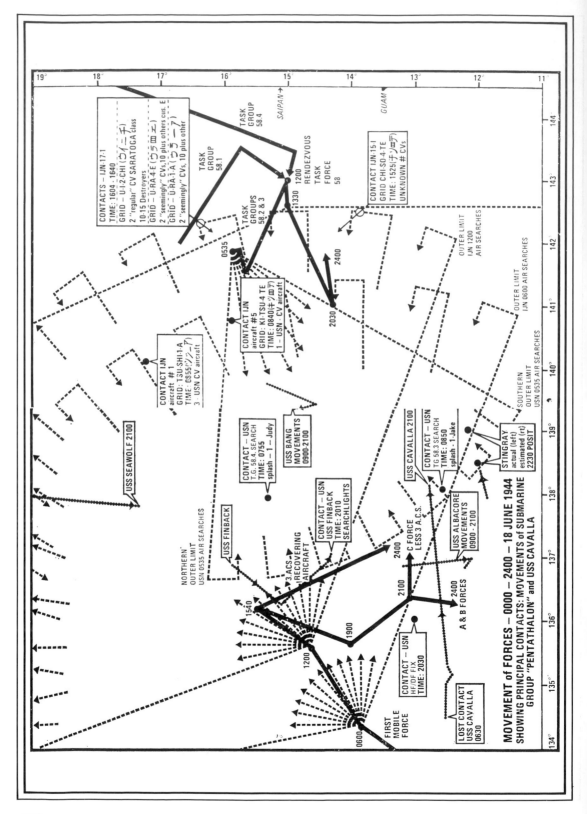

MOVEMENT of FORCES – 0000 – 2400 – 18 JUNE 1944
SHOWING PRINCIPAL CONTACTS: MOVEMENTS of SUBMARINE
GROUP "PENTATHALON" and USS CAVALLA

19° 18° 17° 16° 15° 14° 13° 12° 11°

144° 143° 142° 141° 140° 139° 138° 137° 136° 135° 134°

SAIPAN→

GUAM

TASK
GROUP
58.4

TASK
GROUP
58.1

1200
RENDEZVOUS
TASK
FORCE
58

1330

TASK
GROUPS
58.2 & 3

2400

2030

CONTACTS – IJN-17-1
TIME: 1604 - 1640
GRID – U-I-2-CHI (ウィ二チ)
2 "regular" CV SARATOGA class
10-15 Destroyers
GRID – U-RA-4-E (ウラ四エ)
2 "seemingly" CVs, 10 plus others cus. E
GRID – U-RA-1-A (ウラ一ア)
2 "seemingly" CVs, 10 plus other

CONTACT IJN-15-1
GRID CHI-S0-4-TE
TIME: 1525 (チ/四テ)
UNKNOWN # CVs

OUTER LIMIT
IJN 1200
AIR SEARCHES

OUTER LIMIT
IJN 0600 AIR SEARCHES

SOUTHERN
OUTER LIMIT
USN 0535 AIR SEARCHES

0535

CONTACT IJN
aircraft #5
GRID: KI-TSU-4 TE
TIME: 0840 (キ/四テ)
1 – USN - CV aircraft

CONTACT IJN
aircraft # 1
GRID: TSU-SHI-1-A
TIME: 0855 (ツ/シ一ア)
3 – USN CV aircraft

USS SEAWOLF 2100

CONTACT – USN
T.G. 58.4. SEARCH
TIME: 0755
splash – 1 – Judy

USS BANG
MOVEMENTS
0900-2100

USS CAVALLA 2100

CONTACT – USN
TG 58.3 SEARCH
TIME: 0850
splash - 1-Jake

STINGRAY
actual (left)
estimated (rt)
2230 POSIT

NORTHERN
OUTER LIMIT
USN 0535 AIR SEARCHES

USS FINBACK

3 ACS –
/RECOVERING
AIRCRAFT

CONTACT – USN
USS FINBACK
TIME: 2010
SEARCHLIGHTS

C FORCE
LESS 3 A.C.S.

2400

2100

2400

A & B FORCES

USS ALBACORE
MOVEMENTS
0900 - 2100

1540

1900

1200

CONTACT – USN
HF/DF FIX
TIME: 2030

FIRST
MOBILE
FORCE

0600

LOST CONTACT
USS CAVALLA
0630

on which it was based comprised SC or SK search radars with a range of 60-100 miles. Special SM (height-finding) fighter control radar gave height information and also some idea of the composition and vertical formation of the attackers. SG (surface search) radar could also give warning of low altitude torpedo-bomber attack but the 'Mk1 Eyeball' was, however, usually the best sensor against low level attack and visual FDOs controlled low level fighters.

Fighter Direction Officers were key personnel but they were all young reservists. The force FDO was Lt Joseph R. Eggert whose more normal environment was Wall Street rather than the Philippine Sea. In many ways, however, the management skills of a New York Stock broker, and his capacity to think clearly and make decisions under stress were exactly those required to run a complex three dimensional battle.

The five American Task Groups could fight either independently or in combination. When the Fleet formed into a concentrated force, the three main Carrier Groups were to operate 12 miles apart on a north-south axis: the battle line would operate 15 miles ahead of TG58.3 with TG58.4 to the north. If the air battles led to command of the air then it was intended that the Cruiser Support Groups of the Carrier Groups, plus some of their destroyers, were also to be released for surface action with the battle line.

The American Task Groups were deployed in anti-air circular formations. These were strictly kept and manoeuvres were based on the movement of the guide except in the case of torpedo attack. The powerful Groups could rely on effective fighter and AA gun protection, the latter enhanced by the newly developed radar proximity fuses for the 5in dual purpose guns. The main American deficiency was not in anti-air but in anti-surface unit warfare. There was no efficient American air search doctrine and once the enemy was found there was little experience of the correct way to attack a large enemy fleet. Avengers were too often loaded with bombs rather than torpedoes. Spruance, an essentially surface sailor, did not therefore overestimate the striking power of his carriers. His plan was for his aircraft to knock out enemy carriers and then attack cruisers and battleships 'to slow or disable them'. The surface striking force of battleships and cruisers would then move in for the final kill.

Late on 15 June the submarine USS Flying Fish spotted the carriers of the 1st Mobile Fleet emerging from San Bernadino Strait. Shortly afterwards the Seahorse spotted the battleship group coming northwards 200 miles east-southeast of Surigao Strait. Because of jamming this second submarine sighting report was not received until early on the 16th. Spruance, knowing the enemy fleet was moving in, postponed the invasion of Guam, reinforced TF58 from forces assigned to shore bombardment and ordered the concentration of his Carrier Task Groups 180 miles west of Tinian. TG58.1 and TG58.4 were away striking at airfields on Iwo Jima and Chichi Jima to the northwest. The other two had been attacked on the evening of the 15th. The first wave was composed of 'Betty' twin-engined bombers from Guam and the other a mixed force of 'Judys' and twin-engined 'Frances' aircraft from Yap. Some Japanese torpedo-bombers managed to drop their weapons but all missed. American fighters and AA guns shot down 18 Japanese aircraft — and, sadly, one or two of their own.

On 17 June one of the Japanese supply groups was spotted by the submarine Cavalla but she was unable to attack. Instead, Cavalla followed the tankers towards the expected main fleet. At 1650 that evening Ozawa concentrated his carriers with the battleships coming up from the south. Cavalla duly found the 1st Mobile Fleet that evening and reported the presence of 15 vessels, all the commander could see through his periscope at night. Lockwood ordered the four boats scouting northwest of Saipan, Finback, Dace, Stingray and Albacore, to concentrate to the south; he signalled his submariners that they had 'the chance of a lifetime.'

Less than an hour after Ozawa concentrated his forces Spruance's flagship the Indianapolis joined TG58.3. The Japanese land based air forces tried again to inflict attrition on the Americans but the attacks were misdirected. 17 'Judys', two 'Frances' and 31 'Zeros' mistook the American amphibious support escort carriers for Mitscher's fleet carriers. Neither the CVEs' FM-2 Wildcat fighters nor the fighter direction from the amphibious force HQ ship were of the same quality as TF58's Hellcats and FDOs and the Japanese scored successes. The Japanese hit the USS Fanshaw Bay and near-missed both the Gambier Bay and the Coral Sea. They thought, however, they had attacked the main American fleet and had sunk a number of fleet carriers.

Spruance was much worried about being outmanoeuvred by Ozawa and exposing the amphibious forces to attack. Cavalla's report of only 15 ships, received in the early hours of the 18th, seemed to confirm an all too typical Japanese attempt to use several forces, one as a decoy. Spruance became increasingly convinced that he should not come too far west from Saipan until Japanese movements were clearer. At 0730 Cavalla reported that she was still in contact. Mitscher correctly assessed this as the Japanese main fleet and told Spruance he intended to close it at high

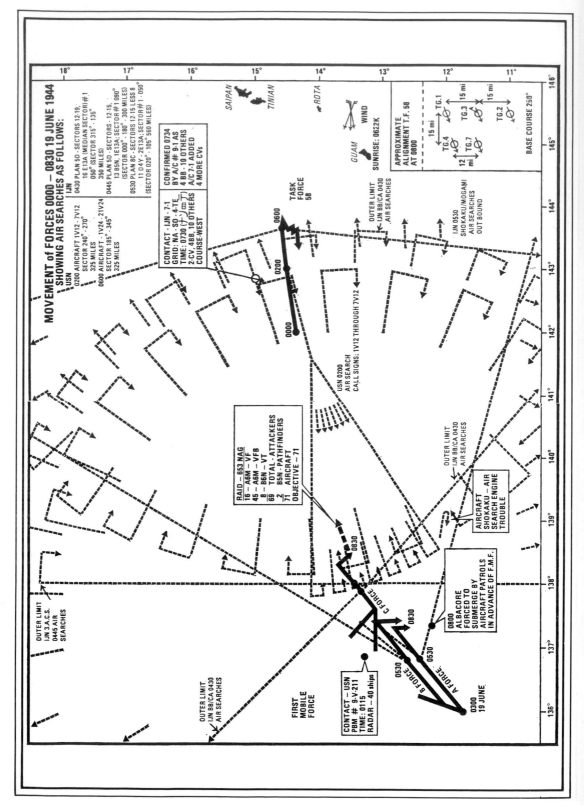

MOVEMENT of FORCES 0000 – 0830 19 JUNE 1944
SHOWING AIR SEARCHES AS FOLLOWS:

USN

0200 AIRCRAFT 1V12 – 7V12
SECTOR 240° – 270°
325 MILES

0600 AIRCRAFT 1V24 – 21V24
SECTOR 185° – 345°
325 MILES

IJN

0430 PLAN 50 – SECTORS 12-19,
16 E13A (MEDIAN SECTOR) #1
050° (SECTOR 315° – 135°
350 MILES)

0445 PLAN 50 – SECTORS – 12-15,
13 B5N, 1E13A, SECTOR #1 090°
(SECTOR 000°, 180° – 300 MILES)

0530 PLAN 8C – SECTORS 12-15 LESS 8
11 D4Y – 2E13A, SECTOR #1 – 050°
(SECTOR 020° – 105° 560 MILES)

CONFIRMED 0734
BY A/C # 9-1 AS
4 BB · 10 OTHERS
A/C 7-1 ADDED
4 MORE CVs

CONTACT · IJN · 7-1
GRID: NA · SD · 4-TE
TIME: 0730 (↑) · ⊡ ☐
2-CV, 4BB, 10 OTHERS
COURSE-WEST

SAIPAN
TINIAN
ROTA
GUAM
WIND
SUNRISE: 0622K

APPROXIMATE
ALIGNMENT T.F. 58
AT 0800

TG.1
TG.3 — 15 mi
TG.4 — 15 mi
TG.7
TG.2 — 15 mi
12 mi

BASE COURSE 250°

0600
TASK FORCE 58
0200
0000

OUTER LIMIT
IJN BB/CA 0430
AIR SEARCHES

IJN 0530
SHOKAKU/MOGAMI
AIR SEARCHES
OUT BOUND

USN 0200
AIR SEARCH
CALL SIGNS: 1V12 THROUGH 7V12

OUTER LIMIT
IJN BB/CA 0430
AIR SEARCHES

RAID – 653 NAG
16 – A6M – VF
45 – A6M – VFB
8 – B6N – VT
69 TOTAL – ATTACKERS
2 B5N – PATHFINDERS
71 AIRCRAFT
OBJECTIVE – 71

0830

C FORCE

AIRCRAFT – AIR
SHOKAKU SEARCH ENGINE
TROUBLE

0830

0800
ALBACORE
FORCED TO
SUBMERGE BY
AIRCRAFT PATROLS
IN ADVANCE OF F.M.F.

OUTER LIMIT
IJN 3.A.C.S.
0445 AIR
SEARCHES

OUTER LIMIT
IJN BB/CA 0430
AIR SEARCHES

FIRST
MOBILE
FORCE

CONTACT – USN
PBM # 9-V-211
TIME: 0115
RADAR – 40 ships

0530

0530

B FORCE
A FORCE
0300
19 JUNE

speed, find it in the afternoon and send the battle-ships in for a night engagement. Lee, however, had too much respect for Japanese abilities in night actions to feel comfortable with this. He signalled thus: 'Do not (repeat *not*) believe we should seek night engagement. Possible advantages of radar more than offset by difficulties of communications and lack of training in fleet tactics at night. Would press pursuit of damaged or fleeing enemy, however, at any time.'

This confirmed Spruance's cautious view that he should remain close to Saipan. He agreed with his Surface Action Group commander that given US material superiority fighting at night was fighting on Japanese rather than American terms. Spruance's preferred option was to use his carriers to cover the islands from attack and to strike at the enemy as soon as they could catch Ozawa in daylight.

Ozawa was, however, cruising out of range, biding his time to strike from somewhere Spruance and Mitscher could not reach. Air searches were sent out by both sides, and at 1525 Ozawa received the first of four reports of carrier groups to the east. He decided to strike at these the following day and communicated this intention to the fleet just as Rear-Adm Obayashi was sending off a strike of 67 aircraft from *Chitose*, *Chiyoda* and *Zuiho*. The raid was recalled.

American search aircraft found nothing but shore based direction finders picked up the Japanese fleet during the night and the more aggressive Mitscher wished to turn the carriers to be within strike range at dawn. Spruance, however, preferred to keep the current northeasterly course. Kurita's force was spotted on radar by an American Martin PBM Mariner twin-engined flying boat at 0115 on the 19th, close to the direction finding fix, but the Mariner's radio signal was not picked up. *Enterprise* launched special radar equipped Avengers which flew together for 100 miles and then split up to search individually; they missed the Japanese force by 45 miles.

Ozawa also sent out search aircraft, a mix of 19 Aichi E13A 'Jake' floatplanes from his surface ships, 13 'Kates' and 11 'Judys' from the carriers. All were in the air by 0600 and the effort reduced anti-submarine patrols around the fleet. Half-an-hour before, TF58 had turned back to the south-west and launched its own dawn search, ASW patrols and combat air patrols. The movement of the American fleet was constantly slowed as the ships turned into the wind to operate aircraft. Fighters were sent to sweep Guam to prevent Japanese air attacks being directed from there. At about 0730 the Japanese air searches spotted three American carrier groups and Ozawa decided to strike. His leading group was 300 miles from the

Americans, with the two main carrier forces 80 miles further west. On the basis of highly misleading reports from Vice-Adm Kakuta, the land-based air commander Ozawa thought that considerable damage had already been inflicted on TF58. Now it was to be finished off. Obayashi again jumped the gun. He launched two 'Kate' pathfinders at 0800, and 45 'Zero' fighter-bombers and eight 'Jill' torpedo-bombers escorted by 17 'Zero' fighters at 0825. Ozawa waited for more contact reports but at 0856 *Taiho*, *Shokaku* and *Zuikaku* together launched 48 'Zeros' escorting 27 torpedo-carrying 'Jills' and 53 'Judys'. The strike was led by two 'Jill' pathfinders and supported by a chaff-carrying 'Judy'. The main Japanese attack thus went in piecemeal. Ozawa kept Force 'B' in reserve.

The battleship *Alabama* picked up 'Raid 1', at 140 miles at 0957. Other ships soon had it on their radar. At 1005 Eggert sent out the signal coined by the old USS *Lexington* in 1942 to recall her fighters, 'Hey Rube'. The Hellcats, claiming 35 aircraft shot down over Guam, returned to defend their carriers. Eggert's main colleagues in the forthcoming battle would be the TG FDOs, Lt C. D. Ridgeway in TG58.1, Lt R. F. Myers in TG58.2, Lt J. H. Trousdale in TG58.3, Lt-Cdr F. L. Winston in TG58.4 and Lt E. F. Kendall in TG58.7. The Americans were also helped by Lt (junior grade [jg]) Charles A. Sims, an intelligence officer in the TF58 flagship, who could understand Japanese radio chatter and gain tactical intelligence.

The carriers had been preparing to attack the Japanese fleet as soon as it was found and the strike aircraft were launched to orbit out of danger while more Hellcat fighters were ranged on deck. Aircraft below in the unprotected hangars were drained of fuel and had any ammunition aboard removed. At 1019 TF58 was ordered to launch its fighters. TG58.1 was due east of TG58.3 and TG58.2 was to the southeast; the groups were 12-15 miles apart. Between 1023 and 1038, 140 Hellcats were launched to reinforce the 60 already on CAP and the 37 returning from Guam. The F6Fs swarmed westwards to intercept the attackers who were orbiting to be assigned targets by the group leader. This both gave Sims the opportunity to listen in to the Japanese plans and the Americans time to launch all their fighters. When the outnumbered Japanese moved in to attack they ran straight into Eggert's Hellcats.

The American fighters scored numerous successes. *Essex*'s Hellcats claimed 20 kills; *Cabot*'s 15 and *Monterey*'s 11. Some 'Zero' fighter pilots proved worthy opponents but the battle was generally one-sided in the Americans' favour; several F6Fs scored four victories each and only three

Hellcats were shot down in return. About 40 Japanese aircraft broke through the outer air defences to be attacked by fighters operating under visual control just out of AA range of the American ships. The 'Jills' proved they could outrun the Hellcats as they split from the main formation and dived down to sea level. Some Japanese aircraft attacked the picket destroyers to the far west but more closed in to attack the battleships of TG58.7. The *South Dakota* was hit by a bomb, the only bomb hit on a US ship that day, although the *Minneapolis* was near missed. At 1057 'Raid 1' was declared over. Only eight 'Zero' fighters, 13 fighter bombers and six 'Jills' were still in the air to return to their carriers.

At 1107 Eggert saw 'Raid 2' approaching from the three Japanese fleet carriers. As the aircraft had flown over their own Force 'C', Kurita's over enthusiastic gunners engaged them, shooting two down and causing eight aircraft to abandon their mission. Again the strike leader tried briefing his crews in the air, allowing the US fighters an easy interception. Cdr David McCampbell, Air Group Commander (CAG) of the *Essex*, claimed five 'Judy' dive bombers. As he looked round he saw the sea dotted with crashed Japanese aircraft and the air filled with coloured parachutes. The rest of McCampbell's aircraft, from squadron VF-15 marked up another 15 kills. Other fighters joined in, the Japanese aircraft demonstrating a tendency to blow up after a few hits. One pilot, Lt (jg) Vraciu from the *Lexington*'s VF-16 claimed six dive-bombers. About 20 Japanese aircraft broke through the F6Fs. One 'Jill' crashed into the side of USS *Indiana* but to no effect. The US AA fire slaughtered the attackers. One 'Judy' dive bomber almost hit *Wasp* and another *Bunker Hill*, both bombs causing limited damage but it was poor return for the 97 aircraft destroyed in this raid. Only 16 'Zeros', 11 'Judys' and four 'Jills' returned.

The massacre of the two Japanese air raids was not the only problem facing Ozawa. The American submarines had struck, and all too effectively. The USS *Albacore* had been allocated a patrol area right in the path of the 1st Mobile Fleet. *Albacore*'s CO, Cdr J. W. Blanchard, first saw one carrier and then another. The second, better positioned for an attack, was the flagship *Taiho*. Blanchard planned to fire a full spread of six torpedoes at 2,000yd but he was disadvantaged by an unserviceable fire control computer and had to fire on an estimated fire control solution. The spread, fired at 0909.32 precisely, was a little wide. One

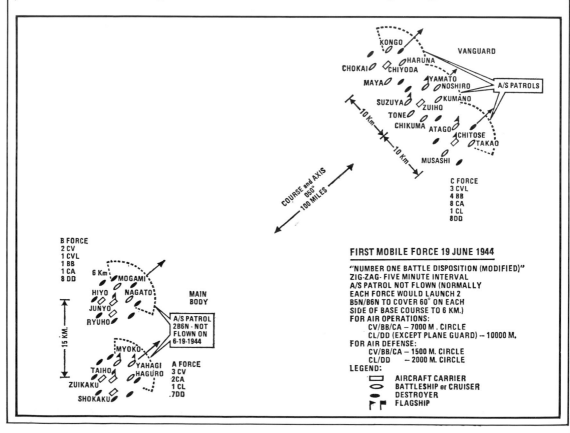

FIRST MOBILE FORCE 19 JUNE 1944

"NUMBER ONE BATTLE DISPOSITION (MODIFIED)"
ZIG-ZAG- FIVE MINUTE INTERVAL
A/S PATROL NOT FLOWN (NORMALLY
EACH FORCE WOULD LAUNCH 2
B5N/B6N TO COVER 60° ON EACH
SIDE OF BASE COURSE TO 6 KM.)
FOR AIR OPERATIONS:
  CV/BB/CA – 7000 M . CIRCLE
  CL/DD (EXCEPT PLANE GUARD) – 10000 M.
FOR AIR DEFENSE:
  CV/BB/CA – 1500 M. CIRCLE
  CL/DD   – 2000 M. CIRCLE
LEGEND:
  ▭ AIRCRAFT CARRIER
  ⬭ BATTLESHIP or CRUISER
  ⬬ DESTROYER
  ⌐⌐ FLAGSHIP

Above:
**USS *Albacore*, the submarine that torpedoed the
Taiho. These big 'fleet' boats lived up to their
name and provided an important reconnaissance
and striking screen to the American main fleet.**
Real Photographs/ Ian Allan Collection

of *Taiho*'s aircraft, a 'Jill', crashed into one torpedo to protect the carrier but one of the six
scored a hit on the *Taiho*'s starboard side forward.
The explosion jammed the carrier's forward eleva-
tor and ruptured her fuel systems but initially the
great ship was slowed by only one knot. The
Japanese damage control officer, however, soon
did *Albacore*'s work for her. As aviation spirit was
pumped out of damaged tanks a large amount
found its way on to the hangar deck and the obvious solution seemed to be to to open the ventilat-
ing ducts to blow the fumes away. Further
thought, or better training, would have demonstrated the folly of this. A dangerous and volatile
mix of petrol and Tarakan crude oil spread

through the ship, which became a floating time
bomb.

As the stage was being set for disaster on board
the Fleet flagship, Force 'B' launched its strike of
seven 'Jill' torpedo-bombers and 25 'Zero' fighter-
bombers escorted by 15 'Zero' fighters. The strike
had to be redirected to a more accurately reported
spot further south, but not all the aircraft got the
message and some continued on to their original
destination to find empty sea. Twenty 'Zeros' did
turn south and became Eggert's 'Raid 3'. It was
engaged by Hellcats, 12 from the *Hornet* and four
F6F-3N night fighters from the *Yorktown*. Six
attackers were shot down and one fighter-bomber
attacked the *Essex*, missing by 600yd. The 'Zero'
was shot down by a *Langley* Hellcat. The Japanese
got away with this attack quite lightly and as many
as 40 aircraft made it back to their carriers.

At 1030 Joshima had another try and launched
10 'Zero' fighter bombers, nine 'Judys', two 'Jills'
and 27 'Vals', escorted by 26 'Zeros'. *Zuikaku*
added another four 'Zeros' and four 'Jills'. The
aircraft were again aimed at a false spot and, when

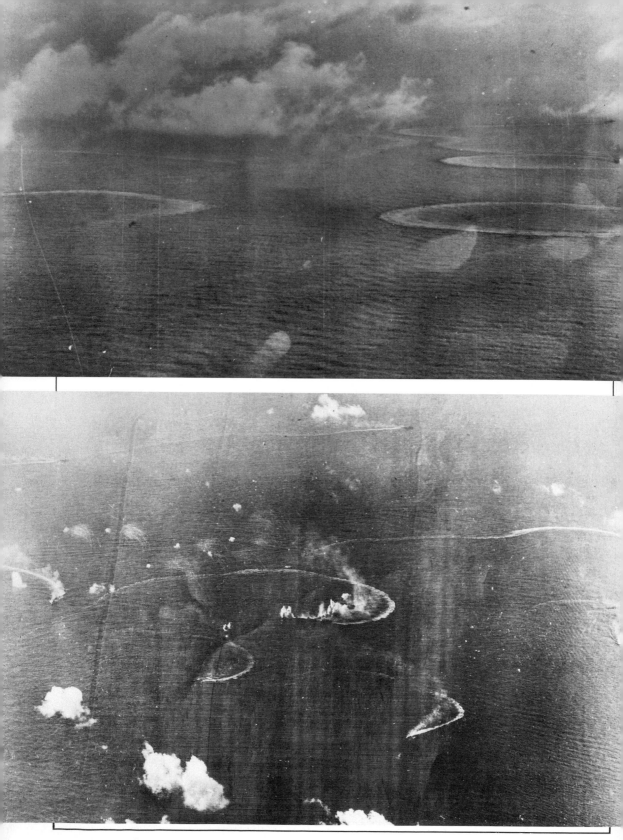

Left:

The wakes of the Japanese ships are clearly traced on the sea. The ships on the right are firing back at the attackers. *US Naval Institute 80-G-231828*

Below left:

The attack on Force 'A' with the damaged *Zuikaku* in the centre surrounded by bomb splashes. *US Naval Institute 80-G-238024*

they found nothing, split up. Most went to land at Guam while the *Zuikaku* aircraft and the eight 'Zero' fighter bombers turned back to the carriers. Some Guam bound aircraft found targets, however, as their course crossed TG58.2's. The aircraft were only just over 50 miles from the American carriers when they were identified as hostile; communications difficulties prevented Myers operating with full effectiveness. *Wasp*'s FDO was put in control and his own fighters made the first intercept but they forgot to confirm the height of the raid to other ships' F6Fs. This allowed 15 'Judy' dive bombers to make glide bombing runs under the CAP; they dropped normal HE bombs and incendiary clusters. *Wasp* was near-missed but her AA gunners claimed three attackers. Another 'Judy' attacked the *Bunker Hill*; its three bombs near-missed but a Hellcat was blown overboard. This intrepid aircraft was shot down as was another, by the light carrier *Cabot*.

As the Japanese aircraft approached Guam, they ran into about 60 Hellcats and Corsairs from *Cowpens, Essex, Hornet, Enterprise, San Jacinto* and *Princeton*. Ensign Wilbur Webb of *Hornet*'s VF-2 put himself into the landing traffic circle, shot down three hapless 'Vals' and then two more of a flight of three. Turning to engage the next trio he claimed a sixth 'Val' in a head-on pass. Another Hornet pilot, Lt Russell L. Reisterer, flying a Hellcat night-fighter with radar under its starboard wing, also got into the landing circuit and lowered his undercarriage to take on the slow, fixed under-carriage 'Vals'. Five more Aichi dive-bombers were shot down as a result. McCampbell also shot down another two aircraft, both 'Zeros', to bring his score to nine. A total of 30 of the 49 Japanese aircraft were shot down and the rest were so badly damaged either in flight or on landing that they were effective losses. Two American fighters were lost.

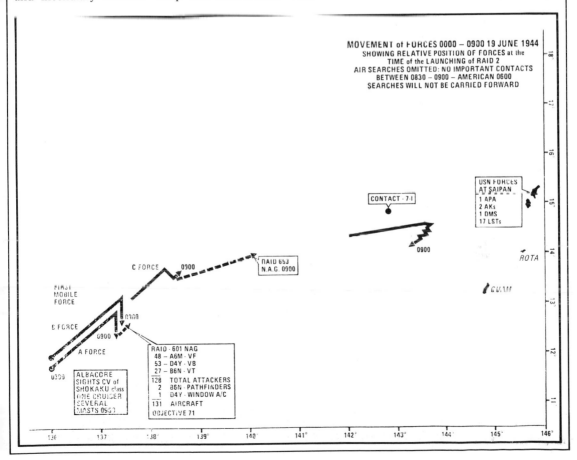

Meanwhile the American submarines had struck again. At 1152 the USS *Cavalla* found Force 'A' and easily penetrated its badly trained and equipped screen; Japanese sonar could not be used above 12kt. The submarine fired a full spread at *Shokaku*, four of which hit. Having thus provided a 'flaming datum' the *Cavalla* was then assailed by the escorting destroyers. She managed to escape the depth charges but her target was less lucky. *Shokaku* was very badly damaged; ablaze, she settled in the water and then at 1500 exploded and sank, taking 1,263 out of her complement of 2,000 to their doom.

Half-an-hour later the floating time bomb that was *Taiho* suddenly exploded as the volatile fumes were somehow ignited. The force of the cataclysm blew holes in the carrier's bottom, bulged the sides of the hangar deck and even split the armoured flightdeck. Ozawa and his staff were quickly transferred to the destroyer *Wakatsuki* and later to the heavy cruiser *Haguro*. Attempts to control the conflagration on board the stricken *Taiho* were futile and, after another explosion just before 1830, the best carrier the Japanese ever built capsized and went down stern first taking with her 1,650 of her 2,150 men.

Below:
**Enterprise was the only survivor of previous
carrier battles to make it to the Philippine Sea,
here seen fighting off the attacks on 19 June.**
US National Archives PO-G-238964

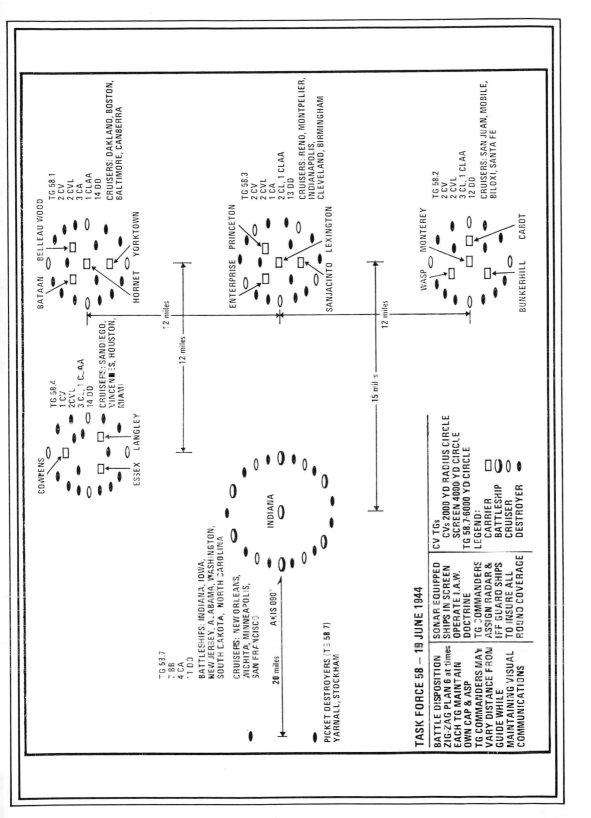

TASK FORCE 58 — 19 JUNE 1944

TG 58.1
2 CV
2 CVL
3 CA
1 CLAA
14 DD

CRUISERS: OAKLAND, BOSTON, BALTIMORE, CANBERRA

BATAAN BELLEAU WOOD HORNET YORKTOWN

TG 58.3
2 CV
2 CVL
1 CA
2 CL, 1 CLAA
13 DD

CRUISERS: RENO, MONTPELIER, INDIANAPOLIS, CLEVELAND, BIRMINGHAM

ENTERPRISE PRINCETON SANJACINTO LEXINGTON

TG 58.2
2 CV
2 CVL
3 CL, 1 CLAA
12 DD

CRUISERS: SAN JUAN, MOBILE, BILOXI, SANTA FE

WASP MONTEREY BUNKERHILL CABOT

12 miles

12 miles

12 miles

15 miles

TG 58.4
1 CV
2 CVL
3 CL, 1 CLAA
14 DD

CRUISERS: SAN DIEGO, VINCENNES, HOUSTON, MIAMI

COWPENS ESSEX LANGLEY

INDIANA

AXIS 090°

20 miles

TG 58.7
7 BB
4 CA
1 DD

BATTLESHIPS: INDIANA, IOWA, NEW JERSEY, ALABAMA, WASHINGTON, SOUTH DAKOTA, NORTH CAROLINA

CRUISERS: NEW ORLEANS, WICHITA, MINNEAPOLIS, SAN FRANCISCO

PICKET DESTROYERS (TG 58.7) YARNALL, STOCKHAM

BATTLE DISPOSITION ZIG-ZAG PLAN 6 at times EACH TG MAINTAIN OWN CAP & ASP TG COMMANDERS MAY VARY DISTANCE FROM GUIDE WHILE MAINTAINING VISUAL COMMUNICATIONS	SONAR EQUIPPED SHIPS IN SCREEN OPERATE I.A.W. DOCTRINE TG COMMANDERS ASSIGN RADAR & IFF GUARD SHIPS TO INSURE ALL ROUND COVERAGE

CV TGs
CVs 2000 YD RADIUS CIRCLE
SCREEN 4000 YD CIRCLE
TG 58.7-6000 YD CIRCLE

LEGEND:
CARRIER
BATTLESHIP
CRUISER
DESTROYER

185

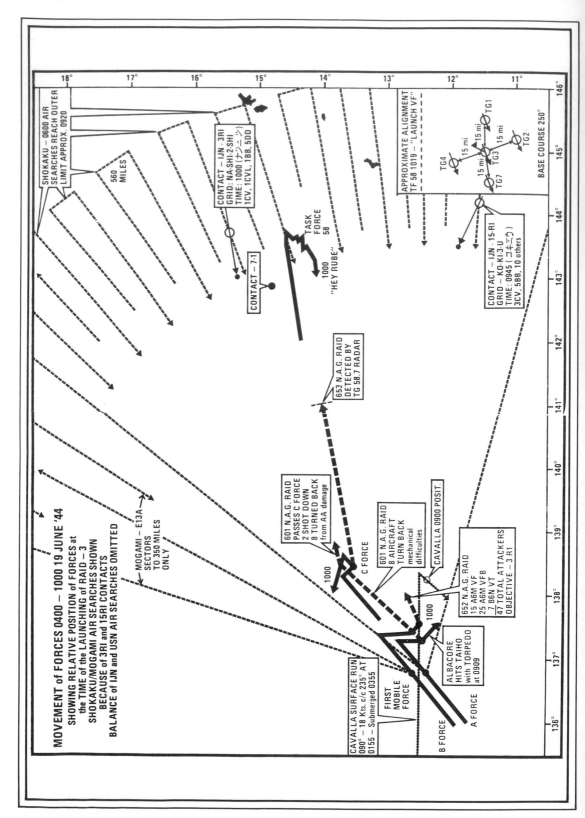

MOVEMENT of FORCES 0400 – 1000 19 JUNE '44
SHOWING RELATIVE POSITION of FORCES at
the TIME of the LAUNCHING of RAID – 3
SHOKAKU/MOGAMI AIR SEARCHES SHOWN
BECAUSE of 3RI and 15RI CONTACTS
BALANCE of IJN and USN AIR SEARCHES OMITTED

SHOKAKU – 0600 AIR
SEARCHES REACH OUTER
LIMIT APPROX. 0920

560
MILES

CONTACT – IJN - 3RI
GRID: NA-SHI:2-SHI
TIME: 1000 (ナゝニゝゝ)
1CV, 1CVL, 1BB, 5DD

CONTACT – 7-1

TASK
FORCE
58

1000
"HEY RUBE"

APPROXIMATE ALIGNMENT
TF 58 1019 – "LAUNCH VF"

TG4   TG1
    15 mi   15 mi   15 mi
         TG2
    15 mi   TG3   15 mi
    TG7
         TG3

BASE COURSE 250°

CONTACT – IJN - 15-RI
GRID – K0-KI.3-U
TIME: 0945 (コキ三ウ)
3CV, 5BB, 10 others

653 N.A.G. RAID
DETECTED BY
TG 58.7 RADAR

601 N.A.G. RAID
PASSES C FORCE
2 SHOT DOWN
8 TURNED BACK
from AA damage

601 N.A.G. RAID
8 AIRCRAFT
TURN BACK
mechanical
difficulties

CAVALLA 0900 POSIT.

1000

C FORCE

652 N.A.G. RAID
15 A6M VF
25 A6M VFB
7 B6N VT
47 TOTAL ATTACKERS
OBJECTIVE – 3 RI

1000

MOGAMI – Ei3A
SECTORS
TO 350 MILES
ONLY

CAVALLA SURFACE RUN
090° – 18 Kts. c/c 235° AT
0155 – Submerged 0355

FIRST
MOBILE
FORCE

ALBACORE
HITS TAIHO
with TORPEDO
at 0909

B FORCE

A FORCE

The day had proved to be one of the worst in the history of the Japanese Navy: 244 of the 374 aircraft of the four carrier strikes had been lost, along with 50 Japanese land-based aircraft. Twenty-two more aircraft went down with the two carriers, bringing total aircraft losses to over 300. On the American side a mere 31 aircraft had been lost, 22 fighters in air combat or by AA fire over Guam, three on search missions and six in operational accidents. On the inspiration of one of *Lexington*'s fighter pilots the day became known as 'The Great Marianas Turkey Shoot'.

The main price paid by the Americans was the disruption of their own air strikes. Congested radio channels prevented directing the American strike aircraft towards the 1st Mobile Fleet. About noon, TG58.1 directed some of its airborne Helldivers to attack Guam and an hour later the commander of *Lexington*'s Dauntlesses organised a strike against Orote field on Guam, supported by Avengers and more Dauntlesses from the *Enterprise*. The armour-piercing bombs fitted to the dive-bombers did little damage but the Avengers carried delayed action high explosive bombs that successfully cratered the runway.

Recovering aircraft delayed the American carriers and they could not turn westwards until 2000. Leaving TG58.4 to refuel, the rest of the Task Force closed the expected enemy position. There was, however, little information as to Ozawa's precise location. Moreover, available intelligence was misleading. Night searches with night fighters and radar equipped Avengers were considered but rejected as both types of aircraft had been used heavily the previous day and the pilots were tired. Operating them would also mean turning back into wind and sailing away from the enemy. At 2207 Mitscher turned westwards and pressed on towards Ozawa at 23kt, his speed of advance being dictated by the maximum economical speed of his destroyers.

Ozawa received orders from Adm Toyoda in the early hours of 20 June. They paid little regard to the realities of the situation and reflected the gross over-estimates of the effectiveness of their strikes that were all too typical of the Japanese.

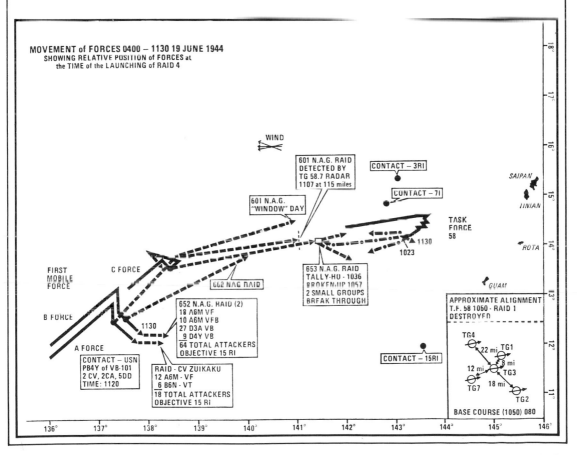

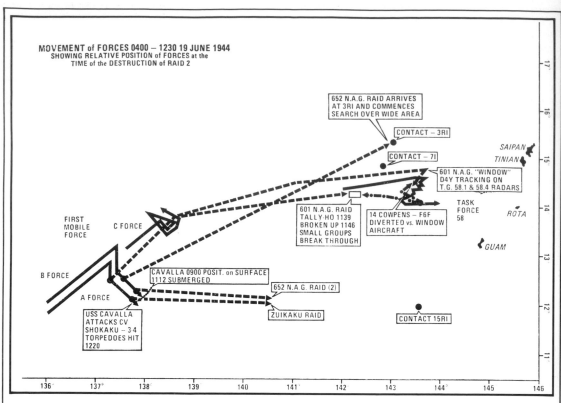

MOVEMENT of FORCES 0400 – 1230 19 JUNE 1944
SHOWING RELATIVE POSITION of FORCES at the
TIME of the DESTRUCTION of RAID 2

652 N.A.G. RAID ARRIVES AT 3RI AND COMMENCES SEARCH OVER WIDE AREA

CONTACT – 3RI

CONTACT – 7I

SAIPAN

TINIAN

601 N.A.G. "WINDOW" D4Y TRACKING ON T.G. 58.1 & 58.4 RADARS

TASK FORCE 58

ROTA

FIRST MOBILE FORCE

C FORCE

601 N.A.G. RAID TALLY-HO 1139 BROKEN UP 1146 SMALL GROUPS BREAK THROUGH

14 COWPENS – F6F DIVERTED vs. WINDOW AIRCRAFT

GUAM

B FORCE

A FORCE

CAVALLA 0900 POSIT. on SURFACE 1112 SUBMERGED

652 N.A.G. RAID (2)

ZUIKAKU RAID

CONTACT 15RI

USS CAVALLA ATTACKS CV SHOKAKU – 3·4 TORPEDOES HIT 1220

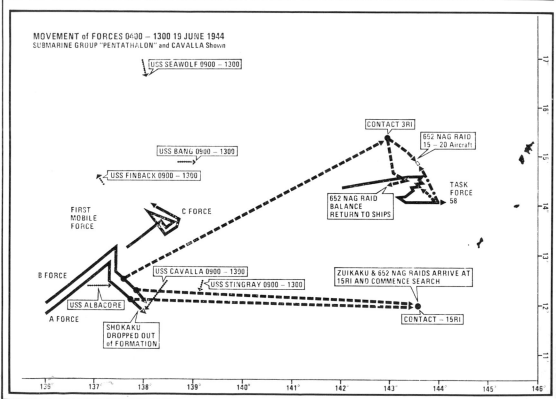

MOVEMENT of FORCES 0400 – 1300 19 JUNE 1944
SUBMARINE GROUP "PENTATHALON" and CAVALLA Shown

USS SEAWOLF 0900 – 1300

CONTACT 3RI

652 NAG RAID 15 – 20 Aircraft

USS BANG 0900 – 1300

USS FINBACK 0900 – 1300

TASK FORCE 58

FIRST MOBILE FORCE

C FORCE

652 NAG RAID BALANCE RETURN TO SHIPS

B FORCE

USS CAVALLA 0900 – 1300

USS STINGRAY 0900 – 1300

ZUIKAKU & 652 NAG RAIDS ARRIVE AT 15RI AND COMMENCE SEARCH

USS ALBACORE

A FORCE

CONTACT – 15RI

SHOKAKU DROPPED OUT of FORMATION

The 1st Mobile Fleet was first to reorganise and replenish on the 21st; disabled ships were then to proceed to Japan and some carriers were to return to Lingga for further training. On the 22nd the surface ships and remaining carriers, with the co-operation of land-based squadrons, would continue their offensive against the damaged US Task Force. The carrier aircraft would then reinforce the shore bases to continue operations against TF58. As the surface ships mopped up what was left, the carriers would all rendezvous at Lingga. Reality could not, however be ignored entirely. On 20 June Kurita sent off 15 search aircraft to the east and when four failed to return and US aircraft were reported he recommended withdrawal to the west. Ozawa, however, shared Toyoda's inflated optimism and determined that his fleet would replenish, as ordered, to fight again.

Below:
TF58 counterattacks: strike aircraft overfly the Lexington. *US National Archives 80-G-255014*

USS *Lexington*

Built: Bethlehem, Quincy (launched 26 September 1942)

Displacement: 27,100 tons standard

Dimensions: 888ft x 93ft x 27.6ft

Armour: 2.5-4in belt; 2.5in hangar deck; 1.5in armour deck over belt

Machinery: four shaft geared turbines, 15,000shp, 32.7kt

Armament: Air group — 38 F6F-3 Hellcat fighters, 34 SBD-5 Dauntless dive bombers; 17 TBF-1C Avenger torpedo and level bombers, 4 F6F-3N Hellcat night fighters; Defensive — 12 x 5in (4 x 2, 4 x 1); 68 x 40mm AA (17 x 4); 52 x 20mm AA (52 x 1)

Sensors: Radars SK-1, SC-2, SM, SG and Mk4

Complement: 3,448 (including air group)

Notes: An exceptionally powerful ship of the 'Essex' class with everything sacrificed to operating the maximum number of aircraft. The class tended to be vulnerable to battle damage but the powerful air group kept hits to a minimum and none of the class was ever sunk. Mitscher's flagship was one of the last equipped with Dauntlesses: by June 1944 most other fleet carriers were equipped with the newer SB2-C Helldiver dive-bomber. The radars were for air search (SK-1 and SC-2), height finding (SM), surface search (SG) and fire control (Mk4). Many of the 'Essex' class perpetuated the names of lost carriers.

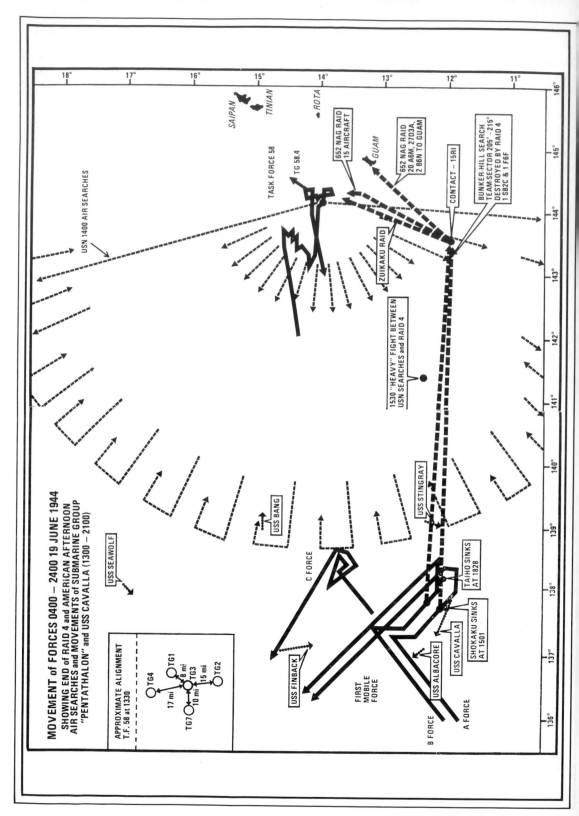

MOVEMENT of FORCES 0400 – 2400 19 JUNE 1944
SHOWING END of RAID 4 and AMERICAN AFTERNOON
AIR SEARCHES and MOVEMENTS of SUBMARINE GROUP
"PENTATHALON" and USS CAVALLA (1300 – 2100)

APPROXIMATE ALIGNMENT
T.F. 58 at 1330

TG1
TG4   8 mi
    17 mi   TG3   15 mi   TG2
        10 mi
    TG7

USN 1400 AIR SEARCHES

USS SEAWOLF

C FORCE

USS BANG

USS FINBACK

FIRST
MOBILE
FORCE

B FORCE

A FORCE

USS ALBACORE

USS CAVALLA

SHOKAKU SINKS
AT 1501

TAIHO SINKS
AT 1828

USS STINGRAY

1530 "HEAVY" FIGHT BETWEEN
USN SEARCHES and RAID 4

TASK FORCE 58

TG 58.4

SAIPAN

TINIAN

ROTA

GUAM

ZUIKAKU RAID

652 NAG RAID
15 AIRCRAFT

652 NAG RAID
20 A6M, 27D3A,
2 B6N TO GUAM

CONTACT – 15RI

BUNKER HILL SEARCH
TEAM-SECTOR 205°-215°
DESTROYED BY RAID 4
1 SB2C & 1 F6F

Ozawa was in fact only partially in control of his fleet because of communications problems from *Haguro*. It milled around the replenishment rendezvous point (15° 20' N, 134° 40' E) in some confusion. The threat of an attack prevented prompt fuelling and a false sighting of enemy aircraft caused further delay still. Only at 1300 was Ozawa able to get to the carrier *Zuikaku*, and reassert control. He also found out for the first time the extent of the previous day's disaster but the admiral still thought the sacrifice had been worthwhile because of the supposed damage inflicted on TF58. As Ozawa boarded *Zuikaku*, the light carriers *Chitose* and *Zuiho* launched three 'Kates' on scouting missions but these did not find the Americans until 1715 that evening. At 1754, knowing that his fleet was within range of the Americans, Ozawa ordered it to assume air defence formation. It was not a moment too soon.

The American air searches sent out in the morning of the 20th spotted nothing. At 1330 eight Avengers and two Helldivers, with Hellcat escort, took off from the *Enterprise* and *Wasp*. At 1538, as his Avenger approached the end of his outward search leg, Lt Robert Nelson spotted something on the horizon: two minutes later he clearly identified Force 'A' with its surviving carrier and caught a glimpse of Force 'B'. Nelson's sighting message was garbled because of radio interference but Mitscher now knew that there was something there. By 1548 with the help of a report from *Yorktown* the rough position of the enemy had been estimated about 15° N, 135° 25' W. A more definite report at 1557 confirmed the range at well over 200 miles but, after checking with his airmen, Mitscher was willing to take the risk. Cdr W. M. Wilhelm, who had led the dive bombers at the Battle of Santa Cruz assured his Force commander that, 'We can make it but it's going to be tight'. Thus advised, Mitscher ordered a large scale attack, hoping that his aircraft would at least damage enemy ships to provide his Surface Action Group with plenty of targets the following day. TF58's commander knew that the possibility of recovery after dark risked heavy losses of pilots untrained in night flying. Nevertheless, he told Spruance that he was launching a deckload strike, to be followed by another, if possible.

Even before the carriers had turned into wind a bombshell of a report was received at 1605 from one of the two Avengers that had joined Nelson over Ozawa. Lt (jg) J. S. Moore corrected his flight commander's longitude to 134° 30', making the range nearer 300 miles than 200. Mitscher decided to hold back his second wave until the morning but at 1615 he decided that the first strike already ranged on deck would be launched

as planned. At 1621 the carriers turned around into wind. Three minutes later the first aircraft began to take to the air at 1624: it took just over 10 minutes for 11 carriers to launch 95 Hellcats (some with 500lb bombs), 54 Avengers (many equipped with four 500lb bombs), 51 Helldivers and 26 Dauntlesses; 240 aircraft in all. At 1636 the carriers turned back to the west to put as short a space between themselves and their aircraft as possible.

The strike did not form up over the carriers as normal, but slowly closed up over the next half-hour as it flew towards the enemy. This conserved fuel and other measures were taken with the same end. The pilots adjusted the fuel mixture of their engines to lean, broaching the limits of safety, and the gunners in the Helldivers and Avengers closed their canopies to minimise air resistance. Such measures became even more important when the squadrons learned the revised position of the enemy. The extra danger, added to the novelty of an assault on the main Japanese fleet, meant that the normally irrepressible Navy pilots were unnaturally silent. There was remarkably little communication between aircraft.

At 1803 Japanese radar picked up the expected incoming strike. The three Japanese forces were now strung out with the reduced Force 'A' to the north, Force 'B' to the southwest and Force 'C' to the south of that. Force 'C' was no longer up-threat of the carrier groups and the American aircraft were flying into an open flank. The supply group was even further exposed to the east of Force 'C' and suffered the first attack. Lt-Cdr J. D. Blitch of Bomber Squadron 14 from *Wasp* decided that his best contribution to a stern chase of the Japanese was to sink their fuel supplies. He therefore led the 12 Helldivers and seven Avengers from his carrier against the tankers. Two of the four converted merchantmen, *Seiyo Maru* and *Genyo Maru*, were bombed so severely that they had to be scuttled; the specialist naval auxiliary *Hayasui* was hit but survived.

Lt-Cdr J. S. Arnold, TG58.1's strike leader, was, like the carrier *Zuikaku*, a veteran of the Coral Sea and was determined that, unlike at that early battle, the American strikes should address all potential targets. He scouted ahead of the Japanese and, after reassuring himself that the other potential targets were being attacked, ordered his aircraft to attack Force 'A'. *Zuikaku*, had *Myoko* and *Haguro* 1,600yd on each bow and *Yahagi* and the seven destroyers in a 2,200yd circle. Two groups of Helldivers from *Hornet* attacked the carrier followed by 12 more SB2Cs from *Yorktown*. Then six Avengers from *Hornet* moved in; four of these carried torpedoes but two of these took on the cruisers and *Zuikaku* escaped

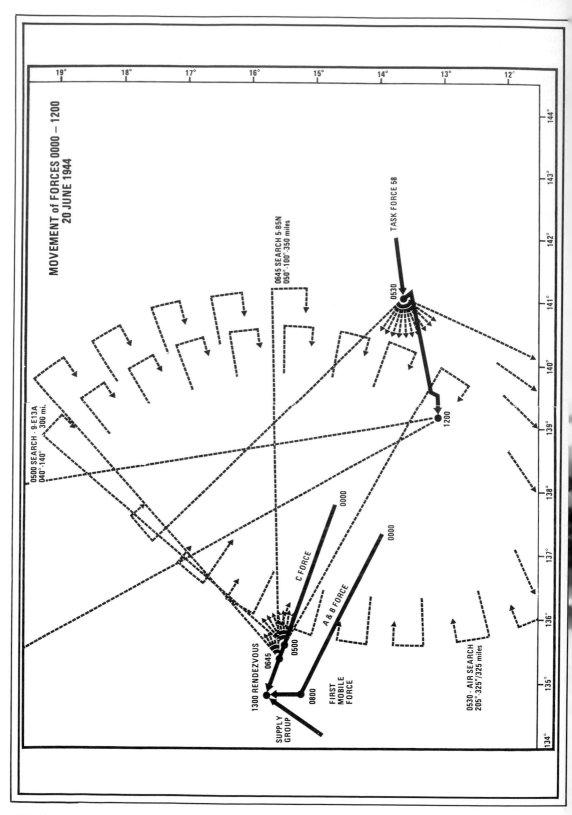

MOVEMENT of FORCES 0000 – 1200
20 JUNE 1944

TASK FORCE 58

0530

0645 SEARCH 5-B5N
050°-100°-350 miles

0500 SEARCH - 9-E13A
040°-140° - 300 mi.

1200

0000

C FORCE

0000

A & B FORCE

1300 RENDEZVOUS
0645
0500

FIRST
MOBILE
FORCE

0530 - AIR SEARCH
205°-325°/325 miles

0800

SUPPLY
GROUP

torpedo hits. Finally, 10 Hellcat fighter bombers from the CVL *Bataan* added to the damage to the carrier which was hit by an unknown but large number of bombs. *Zuikaku*'s aviation fuel was set on fire and orders were given to abandon ship. The carrier was only saved by exceptional damage control, a rarity in the Japanese Navy. *Zuikaku*'s battle hardened officers and men were able to concentrate on controlling the fires; serious flooding from hits by a few torpedo bombers might well have overloaded the system and disposed of the 1st Mobile Fleet's last heavy carrier.

Force 'B' was disposed with the flagship *Junyo* in the centre, with the other carriers 1,500m away on each quarter, *Hiyo* to port and *Ryuho* to starboard. The two heavy surface ships were on station on each bow, the battleship *Nagato* to starboard and the cruiser *Mogami* to port. The destroyer screen was spread out in a 2,000m circle.

Lt-Cdr R. Weymouth, *Lexington*'s dive-bomber commander and group leader co-ordinated his strike with Arnold's and concentrated on Force 'B'. Unfortunately the Avengers accompanying his

Dauntlesses were carrying bombs rather than torpedoes. They hit *Junyo* twice and near-missed her six times. Four Avengers from *Enterprise* carried out glide-bombing attacks on *Ryuho* under fire from the guns of all calibres — including *Nagato*'s 16in main armament. This put the Americans off their aim and *Ryuho* was only near-missed.

Torpedo-carrying Avengers were much more serious threats and three from the CVL *Belleau Wood* took on *Hiyo*. Thanks to the heroism of Lt (jg) George Brown, the flight leader, who deliberately drew down Japanese fire, two hits were scored. The two 600lb charges on the stubby Mk 13 torpedoes caused catastrophic damage to the converted liner's hull and *Hiyo* listed to port, dead in the water and on fire. Two hours later the stricken carrier sank, watched by Radioman E. C. Babcock and Gunner G. H. Platz whom Brown had ordered to bail out. They were floating in the water nearby awaiting rescue by an American submarine; Brown was killed when his heavily damaged aircraft crashed on the return flight.

Group 'C' was the toughest target with its powerful surface ships. The light carriers were recov-

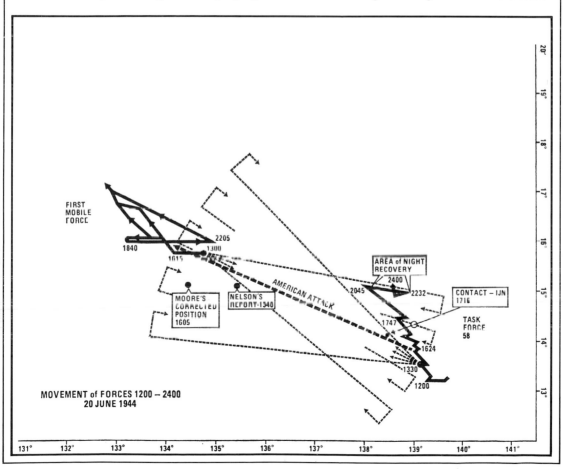

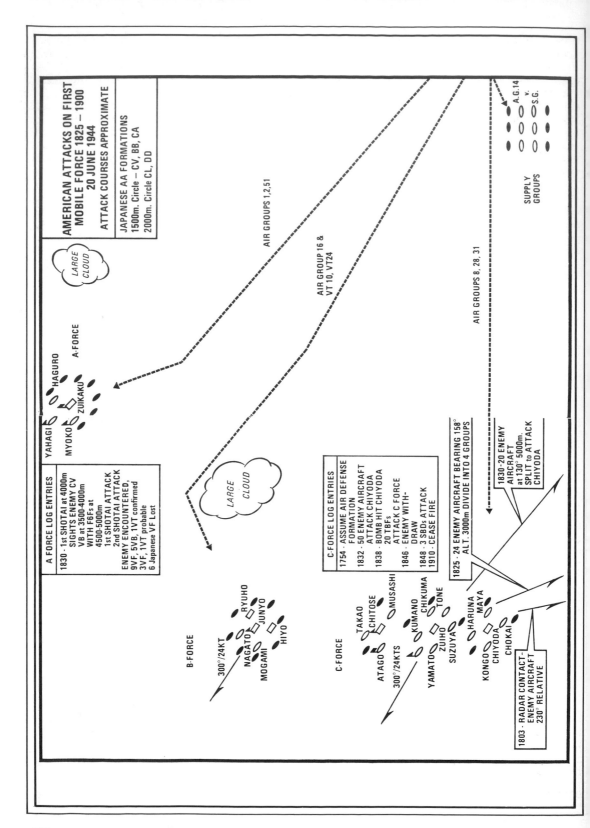

AMERICAN ATTACKS ON FIRST
MOBILE FORCE 1825 – 1900
20 JUNE 1944
ATTACK COURSES APPROXIMATE

JAPANESE AA FORMATIONS
1500m. Circle – CV, BB, CA
2000m. Circle CL, DD

A.G.14
v.
S.G.

SUPPLY
GROUPS

AIR GROUPS 1,2,51

AIR GROUP 16 &
VT 10, VT24

AIR GROUPS 8, 28, 31

LARGE
CLOUD

A-FORCE

YAHAGI
HAGURO
MYOKO
ZUIKAKU

A FORCE LOG ENTRIES

1830 - 1st SHOTAI at 4000m
SIGHTS ENEMY CV
VB at 3500-4000m
WITH F6Fs at
4500-5000m
1st SHOTAI ATTACK
2nd SHOTAI ATTACK
ENEMY ENCOUNTERED,
9VF, 5VB, 1VT confirmed
3VF, 1VT probable
6 Japanese VF Lost

LARGE
CLOUD

C FORCE LOG ENTRIES

1754 - ASSUME AIR DEFENSE
FORMATION
1832 - 50 ENEMY AIRCRAFT
ATTACK CHIYODA
1838 - BOMB HIT CHIYODA
20 TBFs
ATTACK C FORCE
1846 - ENEMY WITH-
DRAW
1848 - 3 SBDs ATTACK
1910 - CEASE FIRE

1825 - 24 ENEMY AIRCRAFT BEARING 158°
ALT. 3000m DIVIDE INTO 4 GROUPS

1830 - 20 ENEMY
AIRCRAFT
at 130° 5000m.
SPLIT to ATTACK
CHIYODA

B-FORCE

RYUHO
NAGATO
JUNYO
MOGAMI
HIYO

300°/24KT

C-FORCE

TAKAO
CHITOSE
MUSASHI
ATAGO
KUMANO
CHIKUMA
TONE
ZUIHO
HARUNA
YAMATO
SUZUYA
MAYA
KONGO
CHIYODA
CHOKAI

300°/24KTS

1803 - RADAR CONTACT-
ENEMY AIRCRAFT
230° RELATIVE

ering a strike of 16 aircraft launched at 1600 against a false contact and seven of the Japanese aircraft were disposed of by the American attackers as they circled for landing. The carrier *Chiyoda* was dive bombed by *Bunker Hill*'s Helldivers but all of them missed. Avenger bombers from the *Monterey* and *Cabot* and Avenger torpedo-bombers from *Bunker Hill* followed the dive-bombers. *Chiyoda* was hit by two bombs aft which started fires and the battleship *Haruna* was hit three times aft and near-missed twice forward. The fast battleship was forced to flood her after magazines and suffered damage to her shafts: nevertheless she could still make 27kt. *Maya* was near-missed, the bomb starting a fire on the torpedo deck that was soon extinguished with no serious damage. The torpedo bombers then carried out a high speed, high altitude attack on *Chiyoda* but all five Mk 13s dropped, missed, and the carrier was left free to put out her fires. The last three torpedo Avengers attacked a cruiser and a battleship but equally fruitlessly. The heavy fire

put up by Force 'C', a spectacular multicoloured barrage including special time fused HE and incendiary shrapnel 18in shells used in the AA mode, had protected the Force from serious damage.

Hiyo was the only Japanese warship actually sunk by the air strike. The main losses were to Ozawa's already reduced air strength; 65 more aircraft were destroyed both in the air and in the carriers. By the evening of 20 June the 1st Mobile Fleet was down to 35 carrier aircraft plus 12 floatplanes. Japanese carriers would never put to sea with fully operational air groups again. It was the end of the Japanese carrier force as an effective unit.

The Japanese had launched 75 'Zeros' in their defence. Hellcats claimed 22 enemy aircraft definitely shot down and seven 'probables'. Dauntlesses from *Lexington*'s VB-15 scored two-air-to-air victories and Avengers another two; *Bunker Hill*'s Helldivers claimed two 'probables', VB-15 another and an Avenger yet another. Some

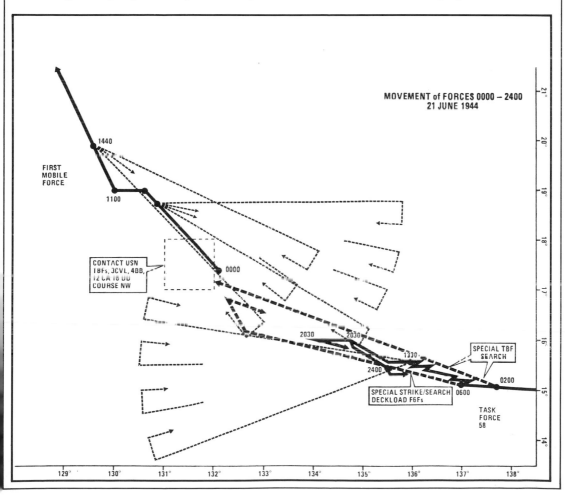

of the Japanese pilots had been good and six Hellcats were lost in air combat. A Helldiver and two Avengers were shot down by AA fire over the Japanese fleet and three Helldivers, two Dauntlesses and an Avenger were lost to fighters — but the main US losses were yet to come.

As the strike aircraft tried to reach their carriers about 250 miles away they began to ditch as they ran out of fuel. The Hellcats were better off with their drop tanks and almost all returned to the carriers, which had turned eastwards to land on and were proceeding at 22kt. Adm Clark ordered his Task Group to turn on their lights and Mitscher soon gave similar orders to the entire Task Force. At 2052 he ordered his aircraft to land on any available carrier and some desperate pilots tried to land on cruisers and destroyers which were firing starshell to help with the illumination. Many aircraft crashed on landing or collided with other aircraft on deck, others had to ditch. Over the entire raid operational accidents claimed 14 Hellcats, 39 Helldivers, four Dauntlesses and 23 Avengers, bringing losses to 99. Excellent rescue work in the succeeding hours reduced the death toll to 16 pilots and 33 crewmen; two officers and four men were killed on board the carriers.

Recovery lasted until 2252 when the carriers turned back both to close the enemy and rescue their ditched aircrew. Ozawa bravely ordered Kurita's powerful surface force eastward for a night attack but no American ships could be found and at 2205 the battleships and cruisers were ordered to turn to the northwest and retire with the rest of the Fleet. Mitscher had suggested that Lee's Surface Action Group be sent ahead as the Carrier Groups rescued aircraft but Spruance preferred to keep his fleet concentrated and in any case TG58.7 would not be able to catch the enemy by the following morning. It seemed better in the circumstances to keep the battleships to deal with any surface threats or damaged enemy warships encountered overnight.

A PBM Mariner flying-boat maintained contact with Ozawa during the darkness as did Avengers with long range tanks, but the need to sail into wind to operate aircraft held back Spruance's pursuit of the fleeing foe. At 0545 and 0615 TF58 launched two armed reconnaissance missions with Hellcat fighter-bombers to search and strike out to 270 miles but nothing was sighted. At 0743 TF58's Avengers finally lost Ozawa when he was 360 miles from Spruance and Mitscher. At 1920 on 21 June Spruance announced that if nothing was spotted that day the fleet was to retire. TF58 duly reversed course at 2030 with the battleships of TG58.7 where the American strike had taken place just over 24hr before the previous evening. As his fleet entered Nakagasuki Bay, Okinawa the same evening a shattered Ozawa offered his resignation to Adm Toyoda — who refused it.

Ozawa had, indeed, handled his forces quite well, only being let down by inferior men and equipment. There were, however, serious recriminations on the American side about Spruance's overly defensive tactics. Spruance admitted:

'that going out after the Japanese and knocking their carriers out would have been much better and more satisfactory than waiting for them to attack us; but we were at the start of a very important and large amphibious operation and we could not afford to gamble and place it in jeopardy. The way Togo waited at Tsushima for the Russian fleet has always been on my mind. We had somewhat the same basic situation; only it was modified by the long range striking power of the carriers.'

It is hard not to agree. Spruance's caution allowed Mitscher to concentrate all his fighters on annihilating the Japanese carrier-based air arm. In a classic demonstration of the defensive form of war allowing attack under optimal conditions, the enemy had been drawn out and destroyed. The Hellcat fighters were no mere defence but as effective a striking force as any other aircraft in Task Force 58's inventory.

The loss of the armament of the Japanese carriers was the most decisive result of the great American victory of the Philippine Sea. On their own estimate the Japanese felt their Imperial Combined Fleet to be powerless. Nothing more could be done to defend the Japanese Empire using conventional forces and tactics. The Tojo Government resigned and any other nation than Japan might have sought peace. But, sadly for herself, Imperial Japan was culturally incapable of making peace. She embarked on an increasingly desperate policy of making the Allied advance too expensive to continue. There were still strong Japanese surface forces, carriers without air groups and landbased aircraft with raw pilots who could at least crash them into enemy ships. Was this a formula to stop the Americans?

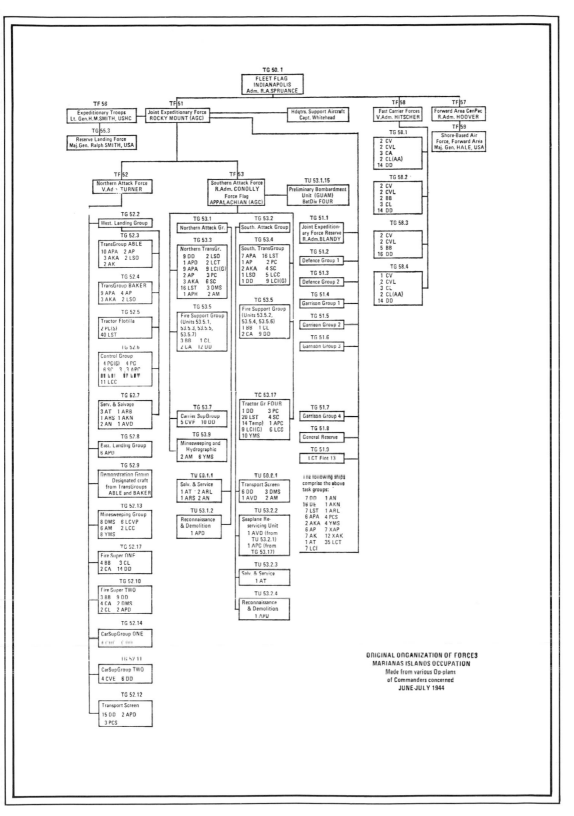

TG 50. 1
FLEET FLAG
INDIANAPOLIS
Adm. R.A.SPRUANCE

TF 56
Expeditionary Troops
Lt. Gen.H.M.SMITH, USHC

TF 51
Joint Expeditionary Force
ROCKY MOUNT (AGC)

Hdqtrs. Support Aircraft
Capt. Whitehead

TF 58
Fast Carrier Forces
V.Adm. HITSCHER

TF 57
Forward Area CenPac
R.Adm. HOOVER

TG 55.3
Reserve Landing Force
Maj.Gen. Ralph SMITH, USA

TG 59
Shore-Based Air
Force, Forward Area
Maj. Gen. HALE, USA

TG 58.1
2 CV
2 CVL
3 CA
2 CL(AA)
14 DD

TF 52
Northern Attack Force
V.Ad TURNER

TF 53
Southern Attack Force
R.Adm. CONOLLY
Force Flag
APPALACHIAN (AGC)

TU 53.1.15
Preliminary Bombardment
Unit (GUAM)
BatDiv FOUR

TG 58.2
2 CV
2 CVL
2 BB
3 CL
14 DD

TG 52.2
West. Landing Group

TG 53.1
Northern Attack Gr.

TG 53.2
South. Attack Group

TG 51.1
Joint Expedition-
ary Force Reserve
R.Adm.BLANDY

TG 58.3
2 CV
2 CVL
5 BB
16 DD

TG 52.3
TransGroup ABLE
10 APA 2 AP
3 AKA 2 LSO
2 AK

TG 53.3
Northern TransGr.
9 DD   2 LSO
1 APD   2 LCT
9 APA   9 LCI(G)
2 AP   3 PC
3 AKA   6 SC
16 LST 3 DMS
1 APH   2 AM

TG 53.4
South. TransGroup
7 APA   16 LST
1 AP   2 PC
2 AKA   4 SC
1 LSD   5 LCC
1 DD   9 LCI(G)

TG 51.2
Defence Group 1

TG 51.3
Defence Group 2

TG 58.4
1 CV
2 CVL
3 CL
2 CL(AA)
14 DD

TG 52.4
TransGroup BAKER
9 APA   4 AP
3 AKA   2 LSO

TG 52.5
Tractor Flotilla
2 PC(S)
40 LST

TG 53.5
Fire Support Group
(Units 53.5.1,
53.5.3, 53.5.5,
53.5.7)
3 BB   1 CL
2 CA   12 DD

TG 53.5
Fire Support Group
(Units 53.5.2,
53.5.4, 53.5.6)
1 BB   1 CL
2 CA   9 DD

TG 51.4
Garrison Group 1

TG 51.5
Garrison Group 2

TG 51.6
Garrison Group 3

TG 52.6
Control Group
4 PC(G) 4 PC
6 SC   3 3 APC
88 LCI 87 LCT
11 LCC

TG 52.7
Serv. & Salvage
3 AT   1 ARB
1 AHS 1 AKN
2 AN   1 AVD

TG 53.7
Carrier SupGroup
5 CVF 10 DD

TG 53.17
Tractor Gr FOUR
1 DD   3 PC
20 LST 4 SC
14 Temp) 1 APC
9 LCI(G) 6 LCC
10 YMS

TG 51.7
Garrison Group 4

TG 51.8
General Reserve

TG 52.8
East. Landing Group
6 APD

TG 53.9
Minesweeping and
Hydrographic
2 AM 6 YMS

TG 51.9
LCT Flot 13

TG 52.9
Demonstration Group
Designated craft
from TransGroups
ABLE and BAKER

TU 50.1.1
Salv. & Service
1 AT 2 ARL
1 ARS 2 AN

TU 50.2.1
Transport Screen
6 DD   3 DMS
1 AVD   2 AM

The following ships
comprise the above
task groups:
7 DD   1 AN
16 DE   1 AKN
7 LST   1 ARL
6 APA   4 PCS
2 AKA   4 YMS
6 AP   7 XAP
7 AK   12 XAK
1 AT   35 LCT
7 LCI

TG 52.13
Minesweeping Group
8 DMS   6 LCVP
6 AM   2 LCC
8 YMS

TU 53.1.2
Reconnaissance
& Demolition
1 APD

TU 53.2.2
Seaplane Re-
servicing Unit
1 AVD (from
TU 53.2.1)
1 APC (from
TG 53.17)

TG 52.17
Fire Super ONE
4 BB   3 CL
2 CA   14 DD

TU 53.2.3
Salv. & Service
1 AT

TG 52.10
Fire Super TWO
3 BB   9 DD
4 CA   2 DMS
2 CL   2 APD

TU 53.2.4
Reconnaissance
& Demolition
1 APD

TG 52.14
CarSupGroup ONE
4 CVE 6 DD

TG 52.11
CarSupGroup TWO
4 CVE 6 DD

TG 52.12
Transport Screen
15 DD 2 APD
3 PCS

ORIGINAL ORGANIZATION OF FORCES
MARIANAS ISLANDS OCCUPATION
Made from various Op-plans
of Commanders concerned
JUNE-JULY 1944

CHAPTER NINE

Leyte Gulf

The Battle of the Philippine Sea destroyed Japanese carrier air power, but the Imperial Japanese Combined Fleet was still an enormously powerful fighting force, with the most powerful gun and torpedo-armed surface warships the world had ever seen. Yet, without carrier aircraft it lacked the weapon that had above all others proved decisive in the Pacific War. The Japanese commanders were faced with the problem of how they could utilise their remaining fighting power when the Americans moved beyond the Marianas to their next objective. Three 'Sho' or 'Victory' plans were created: the first for the Philippines, the second for Taiwan and the third for the Ryukyus. When the blow fell on the Philippines with the invasion of Leyte that began with preliminary landings on 17 October, followed by the main attack on the 20th, SHO-1 was duly activated. The knotty operational problem of how to deal with the American carriers allowed the Japanese to indulge their traditions of elaborate planning with a complex weave of different forces. The basic pattern of SHO-1 was, however, quite simple. Japan would send down from the home islands a decoy force of almost empty carriers to distract the attention of the main American fleet to the north. As the fast carriers and their surface escorts swung northwards, powerful Japanese surface forces would descend on Leyte Gulf from two directions and annihilate the amphibious forces. Such a defeat might just possibly give the Americans pause in their relentless march to impose unconditional surrender on the Japanese Empire. But questions of 'face' and honour were paramount. As Vice-Adm Takeo Kurita, the commander of the surface fleet riding at Lingga Roads just over the Straits of Malacca from Singapore, put it to his captains; 'Would it not be shameful to have the fleet remain intact while our nation perishes?'

Vice-Adm Takeo Kurita, born in 1889, was very much a surface warfare officer. A quiet and taciturn man his background was in destroyers and cruisers and he commanded both types of ship. He reached flag rank in 1938 and was known as one of the Imperial Navy's leading tactical conservatives. His 7th Cruiser Division suffered heavy casualties at the battle of Midway partly due to a collision, but this was lost in the wider disaster and Kurita was promoted Vice-Admiral. After commanding the Close Support Force of two fast battleships and six destroyers at the Battle of Santa Cruz in October 1942, he succeeded Adm Kondo in charge of the whole 2nd Fleet. With seven of the Japanese Navy's most powerful heavy cruisers he was sent to Rabaul where his bad luck held. No sooner had he arrived but the fleet was struck by American carrier planes in November 1943. Kurita eventually ended up as 5th Fleet commander with virtually all the Japanese major surface warships but his leadership continued to vacillate from the overly aggressive to the over cautious. This had come through in the Philippine Sea débâcle. Kurita's judgement was not improved in October 1944 by a nasty bout of dengue fever.

Nevertheless he had a magnificent force at his disposal, with seven battleships, the two 62,300-ton (standard) 18in gun armed monsters *Yamato* and *Musashi*, the 39,000-ton 16in gun *Nagato*, and four much rebuilt veterans of World War 1, all armed with 14in guns: the slow 35,000-ton *Fuso* and *Yamashiro* and the fast 32,000-ton ex-battlecruisers, *Kongo* and *Haruna*. There were no less than 11 8in gun armed heavy cruisers, in one of which, *Atago*, Adm Kurita flew his flag. Two modern 6in gun light cruisers led 19 destroyers, most large vessels of the 'Kagero' and 'Yugumo' classes each armed with four 5in guns , eight 24in tubes for 'Long Lance' torpedoes and up to 28 25mm AA guns. These forces were to go first to Brunei to refuel. Most would then move with Kurita through the Sibuyan Sea and San Bernadino Strait down the east coast of the large island of Samar and then finally 'storm' into Leyte Gulf from the north. Vice-Adm Shoji Nishimura would, however, take a smaller force formed of

Above right:
Major US Naval and chains of command in Leyte operation.

Right:
The Japanese surface fleet before its desperate throw at Leyte. Right to left are *Nagato*, *Yamato* and *Musashi*. *US Naval Historical Center NH73090*

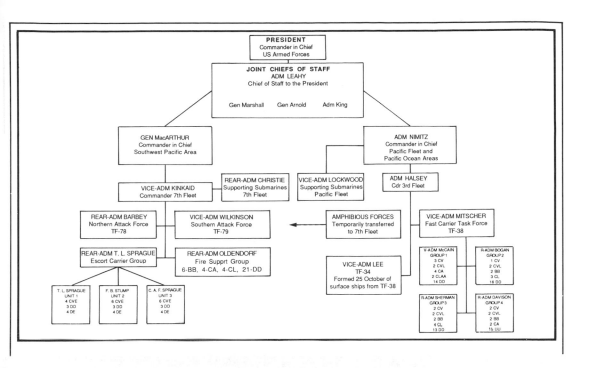

Fuso, Yamashiro, the 8in cruiser Mogami and the four oldest destroyers to form the other half of the pincer movement, entering Leyte Gulf from the south through Surigao Strait. A second portion of the southern pincer would be provided by Vice-Adm Shima with two heavy cruisers, a light cruiser and seven destroyers joining up from the Pescadores islands.

The effectiveness of this massive concentration of surface firepower depended on the success of the northern carrier decoy group. Vice-Adm Jisaburo Ozawa commander of the 1st Mobile Fleet assembled this from the ships and aircraft available in the home islands. Japan was not badly off for carriers, with new 17,000-ton light fleet carriers of the 'Unryu' class just coming into service. However what she did not have were aircraft or trained aircrew. By raiding the air groups assigned

to the new ships, Ozawa was able to scrape together 108 aircraft. The fleet carrier *Zuikaku*, veteran of many battles, carried about 24 'Zero' fighters, 16 'Zero' fighter-bombers, seven 'Judy' dive-bombers and a dozen 'Jill' torpedo-bombers. The light carriers *Zuiho*, *Chiyoda* and *Chitose* would between them carry about 40 'Zero' fighters and fighter-bombers and 17 attack aircraft, 13 modern 'Jills' and four old 'Kates'. Ozawa also had the two old 35,000-ton battleships, *Ise* and *Hyuga*, converted at much trouble and expense into hybrid battleship-carriers, with a flightdeck and hangar for seaplanes instead of the two aftermost 14in gun turrets. Ironically, however, there were now no aircraft for these ships and they were crammed with over 100 light anti-aircraft guns and six AA rocket launchers to support the carriers. These vessels were to form the bait for the trap; they were to be screened by three light cruisers, four large 'Akitsuki' class task force escort destroyers and four new, small destroyer escorts. Ozawa, supported by a group of two tankers screened by seven more escorts, sailed on 20 October.

The Japanese had high hopes that their decoy operation would succeed. They knew that the Philippines operation was covered by Adm William Frederick Halsey. Halsey was the opposite of Kurita, or Spruance for that matter: his ebullient and aggressive nature suited the destroyers in which he spent much of his early career but he was no simple seaman and became a leading expert on the theory and practice of destroyer operations. The new technology of air power appealed to him and, despite advanced years and the rank of Captain, he took aviation training at Pensacola, qualifying in 1935. This meant he could command carriers and he commanded the Pacific Fleet's air forces when war broke out. His early counter-attacks, including the Doolittle raid, helped make his reputation with the press as the aggressive 'Bull' Halsey, although it was a nickname he did not cultivate for personal use. He missed Midway because of a skin infection but was associated with the fighting around Guadalcanal and the offensive in the South Pacific. He was given the South Pacific naval command after initial setbacks especially to insert a little forcefulness into a lacklustre command. Before the Battle of Santa Cruz he confirmed his aggressive reputation by a famous signal to Adm Kinkaid, 'Attack, repeat attack'. This battle had reduced American carrier strength in the Pacific to a single ship. He had already told his subordinates that their job was to 'kill Japs, kill more Japs'. Halsey's charismatic aggressiveness was excellent for morale throughout the war. The South Pacific forces became the 3rd Fleet in 1943 and Halsey remained commander of it after it became one of the two alternative command staffs available for Central Pacific operations. He took over from Spruance after the latter's controversial victory at Philippine Sea and this probably encouraged Halsey to act with determination in the Philippines even at some risk. The change of C-in-C and staff meant that all other designations were altered accordingly but the forces, eg Adm Mitscher and Task Force 38 ('TF38'), remained essentially the same as they had been as TF58.

The Japanese put considerable emphasis on the psychological make-up of their opponents in their planning. Just as their plans in the Marianas had tried to capitalise on Spruance's caution so the Philippines plan counted on the 'Bull's' propensity to charge. Sadly, however, the Americans first missed Ozawa, the force they were meant to find, and found Kurita, the force they were intended to miss! There was an Anglo-American submarine patrol line west of the Philippines and USS *Darter* and *Dace* were in the narrow Palawan Passage that Kurita had chosen to use. At about midnight on 23 October, as the two submarines cruised together on the surface they picked up Kurita on radar; they rapidly closed the contact and confirmed it as the Japanese battlefleet. Cdr David McClintock placed *Darter* on the starboard bow of the leading cruiser, closed to less than 1,000yd and fired his six bow torpedoes at her. He then turned the boat and fired his four stern tubes at the next ship in line; the first torpedoes were already exploding. Four torpedoes hit *Atago*, the 13,400-ton fleet flagship, all the way along her starboard side, causing catastrophic flooding. The cruiser was fatally damaged in her machinery spaces and began to list rapidly to starboard, flames gushing from her air intakes. Adm Kurita and his staff were among the first to leave, to be plucked from the water by the 'Yugumo' class destroyer *Kishinami* but as the *Atago* lurched still

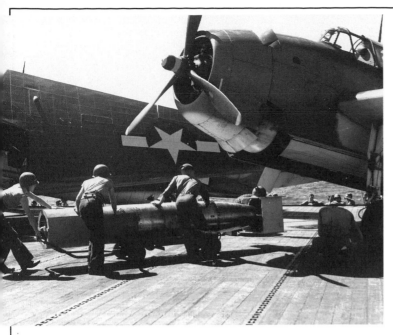

further over on her side her captain gave the order to abandon ship. *Kishinami* and her sister *Asashimo* rescued 711 men, including the Captain: 359 men were lost.

The second cruiser attacked was *Atago*'s sister *Tahao*, struck twice on the starboard side. Two large holes were blown in her but the damage was not so serious and counterflooding corrected the list. Not so lucky was *Maya*, USS *Dace*'s much rebuilt victim. She was blown apart by three hits on the port side. The Japanese were lucky to save 769 of her ship's company of 1,000. Vice-Adm Matome Ugaki in *Yamato* took over temporary command and sorted out the fleet that had been thrown into considerable confusion. Kurita then chose the super battleship as his new flagship and during the afternoon transferred from the *Kishinami*. Ugaki, an ambitious and intelligent officer who had served as the late Adm Yamamoto's chief-of-staff, swallowed his pride and said, 'This I suppose is fate' and welcomed Kurita on board. The US submarines were able neither to renew the assault nor even to finish off *Takao*. Luck

turned against them and *Darter* ran aground and had to be abandoned. Nevertheless the 3rd Fleet's carriers had their targets for the following day.

Halsey was commanding the main striking forces, Vice-Adm Mitscher's TF38, directly from the battleship *New Jersey*. TF38 was, as usual, composed of four Carrier Task Groups. Vice-Adm John S. McCain's Task Group (TG) TG38.1 was made up of the fleet carriers *Wasp* (53 Hellcats, including 10 fighter-bombers, 25 Helldivers and 18 Avengers) and *Hornet* (40 Hellcats, 25 Helldivers and 18 Avengers) and the light carriers *Monterey* and *Princeton* (each with nine Avengers and 23 and 26 Hellcats respectively). Rear-Adm Gerald F. Bogan's TG38.2 deployed the fleet carriers *Intrepid* (44 Hellcats, 28 Helldivers and 18 Avengers), *Hancock* (41 Hellcats, 42 Helldivers and 18 Avengers) and *Bunker Hill* (49 Hellcats, 24 Helldivers and 19 Avengers) and the light carriers *Cabot* (21 Hellcats and nine Avengers) and *Independence* (19 Hellcats — mostly night fighters — and eight Avengers). Rear-Adm Frederick C. Sherman's TG38.3 had *Essex* herself (51 Hellcats, 25 Helldivers and 20 Avengers), Mitscher's flagship *Lexington* (42 Hellcats, 30 Helldivers and 18 Avengers) and the light carriers *Princeton* and *Langley* (both with 25 Hellcats and nine Avengers). TG 38.4 comprised the *Franklin* (39 Hellcats, 31 Helldivers and 18 Avengers) and the veteran *Enterprise* (39 Hellcats, 34 Helldivers and 19 Avengers) along with the light carriers *San Jacinto* (19 Hellcats and seven Avengers) and *Belleau Wood* (25 Hellcats and nine Avengers). The six modern battleships were available for attach-

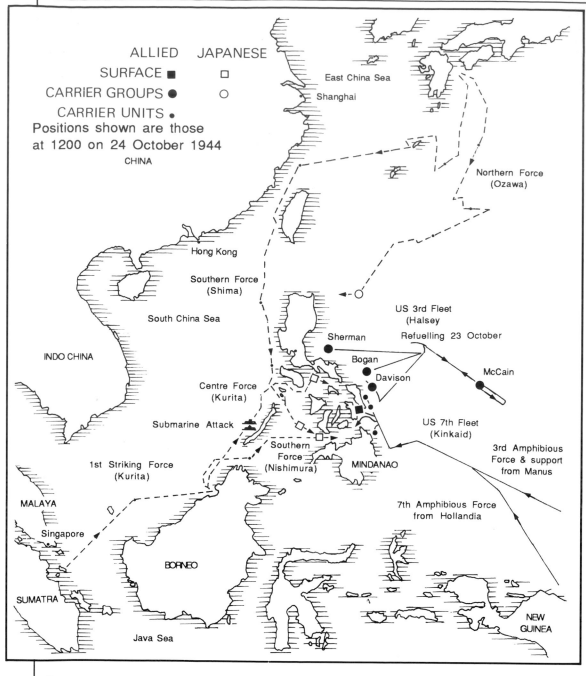

ALLIED   JAPANESE
SURFACE ■   □
CARRIER GROUPS ●   ○
CARRIER UNITS ●
Positions shown are those
at 1200 on 24 October 1944

CHINA

East China Sea

Shanghai

Northern Force
(Ozawa)

Hong Kong

Southern Force
(Shima)

South China Sea

US 3rd Fleet
(Halsey

Refuelling 23 October

Sherman

INDO CHINA

Bogan

McCain

Davison

Centre Force
(Kurita)

Submarine Attack

US 7th Fleet
(Kinkaid)

Southern
Force
(Nishimura)   MINDANAO

3rd Amphibious
Force & support
from Manus

1st Striking Force
(Kurita)

MALAYA

7th Amphibious Force
from Hollandia

Singapore

BORNEO

SUMATRA

NEW
GUINEA

Java Sea

Above:
The approach to Leyte Gulf, 24 October 1944.

ment to Carrier Task Groups for AA cover and surface action support. The Support Task Units contained 13 cruisers and the screen 58 destroyers. Halsey had been in action since 10 October with a series of air strikes that had smashed Japanese land-based air power in the Ryukyus, Formosa and the Philippines. The Japanese had tried to counterattack but their air raids had been chopped out of the sky by Mitscher's formidable Hellcats. The heavy cruiser *Canberra* and light cruiser *Houston* were, however, hit by torpedo-bombers and forced to retire towed by two tugs, screened by the cruisers *Santa Fe*, *Birmingham* and *Mobile* and eight destroyers, and covered by the light carriers *Cowpens* and *Cabot*, the cruiser *Wichita* and a four more destroyers. The losses were soon made up by a new task unit of three more cruisers and six destroyers and the gradual return of the detached ships. The damage might have been significant in 1941 or early 1942, but it did not matter much strategically or operationally in 1944. The US Navy was now just too strong. Saving both ships was however a considerable feat of damage control; *Houston*, hit twice, had filled with 6,500 tons of water, more than any other ship had taken in without sinking.

These air battles completed the work of the offensive strikes in destroying Japanese land-based naval air power and the American landings went in covered by another entire American Fleet, Vice-Adm Thomas C. Kinkaid's 7th, subordinate to Gen MacArthur's South West Pacific Area Command. By concentrating every available aircraft on the morning of 24 October Adm Fukudome in the Philippines was able to mount one last assault on the American fleet carriers to cover

the arrival of Kurita. He got 150 aircraft into the air which attacked Adm Sherman's TG38.3 off Luzon. The American carriers were about to strike at Kurita and the escort fighters were rapidly reassigned to deal with the Japanese raiders. They broke up the Japanese formations but one 'Judy' got through and bombed the light carrier *Princeton* hitting loaded torpedo bombers on the hangar deck. It was a small revenge for Midway when the Japanese had been rather similarly caught and the carrier erupted in smoke and flames. Soon the torpedoes began to explode. Other ships came alongside to help control the conflagration, including the cruiser *Birmingham* newly returned from her previous mercy mission. Charity has a price and during the afternoon a heavy explosion on board the carrier raked the decks of the hapless cruiser killing 229 officers and men instantly and wounding 420, 219 seriously. *Princeton* was abandoned and was finished off with torpedoes by the cruiser *Reno* after the destroyer *Irwin*, also damaged fighting fires, had almost succeeded in sinking herself with errant torpedoes. The carrier disappeared after a final massive explosion in the aviation fuel tanks.

Below:
First blood to the Japanese was the light carrier *Princeton* hit by a lone 'Judy' on 24 October with devastating effect. Here the cruiser *Birmingham* comes alongside to give assistance. A devastating explosion would later sink the carrier and do dreadful execution among the men exposed on the cruiser's upperworks.
US National Archives 80-G-281660-2

TG38 had, however, drawn blood in return. Unaffected by the Japanese air attack, TG38.2 launched its strike of a dozen Avengers, a dozen Helldivers and 21 Hellcats at 0910. The lessons of June had been learned and the Avengers were carrying torpedoes. The strike concentrated on the giant *Musashi* that was damaged by both near-miss bombs and a torpedo hit. Although the ship maintained cruising formation, damage had been quite severe and demonstrated, ominously, that the underwater protection of these behemoths left something to be desired. Four more waves of carrier aircraft attacked Kurita that day and like carnivores around a herd of prey concentrated on the wounded beast. *Musashi* was hit by no less than 20 torpedoes and 17 bombs, while 18 near miss bomb explosions significantly contributed to the underwater damage. Bombing and machine gunning converted her upperworks into a shambles, allowing *Musashi*'s later attackers to take more careful aim. The maddened giant fired her massive 18in guns against her assailants but to no avail. She settled lower and lower in the water as the flooding became more serious and the bows finally dipped beneath the waves. As the ship listed terminally to port, abandon ship was finally ordered and 15min later at 1935 *Musashi* capsized, taking with her 1,023 officers and men of her ship's company of 2,399.

Even before the giant battleship foundered, Kurita, who had also been forced to detach the damaged heavy cruiser *Myoko*, had turned back with his wounded force. Both *Yamato* and *Nagato* were bombed and damaged. Kurita's raging fever had not been helped by his enforced soaking in the ocean. Then he had suffered terrible air attacks from the carriers that should not have been there. No wonder he decided to turn, to allow more attrition to be inflicted on the Americans by land-based aircraft, and the decoy strategy to mature and to deceive the Americans as to his intentions. However at 1815 he received a prompt from Adm Toyoda, the Combined Fleet commander in Japan: 'With confidence in heavenly guidance the combined force will attack'. In Japanese terms this message was a stinging rebuke that brooked no gainsaying. So the fleet sailed once more eastwards, past the sinking wreck of the *Musashi*, towards San Bernadino Strait and the Leyte Gulf landing area.

Kurita's turn brought the Japanese a second chance of success. Shortly before mid-day on the 24th, Ozawa in the decoy force had launched an air strike with 76 aircraft whose main purpose was to advertise the carriers' presence. It was virtually un-noticed as its ill-trained pilots added to the general kills obtained by the American carriers' combat air patrols deployed against attacks by land-based aircraft who claimed about 150 kills in all. What few carrier aircraft survived flew on to the Philippines to make easier landings and swell Fukudome's strength. Only at just after 1600 did a depressed Ozawa obtain clear evidence that at last he had been spotted — by an American Helldiver scout plane. Halsey received news of Ozawa and the carriers just as he received information of Kurita's apparent repulse. He fell for the Japanese trap completely. With his three available Carrier Battle Groups (the fourth was away refuelling) reinforced by the six battleships, he steamed north to meet the new threat. San Bernadino Strait was left completely uncovered. What made it even worse was that Kinkaid whose responsibility it was to cover the landings had listened in to the 3rd Fleet's signals and thought Halsey had left behind a powerful, Surface Action Group to guard the northern entry to Leyte Gulf. He therefore thought he could concentrate on dealing with the southern Japanese pincer.

Kinkaid was a very different officer from Halsey. Thomas Cassin Kinkaid was a surface warfare officer with a background in battleships and cruisers but, despite a lack of carrier experience, he had been chosen as tactical commander in the South Pacific under Halsey. His leadership at the expensive carrier battle of Santa Cruz was not without critics, but his mistakes could be put down to inexperience. Kinkaid's ability with surface forces helped improve American tactical thought in the operations in the Solomons, but he was removed before he could put them into effect and was placed in charge of the Aleutians in January 1943 — something of a backwater, but a command where the emphasis was even more on surface warfare. He pressed for a counter-offensive and recaptured Attu and Kiska. These amphibious successes obtained promotion to Vice-Admiral and command of Gen MacArthur's amphibious forces in the South West Pacific, the 7th Fleet. Kinkaid was in a totally different chain of command from Halsey who reported to Adm Nimitz's Central Pacific headquarters at Pearl Harbor. This contributed to American confusion.

The 7th Fleet was primarily an amphibious formation but contained powerful shore bombardment forces of escort carriers and old battleships, supported by lighter surface units that made it a formidable naval force in its own right. Kinkaid planned to give Nishimura's pair of old battleships and their supporting forces, all spotted from the air on 24 October, a warm welcome. Rear-Adm Jesse B. Oldendorf's bombardment and support group was given the task. Its centrepiece was six old battleships, all but one veterans of Pearl Harbor in the attack on which two had actually been sunk. The centre of the battle line was made up of the three radically rebuilt 35,000 ton ships *West Virginia*, *Tennessee* and *California*, the first named armed with eight 16in guns and the other two with 12 14in. The line was led by the only ship that was not a Pearl Harbor veteran, the *Mississippi*, modernised prewar and armed with 12 14in guns. She was followed by the 16in gun *Maryland*, formerly a sister of *West Virginia* but modernised less extensively. The *Pennsylvania*, the sister ship of the *Arizona* that had blown up on 7 December 1941, brought up the rear with her 12 14in guns.

The battleships commanded by Rear-Adm Weyler patrolled a beat across top of the Strait. Below them on each side were two lines of cruisers, on the left flank was Oldendorf himself with the interwar heavy cruisers *Louisville*, *Portland* and *Indianapolis* , the latter pair sister ships. With Oldendorf was Rear Adm Hayler with the modern light cruisers *Denver* and *Columbia*. On the right was Rear-Adm Berkey with the prewar light cruisers *Phoenix* and *Boise* and the Australian heavy cruiser *Shropshire*.

Two small historical notes are in order here. *Shropshire* was the major White Ensign ship to take part in this the largest naval battle in history; there was now little doubt who was 'top nation' at sea. The second point is almost eerie; Berkey's two 'Brooklyn' class cruisers would pass to Argentina after the war and the *Phoenix*, renamed *General Belgrano*, would achieve a certain notoriety in 1982 by being the first (and so far the only) warship ever to be sunk by a nuclear powered submarine. Having been in at the end of one era in naval warfare — the last clash of super-dreadnoughts in naval history — she confirmed the beginning of another and the emergence of a new form of capital ship; phoenix from the ashes, indeed.

Oldendorf had 22 destroyers to act as pickets, to screen the heavier ships and to rush forward on each side of the strait to add their torpedoes to the maelstrom of steel into which the Japanese would sail. The screen was made up of four 'Fletchers' and two 'Gleaves' class ships, the left flank striking force of nine Fletchers (90 21in tubes all told) and the right five 'Fletchers' and the Australian 'Tribal' HMAS *Arunta* (54 tubes). The right flank destroyers were already patrolling north-south off

USS *West Virginia*

Built: Newport News (launched 19 November 1921)

Displacement: 37,800 standard

Dimensions: 624ft x 114ft x 33.1ft

Armour: 13.5in belt; 5-6.5in total deck; 5-18in turrets

Machinery: four shaft geared turbines, 29,500hp, 20.5kt

Armament: 8 x 16in (4 x 2); 16 x 5in (8 x 2); 40 x 40mm AA (10 x 4); 64 x 20mm AA (58 x 1, 1 x 2, 1 x 4)

Sensors: SK air warning and fire control radar

Complement: 2,375

Notes: Sunk at Pearl Harbor and totally reconstructed along the lines of the 14in ships *California* and *Tennessee*. Used primarily for shore bombardment because of her limited speed, the ship retained formidable striking power coupled with modern radar. In the Surigao Strait action she fired 93 16in rounds, more shells than any other battleship.

the Leyte shore. Seven more 'Fletchers' were disposed as pickets and 39 PT boats acted as a forward screen at the foot of the strait.

The Japanese were suffering their own command problems. Nishimura was supposed to act as overall commander of the southern thrust but Shima, ordered to his support, had gained seniority over his 'simple seadog' classmate in political intrigues in Tokyo. The two men loathed each other and sulkily refused to communicate. Thus it was as two disconnected groups that the greatly outnumbered southern force sailed to its death. The PT boats were brushed aside by the Japanese but they kept Oldendorf informed of enemy movements.

Just after 0200 on the morning of 25 October Capt J. G. Coward of the picket destroyer squadron, DesRon 54, ordered his ships to General Quarters. He left two destroyers to guard the other exit of the strait north of Desolation Point and planned to attack the enemy from both sides with his Divisional commander on the right; with the *McDemutt* and *Monssen* and himself on the left with *Remey*, *McGowan* and *Melvin*. This was a classic prewar type manoeuvre to put the enemy's line into confusion and inflict casualties before the main engagement, and the pickets were ordered

not to engage with gunfire and get out of the way as soon as possible subsequent to their attack. Just after 0300 Coward's division loosed off 27 Mk 15 torpedoes set to run at their intermediate speed setting of 33.5kt. The torpedoes' range at this setting was 10,000yd and the Japanese ships were at most 9,000yd away. The destroyers were engaged by the secondary armaments of the heavy ships and by the Japanese destroyers but made off northeastwards and out of danger. More than one

Mk 15 from the USS *Melvin* hit *Fuso* hard and the old battleship sheered off to starboard out of line, unknown to Nishimura in *Yamashiro* ahead. At 0309 the other American destroyer division began firing its torpedoes, a full broadside of 20. Nishimura took evasive action but this had the unfortunate effect of exposing his destroyer screen to the American Mk 15s. *Yamagumo* was hit and blew up, *Michishio* was crippled, and *Asagumo* had her bows blown off. *Fuso* was also hit but not seri-

Fuso

Built: Kure Dockyard (launched 28 March 1914); reconstructed same yard 1930-33

Displacement: 34.700 tons standard

Dimensions: 698ft x 108.5ft x 31.75ft

Armour: 12in belt; 7in deck; 12in turrets

Machinery: four shaft geared turbines, 75,000shp, 24.7kt

Armament: 12 x 14in (6 x 2); 14 x 6in (14 x 1); 8 x 5in AA (4 x 2); 37 x 25mm AA

Sensors: search radar

Complement: 1,396

Notes: The old super-dreadnoughts were brought up to date in the early 1930s. Kept on secondline duties until desperation forced commitment along with sister *Yamashiro*. Rebuilding allowed reduction to one funnel and the building of very oriental looking 'pagoda' bridge structure. Plans to convert on the lines of the slightly younger *Ise* and *Hyuga* into hybrid battleship carriers shelved after the disappearance of the Japanese naval air arm at the Battle of the Philippine Sea.

ously. It was one of the most successful torpedo attacks in the US Navy's history, 'brilliantly conceived and executed' as Oldendorf later wrote.

Next it was the turn of the first destroyer striking force. Capt McManes of DesRon 24 on the right was flying his pennant in the new USS *Hutchins*, fitted with a proper Combat Information Center (CIC) below decks. McManes directed the

battle from this position, an interesting late 20th century twist to an engagement that was in most ways the end of an era. McManes attacked in two divisions, the second commanded by Cdr A. E. Buchanan RAN in *Arunta*. The explosion of *Yamagumo* illuminated the scene as the attack went in. Buchanan's division fired 14 weapons; *Arunta* missed *Shigure* with her four Mk IXs but the USS *Killen* hit *Yamashiro* again with one of five Mk 15s. McManes went further south and then turned northwards to engage on a parallel course and fired 15 Mk 15s at about 0330. Firing only half the armament was probably a mistake. Torpedoes fired in 'penny packets' are usually ineffective. The intention was to keep torpedoes for a second attack and as McManes' ships circled to make another attack *Hutchins* fired his remaining five tubes at the bowless destroyer *Asagumo* trying to retire, instead they struck the drifting wreck of the *Michishio* which blew up and sank at 0358.

At 0338 *Fuso*'s damage control parties lost the battle to save the stricken old lady; in a shattering explosion the burning, sinking wreck blew into

Below:
The view from USS *Pennsylvania* during the Battle of Surigao Strait with the night lit up by the flashes of the accompanying cruisers' guns.
US National Archives 80-G-288493

two halves which drifted slowly southwards before finally slipping beneath the waves. Three minutes before *Fuso* blew herself apart the final destroyer striking force, Capt Smoot's DesRon 56, went into the attack. The three sections of three 'Fletchers' each sortied from behind the left flank cruisers, two to the east and one to the west. Cdr Conley's Section 2 fired 15 torpedoes, five each, at 0355. Section 3 fired in the same way but on the opposite beam a few minutes later. Neither scored any hits. Smoot himself delayed firing until after 0400. Before they could launch, *Yamashiro* turned hard to port and the destroyers turned to starboard to parallel the target. This eased the fire control solution. Thirteen Mk 15s were fired of which two struck the *Yamashiro* at 0411. The destroyers then retired under fire from both sides.

The gunners in the big ships had held their fire for most of the destroyer phase. Oldendorf's battleships and cruisers mounted combined broadsides of 18 16in guns, 48 14in guns, 27 8in and 43 6in. The cruisers opened fire at 7¾ miles at 0351, the battleships at 11¼ miles at 0353. Sadly this was still over-eager as the destroyer *Albert W Grant* was hit by 11 6in shells from American light cruisers as well as eight Japanese 5in rounds. She stopped dead in the water and was only saved with difficulty. The main American ships in the gunnery action were *West Virginia*, *Tenessee* and *California* whose Mk 8 fire control radar made night into day. They fired 93, 69 and 63 rounds respectively from their limited stockpiles of armour-piercing ammunition. The 16in ship fired broadsides, the other two six-gun salvos to conserve ammunition. The other three ships only had Mk 3 radar and were in trouble finding targets. *Maryland* ranged on *West Virginia*'s splashes and fired six broadsides of 48 rounds. *Mississippi* only fired one broadside, however, and *Pennsylvania* not at all before the situation became so confused that Oldendorf ordered a cease fire. The cruisers were indulging in an amazing outpouring of ammunition. The left flank cruisers fired no less than 3,100 rounds; *Columbia* fired one 6in broadside every 12sec! Their shells added to the damage to *Yamashiro* — and *Denver* disabled the unfortunate USS *Grant*. These cruisers were also taken under ineffective fire by the Japanese. The left flank cruisers were also adding to the bombardment, *Phoenix* firing broadsides every 15sec. All the cruisers seemed to hit *Yamashiro* which turned to port ablaze. Torpedoed once more, as already related she turned back towards the south only to

Below.
On the way to her fate in Surigao Strait the old battleship *Yamashiro* avoids bombs in the Sulu Sea on 24 October.
US National Archives 80-G-281763

capsize and sink at 0419. The cruiser *Mogami*, badly damaged, headed away southwards, escorted by the ever-lucky destroyer *Shigure*, which was hit by only one 8in shell which failed to explode although she was shaken by many near-misses. Shima now appeared on the scene only to have his flagship *Nachi* rammed by the poor *Mogami*. He had already lost the light cruiser *Abukuma* to damage inflicted by a PT boat's torpedo. Shima retired, cautiously followed by Old-endorf's cruisers and destroyers which finished off the destroyer *Asagumo*. *Mogami* fought off surface attacks but finally succumbed to Avenger torpedo-bombers from the escort carriers when dawn allowed flying to begin. Even then a Japanese destroyer had to inflict the *coup de grâce*. *Abukuma* was also finished off by aircraft, in this case USAAF B-24 Liberators and B-26 Marauders on 26 October. *Nachi* made for Manila with her collision damage and was eventually sunk by carrier-based aircraft in early November. Of all the Japanese ships in the southern force, therefore, only one cruiser and five destroyers survived. The southern prong of the Japanese offensive had been well and truly blunted in the last battleship-v-battleship encounter in naval history.

It all now rested on Kurita, whose still powerful northern force of four battleships, six heavy cruisers, two light cruisers and 11 destroyers sailed out of an unguarded San Bernadino Strait in the early hours of 25 October. Kurita heard of the failure of Nishimura's thrust but received no information from Ozawa on the success or otherwise of his decoy mission. Then, shortly after sunrise he seemed to receive confirmation that the 3rd Fleet was still present. The unmistakable silhouettes of carriers appeared over the horizon. These were however not the fleet carriers of TF38 but the 16 escort carriers of the 7th Fleet's TG77.4 operating in direct support of the amphibious landings under the command of Rear-Adm Thomas L. Sprague in three Task Units, known by their call signs as 'Taffy' 1, 2 and 3. It was Rear-Adm Clifton, Sprague's 'Taffy 3', that Kurita had spotted with six CVEs, *Fanshaw Bay*, *St Lo* (formerly the *Midway* but renamed to commemorate the recent victory in Normandy), *White Plains*, *Kalinin Bay*, *Kitkun Bay*, and *Gambier Bay*, all 8,200-ton members of the 'Casablanca' class built by Kaiser using mass production methods in 1942-44 to boost the US Navy's stock of flat tops for various purposes. For amphibious warfare support duties they carried between 14 and 18 General Motors-built Wildcat fighter-bombers and a dozen Avenger general purpose strike aircraft. 'Taffy 3's' escort was composed of three 'Fletcher' class fleet destroyers, *Hoel*, *Heerman* and *Johnston* and four 1,400-ton destroyer escorts *Dennis*, *John C. Butler*,

Raymond and *Samuel B. Roberts*, all of the more heavily armed 'WGT' group with a pair of 5in guns, one forward and one aft; they also carried three 21in torpedo tubes each.

A detached portion of the 3rd Fleet seemed a fair prize and the Japanese opened fire concentrating on the carriers. Sprague could not make off directly southwards as he had to have at least a cross wind to launch his aircraft in self defence. The Avenger bombers and Wildcat fighters were launched with whatever weapons came to hand. The Americans laid a smokescreen but not before the *Fanshaw Bay* and *White Plains* were bracketed with 18in, 16in and 14in shells. The Japanese battleships had different coloured dyes in their shells to mark fall of shot and the sea around the Americans erupted in yellow, blue, green and red waterspouts. By sheer luck no direct hits were scored before the carriers obtained the cover of a rain squall

The CVEs' aircraft, together with those of 'Taffy 2' redirected from strikes ashore, began to peck at their mother ships' assailants with machine gun fire, bombs, rockets — and even depth charges from aircraft that had been assigned to anti-submarine patrol. The cruiser *Suzuya* was

---

USS *Samuel B. Roberts*

Built: Brown Shipbuilding, Houston (launched 20 January 1944)

Displacement: 1,430 tons standard

Dimensions: 306ft x 37ft x 11.2ft standard

Machinery: two shaft geared turbines., 12,000shp, 23kt

Armament: 2 x 5in (2 x 1); 4 x 40mm (2 x 2); 10 x 20mm (10 x 1); 3 x 21in torpedo tubes; Hedgehog ahead throwing weapon; eight depth charge throwers, two depth charge racks

Complement: 178

Notes: Never intended for major surface action this little destroyer escort (DE413) was torn apart by 14in shells from the battleship *Kongo* as she struggled to protect the escort carriers off Samar. She followed the fleet destroyers and launched three torpedoes at Japanese heavy cruisers but none seem to have hit a target.

Above right:
The 'Fletcher' class USS *Heerman* lays a protective smoke screen in her classic defence of the escort carriers off Samar.
US National Archives 80-G-270517

Right:
The brave destroyer escort *Samuel B. Roberts* that supported the more powerful fleet destroyers and met her end off Samar protecting the escort carriers. She was photographed from the USS *Walter C. Wann* a week or two before the battle.
US Naval Historical Center NH96011

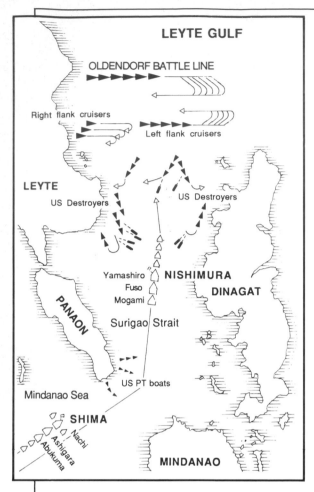

LEYTE GULF

OLDENDORF BATTLE LINE

Right flank cruisers

Left flank cruisers

LEYTE

US Destroyers

US Destroyers

Yamashiro
Fuso
Mogami

NISHIMURA

DINAGAT

PANAON

Surigao Strait

US PT boats

Mindanao Sea

SHIMA

Nachi
Ashigara
Abukuma

MINDANAO

Above:
Oldendorf's trap, Battle of Surigad Strait, positions at 0330, 25 October 1944.

damaged and slowed by a near miss aft and the *Haguro* was also hit, losing one of her 8in turrets. Sprague also ordered his escorts to attack the enemy and there followed one of the most heroic such actions of the war. Cdr Ernest E. Evans of the USS *Johnston* had already decided to close the enemy as he laid the smokescreen. He scored hits on the cruiser *Kumano* with 5in shells and then, covered by the air attacks, launched 10 torpedoes which blew off the cruiser's bows. The destroyer was heavily hit but many of the Japanese armour piercing shells passed clean through the 'tin can' without exploding and the brave ship was soon giving fire support to the torpedo attack being made by the *Hoel* and the *Heerman*. Five-inch fire support was also given by the pair of guns carried

by the little *Samuel B. Roberts*. *Hoel* fired five torpedoes at the battleship *Kongo* which had to turn away while her guns smashed the destroyer's upperworks. Nothing daunted, however, *Hoel* fired his remaining five Mk 15s at *Haguro*. These missed their primary target but caused *Yamato* and *Nagato* to turn away, putting them out of the battle. Then *Heerman* also fired a spread of seven torpedoes at *Haguro*. Again the cruiser bore a charmed life and the US destroyer moved on to the fast battleships *Kongo* and *Haruna*. She hit them with gunfire and fired her remaining three torpedoes before retiring together with the other American ships. Even the little *Samuel B. Roberts* had got off her three Mk 15s as did the *Raymond* and *Dennis* in independent attacks.

The Japanese chase had been seriously disrupted by brave efforts of the three DDs and three DEs. Kurita and his captains were forced to take avoiding action and were so impressed they thought the 'Fletchers' were cruisers and the DEs destroyers. It all confirmed them in their belief that they were in contact with the main American fleet. *Hoel* was the first of the 'cruisers' to be fatally damaged. She gradually lost way and was caught by a hail of heavy gunfire that brought her to a standstill and then sent her to the bottom. Every Japanese ship in range engaged the wreck of the brave destroyer, venting their frustration on the only easy target.

When the escort carriers came out of the squall they were immediately assailed by the Japanese ships once more. Sprague was now racing southwest and his two most northeasterly escort carriers, *Gambier Bay* and *Kalinin Bay* were the most exposed. Their aft single 5in mountings spat back defiance at an enemy whose shooting was all too accurate. Again, heavy Japanese armour-piercing shells often passed through with little effect but the *Kalinin Bay* was seriously damaged by repeated effective 8in hits. *Fanshaw Bay*, Sprague's flagship, was also hit but the worst sufferer was the *Gambier Bay*. The heavy cruiser *Chikuma* closed to 10,000yd and her accurate 8in salvoes cut the CVE's speed to 11kt and then stopped her completely. Other Japanese ships had joined in by this time and their joint efforts made the *Gambier Bay* capsize at 0907. Attempts were made by the escorts to draw the Japanese fire which led to both the *Heerman* and the *Dennis* being seriously damaged and the brave little *Samuel B. Roberts* being sunk by devastating hits from 8in and 14in shells. The *Johnston* was also sunk in a brave and successful attempt to disrupt a torpedo attack by the cruiser *Yahagi* and four of her destroyers. The 'Long Lance' torpedoes were fired at the escort carriers at extreme range and as they slowed one of the big torpedoes was

destroyed by the carrier *St Lo*'s gunfire and
another by a strafing by an Avenger. The heroic
Johnston was hit from all sides and circled by
Japanese destroyers which poured shells into the
wreck until she sank at 1010; 189 men including
her captain Cdr Evans were lost.

By then, however, these destroyers were the
only Japanese ships in action. The American air
attacks had begun to cause the Japanese real problems. There was time to begin arming 'Taffy 2's'
Avengers with torpedoes and 'Taffy 3's' aircraft
put down on the other group's six carriers
(*Natoma Bay*, *Manila Bay*, *Morcus Island*,
Kadashan Bay, *Savo Island* and *Ommaney Bay*) to
receive the weapons. Cdr R. L. Fowler of 'Taffy 3'
circled the battle in his Avenger to act as a strike
co-ordinator. 'Taffy 2' used 43 Avenger torpedo-
bombers to launch 49 torpedoes in five strikes as
Wildcat fighters desperately supported the torpedo aircraft with .5in machine guns and rockets.

The fat little 22.4in Mk 13 aerial torpedo with its
600lb head could be just as deadly from a CVE's
Avenger as from a CV's and *Chikuma*, *Gambier
Bay*'s main assailant, was seriously damaged by a
hit on the stern. Unable to manoeuvre properly
she lost contact with the main force and had eventually to be sunk by her escorting destroyer. The
cruiser *Chokai* was also crippled by bombs and
torpedoes and had to be abandoned. Yet the
cruisers *Haguro* and *Tone* still had their tails up
and were within 10,000yd of Cliff Sprague's ships
discussing a 'Long Lance' attack. Kurita, however, well astern, was troubled by news of more
carriers in the distance, the steady attrition his
forces had received and the confusion into which
they had fallen. The floatplanes he launched were
quickly despatched by Wildcats. At 9.14 he
ordered his ships to turn and regroup.

The American airmen kept up the pressure as
the Japanese ships tried to reform. The damaged
cruiser *Suzuya* was hit again by bombers and
abandoned as her torpedoes began to explode.
Again a Japanese destroyer gave the *coup de grâce*.
Nevertheless, Kurita began one more charge at
1120. Another air attack from the escort carriers
dented Japanese resolve and a supposed sighting
of an American battleship was the final straw. At
1313 Kurita finally turned back rationalising his

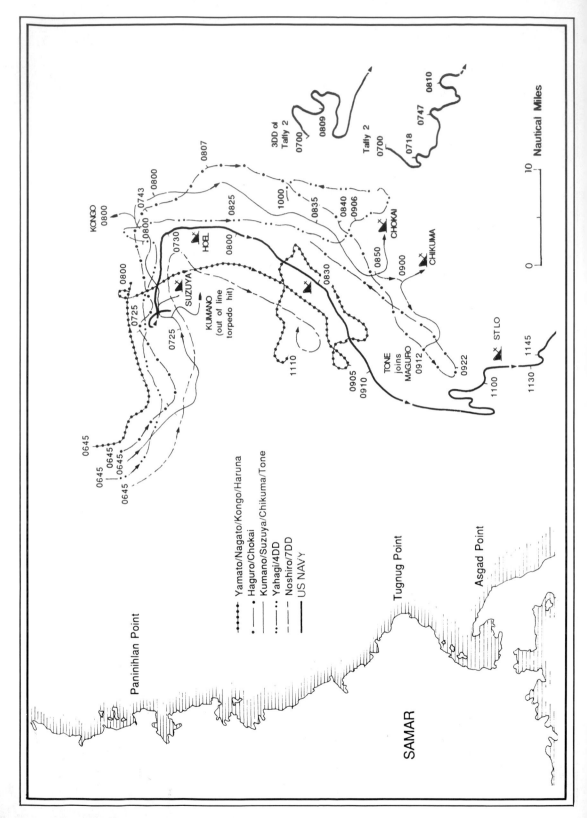

Paninihlan Point

KONGO 0800

0800
0743
0800
0800
0807

0800
0725
0725

SUZUYA
0730
HOEL
0800
0825

KUMANO
(out of line
torpedo hit)

0645
0645 0645
0645
0645

1110

0905
0910

1000

0835

0840
0906

0850

CHOKAI

0830

CHIKUMA
0900

TONE
joins
MAGURO
0912

0922

ST LO
1145

1100
1130

3DD of
Tally 2
0700
0809

0718
0747
0810

Tally 2
0700
0718

Tugnug Point

Asgad Point

SAMAR

Yamato/Nagato/Kongo/Haruna
Haguro/Chokai
Kumano/Suzuya/Chikuma/Tone
Yahagi/4DD
Noshiro/7DD
US NAVY

0   10   Nautical Miles

decision and, perhaps saving face, by signalling Tokyo that he was going after enemy forces reported to the northeast. Ironically, almost at that very moment one of Halsey's task groups, Vice-Adm McCain's TG38.1, which had been called back from replenishment to give support to the escort carriers, put in an air strike on Kurita at extreme range. The attack, by bomb-carrying aircraft, was almost completely ineffective but it increased pressure on Kurita to make only half-hearted efforts to go after the forces to which, supposedly, he had shifted his attention. After a search operation that received better land-based air support than any part of his attack so far, Kurita, his destroyers short of fuel, turned back to San Bernadino Strait. SHO-1 was over.

Left:
Battle off Samar 25 October 1944.

Above:
The Japanese decoy force is attacked off Cape Engano as viewed by an aircraft from the USS Essex. The light cruiser *Oyodo* is in the foreground and the carrier *Zuiho* to the right above it.
US Naval Historical Center NH95541

And what of Halsey who had swallowed the Japanese bait whole? That, or at least the presence of TF34, Halsey's proposed Surface Action Group, was the question uppermost in the mind of Adm Nimitz and his Pacific Fleet staff at Pearl Harbor. At about 10 in the morning they sent a message to the *New Jersey* that infuriated Halsey; 'From CINCPAC Action Com Third Fleet Info

Below:
Adm Ozawa's flag is transferred from *Zuikaku* to the light cruiser *Oyodo* as the carrier lists to port.
US Naval Historical Center NH73068

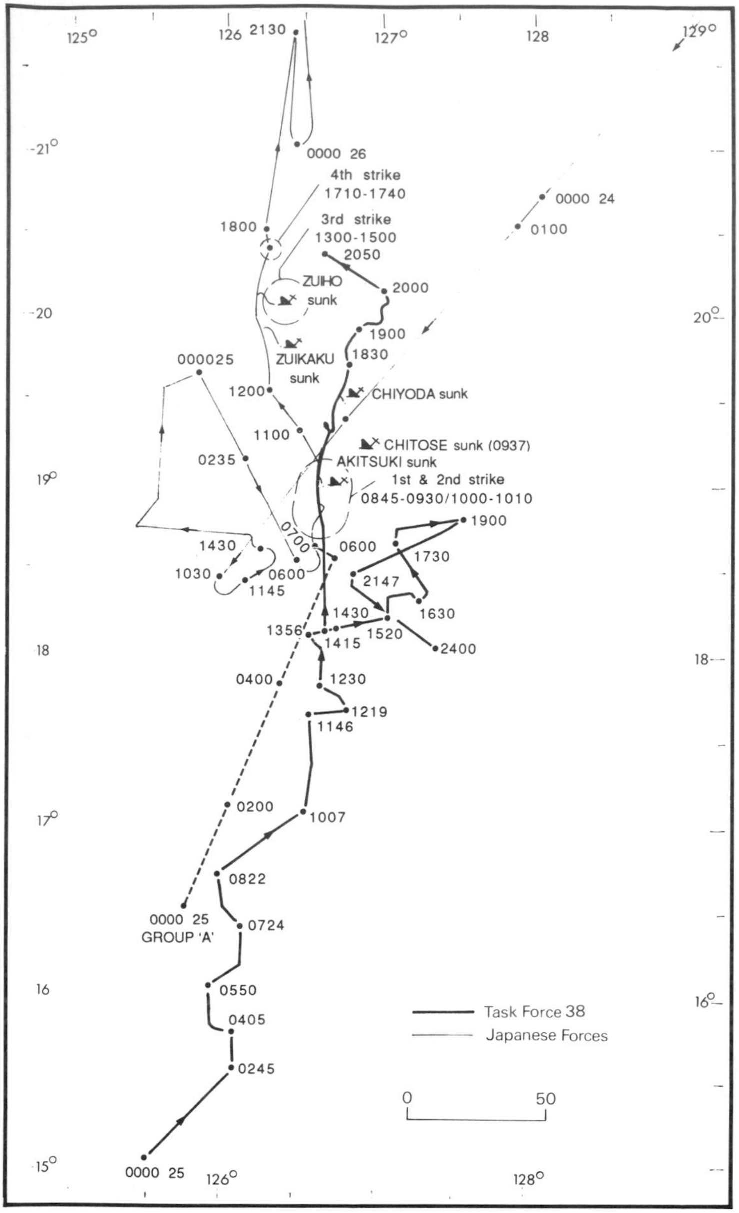

125°
126
127°
128
129°
21°
20
20°
19°
18
18
17°
16
16°
15°
126°
128°
2130
0000 26
4th strike
1710-1740
3rd strike
1300-1500
0000 24
0100
1800
2050
2000
ZUIHO
sunk
1900
1830
ZUIKAKU
sunk
000025
1200
CHIYODA sunk
1100
CHITOSE sunk (0937)
AKITSUKI sunk
0235
1st & 2nd strike
0845-0930/1000-1010
1900
0700
0600
1430
1730
1030
0600
2147
1145
1430
1630
1356
1520
1415
2400
0400
1230
1219
1146
0200
1007
0822
0000 25
GROUP 'A'
0724
0550
0405
0245
Task Force 38
Japanese Forces
0
50
0000 25

Left:
Battle off Cape Engaño detail track chart, 25 October 1944.

COMINCH CTF Seventy Seven X Where Is Rpt Where Is Task Force 34 RR The World Wonders.' The message was more pointed both because of the routine repetition of the important part of the signal and the irregular adding of 'padding' that could be construed as part of it to the end by the encrypting officer at Pearl Harbor. Halsey also did not like the message being repeated to Adms King (Cominch) and Kinkaid (CTF77). At that moment his flagship was part of that very TF34 speeding ahead of Mitscher's carriers to finish off any survivor of the morning's air strikes against Ozawa's forces. A strike of 180 aircraft had been flown off at dawn and the escorting Hellcats had brushed aside the handful of defending 'Zeros' left in the Japanese carriers. Helldivers sank the light carrier *Chitose* and an Avenger's torpedo hit the *Zuikaku* aft putting out of action both her communications and her steering. Ozawa transferred his flag to the light cruiser *Oyodo*. The large fleet escort destroyer *Akitsuki* was also torpedoed and blew up. A later strike by 36 aircraft disabled *Chiyoda* and torpedoed the covering light cruiser *Tama*.

Although not able to protect the carriers, the formidable batteries of the battleship hybrids *Ise* and *Hyuga* were at least able to protect themselves. How they would have coped against the 36 16in guns of TF34 is unknown for at 1115, with the enemy only 42 miles away Halsey gave in to the pressure from above and turned back. The Japanese to the north were left to the carriers of TG38.3 and TG38.4 that put in a massive air strike of over 200 aircraft. It took off just before mid-day and attacked at 1310. *Zuikaku*, the last survivor of Pearl Harbor, was torpedoed three more times by Avengers and hit repeatedly by Helldivers. She heeled over and sank just before 1415. The smaller *Zuiho* proved surprisingly tough but eventually succumbed to repeated Helldiver attacks. *Chiyoda* had to be left to her fate as Ozawa retired to the north. She was sunk by a Surface Action Group of four American cruisers and 12 destroyers sent north to deal with any 'cripples'. More air strikes were put in on *Ise* and *Hyuga* but the tired American pilots were again beaten off. Less lucky was one of the three Japanese destroyers left behind to pick up survivors. After a brave night battle against overwhelming firepower the *Hatsuzuki* was sunk by the Surface Action Group. A pack of submarines mounted the final attack on Ozawa's force and dealt with the damaged *Tama*. But no one was more surprised than Ozawa to return to Japan still with *Oyodo*, *Ise* and *Hyuga* and five destroyers.

Halsey divided TF34 and rushed down to San Bernadino Strait with his two fastest battleships, *Iowa* and *New Jersey*, three light cruisers and eight destroyers. This was yet another flawed judgement as it put him at a disadvantage to Kurita, especially in a night action for which the Japanese were usually renowned. Alas, however, there was to be no trial of strength between the world's most powerful battleships ever. Halsey missed Kurita by over two and a half hours and his ships had to be content with sinking the straggling destroyer *Nowake* which had been left behind to look after the doomed *Chikuma*. The following day the 3rd Fleet's carriers put in their final blows on the retreating Kurita adding to the poor *Kumano*'s wounds and sinking the modern light cruiser *Noshiro*. Kurita still had four battleships, two heavy cruisers, a light cruiser and seven destroyers afloat, a powerful force to act as a fleet in being and affect allied calculations in succeeding months.

Leyte Gulf was therefore not the end of the Japanese Navy although it had suffered grievous wounds; one of its pair of super battleships, two older battleships, four carriers, no less than 10 cruisers and nine destroyers. It never mounted a complex main fleet operation again. Leyte was the largest naval battle ever, in which all types of forces were engaged, surface, air and subsurface. It was an extraordinary affair of missed opportunities, command errors and great heroism, especially from Clifton Sprague's 'Taffy' and its escorts. They, and the American destroyers at Surigao Strait emerge as the main victors. But the Japanese were never going to carry off a major victory in conventional terms. Even if Kurita had carried on into Leyte Gulf he might have created chaos but eventually he would have been destroyed. The Japanese surface navy was clearly still too valuable to become a suicide force. Not so the Navy's aviators. Even as SHO-1 was being put into effect Vice-Adm Onishi the new commander of the 1st Air Fleet was organising his first 'Special Attack' units of Kamikaze suicide pilots. On 25 October, just as Kurita was considering withdrawing in a last act of conventional Japanese naval wisdom, the first unit of Kamikazes to find targets struck against 'Taffy 1'. Six 'Zeros' attacked and two scored hits on the 10,500-ton 'Sangamon' class escort carriers *Suwanee* and *Santee*. Despite holed flight and hangar decks, and a submarine torpedo hit on the *Santee* the tough converted tankers were soon back in action.

Then the suicide pilots turned to Clifton Sprague's already battered 'Taffy 3'. After escaping from the might of the Japanese battlefleet the remaining five escort carriers were attacked by five Kamikaze 'Zeros'. One narrowly missed the *Kitkun Bay* but its bomb did not and caused serious damage. Another Kamikaze exploded alongside the *White Plains* and the two that attacked the *Fanshaw Bay* were shot down. The last pilot seemed to be attacking the *White Plains* but swerved into the USS *St Lo*. The Kamikaze plunged through the centre of the flightdeck, causing explosions that almost tore the ship in half. She sank in less than half-an-hour. Then 15 Kamikaze 'Judy' dive-bombers mounted a third attack. This concentrated on the shell-damaged *Kalinin Bay* which took two hits but nevertheless survived. Sprague could not really believe that he still had four carriers at the end of that terrible morning. He put it down to the 'definite partiality of Almighty God'.

Halsey always insisted that he would act in the same way again if presented with the same information. He insisted that he thought the escort carriers could look after themselves, against a foe his carriers had demoralised the previous day. But the margins of risk he was willing to accept were dangerously wide for a commander in his position. He thus verged on the incompetent and was too proud and stubborn to learn from his mistakes — which got worse. Halsey's attempts to maintain

'Fletcher' class destroyers

Displacement: 2,325 tons standard

Dimensions: 376.5ft x 39.5ft x 17.75ft

Machinery: two shaft geared turbines, 60,000shp, 37kt

Armament: 5 x 5in (5 x 1); 6- 10 x 40mm AA (3 – 5 x 2); 11-7 x 20mm (11-7 x 1); 10 x 21in torpedo tubes (2 x 5); six depth charge throwers, two depth charge racks

Sensors: radars, SC air-warning, SG surface search, Mk 4 fire control; sonar.

Complement: 300

Notes: The standard American fleet destroyer of 1944, well equipped for three dimensional naval warfare.

Above:
The hybrid seaplane carrier/battleship *Ise* was able to use her massed anti-aircraft batteries to keep the Americans at bay off Cape Engano. She carried no less than 104 25mm light AA guns and six AA rocket launchers.
US Naval Historical Center NH63440

the offensive against the Japanese helped expose the 3rd Fleet to the great Typhoon of 18 December 1944 which caused the loss of three destroyers and almost 800 men. The Court of Enquiry blamed Halsey for 'errors in judgement'. The US Government also had to apologise for a strike he delivered on neutral Macao. Thankfully Halsey handed over to the far more able Spruance again in January 1945. Spruance was to plan the invasion of Japan but Nimitz delayed relieving him by Halsey until the Okinawa campaign was virtually over; the 5th Fleet became the 3rd Fleet again at the end of May 1945. It almost immediately encountered another Typhoon but this time no ships were lost. Nevertheless it was recommended that Halsey be transferred to other duty and this

was only overruled for reasons of fleet morale. Halsey spent the final weeks of the war in his element operating off the Japanese coast but his promotion to Fleet Admiral was delayed to the end of 1945, after the war was safely over. There was no place for a sloppy planner like 'Bull' Halsey in the postwar Navy and he finally retired from active duty in early 1947, after a career in which he had been lucky to avoid responsibility for a truly major disaster.

And Kurita? He recovered from his fever and from the strain and lack of sleep that must have had a considerable negative effect on his judgement and decision making abilities; as the operation wore on they emphasised the schizophrenic tendencies in his nature. Kurita's lack of willingness to press on off Samar looked increasingly bad as the Japanese surface navy joined in the suicide operations of its aviators or was sunk in other ways for little purpose. He must have remembered his brave words at Lingga before the Leyte drama began. It cannot have been a very happy admiral who lived on after the war, one who always remained silent, even under interrogation, about his decisions of 25 October 1944.

Select Bibliography
Compiled by D. G. Law

General
Barnett, Correlli; *Engage the Enemy More Closely*; London, Hodder; 1991
Broome, Jack; *Make Another Signal*; London, Kimber; 1973
Campbell, John; *Naval Weapons of World War Two*; London, Conway; 1985
Conway's All The World's Fighting Ships 1922-1948; London, Conway; 1990
Dull, Paul S.; *A Battle History of the Imperial Japanese Navy 1941-1945*; Cambridge, PSL; 1978
Friedman, Norman; *Naval Radar*; Greenwich, Conway; 1961
Gill, G. Herdman; *Royal Australian Navy 1942-45*; Canberra, Australian War Memorial; 1968
Ladd, J. D.; *Assault From The Sea*; Newton Abbot, David & Charles; 1976
Morison, S. E.; *History of US Naval Operations in WW2*; New York, Little Brown; 1947-62
Poolman, K.; *Allied Escort Carriers of World War Two*; London, Blandford and Annapolis, Naval Institute Press; 1988
Roskill, S. W.; *Churchill and the Admirals*; London, Collins; 1977
Roskill, S. W.; *The Navy at War 1939-1945*; London, Collins; 1960
Roskill, S. W.; *The War at Sea;* London, HMGO; 1961
Van der Vat, Dan; *The Pacific Campaign;* London, Hodder; 1992
Whitley, M. J.; *German Destroyers of World War Two (2nd Edition)*; London, Arms & Armour; 1991
Winton, John; *Ultra at Sea;* London, Cooper; 1988

Narvik
'First and Second Battles on 10th and 13th April 1940', respectively supplement to the *London Gazette* of Thursday 3 July 1947, Number 38005, pp3047-3056.
'Norway Campaign; 1940 Supplement to the *London Gazette* of Tuesday 8 July 1947, Number 38011, pp3167-3196.
Brookes, Ewart; *Prologue to a War: the Navy's Part in the Narvik Campaign;* London, Jarrold's; 1966
Connell, G. G.; *Valiant Quartet;* London, Kimber; 1979
Derry, T. K.; *The Campaign in Norway*; London HMSO; 1952
Dickens, Peter; *Narvik: Battles in the Fiords* (Sea Battles in Close up, 9)*;* London, Ian Allan; 1974
Gasaway, E. B.; *Grey Wolf, Grey Sea;* London, Barker; 1972
Healiss, Ronald; *Adventure Glorious;* London, Muller; 1955
MacIntyre, Donald; *Narvik;* London, Evans; 1959
Moulton, J. L.; *The Norwegian Campaign of 1940*; London, Eyre & Spottiswoode; 1966
Winton, John; *Carrier Glorious;* London, Cooper; 1986

Crete
'The Battle of Crete' supplement to the *London Gazette* of Friday 21 May 1948, Number 38296, pp3103-3118
Davin, D. M.; *Crete*; Wellington, Department of Internal Affairs; 1953
Pack, S. W. C.; *The Battle for Crete* (Sea Battles in Close-Up, 5); London, Ian Allan; 1973
Stewart, I. McD. G.; *The Struggle for Crete, 20 May - 1 June 1941*; Oxford University Press; 1986
Thomas, David A.; *Crete 1941: the Battle at Sea;* London, Deutsch; 1972

Force K
Bailey, E. A. S. ed.; *Malta Defiant and Triumphant: Rolls of Honour 1940-1943*; illus. Bridgewater [author]; 1992
Bradford, Ernle; *Siege: Malta 1940-1943*; London, Hamilton; 1985
Kemp, Paul. J.; *Malta Convoys 1940-1943* (Warships Illustrated No 14); London, Arms & Armour; 1988
Poolman, Kenneth; *Night Strike from Malta: 830 Squadron, RN & Rommel's Convoys*; London, Jane's; 1980
Smith, Peter C. & Walker, Edwin; *The Battles of the Malta Striking Forces* (Sea Battles in Close-Up, 11); London, Ian Allan; 1974
Spooner, A.; *In Full Flight*; London, Macdonald; 1965
Van Creveld, M.; *Supplying War*; Cambridge University Press; 1977

Java Sea
'Battle of the Java Sea, 27th February, 1942'; supplement to the *London Gazette* of Tuesday 6 July 1948. Number 38346, pp3937-3947
Cain, T. J.; *HMS Electra*; London, Muller; 1959
Gordon, Oliver L.; *Fight it out*; London, Kimber; 1957

Johns, W. E.; *No Surrender;* London, Harrap, 1969 [reprinted 1989]
McKie, Ronald; *Proud Echo*; London, Hale; 1954
Thomas, David A.; *Battle of the Java Sea*; London, Deutsch; 1968
Van Oosten, F. C.; *The Battle of the Java Sea* (Sea Battles in Close-Up, 16); London, Ian Allan; 1976
Van Oosten, F. C.; *Her Netherlands Majesty's Ship De Ruyter* (Profile Warship 40); Windsor, Profile; 1974
Winslow, Walter G.; *The Fleet the Gods Forgot*; Annapolis, Naval Institute Press; 1984

Sirte
'The Battle of Sirte of 22 March 1942' supplement to the *London Gazette* of Tuesday 16 September 1947, Number 38073, pp4371-4900
Pack, S. W. C.; *The Battle of Sirte*; (Sea Battles in Close-Up, 15); London, Ian Allan; 1975

Tirpitz
'The Attack on the Tirpitz by Midget Submarines on 22 September 1943' supplement to the *London Gazette* of Tuesday 10 February 1946, Number 38204 pp993-1088
Brennecke, Jochan; *The Tirpitz: the Drama of the 'Lone Queen of the North';* London, Hale; 1963
Brown, David; *Tirpitz: the Floating Fortress*; London, Arms and Armour; 1972
Cooper, Alan W.; *Beyond the Dams to the Tirpitz;* London, Kimber; 1983
Frere-Cook, Gervis; *The Attacks on the Tirpitz* (Sea Battles in Close-up, 8); London, Ian Allan; 1973
Kennedy, Ludovic; *Menace: the Life and Death of the Tirpitz*; London, Sidgwick & Jackson; 1979
Peillard, Leonce; *Sink the Tirpitz!*; London, Cape; 1968
Walker, Frank; *The Mystery of X5*; London, Kimber; 1988

Neptune
'The Assault of the Normandy Landings', supplement to the *London Gazette* of Tuesday 28 October 1947, Number 38110, pp5109-5124
Belchem, David; *Victory in Normandy;* London, Chatto & Windus; 1981
Edwards, Kenneth; *Operation Neptune*; London, Collins; 1946
Eisenhower Foundation; *D-Day: the Normandy Invasion in Retrospect*; Lawrence, University Press of Kansas; 1971
Hartcup, Guy; *Code Name Mulberry*; Newton Abbot, David & Charles; 1977
Hastings, Max; *Overlord: D-Day and the Battle for Europe*; London, Joseph; 1984
Hoyt, Edwin P.; *The Invasion before Normandy: the Secret Battle of Slapton Sands*; London, Hale; 1987
Paine, Lauran; *D-Day*; London, Hale; 1981
Schofield, B.B; *Operation Neptune* (Sea Battles in Close-Up, 10); London, Ian Allan; 1947
Taylor, J. E.; *The Last Passage*; London, Allen & Unwin; 1946
Tute, Warren; *D-Day;* London, Sidgwick & Jackson; 1974

Philippine Sea
Buell, T. B.; *The Quiet Warrior: A Biography of Admiral Raymond A Spruance* (with new introduction by J. B. Lundstrom); Annopolis Naval Institute Press; 1987
Dickson, W. D.; *The Battle of the Philippine Sea* (Sea Battles in Close-Up, 13); London, Ian Allan; 1974
Lockwood, Charles & Adamson, Hans C.: *Battles of the Philippine Sea*; New York, Crowell; 1967
Taylor, Theodore; *The Magnificent Mitscher*; Annapolis, Naval Institute Press; 1992
Tillman, Barrett; *Hellcat: The F6F in World War 2*; Annapolis, Naval Institute Press; 1979
Y' Blood, William; *Red Sun Setting: Battle of the Philippine Sea*; Annapolis, Naval Institute Press

Leyte Gulf
Falk, Stanley L.; *Decision at Leyte*; New York, Norton; 1966
Field, James A.; *The Japanese at Leyte Gulf;* Princeton University Press; 1947
Hoyt, Edwin P.; *The Battle of Leyte Gulf*; New York, Weybright; 1972
Potter, E. B.; *Bull Halsey*; Annapolis, Naval Institute Press; 1986
Potter, E. B.; *Nimitz*; Annapolis, Naval Institute Press; 1976
Stewart, A; *The Battle of Leyte Gulf*; London, R. Hale; 1979
Vann Woodward C.; *The Battle of Leyte Gulf*; New York, Macmillan; 1947
Y' Blood, W.; *The Little Giants: US Escort Carriers Against Japan;* Annapolis, Naval Institute Press; 1987